AFRICAN STUDIES
HISTORY, POLITICS, ECONOMICS, AND CULTURE

Edited by
Molefi Asante
Temple University

A ROUTLEDGE SERIES

African Studies
History, Politics, Economics, and Culture
Molefi Asante, *General Editor*

MISSIONS, STATES, AND EUROPEAN EXPANSION IN AFRICA

Edited by Chima J. Korieh
Raphael Chijioke Njoku

Routledge
New York & London

Routledge
711 Third Avenue, New York, NY 10017
2 Park Square, Milton Park, Abingdon, Oxfordshire OX14 4RN

© 2007 by Taylor & Francis Group, LLC
Routledge is an imprint of Taylor & Francis Group, an Informa business

First issued in paperback 2011

ISBN 978-0-415-95559-1 (hbk)
ISBN 978-0-415-51469-9 (pbk)

Library of Congress Cataloging-in-Publication Data

Missions, states, and European expansion in Africa / edited by Chima J. Korieh and
   Raphael Chijioke Njoku.
      p. cm.
   Includes bibliographical references and index.
   ISBN 0-415-95559-9
   1. Missions--Africa--History--19th century--Congresses. 2.
Church and state--Africa--History--19th century--Congresses. 3.
Europe--Colonies--Africa--History--19th century--Congresses. 4.
Africa--History--19th century--Congresses. I. Korieh, Chima J. (Chima Jacob),
1962- II. Njoku, Raphael Chijioke.

BV3500.A35M57 2007
266'.0234067--dc22   2006102737

Visit the Taylor & Francis Web site at
http://www.taylorandfrancis.com

and the Routledge Web site at
http://www.routledge.com

To

Felix K. Ekechi and Innocent F.A. Uzoechi

Contents

List of Tables

Acknowledgments

This project has accumulated many debts since it was conceptualized. We cannot mention many of those we are indebted to individually here. However, we would like to express our sincere gratitude to everyone whose essay appears in this book. From the inception of this project at the African Studies Association Meeting held in Washington DC in 2005, to the time of going to press, the contributors have patiently offered their time and expert ideas towards the completion of this volume.

We highly appreciated the financial support provided by our institutions that made this project possible. In this regard, we would like to thank the Departments of History and Pan African Studies, the University of Louisville, Kentucky. We would also like to acknowledge the enthusiasm shown by Mr. Benjamin Holtzman of Routledge from the inception of this project to its final production. We are grateful to the production team, including Jennifer Genetti and Alicia Solsman, for their professionalism and patience.

Finally, we would like to thank the two individuals to whom we have dedicated this volume for their support and mentoring over the years. Professor Emeritus Felix K. Ekechi remains one of African pioneers in the field of Christian mission history in Africa. Our able teacher, Professor Emeritus Innocent F. A. Uzoechi provided both of us an immense fountain of knowledge from which we drank in abundance.

Introduction

Raphael Chijioke Njoku and Chima J. Korieh

A significant shift in both imperial and mission historiography has emerged in recent times as the ideology, which prompted missionary enterprise, is (re)conceptualized in the context of imperialism. Indeed, critical and nationalist approaches to African history and a narrative of collaboration, which underlies the work of many Africanist scholars, have increasingly characterized Christian missions as agents of colonial governments.[1] Few will debate the historical role of missionaries in extending the frontiers of empire and their contribution to the remaking of African societies, yet the depictions of Africa's encounter with Europe since the nineteenth century have not often emphasized the centrality of the collaborations between missions and imperial authority as much as the centrality of the colonized population, who in most cases straddled different ideological frontiers. A panel at the 48th Annual Meeting of the African Studies Association, held in Washington DC (17–20 November 2005), provided an opportunity to re-examine some of these issues. Most of the essays in this volume emerged from that panel. We acknowledge the limited coverage in this volume in regards to regional representations and the uniqueness of the colonial/missionary encounter, which cannot be generalized for all of Africa. In each of the areas covered, however, the contributors analyzed specific cases of collaboration between missions, state and colonial expansion in late nineteenth century Afro-European relations.

The European attempt to penetrate the African interior and extend their political and commercial influence from the late nineteenth century created a more favorable climate for Christian evangelical expansion. The imperial intrusion heralded new forces of change that would rudely alter the colonized people's ways of life. These forces have continued to exert influences on the continent.

As one of the most powerful forces of transformation in Africa, the nineteenth century Christian missionary movement has received more than a fair scholarly interest. The extant studies on both missionary enterprise and colonial conquest provide the starting point upon which the essays in this book proceed. Collectively, the various chapters here explore a set of ideas that touch on the complex nature of the encounter between European missionaries and their African converts; missionaries and imperial officials; and between colonial administrators and their African subordinates. Since this encounter involved exercise of power and the authority to impose rules on, as well as compel the obedience of the colonized people, the essays analyzed the dialogue between two different cultures and their attempt to understand, contend with, and accommodate each other. While the alien culture arrived with imperial intents, the indigenous people responded in ambivalent contexts, resulting in changes and cultural hybridities that may defile any grand or simple analysis.

In the chapters that follow, the authors highlight several aspects of the critical role played by the missionaries in the establishment and con- solidation of colonial control in Africa. Our focus centered on the motives, practices, and processes of the collaborative hegemony (although not often successfully) imposed on African societies by missions and colonial rulers. The mutual linkages among missions, colonial state institutions, as well as the role of Africans in the remaking of African societies are well covered. To think of the intersection between evangelism, and colonial expansion across Africa, however, is not to state the obvious, but to explore the processes and outcomes of this partnership, including the conflicts of collaboration and the induction of some Africans as agents of imperial control. Under- standing the nuances of collaboration and ambivalences that emerged also require us to acknowledge the wide scale use of language, imagery, technol- ogy, and European epistemology in legitimizing relations of inequality with Africans. Additionally, it is important to underline the impetus provided by the foreign trading conglomerates operating in Africa. The European mer- chants supported colonial rule in order to have a free reign in consolidating their commercial interests and investments—hence their active teamwork in the "civilizing" mission to transform African societies after the alien's image.

The framework for this collection revolves around the complex inter- actions—rather than the oppositions—between the missionary and the imperial impulses in Africa. We can understand both processes through a dialectics of cultural imposition and the implicit notions of racial superi- ority or inferiority, exercise of power and its ability to corrupt, and ide- ology and consciousness that together shaped the historical processes of the encounter. As a matter of fact, each of the essays in this volume transcends the narrow boundaries that often separate the diverse elements of the encounter in arguing that missionary endeavors and official colonial actions, including the intention to protect trading interests—could all be conceptualized as different dimensions of the grand hegemonic project in the sense that all the European actors pursued same civilizing agenda, at least at the ideological level, even though each of these interest groups may have sometimes followed different strategies in their dealings with the Africans.[2]

In this volume, Roger Becks adopts the concept of "imperial fault line," as first proposed by Jeffrey Cox, and applies it to the position of Christian missionaries in southern Africa in the early nineteenth century.[3] The position of European missionaries was extremely paradoxical as it related to frontier trade and government policy. As British colonial officials attempted to regulate commercial contact across the Cape colonial border, missionaries, resident hundred miles beyond the official colonial borders, found themselves literally straddling a line with their feet in both African and colonial camps along the border. Colonial officials increasingly called on the missionaries to facilitate and advance cross-border exchanges and trade fairs, and in this capacity they were obligated to interpret colonial laws; to issue passes to enter the colony; occasionally to distribute arms and ammunition to those favored by the Cape government; and to inculcate the inhabitants of their mission stations with Christian ideals and the rudiments of European civilization. They were also expected to keep the governor and his officials informed about events in the interior, and about the attitudes and actions of the African peoples who lived both on and off their mission stations. By serving as informants and advisers to both the Cape government and the peoples among whom they lived, the missionaries could be valuable participants in the making of frontier policy. By attempting fairly to represent both sides of the imperial fault line, however, they opened themselves to suspicion and mistrust from everyone.

A similar result emerged from Waibinte Wariboko's study on missionary/colonial activities in the Niger Delta, particularly in the trading states of the Eastern Niger Delta, where secular officials of the British Crown and Christian missionaries came after the trading merchants in the nineteenth century. These extra-territorial forces of change were united by one grand ideological interest: the imposition of "Whiteness" on the Niger Delta for the ultimate sociopolitical, economic and cultural benefits of Great Britain as it attempted to establish its empire in West Africa during the nineteenth century. On the strength of the result of this investigation, Wariboko disputes the perception previously suggesting that the Christian missions and secular administration, as the two most important bastions of British colonial rule in southeastern Nigeria, were often locked in conflict. Rather he emphasizes three mutually reinforcing points. First, subtle differences aside, the relationships between the tripartite forces of change were marked by a strong sense of mutual respect, friendship and support in the Niger Delta throughout the nineteenth century. Second, the creation and sustenance of the colonial state has to be seen, therefore, as the collaborative effort of the three "Cs" in the Niger Delta before the British established a foothold in the Igbo-speaking hinterland of southern Nigeria after the Aro conquest of 1901/2. Third, this study contends that the triumph of "Whiteness" over "Blackness" would have been more difficult to achieve if the extra-territorial forces and the missions "were often locked in conflict" before the consolidation of the colonial state in southern Nigeria after the first decade of the twentieth century.

Obviously we cannot understand why peculiar policies and approaches were adopted, or why some African societies responded in certain ways, without looking at the larger context of nineteenth century imperialism and the ideology of a duty to civilize pursued by the Europeans. We must also consider how decisions made in the process affected both the colonizer and the colonized. This perspective informs Raphael Njoku's analysis of the intriguing, but botched, circumstance in which the pre-colonial Ganda monarchy attempted to appropriate the new religion for its power aggrandizement. This important contribution to the increasing body of literature on the history of the missions to Africa corroborates earlier works, including that by Jean and John Comaroff who have argued that both facets of European encounter and the interplay between religion and political economy that arose in their wake gave rise to "cultural struggles, accommodations, hybridities, and new hegemonies."[4] As the Comaroffs used a wide range of analytical approaches in their examination of Christianity, colonialism, and the Tswana of Southern Africa to explicate what they call the "colonization of consciousness and the consciousness of colonization,"[5] so did Njoku's investigation of Christian missionary engagements in what later became modern Uganda reveal a complex process of inventiveness resulting in a wholesome cultural sale-out that secured the interest of the Christian (*Bagungu*) chiefs as co-inheritors of the colonial state. Indeed, as witnessed in Tswana, the Protestant and Catholic missions in Uganda first colonized the consciousness of the former pageboys (later Christian chiefs) and thus, prepared them as partners in the collaborative hegemony.

Elsewhere, other studies have shown that missions abetted the formal occupation of Africa, despite the bloody nature of the wars of conquest.[6] A. E. Ayandele in *Missionary Impact on Modern Nigeria* had qualified the missionaries as pathfinders of British influence, arguing that their propaganda not only prepared the way for the government and exploiters but also ensured the smooth and peaceful occupation of African territories. Anyandele further observed that the political environment, patriotic instincts and the logical outcome of the activities of the missionaries made them emissaries of both the government and chiefs. In fact the politics of race in the nineteenth century, the flows of public opinion in Europe, the ebbs and flows of trade, the tides of the scramble and partition of Africa in the last quarter of the century, and the nature of responses of the indigenous people made this ambivalent triumvirate inevitable.[7] As an agent of imperialism, Christianity was crucial in establishing and maintaining political, cultural, and economic domination. In most cases the missionaries tried to impose upon the Africans some particular ways of seeing and being or values and attitudes that betrayed not only their self-righteousness but also limited understanding of African societies. Since cultural assimilation was a crucial part of the European civilizing endeavor, the belief in the superiority of the alien culture to the indigenous practices provided the lens through which many missionaries—and later colonial officials—interpreted and pursued their missions in Africa.

From this standpoint, Yolanda Covington-Ward's study of the Kongo reveals that at the center of the local people's encounter with the aliens, cultural practices constituted a contested arena of both religious and political domination. In this Central African region, the shifting nature of the uses and meanings of embodied practices in the milieu of the many sociocultural transformations that defined the colonial period reveals a struggle between the local and the alien cultures as they sought for a common ground for adaptation and co-existence. Initially, Kongo non-secular performances within the independent *ngunza* churches—including practices such as trembling, jumping, and using traditional instruments—were seen as subversive movements that menaced the smooth running of the colony and the hegemony of the European-led missions. However, attitudes towards these practices and the manner in which they were used for different purposes changed over time and in varying contexts. Over the period of colonial rule, the colonial officials succeeded in altering, to certain degrees, some of the embodied practices such as dance in much the same way that the economy, social and political structures, language, and manners of dress of indigenous populations were subject to changes.

Yet, the engagements and interactions of missionaries as well as their understanding of the local societies they encountered sometimes diverged from imperial interests. Mission education and the ideologies they brought were sometimes constructive and accommodative in their engagements with Africans—a process that perhaps enhanced the ability of the missionary agents to successfully translate their experiences to the general enhancement of colonial administration. Therefore, a balanced perspective on the activities of the Christian missions would acknowledge their multiple roles as agents of modernization despite their often ethnocentric and racist views of other societies. The evangelical missions used the provision of western-style education and health services as an extra-doctrinal technique for winning African souls.

Ogbu Kalu expertly picked up this important factor in missionary/colonial expansion in Africa by revisiting the Edinburgh Conference on African education of 1910. Kalu reexamines, in details, the report of "Committee Three" on education from the African's lens—asserting that the role of Christianity in the colonization enterprise, colluded with the racist imperial mental structures of colonialism, and acted out the script designed to transform the African's mind and worldview into Western molds. The chapter also considers the encounter as an example of Africans' encounter with the rain of the gospel and agency in the appropriation, gestation, and responses to the missionary strategies.

As the chapter by Jude Aguwa further elucidates, the humanitarian approach to mission work in Africa provided the Europeans with important but subtle avenues for interaction with the ordinary people.[8] However, Aguwa strongly emphasizes that the introduction of Western medical system by the missionaries resulted in the destruction of the indigenous healthcare system—just as other elements of the Western culture impacted on indigenous ways of life. Chima Korieh extends this perspective on the remaking of African societies with a discourse on the early period of the twentieth century that focuses both on Nigeria in particular and Africa in general. As the study reveals, mission education, denominational affiliation and choice of either monogamous or polygamous marriages were new forces in the remaking of African identities. While the mission presence provided a new impetus for identity formation, the new identities were, however, contested by the Africans. Elsewhere, Carol Summers' work in Zimbabwe has shown how African converts appropriated missionary impositions to suit their own interests. Like many in other parts of Southern Africa, the Africans embraced mission education in the early twentieth century in order to create new identities and relief themselves from the extractive colonial labor demands. African funded schools provided the people with opportunity to construct new identities and ask for membership in the new mission community.[9]

While most African societies were conquered in theory and in practice, complete conversion was rare, as "new converts" adapted Christianity to fit in with local practices, beliefs, and rituals—a dynamic which often produced divergent and sometimes contradictory results.[10] The resilience of indigenous cultural practices in the face of corroding alien influences and the ability of Africans to selectively appropriate European ideas and opportunities for survival were particularly remarkable. Elsewhere, Chukwudi A. Njoku has elaborated upon this local initiative: "In the midst of their powerlessness before their oppressors, the elders perceived even if vaguely that perhaps their hope for eventual survival and triumph lay in the strange paradox of embracing, understudying and mastering the power and knowledge of their oppressors. Nothing seemed to separate the two, the oppressed and the oppressor, more than orality and literacy."[11]

Both colonial powers and missionaries were concerned with boundaries and frontiers of all kinds: physical and psychological, real and imagined—not only between themselves and Africans and among Africans, but also between different imperial powers and missions. Elsewhere, Wariboko's work on Caribbean missionaries in Southern Nigeria exemplifies the ways notions of race permeated missionary endeavors. Race, for Afro-Caribbean missionaries, as it was for their American counterparts, was essentially a process of self-identification with their African origins. Although both European and Afro-diaspora missionaries assumed moral and spiritual superiority over Africans, the latter, to whom race mattered much, were particularly influenced more by a sense of Pan-Africanism.[12] In this volume, Wariboko also highlights that the evangelization of West Africa was a European initiative pursued under the auspices of missionary organizations such as the Church Missionary Society and the Society for the Propagation of the Gospel during the nineteenth and early twentieth centuries. But the Pongas Mission, also known and called "The Mission from the sons and daughters of Africa in the West Indies to Africa," was the first and only collective Caribbean initiative designed and funded almost entirely by the Anglican Communions in Antigua, Barbados and Jamaica to "civilize" the "benighted" Susu speaking peoples of Conakry, Dominga, Fallangia, Farringia, Isles de Los and Dubrica—all in present day French-speaking Guinea-Conakry, West Africa—between 1855 and 1935. The West Indians of African descent in this program, informed and motivated by the notion of race, pride and belonging, argued that the redemption of Africa from its spiritual and sociocultural degradation cannot be left to European missionary organizations alone; it was, they also argued, the moral and political responsibility of the black populations in the New World diaspora to rescue their ancestral homeland. The purpose of this essay is to discuss the evangelical and sociopolitical accomplishments of the Pongas Mission, including its impact on the black personhood in the Caribbean. Colonial administrators encouraged such endeavors because they hoped that Christianity would provide support for colonial rule as African converts increased.

COLLABORATION AND CONTAINMENT

The mutual interests of missionaries, traders, and imperial officials led to the successful subjugation of African societies. This, of course, is not to argue that these vested interests that sustained the shared hegemony remained static. Rather, the nature of the alliance evolved and shifted based on a number of factors including (but not limited to) the local context prior to contact. Also the nature of rivalry existing amongst the various participating Christian missions—not particularly the peculiar rivalry between Catholics and Protestants—but that between imperial powers like Britain and Germany for instance—often created social cleavages among Africans while providing opportunity for official intervention. In this volume, Michael McInnishin describes how the colony's British missionaries and German officials found themselves competing in their claims over the colony and its subjects, yet how they ultimately collaborated in their treatment of the territory's subjects, due to shared ideologies about the landscape.

Also the collaborative endeavor between colonial governments and Christian missionaries was strongest in those areas that did not have large Muslim populations. Indeed the progress of Christianity in Africa from the nineteenth century was linked to the Muslim factor. Elsewhere, Kalu has argued that

> Islam benefited from colonialism and expanded south of the Sahara, not just because of jihads that led to state formations but because Europe shifted from an idea that Islam was a form of superstition to the acceptance that since it acknowledged one God, it was superior to African religions. . . . For other political reasons enshrined in the Indirect Rule strategy, the official policy protected Islam that used improved modes of communication to trade and spread."[13]

For colonial officials, Islam and prohibitive injunctions, including the use of alcohol, was best suited for "natives." In areas with large Muslim populations, colonial governments discouraged Christian missionary work. Islamic institutions, in most cases, were indispensable in the functioning of the colonial state. The collaborative hegemony with the Muslim oligarchy defined colonial and missionary relationship early in the colonial period. So while British pacification, for example, ended the Sokoto Caliphate in 1903 and curtailed the power of the old Muslim aristocracy, Imperial policy of

Britain stopped short of dismantling the Islamic structures and social institutions of the Caliphate. Many aspects of the Caliphate's system, including the Islamic legal code, were retained and incorporated into the colonial hegemony in a deliberate policy to win the cooperation of the Muslim elite and to protect imperial interests.

In this volume, Gideon Mailer argues that this "dichotomy" was consciously harnessed, so that, in the contact between the indigenous communities of Southern Sudan and the missionaries the former were no real function in society as a whole, both in relation to the British rulers, and the Sudanese Arab elites in the North, who these colonial rulers sought to keep separate from those black Southern Sudanese who were given the empty vehicle of religious choice. Mailer, nonetheless, modified old assumptions in relation to Sudan—with the contention that in late nineteenth and twentieth century Sudan, the kind of individual religious choice that previous studies on Sudan link to a diminishment of individual agency in relation to ascendant power structures, led to anything but such a phenomenon. It was precisely a post-Enlightenment notion of individual choice that led to heightened anxiety by ruling British authorities regarding the missionary presence in the colonial state. Moreover, as evident in the postcolonial order, the ruling Arab North has maintained many elements of the previous British hegemony, so that a similar anxiety could come about on their part regarding the missionary influence and Southern Sudanese agency. One of the aftermaths of this policy remains the religious conflict between African Christians and their Muslim neighbors, in which the state has often been a biased umpire.[14]

Overall, we must reemphasize that developments within colonial and missionary circles could not occur without African participation, influence, and compromise because African societies were not just passive recipients of change. Colonialism took many forms and the political, economic, and cultural processes of domination that emerged were different for many African societies. As active participants, the local people accepted some of the alien cultural trends and subverted others. This complexity gave rise to what Comaroff and Comaroff regard as "conversation between indigenous people and Europeans rather than 'conversion' by an unequal colonizing force."[15] Indigenous African societies were pragmatic in the emerging dialectic of domination and resistance. For those scholars who have formulated the "cultural imperialism" thesis, including Lamin Sanneh, Christianity, from the outset, has been an enterprise of translation of its message into the vernacular languages and assumptions of other cultures, rather than an enterprise of dominating them or bending their ways to a foreign notion of "civilization." Sanneh argues persuasively that the attempt to translate also sets up an unequal relationship, but one that gives greater power to the indigene rather than the missionary—a view not entirely different from Comaroffs.[16]

POST COLONIAL LEGACY

While the essays in this volume are largely about the actions of European missionaries and colonial states rather than African Christians, this should not lead one to conclude that the church became irrelevant in the post-colonial era. Since Christianity spread in conjunction with the expansion of colonialism, the emergent African political elites associated Christianity with authority and power. Thus, just as Africans appropriated the gospel in the nineteenth century under the colonial order, the postcolonial states in Africa have tried to appropriate the church soon after the end of colonial rule. However, the relations between Christian churches and the state in many African societies in the postcolonial period have been marked by intense conflicts. Secularism—the division between religion and state—and a Christian concept and belief was challenged. This conflict emerged in the larger framework of political uncertainties and the churches' engagement, pronouncements and positions on major national issues, which have often been at variance with those of the state—thanks to liberation theology, which has become a viable strategy in the churches' desire to promote democracy. This relationship has become even more conflictual in societies with Islamic population. Its root, however, lies in the colonial legacy. The ambivalent nature of colonial attitude towards religion introduced two significant currents that retained the old politico-religious order in many Muslim societies and allowed a Christian expansionist policy amongst the so-called African pagans.

Chapter One
All Things to All People: Christian Missionaries in Early Nineteenth Century South Africa

Roger B. Beck

INTRODUCTION

In his recent study of missionary activity in the Punjab, Jeffrey Cox characterizes the ubiquitous and unbridgeable divide between British Christian missionaries and Indians as an "imperial fault line." As they ministered to, and interacted with Christians and non-Christians alike, missionaries struggled with the conflict between their "universalist Christian religious values and the imperial context of those values. One audience might describe this relationship as a conflict between faith and power, another as the relationship between universal egalitarian ideals and an exploitative imperial presence."[1] Although the British Raj was a far different context for nineteenth century Christian missionary evangelism than southern Africa in the same period, missionaries in Africa were no less torn between a sense of universal brotherhood in Christ and their identification with an imperial overlordship that accepted no such equality. And, as in India, this "imperial fault line" influenced every facet of their mission.

The imperial fault line in South Africa may be found in many places and in many forms, some quite obvious and others more subtle.[2] Andrew Porter, for example, argues that even before they left English shores, the first London Missionary Society (LSM) missionaries to South Africa found themselves dependent on imperial assistance and sanction. The first four LMS missionaries arrived at the Cape in March 1799 on the convict transport, *Hillsborough*, bound for Botany Bay. Porter observes that the circumstances of their free passage to the Cape reflect in a stark but simple way "the impossibility for missionaries of escaping the embrace of government, whatever illusions they might entertain as to the likelihood or desirability of independence." LMS missionaries were anxious to get out in the field and collusion with government provided them with a quick departure, it satisfied their thrifty use of funds, and allowed them an "expectation that they could take advantage of a government offer or facilities (however apparently 'providential') without risk of compromise or obligation." These proved to be "perennially recurring features of missionary thinking and much traveled pathways to 'political' involvement with government."[3]

This paper will focus on an imperial fault line in southern Africa that placed missionaries in the position literally of straddling a line with their feet in both camps along the colonial border. Beginning in the 1810s British colonial authorities set about to regulate commercial contacts between the various peoples living in the Transorangia region north of the Cape colony and the colony itself. In establishing these links colonial administrators called on Christian missionaries living beyond the Cape border to serve in a variety of roles as intermediaries to facilitate and advance this commerce. Since, as Jean and John Comaroff have pointed out, the first generation of LMS missionaries placed a good deal of stress on things material,[4] this was not something viewed by them as necessarily a bad thing. However, on both sides of the imperial fault line the missionaries frequently found themselves as "the ruled among the rulers."[5] This was certainly the case vis-à-vis the colonial authorities. But on their mission stations beyond the Cape colonial borders as well, missionaries often lived a very tenuous existence, dependent upon the peoples among whom they resided and in many respects under their authority.

THE GRIQUA AND THE NORTHERN CAPE FRONTIER

After 140 years of Dutch rule, the British occupied the Cape Colony in the late 1790s for the first time. Accompanying them were the first permanent groups of Christian missionaries, led by the London Missionary Society (LMS). These early missionaries headed out to the edges of the colony and beyond to minister to the African, Khoisan, and Griqua peoples. Other missionary societies continued to arrive throughout the nineteenth century, most of whom came from the British Isles, but there were, among others, both Protestant and Roman Catholic French, American, Swedish, German, Dutch and Norwegian missionaries also. There is no doubt that these missionaries played a critical role in effecting change among the African peoples with whom they came into contact. They made southern Africa "among the most intensively missionized parts of the world."[6] William Freund has written that "the expanding mission movement, which would dramatically affect the culture and society of brown and black peoples at the Cape, was perhaps the most striking new social phenomenon of the period, and the one with the greatest long-range significance." Richard Elphick has suggested that the reorientation of thought and behavior that the missionaries demanded of the Africans "can only be called revolutionary."[7]

In the northwestern and northeastern frontier zones the official boundary of the colony in the early nineteenth century lay well south of the Orange River, but mission stations and the settlements of former colonists of mixed descent created an open and fluid frontier much further to the north. As one moves north from the colony, the land becomes progressively dryer and harsher. The Orange River is the least navigable of all the rivers in South Africa as it is reduced to a series of pools during the dry winter months.[8] The various peoples in Transorangia and the missionaries who settled among them depended upon irrigation for agriculture.[9]

In its initial stages in the late 1600s and early 1700s, the European expansion from Cape Town progressed east and north, following the coastal plains. Beginning roughly in the middle of the eighteenth century the two thrusts turned inland to meet by 1820 in central Transorangia. Although the original expansion had been led by white colonists north to the Orange River, into the area known as Little Namaqualand, by the 1730s the eastern advance along the Orange through Bushmanland and into Transorangia was made predominantly by the Griqua (or, as they originally called themselves, Bastaards). Unlike the eastern frontier which was "closed" by the colonial government, and subsequently occupied almost exclusively by white farmers, the northern frontier was closed by the Griqua who initially attempted to normalize relationships among the various societies in the northern frontier zone, with and without the cooperation of the Cape government.[10]

The Griqua were a multifarious assemblage comprised of the descendants of unions among Europeans, Khoikhoi and slaves. There were also free blacks and runaway slaves as well as individual, or groups of, Khoikhoi and other indigenous peoples displaced by white encroachment, war, famine, disease or free choice, who were assimilated into the Griqua communities. The Bastaards were of a mixed-race ancestry, but enjoyed a higher economic and social status within the colony than Africans because the white colonists considered them more "civilized." The outward manifestations of this higher status were Christianity, literacy, Dutch as their native tongue and the possession of jobs requiring skill or responsibility. Bastaards were transport riders, day laborers, and craftsmen. They acted as overseers for white farm owners, and some were owners of small farms in their own right. They saw themselves as "swarthy Hollanders."[11]

The Bastaards' special status did not protect them, however, from racial prejudice. Throughout the eighteenth century the property owners and farmers among them were pushed to the colony's periphery and beyond by white expansion and alienation of land.[12] The desire to protect their privileges and possessions made them more vulnerable to these pressures than for the Khoisan. Initially they moved east and north, settling on farms along the fertile coastal belts. Toward the end of the eighteenth century they began to trek into the interior. Between 1800 and 1820, under the leadership of the wealthy and powerful Kok and Barends families, they occupied an area of fresh water springs in central Transorangia near the Orange River's junction with the Vaal River. Their main settlement was at Klaarwater (Griqua Town), but they also founded villages at Danielskuil and Campbell. These latter two increased in importance after 1820 because they possessed greater agricultural potential than did Griqua Town.[13] The Bastaard population in 1805 numbered perhaps 400 to 500.[14]

THE LONDON MISSIONARY SOCIETY IN THE NORTHERN CAPE

In 1801 the Bastaards invited the London Missionary Society (LMS) to send missionaries to live among them and William Anderson arrived at Klaarwater in that year. He and his fellow LMS missionaries induced profound changes within Bastaard society, not the least of which were the introduction of agriculture among these pastoralist peoples and the centralization of their political organization.[15] As Andrew Porter observes, however, "Anderson found his influence with the local Bastaard (Griqua) leaders growing as a result of missionary marriages, colonial contacts and the development of a church. However, while attempting to nurture their independence, he also found himself under tightening controls and growing pressure from Cape Town to act, against both his instructions and personal inclination, as an agent for the colonial government."[16]

In 1814, the Bastaards, with missionary prompting, changed their name to Griqua, to reflect a supposed genealogical connection to an ancestor of that name and to the Chariguriqua, a Khoikhoi community who had lived north of Cape Town. This change signaled a shift away from their traditional orientation toward the colonial and European ties of the "swarthy Hollanders" to an emphasis on indigenous ancestry and heritage.[17] The Griqua by about 1815 numbered from 2,000 to 3,000, reflecting not only natural increase, but also significant additions of slave and Khoikhoi deserters from the colony, and the gradual assimilation of neighboring Khoisan.[18] Klaarwater, now known as Griqua Town, was the center of the Griqua community, the center of LMS mission activity in the north, and the government agent's post after 1822.

While separating themselves geographically from the Cape authorities, the Griqua nevertheless sought to maintain and even strengthen certain ties with the colony. This paradox explains why the Griqua invited missionaries to settle among them almost immediately after their arrival at Griqua Town. The missionaries brought with them Christianity, the symbol of civilization and status within the colony. They also served as representatives to the colonial government and presented to the Cape Town authorities Griqua wishes as they perceived them in matters of commerce and frontier politics.[19] The tensions created by Griqua efforts to remain politically independent, however, while maintaining certain economic and social ties with the colony were a hindrance to the development of a truly stable, trusting and reciprocal relationship between the Griqua and the British authorities. It also placed the missionaries in an uncomfortable middle position where they were answerable to both sides but unable to please either.[20]

As Legassick has noted, the missionaries remained deeply dependent "on their attachments to the colony, logistically, culturally and personally," and the government frequently took advantage of this dependency to control the missionaries and their mission station residents.

> Thus sanctions could effectively be imposed on them by the colonial authorities and through them on the Bastaards. Indeed, the missionaries were quick to make use of the authority thus bestowed upon them by the colonial authorities. People who refused to help build a missionhouse were threatened with government retribution; potential dissidents were warned that leaving the station would mean loss of their guns and of access to the colony. Missionaries distributed powder to ensure the loyalty of those at the settlement and to encourage the adherence of new members. They negotiated with groups hostile to the settlement, allocated and redistributed land and water resources, adjudicated disputes, and punished crimes.[21]

MISSIONARIES AND TRADE ON THE NORTHERN CAPE FRONTIER

Between 1800 and 1814 mission Griqua had access to guns, powder, and ammunition and to the colonial market at Cape Town through passes issued to them by the missionaries at Griqua Town. Those Griqua not attached to the mission traded illegally with the Boers and itinerant traders who met them along the colonial border. These illegal activities angered the mission Griqua. First, by illegally obtaining supplies of weapons from colonists, the non-mission station Griqua were able to maintain a strong position politically and militarily relative to the Griqua at Griqua Town and to the other Transorangian societies. Second, the illegal trade discouraged those Griqua who were loyal to the missionaries because they saw no advantage to obeying the regulations and rules laid down by them and, *de facto*, by the colonial government who had no legitimate power over them. Third, it disturbed the price and supply structure for goods traded along the northern frontier and often left the mission Griqua with inadequate supplies of goods for which they were forced to pay exorbitant prices.[22] In 1814 some of the mission Griqua at Griqua Town openly rebelled and returned to their pre-1800 practices of roaming about the frontier in trading and raiding parties.

The Griqua Town missionaries' inability to construct a viable, independent polity in Transorangia, and to bring all the feuding factions together following the rebellion of 1814, provoked the colonial government into taking action. Believing that desertions by slaves and Khoi servants across the northern border were increasing, and that there was a proliferation in the illegal arms and ammunition trade as well as raids on colonial cattle, the government reacted against the missionaries, rather than the illegal traders. It closed a number of outstations staffed by African lay ministers along the upper Orange River and refused to allow four recently arrived LMS missionaries, including Robert Moffat, to establish new stations beyond the colonial borders.[23] It sought to bring the Griqua Town mission within the colonial orbit, subject to colonial law and answerable to the nearest landdrost (magistrate) who, from November 1818, resided at the newly established sub-drostdy (sub-magisterial district) of Beaufort.[24] Because the government did not possess any official authority over the Griqua, they attempted to pressure them to abide by the colonial regulations by controlling their access to the colony. These policies proved just as ineffectual as the missionaries' efforts, however, when applied across the vast expanses of the northern frontier. In the 1820s Cape authorities began to treat the Griqua more as a polity in their own right and to deal with them accordingly.

The Griqua were not the only peoples settled along the middle stretches of the Orange River. The area was also inhabited by groups of cattle-keeping Kora Khoi, or Coranna as they were then known, and numerous small bands of San, who were hunter-gatherers.[25] As the Griqua gradually established a quasi-hegemony over this area in the early 1800s and took possession of the few springs, the Khoikhoi and the San faced a choice between assimilation into the Griqua community or moving deeper into the interior. Some of each group remained; some scattered further to the north and east.[26] Until 1814 the dominant Griqua generally treated the San and Kora who remained as dependents, but in that year, according to a constitution drawn up by the visiting LMS missionary John Campbell, all members of the community were to be treated as equals. Although the distinctions did not immediately die away, in 1820 Andries Waterboer, of San descent, was elected *Kaptyn* at Griqua Town.[27]

Beyond the Griqua to the north resided several communities of Sotho-Tswana, divided into a number of clan groupings: the Tlhaping, Rolong, Kwena, Hurutshe, Kwena-Fokeng, and Ngwaketse. Between 1800 and 1820 a stable trading relationship was established between the Griqua and the Tlhaping. This relationship brought the Tlhaping and other Sotho-Tswana communities within the "southern catchment area." That is, the people in this area by 1817 had turned their trade more to the south and the colony, and away from their traditional trading partners farther to the north. There was little penetration by European, or for that matter Griqua, traders into those areas controlled by the Sotho-Tswana until after 1820. The Griqua acted as middlemen for this Sotho-Tswana trade with the colony. Sotho-Tswana trading parties brought ivory, iron, and other goods from the north, and exchanged them with the Griqua for sheep, tobacco and European manufactured goods, including guns and ammunition. The Griqua then passed these goods on to the Cape market.[28]

Policy regulating cross border trade under the Dutch East India Company (VOC) had consisted mainly of monopoly and threat. Although at different times during its 150 year rule private traders were given permission to barter for cattle and ivory with the Khoikhoi, and later the Xhosa, the VOC generally tried to restrict the right of trade to company representatives only, usually licensed butchers or official trading expeditions. They adopted this policy partly in response to the violence that was sometimes engendered by illegal trade, but mainly in order to secure to themselves a monopoly on the supply of meat and other valuable commodities brought to Cape Town.

Of course, this did not prevent individuals from illegally transporting wagonloads of goods beyond the colonial boundaries to trade. The VOC reaction to this illicit barter was to issue *placaaten* (proclamations), in 1677, 1727, 1739, 1770, 1774 and 1786, and threaten to execute anyone caught trading with the indigenous peoples. The sheer number of *placaaten* testifies to their ineffectiveness.[29] When the British first occupied the colony in 1795 they replaced the monopolistic practices of the VOC with a policy encouraging entrepreneurship and free trade.[30] Initially, however, the new government's policy relating to transborder trade with the colony's neighbors did not change. The old *placaaten* were invoked and the only barter permitted beyond the colonial boundaries was that carried on by officially recognized exploration/trading expeditions.

MISSIONARIES AND COLONIAL REGULATION OF FRONTIER TRADE

But, like the Dutch officials before them, the British were unable to enforce this policy of separation. Colonists continued to trade relatively freely with the Griqua, Kora, and Nama in the north and with the Xhosa in the east. It is impossible to measure the extent of this illicit barter but it was enough by the mid-1810s to draw complaints from missionaries and government officials and to draw the attention of the newly-appointed colonial governor, Lord Charles Henry Somerset.[31]

Somerset believed the resentment and violence that often accompanied illegal trade increased the possibility of border hostilities. He also discerned the economic advantages offered by the establishment of commercial links with the Griqua and African societies beyond the borders. In order to lessen the violence and reap the economic benefits, however, he had to reverse the old policy of separation and establish formal and official contacts with the colony's neighbors.

Within six years of his becoming governor Somerset had established several new policies affecting frontier trade and contact between the peoples on both sides of the colonial border. That segment of the colonial population, however, that resided along the imperial fault line between the two communities, the missionaries, remained a major source of anxiety for the governor. Somerset's conflict with the missionaries resulted from fundamentally opposite views about the missionary's role while serving at mission stations beyond the colonial border.

According to Somerset, the missionary was to maintain social order while harboring a labor pool for neighboring farmers and inculcating in the mission residents the value of wage labor. The missionaries were answerable to the colonial government and obligated to implement and enforce governmental policy. They were responsible, for example, for issuing passports permitting Griqua and Africans to enter the colony for purposes of trade. The missionaries, on the other hand, maintained a spirit of independence that often led them to question government policy, particularly the treatment of Khoisan, Griqua, and Africans within and without the colony. They complained about the deception, fraud and even theft perpetuated against Griqua traders by colonial traders. They believed that the missions should develop agriculture so that the mission residents could become self-sufficient, own property, and decrease their dependence on laboring for colonial farmers.[32]

The Cape's northern frontier zone witnessed the most extensive trading activity between the colony and its Griqua and African neighbors prior to 1824 when trade fairs were established at Fort Willshire in the Eastern Cape. A portion of this exchange was officially sanctioned by the government, permitting licensed merchants or butchers to travel into the interior to obtain meat for Cape Town and the ships in port.[33] The colonial authorities also appointed some of the missionaries to act as government agents and allowed them to issue passes for certain groups, such as the Griqua, to enter the colony to trade. There was also an extensive missionary trade carried on by all the missionaries,[34] which was also greatest beyond the northern frontier prior to 1824. And finally, there was the illegal trade, much of it involving the illicit barter of guns, ammunition and powder. As all commercial contact between colonist and peoples living outside the Cape colony was illegal, apart from the exceptions previously mentioned, the majority of trade across the Cape frontier at this time probably took place in defiance of colonial law.[35]

THE ESTABLISHMENT OF FRONTIER FAIRS

In order to establish some measure of control over trade along the northern frontier, the Graaff Reinet landdrost, Andries Stockenstrom, suggested in April 1817 the creation of a new sub-district named Beaufort, attached to the largest district in the Cape colony, Graaff Reinet. In addition, he proposed a frontier fair be held at the new deputy landdrost's residence. Stockenstrom noted that for many years the government had attempted, unsuccessfully, to make contact with the African interior where "the more savage nations . . . are most anxious to trade with the colony." Mission station residents beyond the Orange River had already made a "vast deal" from bartering for the abundant ivory found in the transborder country. He believed a fair could attract this ivory trade to the colony, as well as other useful trade articles, such as local produce, if a market were established in the region. Once the northern societies were aware that this was the only place where trade might legally be carried on Stockenstrom expected that the "Smuggling and dangerous sort of traffick . . . by which the lawless Bastaards are provided with a great number of Arms, and a vast quantity of ammunition," would stop; the incitement of slaves and Khoi to leave their masters checked; and, of course, "civilization" and Christianity brought to the region.[36]

Somerset acted on Stockenstrom's suggestion and in November 1818 created the sub-district of Beaufort (which became Beaufort West) and a new mission station named Kookfontein, where Somerset hoped the "wandering

Bosjesmen or Bastaards . . . [would] settle . . . , and receive instruction in the principles of Christianity." Somerset also directed that a fair be instituted at the new mission as soon as possible, so that Griqua and other "northern tribes" could frequent this fair and barter their produce, mainly ivory and draught oxen, for basic necessities.[37] Clearly Somerset viewed the fairs as part of a larger policy to encourage the development of European culture and industry among the inhabitants living on the mission station, and hopefully among non-mission residents who visited the fairs as well. Each mission family was to receive a plot of garden land to cultivate. It was Somerset's wish that "wants will be created which Industry and Industry alone will gratify," including a desire among both men and women for "the usual clothing used by the lower classes . . . of this Settlement, and . . . the uncleaning [sic] kaross [skin blanket] should be thrown aside."[38] Stockenstrom believed through fairs the colony could "much sooner get acquainted with the Tribes, inhabiting the higher Parts of Africa, and with their Country, their mind would be much sooner enlightened, and render it susceptible of the Precepts of Christianity, than by all the missions as yet projected."[39]

Somerset asked that "neighbouring Tribes" be invited to Kookfontein to barter cattle and other valuables for any colonial articles they might wish or need. He wanted to demonstrate to them "the paternal Care . . . extended to their Brethren within [the colony] . . . the fairness of dealing . . . and the improvement . . . in those who live in better regulated society than those to which they have been accustomed," thereby creating a "desire to participate in the Benefits of Civilization." Somerset asked Stockenstrom to frame the necessary regulations to insure "the preservation of order, regularity and fair dealing at these markets."[40]

Colonial hawkers, that is, licensed itinerant traders, who were predominately Afrikaners, were to provide the goods necessary to satisfy Griqua and African desires at these markets. These hawkers were licensed to travel within specified districts and exchange their merchandise, generally for cattle, with local farmers.[41] Somerset also proposed to send the newly-appointed Beaufort deputy landdrost, John Baird, a supply of trade items to insure that the visiting Griqua and African traders, having come long distances, would be guaranteed a market. Baird was not to interfere with the colonial traders, but was to use these goods for barter, "should the hawkers not attend or not have it in their power to satisfy the demands made upon them."[42]

The Griqua Town missionary, William Anderson, was to communicate to the northern border societies the times and arrangements for the fairs, and that they could now have their necessities supplied at these markets.[43]

Stockenstrom advised Anderson that the "bordering Tribes" could bring whatever they wished to exchange at the fairs and "every facility [was to be afforded] to the Griquas, Bricquas and other neighbouring Hordes to add to their comfort and improve their ways of living." Anderson was to confer with the peoples in his area and determine the dates and times that they considered most suitable for holding the fairs. He was also to ensure that no one entering the colony to attend the fairs would be pressed into service, either for the military or as laborers on colonial farms. Many Griqua had left the colony for just these reasons and the fair's success now depended on the government guaranteeing their security should they return.[44]

Anderson promised to promote the fair with everyone with whom he came into contact. He had explained the plan to some of the people and some approved of the idea while others viewed it as an attempt by the government to take away their liberty.[45] He proposed 4 August 1819 as the date for the first fair. Anderson expected a large quantity of ivory brought to the market, "for which many will like to have money, being indebted."[46]

The date of the first Beaufort fair—4 August—as it turned out, was not an optimum time to commence the fairs.[47] The eastern frontier was in a state of war, and all the able bodied white men in the Graaff Reinet district had been called away to fight, including Stockenstrom, who was engaged with his commando unit in battle against a party of Xhosa.[48]

Baird, left to manage the fair alone, requested the presence of a small military presence to enable him to enforce good order. He was particularly anxious about the "considerable number of muskets" possessed by the Griqua and the "implements of war," that might be brought by the Tswana and others to this first fair. Baird estimated that there were about 200 settler farmers together with some 60 or 70 Griqua or Khoikhoi on commando or guarding cattle, and he doubted whether he could conscript more than one hundred willing and able farmers into the field if required. In fact, he noted, "at present, this District is inhabited with old and worn out, lame, and otherwise debilitated People." Baird also worried that the hostilities might discourage the colonial merchants and hawkers from entering into trade with the Griqua and Africans attending the fair.[49]

Initially Stockenstrom did not view the Kookfontein fair as so "intricate and serious" an event as did Baird. Although his commando activities prevented him from giving the fair much attention, he had never intended to do more than "ensure a supply of merchandise at the market, appoint the clerk . . . to keep a list of what was brought to Market, the average price of the articles &c, and send . . . a few instructions. . . ."[50] As the event date drew closer, however, he expressed concern that the people coming from beyond the colony's boundaries receive a fair deal and not return empty-handed. For this reason, and to support missionary efforts to encourage and regulate frontier trade, Stockenstrom made special allowances to the missionaries accompanying the Griqua and Africans traders. Should the fair not be sufficiently stocked with those items that the Griqua and Africans were most anxious to procure, Anderson, or any other missionary, could journey to Cape Town or wherever he wished to purchase the desired merchandise. Stockenstrom also gave permission to the Graaff Reinet and Cradock merchants to attend the fair in order to ensure its success. They were to carry with them sufficient goods so that Stockenstrom would not have to provide Baird with any trade items.[51]

At the same time Stockenstrom wrote to Anderson with the wish that he attend the August fair and pass on any suggestions he might have for improving future fairs.[52] Anderson, however, was prevented by "pressing circumstances" from attending. In his absence he requested that Baird look after some ivory tusks he was sending to the market. He hoped his example would encourage the Griqua Town residents to take their produce to the fair as well. Anderson asked Baird to dispose of these teeth and give the profits "to his man who has a list of articles . . . to purchase."[53]

Stockenstrom intended the market to be open to everyone. All African peoples, by which he included the Griqua, to the north of the colony were entitled to sell their wares at the market, and all inhabitants of the colony had the same right to bring and sell colonial produce. Everyone coming from the northern interior had to carry a pass issued by the missionary, William Anderson, or be turned away. Those possessing passes and allowed into the colony, could travel no further than Kookfontein, and were to be unarmed, or armed only to the extent allowed by Baird. On their return passage home, they were to follow a route fixed by the deputy landdrost. If they were found to have taken with them "Slaves, hottentots or others, deserting this Colony," or to have committed other transgressions, they would be pursued, punished, and never again allowed access to the market. Likewise, no arms or ammunition were to be sold to any person who resided outside the colony, and any transgressor was to be immediately arrested.

Considering the circumstances, colonial officials regarded this first fair as fairly successful. It commenced at sunrise on 5 August and continued daily, except for Sunday the 8th, until sunset on the 10th.[54] Baird, who was in daily attendance, reported that "transactions on both sides were regular liberal and fair." He was "highly satisfied with the conduct of the Colonists and . . . Bastards." He noted that there were very few of the other neighboring societies, and these few were in the service of the Griqua and brought no articles for barter.[55]

In Anderson's absence the Griqua traders, numbering about 120, entered and left the colony under the leadership of captains Berrends and Kok. They brought with them twenty-five wagons and some fifty team of oxen. On the colonial side there were but "six waggons with merchandise, and about 16 more with Tabaco, fruit and Brandewyn." Baird calculated that altogether about fifteen thousand rixdollars worth of goods were bought and sold."[56] On the 14th the captains with their people took leave, according to Baird, "full of expressions of unfeigned and heartfelt gratitude for his Lordship's magnanimous and benevolent provision made, which they Saw, and acknowledged to be solely for their benefit."[57]

Early in 1820, Stockenstrom suggested that future fairs be held at the new village of Beaufort, rather than the Kookfontein mission station. He pointed out that societies coming from the north had to pass the village on their way to the mission, an additional twenty mile journey with their cattle over a sharp stony road. The mission was also off the regular route taken by colonists and merchants. Locating the fair in Beaufort would allow the magistrate and police to perform their regular duties while watching over the fair, and enable the "visitors from far . . . [to] leave their Waggons &c [for] repair while the fair goes on."[58] Stockenstrom also hoped the Beaufort fair, would aid the growth of the new town, which it did. Twenty-one plots of land were sold in the village valued at 12,149 rixdollars in 1820.[59]

The second northern border fair was held at Beaufort in April 1820.[60] On the evening of 23 April there arrived at the new village "Bastards or Griequas [sic], and Korannas under the Chiefs Kock, & Barend, and the Bootchoanas or Breequas under the Chiefs Chaka & Maklanaka altogether about two hundred in number."[61] They brought with them "twenty Seven Waggons laden with Elephants Teeth, Salt, Skins of all kinds, wheat, honey, and various Curiosities driving before them upwards of Seven hundred Oxen."[62]

According to Stockenstrom the colonial traders and those from the interior left the fair, "highly Satisfied with the Mutual fair dealing and Confidence which had prevailed throughout, . . . as well as of the regular peaceable Conduct of them all." He observed that the "Briequa Chiefs" were delighted with the reception afforded them and thanked him "in the name of their King Mateebee," who intended to come to the next fair in person with "numbers of his People who possessed an abundance of Ivory."[63]

RESULTS AND CONSEQUENCES OF THE FRONTIER FAIRS

While colonial officials were pleased with the Beaufort fair's outcome, these frontier markets did cause some unforeseen hardships for the Griquas and others who attended them, and missionaries became the scapegoats. For one, it was not always safe for the northern peoples to leave their villages unattended. In July 1820, John Philip, superintendent of the London Missionary Society, reported to his London superiors that "We have heard that another party of Bushmen have robbed the Griquas at the same time and manner [as the other night], perhaps taking advantage of so many Griquas being at the Beaufort fair."[64] The fairs also created problems for those remaining at the mission stations by tying up scarce manpower, wagons, and oxen. Moffat complained that the "fairs attract [the Tswana] from their farms in too great numbers, it becomes a species of emigration, their homes are left defenseless, and their agriculture neglected perhaps at the proper season."[65] There were also no oxen left at the station to pull wagons for they had all been taken to the fair.[66]

In a journal entry for 22 June 1820 the missionary Robert Hamilton noted that two Tswana returning from the fair that day brought the news that three of their number had drowned in the Orange River while returning from the Beaufort market. On hearing this the women cried and the people "cursed the Dutch people as the cause by advising the Bootchunnas to go." Six days later, when Campbell returned, Hamilton informed him that 'in his absence we had had almost no Bootchunnas in Church as they were displeased with us for advising them to go to the Market . . ."[67]

Easy access to alcohol was a constant problem at the fairs. The missionaries believed they could discern an increasing amount of crime, corruption and violence among the mission residents that could be traced to this source. LMS missionary Henry Helm felt the fairs revealed the "sinful tendencies" of the members of his Griqua Town congregation, who generally returned from the fairs filled with stories of "drinking themselves drunken, quarreling, [and] fighting."[68] One Griqua teacher, Barend David, had been expelled from the church for becoming intoxicated one evening while attending the fair.[69] The government representative in Griqua Town, John Melvill, complained that liquor bought at the fairs and from the farmers on the road resulted in "evil effects" that could be witnessed from Graaff Reinet to the Orange River.[70]

Moffat also felt the Griqua Town residents were charged unfair prices for goods and that the fairs afforded little relief to either missionaries or Griqua as long as every article continued to be so expensive. He offered, as example, a great coat costing seventy rixdollars, a hat ten to fourteen rixdollars, or an ox, a handkerchief three rixdollars and "een Boschlimmer Mess," a kind of knife, 2 rixdollars.[71]

Despite these problems the missionaries were not totally displeased with the fairs and often took advantage of them themselves. John Philip was an early supporter of the fairs, noting that they might prove "a profitable speculation for Messrs. Toomer and Rutherford, . . . could they send a Waggon load [of beads] to the next Beaufort fair in 12 months."[72] Robert Hamilton bought "a beautiful cat skin Kaross . . . the only one that was brought to the market" that cost him 42 Rixdollars."[73]

In addition the articles[74] that the Griqua asked be made available for their purchase included 400 pounds of beads, ploughshares, spades; picks, files & rasps, chisels, smith's and other hammers, axes and hatchets, saws, planes, tar, and iron. This list of predominantly agricultural implements and ironware reflects the Griqua's colonial cultural heritage as well as some missionary influence.

For the missionaries on the northern frontier the fairs were their only link with the colony until a regular post was established in the mid-1820s. Melvill defended Helm's failure to forward his journal on schedule to the LMS directors in London by informing them that before a regular mail service was established between Griqua Town and Cape Town, the Griqua entered the colony but once a year to attend the fair. This visit did not always occur at the proper time for the journal to reach England in time for the director's meeting.[75]

A planned fair for September 1820 was cancelled, and no other fairs were held in 1820. In February 1821 the Griqua Town missionary Henry Helm informed Stockenstrom that a Griqua party planned to visit Graaff Reinet.[76] The intended Griqua visit caused much anxiety among Beaufort officials. They feared for the Beaufort fair's future success and existence were the Griqua to extend their stay in Graaff Reinet. Sir Rufane Donkin, the acting governor, sought to allay their fears by assuring them that he would not encourage such visits and that all commercial dealings with the Griqua should be restricted to the Beaufort fairs.[77]

Stockenstrom approved of the Griqua trip, explaining to Donkin that the object of their visit was, in fact, to enable them to maintain the Beaufort fairs. They reasoned that as they had had nothing to bring to the cancelled fair the previous September, they would visit the colony now to try and procure on credit from the numerous Graaff Reinet and Uitenhage merchants those articles that were required in their barter with the Tswana, and thus enable them to collect cattle and ivory to bring to a fair that year. If the governor determined to hold to his decision to limit trade to Beaufort, then Stockenstrom would abide by his wishes and request that Anderson communicate that decision to the Griqua leaders. He observed, however, that there was no definite law forbidding Griqua visits to the colony and Griqua had trafficked with every part of the colony, exclusive of the fair.[78]

Helm did not receive notification in time to prevent the Griqua from heading to Graaff Reinet, but promised in future to issue no passes except for the Beaufort fairs.[79] The missionary Stephen Kay crossed paths with these people on their way to Graaff Reinet in April 1821, although he assumed they were going to the Beaufort fair. He reported meeting a caravan of nineteen wagons and between two and three hundred people, principally Griqua and Tswana, "recently come down the country . . . to trade with the Colony at the Annual Fair."[80]

The next Beaufort fair, set for May 1822, was cancelled. In April 1822, Helm informed the government that the Griqua had nothing to bring to the fair and only a few of them wanted it to be held.[81] The Griqua Town *Kaptyn*, Andries Waterboer, did journey to Beaufort with three wagons to meet Melvill who was returning from Cape Town. They met at Israels Poort, and, having but a few articles for sale at Beaufort, Waterboer instead traded them with the farmers at that place. In June 1822 Melvill requested that an October fair be scheduled as the Griqua Town residents had a good number of elephant tusks. They were in need of many articles and could not conveniently wait till the following year. Ironically, considering the efforts of colonial officials and missionaries to encourage the Xhosa on the eastern frontier to trade for agricultural and industrial tools, Melvill complained that the Griqua "seldom procure at the fair the articles they most stand in need of." The scarcity of such articles compelled them to pay extravagant prices wherever they could get them. As examples he cited a "great coat of common duffel," that cost twenty-five to thirty rixdollars in Cape Town, costing seventy at Beaufort, and beads being raised in price from 1 1/2 to 2 rixdollars a pound to 6 to 10. As a result of these high prices some persons had traded away nearly all their cattle and had received little or nothing useful in return. Some told him that they had given up going to the fair as it "had made them quite poor."[82]

Stockenstrom, however, believed the Griqua's real objection to the fair was the prohibition against the free sale of firearms, ammunition and spirits. He observed that these were no doubt secretly procured by the Griqua at such high prices as might "make them poor."[83]

As it turned out, the intended October fair never materialized either as the Griqua oxen contracted the *Klauw Siekte* (foot disease). Eight wagons set out for the fair, with not less than 2500 elephants tusks, but only one was able to proceed. Melvill requested that these facts be made public in the colony as he realized what displeasure had been caused by the Griqua absence.[84] Before another fair could be arranged Melvill informed the colonial authorities that a Mr. Oliver from Graaff Reinet had come to Griqua Town to collect money due him and had taken all the elephant tusks as well as a good number of cattle.[85]

MISSIONARIES, TRADE, AND FRONTIER POLITICS

This was the last attempt to hold a fair at Beaufort. By 1824 inconsistent government policies directed toward the different Griqua groups had caused much resentment and hostility. Officially Griqua were only to trade at the Beaufort fairs, and were allowed into the colony only if they possessed a pass signed by the government agent or a missionary. But those Griqua who had revolted against the colony, and broken away from the mission stations, traveled freely across the long stretches of unguarded border to trade for arms, ammunition and powder with the colonial farmers. This created an atmosphere in which the Griqua who obeyed the colonial regulations felt they were receiving nothing in return for their good behavior while their enemies were illegally amassing a large supply of arms. The Griqua *Kaptyn* Andries Waterboer, expressed his anger and resentment to the missionaries Helm and Christopher Sass in May 1824. He complained that the Griqua Town residents were not able to purchase necessities from the white farmers, who told them that though they had passes from Melvill, colonists were not allowed to trade with Griqua except at the Beaufort fair. Other Griqua, however, who entered the colony without such passes, were able to trade with the farmers for whatever they wished.[86] He asked the missionaries to write to the governor and request that the fair at Beaufort be abandoned and his followers be allowed to go into the colony when and where they pleased. Helm and Sass explained to him that this would have to be done by the government agent Melvill.[87]

The political situation in the northeastern frontier zone was exacerbated between 1820 and 1825 by the division of the Griqua into competing factions following Andries Waterboer's election as Griqua Town captain at the end of 1819.[88] The older Griqua families under the leadership of Barend Barends and Adam Kok II moved away from Griqua Town to form their own settlements at Daniels Kuil and Campbell respectively. A third group, the so-called "Bergenaars," composed of disaffected Griqua and a number of Kora and San who joined them, collected at a site along the Modder River.[89]

Throughout this period Waterboer had the support of the government agent, Melvill, and through him, the colonial government. In return for his cooperation Waterboer expected to receive certain privileges, including a steady supply of weapons and ammunition, free access to the colony and government action to halt the illegal activities of the other factions. Had the government granted these requests the dissident parties might have sought accommodation with Waterboer and recognized colonial authority. Cape officials accorded Waterboer few special privileges, however, and had but limited success in halting the illegal activities of the other groups. Griqua Town residents were allowed to obtain passes to travel into the colony, but only to specific places at certain times of the year. They had placed themselves under colonial protection with the government agent living in their midst but remained less well off than those who recognized no colonial authority. Increasingly dissatisfied with Waterboer's collaboration with the colonial government, they watched with a jealous and resentful eye as the Bergenaars entered the colony without passes and traded illicitly and relatively freely with Afrikaner pastoralists as well as hawkers transporting goods from Cape Town and Stellenbosch.[90]

In May 1824 Lord Somerset ended the Beaufort fair and gave permission to "Griquas of good character," as determined by the government agent or a missionary, to purchase small quantities of gunpowder at Graaff Reinet. Such actions were intended to affirm the government's approval of the mission Griqua's loyalty while retaining tight control over their movements and actions. The Bergenaars' example of an unrestrained intercourse in arms and ammunition with the colony had created such a spirit of insubordination, however, that few of the mission Griqua applied for certificates to obtain the powder.[91]

The hostility between the opposing Griqua factions intensified from July to September 1824 when raids and counter raids were carried out. Waterboer struck first, leading a surprise attack against the Bergenaars' main camp near present day Fauresmith, and capturing their entire herd of 5000 cattle. This was followed by a Bergenaar raid against Griqua Town in September while both Waterboer and Melvill were in Cape Town.[92] The latter had returned to Cape Town, disheartened and frustrated by his inability as government agent to influence government opinion and action, or to bring the warring factions together.[93]

A primary reason for the government's failure to meet Waterboer's requests, and to halt the illicit trade, was that several government officials in the northern frontier zone, particularly the Graaff Reinet landdrost, Andries Stockenstrom, were sympathetic to the old leaders, Barends and Kok, and to the grievances presented by the Bergenaars regarding their treatment by the Cape government. In late 1824 and early 1825 Melvill and Stockenstrom presented their respective positions to government. Melvill, during a visit to Cape Town, argued that trading rights should be granted exclusively to Waterboer. He complained that the Bergenaars continued their illicit trade, obtaining guns and ammunition freely. He believed all Griqua should be forced to join together in one polity under Waterboer's leadership at Griqua Town. This could only be accomplished by granting certain privileges to "persons of good Character," and excluding all others

from these advantages. The ones so favored would then cease their depre-
dations and live in peace under their lawful leaders in order to retain their
special rights.[94]

Stockenstrom argued, in a report following a visit to the Bergenaar
camp in October 1824 that the majority of the Griqua did not support Waterboer. He believed if Waterboer received special privileges, and was supplied
with arms and ammunition, his followers would quickly abandon him and
join with the rebellious groups to use these weapons against him. The Bergenaar leaders promised Stockenstrom that they bore no animosity toward the
colony and that they wanted to live in peace with all their neighbors. They
would not, however, submit to Waterboer's authority. Stockenstrom warned
them of the consequences should they continue raiding their neighbors, but
gave them permission to enter the colony in small numbers to trade provided
they first obtain passes from the lay minister Goeyman, cross the border only
at Meyers Drift, and carry on their barter only under the supervision of a
local field cornet. They were not allowed to trade in weapons or ammunition.[95]

THE 1825 PROCLAMATION REGULATING FRONTIER TRADE

As Stockenstrom presented his arguments from a distance, while Melvill and
Waterboer were in Cape Town consulting directly with the governor, it was
no surprise that Somerset followed Melvill's advice. On 27 January 1825 he
issued a proclamation intended to better regulate trade between the colony
and its neighbors along the northern border and put an end to the illicit traffic
in that region. According to the new law, which was to take effect on 27 July
1825, all trade or contact of any kind with the Griqua or other neighboring
societies beyond the colony's northern frontier was strictly prohibited except
by means of passports. Each person or party intending to enter the colony to
trade had to possess a passport signed either by the government agent at Griqua Town, or the resident missionary in his absence, or by the Graaff Reinet
landdrost or Beaufort deputy landdrost. The passports were for "persons of
good character" who could then proceed to any of the principal towns in the
colony, including Cape Town. The passports stated the exact place or places
the bearer intended to go, and were valid only for traders.

Individuals from beyond the frontier in possession of such passports
were permitted to trade with the colonists at the chief towns, under the
control of the local authorities who were to ensure that the visitors received
a fair deal. Persons not furnished with such passports would be detained
and could have their property confiscated.

Hawkers or other colonists could also obtain passports from the Graaff Reinet landdrost or Beaufort deputy landdrost. They were to limit their trading activities beyond the frontier, however, to those places where a government agent resided and place themselves under his direct control.

The proclamation's final clause demonstrates the dominant influence that Melvill had with government in January 1825 and also offers some insight into Somerset's understanding of conditions on the northern frontier. Stockenstrom was instructed to call upon the Bergenaar leaders and explain to them the new law. The Bergenaars were to submit to the elected Griqua chiefs, that is, Waterboer, and place themselves on good terms with the Griqua people generally, or be "shut out entirely from all Traffick with the Colony." Stockenstrom was also to give a guarantee to the neighboring chiefs that the British government had no intention of interfering with them in any manner, but sought only their "peace and happiness."[96]

Asked to comment on these regulations, Stockenstrom observed that he had no objections but there was also a missionary establishment nearby the Bergenaar settlement, from where the local missionary might dispense passports to visit the colony as long as the Bergenaars remained peaceful. Their kraals were much nearer the colony than to Griqua Town. It would be a great inconvenience for them if they had to journey to Griqua Town to obtain passes when their settlement was only a fourth or a third of that distance from the colony.[97]

Somerset's response to Stockenstrom's suggestion was that, as the Bergenaars continued to live in opposition to "legal power and good order," it did not appear sound policy to extend to them any privileges. They would be able to obtain passes only through acknowledged authorities. J. Goeyman, the missionary assistant established among them, would therefore not be allowed to issue passports for entry into the colony to trade.[98]

In May 1825, according to his instructions as set down in the proclamation, Stockenstrom visited the Bergenaar camp near Goeyman's mission, but found nearly all the camp's inhabitants departed. He was informed by Goeyman that since Stockenstrom's visit the previous October, the Bergenaars had been peaceful, had made no raids against their neighbors, and had respected the agreement they made with Stockenstrom at that time. When they learned, however, of the government's support for Waterboer, as contained in the January proclamation, they began to pack their belongings and leave, heading toward the Riet River. Goeyman believed they would never submit to Waterboer and would resume their attacks on neighboring African societies.[99]

One Bergenaar leader, Andries Hendrik, remained behind in order to hear from Stockenstrom himself what the colonial government's real views were toward themselves and Waterboer. Stockenstrom convinced Hendrik to recall the other Bergenaar leaders and on 20 May Stockenstrom met with Gerrit Goeyman, Adam Kok and Hendrik and read to them the January proclamation. They responded that they did not question the Cape government's good will toward them, and had no objections to living under the government of the old chiefs, Barends and Kok, but they would never accept Waterboer as their leader. They argued that he had been elected in 1819 by a small number of Griqua Town inhabitants to manage affairs there, but with the support of Melvill and the missionaries he now pretended to rule over all the Griqua. Only their respect for the colonial government, and a fear of injuring the missionaries and government agent at Griqua Town, prevented them from crushing Waterboer. On his return Stockenstrom reported that in his opinion it would require considerable mismanagement to alienate the Bergenaars and make them enemies of the colony. He believed Waterboer intended to use government weapons to usurp power and that, if successful, it would lead to war between the various Griqua factions on the northern frontier.

Leaving aside the ill-feelings aroused by granting certain privileges to one group and not to others, Stockenstrom believed that if the Bergenaars were not allowed to purchase goods and supplies fairly and legally at colonial markets then they would smuggle them in illegally, or buy them at exorbitant prices from the privileged Griqua. To make these purchases the Bergenaars would take as many cattle as they required from their weaker neighbors further in the interior. Thus, according to Stockenstrom,

> The evils which some wretched and weak Hordes will ultimately suffer from the depredations . . . committed upon their Stock (their principal means of Subsistence) for the purpose of supplying our Markets, are incalculable and cannot miss the consideration of our Government . . .

Stockenstrom suggested that the trade in cattle between the colony and the societies living on its northern border be halted altogether.[100]

Somerset's reply to Stockenstrom's report marked the beginning of a change in attitude by the Cape government toward Waterboer and the dissident Griqua groups. Somerset appeared shocked that the Bergenaars had received his proposal unfavorably. He had issued the January proclamation hoping it would unite the various Griqua leaders, and had based it principally on Melvill's report of the situation the previous December. Somerset acknowledged that Waterboer had long been recognized as one of the Griqua leaders approved of by government and had received special attention on his recent visit to Cape Town. Somerset had not intended this as a rejection of the other Griqua leaders' authority, however, and argued that any of them would have received such attention had they come to Cape Town.

Somerset now reversed his position and declared that he did not wish to support Waterboer over any other Griqua leader. If the Bergenaars were determined to be independent from the Griqua Town faction, he would consider allowing the missionary settled among them to grant licenses as prescribed in the January proclamation. Somerset also agreed with Stockenstrom about the need to prohibit a trade in cattle and ordered that all officials granting licenses in the future were to strictly forbid such barter.[101]

Melvill returned to Griqua Town in May, believing he had convinced government of the correctness of his views, but apprehensive about the success of the new measures because so much depended upon Stockenstrom's cooperation. His misgivings were confirmed when he learned shortly after his arrival that two of the first colonial hawkers receiving trading licenses under the January proclamation had proceeded directly to the Bergenaar camp without making an appearance in Griqua Town. Another hawker went first to trade with the Bergenaars and then brought the remainder of his goods, "scarcely anything that the people wanted," to Griqua Town. Melvill also received reports that two wagons loaded with brandy had been illegally trading near the salt pans about fifty miles southeast of Griqua Town.102

The cattle trade prohibition aroused great discontent among the "orderly part of the Griquas" for it left them with nothing to barter for colonial goods. They therefore abandoned agriculture, despite the missionaries' protestations, and returned to their old practice of hunting in order to obtain skins and ivory for trade. Melvill believed the prohibition against the cattle trade negated what little authority he had among the Griqua people because they now realized he had no influence with the government and could not offer them sound advice.103 These new developments did not change Melvill's opinion, however, that Waterboer and his followers should receive the full support of the government and that they were being punished and restricted in their colonial dealings "while a set of Plunderers have received encouragement and are still supported."104

The end to this dispute was decided not by the exertions of Melvill or Stockenstrom, but by the superintendent of the LMS in South Africa, Dr. John Philip. In August 1825 Philip crossed the Orange River and visited several of the Griqua settlements: Philippolis, Ramah, and Adam Kok and thirty to forty Bergenaars on the Modder River. As a result of these travels he concluded that Stockenstrom's analysis of the situation on the northern frontier was more accurate than Melvill's and called for a meeting to be held at Griqua Town toward the end of September to which all the Griqua leaders were invited. The outcome of this meeting was a recognition that there were three legitimate polities, Waterboer, Adam Kok II at Philippolis and Barend Barends at Boetsap, and that each should be allowed to trade and negotiate directly and independently with the colony and the colonial government.105

CONCLUSION

This study has focused on missionaries in southern Africa in the early nineteenth century who served as commercial intermediaries and government emissaries across an imperial fault line. As shapers of frontier trade policy they were often ineffectual. They disagreed with the government about the role of the missionary in the interior, and among themselves about the advisability of frontier fairs, or even frontier trade in general. These disagreements, the questionable activities of some missionaries, and the continuous disputes in support of one Griqua leader over another alienated the Cape governors and weakened the missionaries' position.

The Griqua on the northeastern frontier were anxious to develop commercial relations with the colony but not at the expense of their independence. Their requests for trade and support in fighting their enemies were communicated to the government by missionaries and local colonial officials representing one Griqua faction or another. Although the government made several attempts to establish a legal trade, and to allow the Cape colony's northern neighbors access to colonial markets, they were largely unsuccessful in their efforts. The disagreements among the different Griqua factions created a great deal of distrust among government officials and reinforced the view that the Griqua were incapable of self-government. The illegal trading activities of the Bergenaars and their forays into the colony also angered many officials and alienated the missionaries and government agent.

Matters were made even worse by colonial authorities who sought to encourage trade on the northern frontier but required that trade fairs be held within the colony, as at Beaufort. A market at Griqua Town, or Kuruman, would have taken advantage of the Griqua desire to trade with the colony and attracted colonial butchers and itinerant merchants. This would have freed the Griqua of having to drive livestock to the colonial fair and placed the responsibility on the butchers and merchants to return the livestock in good condition to the colony. Since many colonial traders carried on an illegal trade anyway, the government's contention that they did not want colonists traveling beyond the colonial borders for fear of violence and an illicit arms and ammunition trade, was not a valid one. A Griqualand fair would have allowed them to monitor trade more closely, and removed other obstacles as well, such as pass requirements for Griqua and Africans.

LMS missionaries in the first decades of the nineteenth century found themselves in an extremely paradoxical position as it related to frontier trade and government policy along the Cape northern frontier. Their residency hundreds of miles beyond the official colonial borders placed them outside the pale of colonial law and allowed them to carry on an extensive exchange of goods in their own right with the indigenous peoples of southern Africa years before the colonial settlers were allowed such contact. At the same time, they were expected to act as official or unofficial representatives of the Cape government in the interior. In this capacity they were obligated to interpret colonial laws; to issue passes; occasionally to distribute arms and ammunition to those favored by the Cape government, as in the case of the Griqua; and to inculcate the inhabitants of their mission stations with Christian ideals and the rudiments of European civilization. They were also expected to keep the governor and his officials informed about events in the interior, and about the attitudes and actions of the Griqua and Africans who lived both on and off their mission stations. By serving as informants and advisers to both the Cape government and the peoples among whom they lived, the missionaries could be valuable participants in the making of frontier policy. By attempting fairly to represent both sides of the imperial fault line, however, they opened themselves to suspicion and mistrust from everyone.

Chapter Two

The CMS Niger Mission, Extra-Territorial Forces of Change, and the Expansion of British Influence in the Niger Delta during the Nineteenth Century

Waibinte Wariboko

INTRODUCTION

Throughout the Niger Delta, particularly in the trading states of the Eastern Niger Delta, missionaries and secular officials of the British Crown came after the trading merchants in the nineteenth century. A very considerable amount of British capital, with the abolition of the trans-Atlantic slave trade, was invested in the Eastern Niger Delta trading states of Bonny, New Calabar, Nembe-Brass, Opobo and Okrika, including Old Calabar, in order to encourage the growth and development of the nascent commerce in palm oil. Between 1807 and 1830, the critical years of transition from slave to produce trading, the aforementioned states supplied the bulk of produce consumed by Great Britain.[1] The value of British trade at both Bonny and New Calabar alone, for example, amounted to 500,000 pounds in January 1854; this represented an increase of forty-seven per cent from the 1850 level of 235,000 pounds.[2] This volume and value of trade underscored the significance of the Niger Delta, particularly the Eastern Niger Delta, in the overall Anglo-African sociopolitical and economic relationship before the new imperialism.

However, the private capital investments in produce trading, including Britain's overall political and ideological commitment and determination to abolish slave trading in the Niger Delta, were being threatened and undermined by the activities of those Europeans and Africans still interested in perpetrating the outlawed commerce. To guarantee political security for that investment, including the proper management of the overall transition process, John Beecroft was appointed in 1848 as Her Majesty's Consul to the Bights of Benin and Biafra. Thereafter, in concert with the anti-slave trade Naval Squadron, Beecroft and his successors—T. Hutchinson (1853–1855), R. Burton (1855–1861), C. Livingston (1861–1867), G. Hartley (1867–1873), D. Hopkins (1873–1878), and E. Hewitt (1878–1882)[3]—worked assiduously to exterminate those seeking to undermine British commercial, ideological and political interests in the Niger Delta. The pursuit of British self-interests under the cloak of civilizing Africa through the abolition of the slave trade and the introduction of "legitimate commerce," as many scholars such as J. C. Anene and W. I. Ofonagoro have demonstrated, prepared the foundation for the eventual imposition of British colonialism in the Niger Delta after 1884.[4]

By the beginning of the mid-nineteenth century, the Church Missionary Society, among other missionary organizations, had concluded arrangements to participate in the civilizing mission to southern Nigeria. Working through the Niger Mission headed by Bishop Samuel Crowther, the CMS established mission-stations in the following coastal trading states within and outside of the Niger Delta in southern Nigeria: Onitsha (1857), Rabba (1857), Gbebe (1857), Akassa (1860), Idah (1865), Lokoja (1865), Bonny (1864), Nembe-Brass (1868), Osomari (1873), New Calabar (1874), Asaba (1875), Kippo Hill (1876), Alenso (1878), and Okrika (1882).[5] Before the end of the empire of informal sway, therefore, the extra-territorial forces of change were well established and entrenched in the Niger Delta to pursue the goals of the British civilizing mission to West Africa.

In "Christian Missions and Secular Authorities in Southeastern Nigeria from Colonial Times," Adiele Afigbo has argued that: "[T]hough the Christian missions and the secular administration were probably the two most important bastions of British colonial rule in south-eastern Nigeria, the two were often locked in conflict."[6] This essay argues that, unlike the colonial period in the Igbo-speaking hinterland of southern Nigeria, the relationship between the extra-territorial forces in the decades leading up to formal colonialism was overwhelmingly marked by a strong sense of mutual respect, friendship and support in the Niger Delta. They had their differences, but they were not "often locked in conflict." Instead of being "often locked in conflict," they worked concertedly to impose the British colonial state on the indigenous populations of the Niger Delta. To effectively articulate this position, this essay intends to discuss the ideological basis of cooperation among the extra-territorial forces of change before doing a narrative on the nature of their alliance as it evolved over time in two chronologically related phases—the empire of informal sway and the formal empire. Because the primary focus of the essay is on the Niger Delta, discussions pertaining to the formal empire will be terminated after 1900–the beginning of the decade when the Niger Delta became part of Southern Nigeria and the Crown Colony of Lagos in the evolution of the colonial state in Nigeria.

THE IDEOLOGICAL BASIS AND IMPETUS OF COOPERATION AMONG THE EXTRA-TERRITORIAL FORCES

A number of interrelated ideological factors accounted for the alliance between the extra-territorial forces of change in the Niger Delta in the decades leading up to formal colonialism in 1891: consciousness of a common mission—the civilizing mission—and the desire to elevate and promote "Whiteness" above "Blackness." Otherwise called the "white man's burden," the civilizing mission was firmly predicated on the notion that Europeans were racially superior to non-Europeans—in this case Africans. The British invasion, conquest and annexation of West Africa, a process that began immediately after the abolition of the slave trade through to the beginning of the twentieth century, was thus conceived and described by Joseph Chamberlain of the British Colonial Office as a civilizing mission intended to transform the barbarous indigenous socio-cultural and religious heritage of African societies. This race-oriented cum culturally chauvinistic notion, which informed and underpinned the civilizing mission before and after the Berlin Conference of 1884, was vividly expressed in the famous "omelette speech" given by Chamberlain in 1897.

> You cannot have omellete without breaking eggs; you cannot destroy the practices of barbarism, of slavery, of superstition, which for centuries have desolated the interior of Africa, without the use of force; but if you fairly contrast the gain to humanity with the price which we are bound to pay for it, I think you may well rejoice in the result. . . .[7]

In varying degrees all the officials of the Crown generally believed that, to achieve the goals of the civilizing mission to the Niger Delta, the indigenous societies must be fully exposed to the benign influences and values of British civilization, commerce and Christianity—the three "Cs," as they were sometimes called. There was an unwritten understanding pertaining to the division of labor in the business of pursuing and implementing the goals of the civilizing mission: the consuls must militarily subjugate the people with a view to creating the political atmosphere and environment for the merchants and missionaries to implant the values of mercantile capitalism and Christianity without let or hindrance.

Some missionaries, however, did question the ideological appropriateness of this unwritten understanding and division of labor among the extra-territorial forces seeking to introduce European civilization to non-European societies. According to the chief accounting officer of the CMS Niger Mission and one of the most out-spoken propagandists of the British civilizing mission to West Africa between 1899 and 1931, James Norris Cheetham: "Where ever the civilization of the West penetrates, without being accompanied by its religious atmosphere and sanctions, it exercises a blighting and fatal influence on other people."[8] For this reason Cheetham often argued that it was imperative for Christian missions, as partners in the civilizing mission, to introduce the requisite socio-cultural and religious framework "before (non- European societies come) . . . into contact with the darker side of our civilization. . . ."[9] Some European merchants, in Cheetham's view, represented "the darker side" of British civilization. According to him: "A larger number of the younger clerks sent out by the mercantile firms were careless, selfish, and lived loose lives, and this causes the prestige of the white man to be lower than it should be."[10]

The Niger Mission under the Episcopal superintendence of S. A. Crowther also endorsed this view about traders, particularly those referred to as "palm oil ruffians" in the first three decades of the commercial transition in the Niger Delta. When invited to build a mission-station in the area occupied by the mercantile community at New Calabar in 1874, D. C. Crowther replied: "We do not want to build among merchants for their sons' and daughters' sake, for merchants cannot be held responsible for the conduct of their men."[11] Most missionaries, as D. Fraser of the United Free Church of Scotland in Nyasaland noted, wanted to see Africa "covered with the white robe of Christian commerce."[12]

Aside from missionaries, some officials of the Crown in the Niger Delta also expressed dissatisfaction with the moral behavior of merchants during the period under review. This was the perception of Vice-Consul Harry Johnston in 1888: "The trader civilizes, but he does not go to Africa for that purpose, he goes to trade (profit)." For that reason, Johnston argued, the British Empire's "moral obligations towards uncivilized or backward peoples [could] never [be] served by . . . traders."[13] Over and above these, however, there were some European commentators cum traders in West Africa who opposed the goals of the civilizing mission as perceived and pursued by the missionaries. E. D. Morel, a trader and commentator on West African affairs in the latter part of the nineteenth century, could be taken to represent the voice of opposition. Morel, in the words of

Cheetham, had argued "that native life is interfered with by the missionary propaganda; that its unity is destroyed; and that the result of (missionary) work is to Europeanize the people and make them . . . disloyal to their chiefs."[14]

For Morel and other critics, the civilizing mission was just a cloak for imposing whiteness on non-European societies globally during the nineteenth century. According to C. W. Mills, from about the beginning of the nineteenth century, or even earlier, "race" had become for Europeans "the common conceptual denominator that gradually came to signify the respective global statuses of superiority and inferiority, privilege and subordination."[15] The very construction of "race" as several scholars, including P. Gilroy and K. A. Appiah, have pointed out in recent times was a European creation rooted in attempts to rationalize the social and psychological domination of non-European peoples.[16] For this reason, it is being argued that white supremacy from the outset was constitutive, not additive, to the makings of the civilizing mission. The position of this essay, in view of the foregoing is as follows: in spite of those subtle differences noted earlier, the desire to exalt and promote "Whiteness" in non-European societies provided the ideological foundation and impetus for the alliance between the extra-territorial forces of change in the Niger Delta.

Bishop S. A. Crowther, the man who led the evangelization of the Niger Delta under the auspices of the CMS Niger Mission from 1864 to 1891, fully endorsed the goals of the civilizing mission to impose "Whiteness" on Africans. This, for example, could be taken to represent his socio-cultural perception of Africa:

> The 'Dark Continent' is properly applied to Africa. The inhabitants of a great portion of it are very ignorant, being *illiterate, unlettered, untaught,* all what they know is what was got by tradition from their forefathers, and handed down from generation to generation; they are therefore *rude,* barbarous, unmerciful (and) superstitious.[17](Crowther's emphasis)

The proselytizing activities of Crowther, particularly his comments about the indigenous socio-cultural and religious heritage, undermined the black personhood and also facilitated the ends of British political and economic domination of the Niger Delta before his demise in 1891. The comments, for example, could be taken to substantiate the opinion of Mills when he argued that: "there should be no essentialist illusions about anyone's intrinsic 'racial' virtue. All peoples can fall into Whiteness under the appropriate circumstances."[18] The term "functional Whites," Rex Nettleford has noted, not only "covers a range of skin-hues," but it "also refers to the cultural commitments such persons betray."[19] Along the lines of thought articulated by Mills and Nettleford, it could be argued that people are just "white" or "black" solely on grounds of skin colour. Crowther—a Yoruba by birth and an ex-slave—and the Sierra Leonian missionaries in the Niger Mission before 1891 were "functional whites;" hence they easily identified with the European merchants and secular officials of the Crown to enthrone "Whiteness" over and above "Blackness" in the Niger Delta–this process, in part, meant undermining African sovereignty.

THE EXTRA–TERRITORIAL FORCES AND THE EASTERN DELTA DURING THE PERIOD OF INFORMAL EMPIRE

It was a very popular and wide-spread conviction among missionary strategists during the nineteenth century that the development of trade, agriculture, and industry in Africa were essential conditions for the success of evangelization in the continent. Bishop Crowther, notwithstanding the unscrupulous commercial practices of some palm oil traders in the Niger Delta, believed that commerce and Christianity had one united purpose: " . . . the Christian civilization of the ignorant teeming populations. . . ."[20] In southern Nigeria generally, the desire to promote agriculture and industry, among other factors, influenced the location of mission-stations. The comments of S. A. Crowther in 1888 for locating the mission at Abonnema, rather than Buguma or Bakana in the New Calabar missionary field, are very instructive and revealing.

> [O]f these . . . places (Bakana and Buguma) Abonnema presents the greatest advantages for our mission work, as being the more open and salubrious, more populous, the ground elevated and dry; the soil affords opportunity to introduce habits of industry such as brick making and farming; coffee, cocoa and cotton can be planted as examples for the benefit of the country in general.[21]

The preference for Abonnema was also influenced by another factor. Throughout the latter part of the nineteenth century, including the first three decades of the twentieth century, Abonnema was a booming commercial emporium in the Eastern Delta with the following European trading companies: Company of African Merchants Limited, G. B. Olivant and Company, African Traders Company Limited, Alexander and Miller Brothers Limited, and Niger Company Limited.[22]

These companies constituted a source of material assistance to the missionaries in three ways. First, merchants within West Africa and Britain contributed money occasionally for various missionary projects—school and church building projects. By the time Crowther was permitted to establish the church at the age-old New Calabar settlement before their migration to Abonnema, Buguma, and Bakana between 1881 and 1882, the "Bishop of the Niger Funds"–the funds set aside for church and school building projects—had been exhausted. On appeal, however, W. Jones, the executive administrator of the British and African Steamship Company, replenished the coffers of the Niger Mission.[23] This enabled Crowther to immediately commence the evangelization of the Kalabari-speaking people in 1874 before the above migration took place. In 1893, shortly after the demise of Crowther and the separation of the Niger Delta Pastorate Church from the Niger Mission, Jones also agreed on request to annually contribute five hundred pounds to the coffers of the Niger Mission-the "Niger Bishopric Funds"-under Bishop Hill.[24]

Second, from these merchant houses the missionaries procured assorted commodities on "drafts" or bills of credit; thereafter, these bills of credit were presented for payment by the parent company in England to the headquarters of the CMS Niger Mission at Salisbury Square in London. Finally, until the establishment of the West African mail boat in 1853, every missionary organization depended on the vessels belonging to these trading companies for passage, freight and correspondence between their mission-stations in West Africa and Europe. "Passages and freight," as J. F. A. Ajayi has noted, "were taken as a favour because it was more profitable for the traders to carry trade goods than missionary houses, gift boxes and other equipment. They were quite often taken free."[25] However, even during the last quarter of the nineteenth century, as part of a letter from D. Crowther to the directors of the British and African Steamship Navigation Company indicates, the Niger Mission still relied on the merchants for freighting their commodities from England.

> My object, gentlemen, in writing is to ask you kindly to help us on this point of freights. . . . We hope that the boxes from [the Missionary Leaves Association] for the Niger and the Coast stations via Bonny, New Calabar and Benin, can by your kindness be allowed freight free in any of your steamers. If so you will be doing a good part in helping to further the gospel among those who are sitting in darkness, and facilitating our work to afford more home advantages to those whose lot it is to labour out here.[26]

Within the Niger Delta itself these trading companies assisted missionaries intending to travel from one coastal community to another. In April 1865,

Bishop Crowther's first visit from Bonny to the age-old New Calabar settlement was made possible through the generous assistance of two European traders—Captain Babington and Captain Henryway—who were stationed at Bonny and New Calabar respectively.[27] With these instances illustrating support for the Niger Mission by merchants, let me examine how the secular officials of the Crown perceived and assisted the missionaries during the period under review- the empire of informal sway.

All of the secular officials of the Crown recognized the socio-cultural significance of the CMS agenda for the civilizing mission; and, for that reason, they related to the missionaries as invaluable partners in the creation and sustenance of the British West African Empire. In the words of Harry Johnston, one of the vice-consuls to the Niger Delta: "The native populations of the Niger Delta area are in a transition state. For a long time civilization has knocked at their door unheeded and until, getting impatient, she may be said to have kicked the door open and come face to face with the surprised inmates."[28] The consuls and traders realized that the campaign against the alleged barbarism of the indigenous populations, who were "unheeding" to the knocks on their door by civilization, needed an ideological base which the missions provided. Edward Hewitt, among the consuls and vice-consuls to the Niger Delta, was arguably the most successful in putting measures in place to assist and facilitate the missionaries in their onerous task of transforming the indigenous socio-cultural heritage.

In 1881, according to the Niger Mission agent at New Calabar, Rev. Ebenezer Carew, Hewitt announced that: " . . . so long as he is Consul for the Bights of Benin and Biafra, he will most certainly defend the cause of (the Christian) religion and will always help the missionaries in their work, and if there are any obstacles in their way to retard the progress of their work, he will do all in his power to break through it and clear the missionary's way and will help them to see that everything goes well."[29] Hewitt promoted and defended the cause of Christianity in the Eastern Niger Delta in many and varied ways. In addition to providing the much needed political and military security for missionaries, he often threatened to impose sanctions on those parents who expressed reluctance to pay prescribed fees for their wards in the missionary educational institutions. His greatest contribution to the process of implanting the church, however, came through the provision of a legal instrument—article seven of the "Treaty of Protection" signed between New Calabar and Britain in 1883—to guarantee religious tolerance and liberty of worship at New Calabar. Exited by Hewitt's inclusion of this provision, which the missionaries had lobbied for, Bishop S. A. Crowther exclaimed: "This is God's doing, and is marvelous in our eyes!"[30] Carew also expressed happiness over Hewitt's action in these words: "If every Consul could follow his example, I am sure that great things could be done."[31] To proceed further it is pertinent to ask one question: how did the Niger Mission under Bishop S. A. Crowther pay back the traders and officials of the Crown for all the aforementioned benefits before the end of the informal empire?

To begin with missionaries facilitated the process of incorporating West Africa into the evolving global capitalist economy; and, at the conference of West African Protestant missionaries held at Gabon, in 1875, they took an early opportunity to emphasize their role in this process.

> Commerce is materially indebted to missions for the development of natural resources. . . . Again missions contribute to the interest of commerce, by creating extensively a demand for foreign manufactures of almost every variety, from needles to sewing machines and cooking stoves. In addition to these financial benefits, missions have extended at great expense and labour, a generation of young men through whose agency as clerks, interpreters and traders, commerce is being prosecuted on the coast, and pushed up the rivers, creeks, and lagoons, where the white man cannot go with safety to health and life.[32]

In a sense the missionaries were arguing that investing in evangelism was not counterproductive to the economic objectives of British traders in West Africa.

Available evidence suggests that missionaries also contributed immensely to the realization of Britain's political objectives in West Africa during the period of the informal empire in the Niger Delta. They acted as informants and spies for the Crown and also helped generally to build up the prestige and image of the Crown's representative, the consul, in the Niger Delta. On 15 June 1876 king Ockiya of Nembe-Brass, who had been converted to the alien faith at this time by the Niger Mission, wrote to Bishop Crowther about a plan to attack European trading vessels in the Lower Niger. The Lower Niger, it may be noted, was considered by the king as a primary producing palm oil market for the exclusive exploitation of Nembe-Brass in southern Nigerian.

> I have heard that the Idzo (Ijo) men are bent to fight the ships this year not in that ordinary way they use to do it, when the ships passing they hide and fire *poo, poo, poo*, but they are prepared to fight desperately this year. Therefore I come to tell you . . . by way of advice from me not to go up this year (to the Niger). It is a secret, I do not see, neither know, I only heard.[33]

Interestingly, by 26 June 1876, Crowther's report on this matter to the CMS headquarters at Salisbury Square had been compiled and dispatched. It contained these words of warning and advice for the British imperial government.

> This is a very important subject. There is a strong combination between the chiefs of Brass and Idzo people at the Delta to put a stop to navigation of the Niger. I hope the Home Authorities will enquire with promptness into the matter, and deal with it accordingly, so as to put a final stop to these barbarous outrages on human lives and against endangering . . . legitimate trade by stopping of access to the interior. . . . [34]

In another letter to Commodore Sir W.N.N. Hewitt, the commander of the British Naval Forces on the West Coast in 1876, Crowther had commended the efforts of the British Navy, including the secular officials of the Crown, for the military and political protection offered to the Niger Mission in the Niger Delta. Here is the relevant excerpt of that letter.

> Since the treaties for the abolition of the slave trade and the introduction of legitimate commerce were made with the kings and chiefs in the Bights of Benin and Biafra, Old and New Calabar Rivers, Cameroons, Bonny, Brass have become accessible to Christian missionaries, and a visit now and then from the Consul in a gunboat has served to keep the people quiet from molesting the missionaries and their establishments.[35]

After these complimentary remarks Crowther went on to make the following appeal: "I sincerely hope the present actual results of past fostering care of Her Majesty's Government would be favourably considered; that it may be restored by a resident Consul, or an annual visit of a gunboat, and continued for some years till a large portion of the native chiefs themselves will see the necessity of taking in hand, the care and protection of merchants and missionaries, with their properties, as their true interest."[36]

These comments, for our purposes, are significant for a number of reasons. First, they vividly express the endorsement of the Niger Mission for the gunboat diplomacy that characterized the era of consular imperialism in the Niger Delta before 1891- the year the formal colonial state was inaugurated under Major Claude MacDonald. Second, they convey gratitude to the secular department of the imperial mission for its strong-arm tactics against the indigenous potentates of the Niger Delta in defense of merchants and missionaries. Third, like the European managers of the Niger Mission after him, it is evident that Crowther was prepared and willing to endorse punitive expedition as a way of facilitating the socioeconomic, cultural, religious and political transformation of African states. To put the matter squarely: Crowther, like Chamberlain of the Colonial Office, did not see any thing wrong in breaking African "eggs" in order to prepare a British "omelet." According to A. Toynbee, missionary enterprise ceases to be a legitimate exercise performed for its own sake when it engages in "building up a 'fifth column' in one country for the purpose of assisting the people of another country to bring the (propagandized) country under their political country."[37] Covertly and overtly, as the evidence overwhelming suggests, the CMS Niger Mission worked in concert with the merchants and consuls in creating the auspicious background conditions for the imposition of British colonialism in the Niger Delta after 1891.

RELATIONS UNDER FORMAL COLONIALISM, 1891–1900

The relationship between the extra-territorial forces after 1891 and the Eastern Delta states could be laconically summarized in the following way: continuity amidst change. In assuming office as the first Consul-General of the Niger Coast Protectorate in 1891, MacDonald took an early opportunity to spell out the goals to be pursued by his administration: "The whole of the Consular staff will endeavour by developing legitimate trade, by promoting civilization, by inducing the natives to relinquish inhuman and barbarous customs, and by gradually abolishing domestic slavery, to pave the way for placing the territories over which Her Majesty's protection is and may be extended directly under British rule."[38] Implementing this agenda, which in many respects echoed the goals of the civilizing mission before 1891, required the support and cooperation of merchants and missionaries in the Niger Delta.

Developing legitimate commerce, among other things, involved the elimination of the Eastern Delta middleman trading states because they were perceived as obstacles to the European penetration of the hinterland primary-producing markets. T. N. Tamuno has noted that "from the 1890s the (British) Chamber of Commerce had advocated for the penetration of the hinterlands of British West Africa, and punitive expeditions represented some of the bloody consequences of this policy."[39] In the first decade of the formal empire, according to W. I. Ofonagoro, the "refusal to sign a treaty guaranteeing free trade, as well as the breaking of a treaty so signed, were deemed adequate justification for a punitive expedition."[40]

The policy of enforcing free trade through punitive expeditions represented one element of continuity in Anglo-African relations between the informal and formal empires. The overthrow and deportation of king Jaja of Opobo to the Caribbean Island of St. Vincent was conceived and implemented by officials of the Crown—Hewitt and Johnston—working in concert with merchants—G. Watts and J. Holt—because he was considered the greatest threat and obstacle to free trade in the Niger Delta between 1879 and 1887.[41] Between 1891 and 1900 many Eastern Delta potentates, including Ibani Chuka of Okrika,[42] experienced the fate that befell Jaja. Unlike Jaja, however, Chuka was deported to Degema in the Niger Delta. There were, admittedly, those European traders who had objected to punitive expeditions and deportations in order to eliminate the perceived obstacles against free trade; but their views and protestations had no effect on the determination of the colonial state to carry through its policies in the Niger Coast Protectorate.

Beyond these punitive expeditions, however, other measures were put in place to enforce the principles of free-market enterprise in the Niger Delta. The Customs Regulations Ordinance of 1891,[43] which spelt out elaborate rules for the import-export trade, represented one of these measures. In order to enforce some of these regulations—for example, the law prohibiting the payment of fees to Delta kings known as *comey* before they could commence trading with Europeans—the officials of the Niger Coast Protectorate required the support and cooperation of the European traders. Over time the colonial state secured the support and cooperation of the British mercantile community to eliminate the Eastern Delta trading states as brokers in the trans-Atlantic commerce between Africa and Europe.

MacDonald, like all officials of the Crown before him, realized that inducing "the natives to relinquish inhuman and barbarous customs," including "abolishing domestic slavery," could not succeed if based alone on stringent state regulations and on prosecutions for their breaches through the secular courts. This was why he needed the support and cooperation of the missionaries. In order to strengthen the political alliance between the nascent administration of the Niger Coast Protectorate and the missionaries, MacDonald accepted an invitation from the Niger Delta Pastorate Church—a breakaway movement from the Niger Mission headed by Archdeacon Dandeson Crowther—to become its grand patron in 1894. That invitation, which was accepted on the note that the missionaries of the Pastorate Church "do most excellent work in these Rivers,"[44] signaled the beginning of the cordial relationship between church and state during the period under review.

In pursuit of the administration's policy to promote education, particularly industrial education, through mission schools, MacDonald promised an annual grant of 200 pounds to Archdeacon D. C. Crowther. The aim of the grant was to enable Crowther subsidize the cost of industrial training programs in the schools operated by the Pastorate Church.[45] Like Hewitt and Johnson before him, MacDonald worked assiduously to protect missionaries and mission property from the predatory activities of those who perceived them as disturbers of society. In 1892, at no cost to the CMS, he allowed an employee of the Protectorate administration, Isaac O. Mba, to fully oversee the CMS Niger Mission establishments at Abonnema in New Calabar. This was because, for various reasons outside the purview of this paper, the Onitsha-based Niger Mission could not find a trained parson to man the Abonnema station. As a result, the Christian converts there, including the church and school buildings, were being abused.[46]

Notwithstanding the magnanimity and support of the colonial state, the Niger Mission and the Pastorate Church began to express unease with some of the secular policies formulated during the successive reigns of Ralph Moor [1893–1900] and W. Egerton [1904–1906] as High Commissioners in southern Nigeria. Several factors were responsible for this situation; but, in the interest of this paper, I will discuss two factors alone. The school, throughout the nineteenth century, was perceived and utilized as the most potent instrument for the evangelization and cultural invasion of West African societies, including the Ijo-speaking societies of the Niger Delta. This was how Bishop Johnson of the CMS Niger Mission put it in 1905:

> The Boarding school system was in the early days of mission work in the Niger Delta a prominent feature because of the promise it gave and the hope it held out of being quickly very helpful in detaching the more youthful sections of the different communities from heathenism and its idolatry and winning them over to Christianity and through them influencing the different households which they severally represent.[47]

The nascent colonial state, particularly after MacDonald, began to question this policy. "When Ralph Moor," according to A. E. Afigbo, "decided that his administration would join the Presbyterian mission in making the Hope Waddell Institute [at Old Calabar] a center for raising qualified teachers and better educated pupils than the local schools had so far produced, he made it a condition for government participation that instruction in Christian dogma would not be compulsory for students."[48] The advice that religious instruction should not be compulsory for pupils remained a sore point in church-state relationship throughout the period leading up to the demise of colonialism in Nigeria.

The second sore point had to do with the decision of Moor and Egerton to administer the colonial state through the preexisting sociopolitical and cultural institutions. Missionaries felt unhappy with this policy, which became known as the indirect rule system of colonial administration, for the following reason. Since the nineteenth century they had argued that: "[A] new social order, a new political economy and a new culture must accompany the change to a new moral order. Proper European civilization was Christianity, and the only way to bring about conversion was to establish this cultural framework."[49] This was the concept of church-culture that informed proselytizing throughout the nineteenth and early twentieth centuries; and the missionaries insisted that what was Christian could not abide with what was African. For this reason they were not looking forward to any form of preservation of the preexisting indigenous sociopolitical and cultural institutions.

Now, during the period of the informal empire, this perception and position of the missionaries never came under close scrutiny because the secular officials of the Crown were yet to formulate a policy for the administration of the indigenous populations under their sway. With the inception of the colonial state, however, the policy of indirect rule was evolved. For purposes of indirect rule, as the colonial state argued, aspects of the indigenous sociopolitical and cultural institutions must be preserved and sustained, especially those aspects that were not considered barbarous and repugnant to the British sense of natural justice. This was how, for example, A. F. E. P. Newns, the district officer at New Calabar, put it: "Whatever there is of value in the indigenous organization should be retained and built upon but whatever has been proved worthless must be ruthlessly discarded."[50] The missions campaigned, but without success, against these policies because they were perceived as obstacles to the attainment of their grand evangelical objectives in southern Nigeria.

All of these sources of disquiet in state-church relationship notwithstanding, the latter at the beginning of the twentieth century continued to rely on the former in order to expand their activities beyond the coastal trading states of the Niger Delta. At the end of the Aro expedition of 1901/2, D. C. Crowther wrote to the secretary of the CMS, F. Baylis, on the advantages of the expedition for the expansion of Christianity in southern Nigeria. Here is the relevant excerpt of that letter:

> I hope you will excuse the liberty I now take in addressing you the following lines, knowing how happy you would be to learn that the

interior of the Ibo country is quite open to missionary operations. Hitherto, we have been more or less confined to the coast: the expedition undertaken by the Government some three years ago, has resulted in the throwing open of the hitherto closed doors of the Isuama country, and today its two most important towns, Bende and Aro, so well known to the Ibo people are ready to welcome missionaries.[51]

In order to set the stage for the concluding remarks later, it is pertinent to pose this question again: how did the missions pay back the colonial state for this benefit? In 1902, just before the completion of the Aro expedition in the Igbo-speaking hinterland of southern Nigeria, the Niger Mission under Bishop H. Tugwell was allowed into Bida with the full cooperation of the British Resident and the Emir.[52] Regarding the final British conquest and pacification of northern Nigeria between 1901 and 1910, P. D. Gordon and D. A. MacFarlane—black West Indian missionaries engaged to the Niger Mission—had assisted in intelligence gathering under the superintendence of a European missionary, A. E. Ball. They were required, among other things, to "report on all the principal towns in that neighbourhood (Bida and Nupe) with a view to permanent settlement in that province at the earliest opportunity."[53]

In 1932 the British Resident in charge of Ondo province in Western Nigeria, by way of showing his gratitude to L. A. Lennon—another black West Indian missionary attached to the CMS Yoruba Mission—made the following comments: "I have known Canon and Mrs. Lennon for some years and consider the good work they have done in the Akoko district has greatly helped me and my administration in our political work."[54] Missionaries, because of the moral values they preached and the close relationships they maintained with their converts in the mission-stations, were often considered as custodians and guardians of the people's moral conscience, including their political conscience. For this reason the secular authorities used them as one other means of keeping a close surveillance on the political pulse of society throughout the period of the informal empire, including the initial decades after the imposition of colonial rule. In southern Nigeria missionaries were occasionally invited to assume political and/or judicial responsibilities on behalf of the colonial state. In that capacity missionaries often acted as confidential advisers to the colonial state on several socio-cultural matters. In 1913 James Norris Cheetham— a European missionary in the Niger Mission from 1899 to 1931—was appointed as one of the assessors for the Onitsha Assize Court in southern Nigeria.[55] This level of mutual cooperation and interpenetration between church and state, their subtle differences over certain administrative policies notwithstanding, illustrated the fact that they were more often united by one grand ideological objective: the promotion of British imperial interests in southern Nigeria.

CONCLUSION

The three "Cs" collaborated, despite their subtle differences, to extend and consolidate British influence in the Niger Delta between 1864 and 1900. C. G. Baeta has noted that: "On the relations between missions and colonial administrations . . . interest was greater and support more generous for national missions operating in colonies of the countries concerned, than for other missions."[56] Several factors accounted for this. The black West Indian missionaries in the Niger Mission, for example, held the view that "the British Empire (was) an instrument of Divine Providence (and a benign force of fate) to make possible the enlightenment of benighted Africa."[57] This ideological perception of the British Empire compared very well with that of Bishop S. A. Crowther and Archdeacon D. C. Crowther during the period of the informal empire. Cheetham commented as follows in 1908:

> One sees abroad more clearly than at home the use of 'red tape,' and I fully agree with Rudyard Kipling that it is those who see the British Government at work in distant lands who admire and respect it most. By this I do not of course mean that government officials are invariably pleasant men to deal with, neither do I mean that their methods are always right; *but I am fully prepared to uphold the principle that no other body of men on the face of the earth could provide a better administrative force for Nigeria than the British Government.*[58](My emphasis)

Given this sense of jingoism and imperial pride, it is not surprising that missionaries often recommended obedience to colonial regulations while proselytizing. In this way they assisted tremendously in building up the prestige of the British Empire after the imposition of formal colonialism in West Africa.

This sense of empire and jingoism could also explain why the French colonial administration—a competing and rival imperial power in West Africa—was reluctant to show generous support for missions associated with the furtherance of Victorian values in its own colonies. The relationship between the Pongas Mission—a mission associated with the Church of England in the West Indies—and the French colonial administration in Guinea-Conakry between 1896 and 1935 illustrates this point. According to L. E. P. Erith, a commentator on the Pongas Mission: "[T]he French colonial government, if not actively hostile has always been passively unsympathetic towards missionaries of another nation,"[59] including the Pongas Mission. The unsympathetic attitude of the French colonial administration, including other socioeconomic and cultural factors, eventually contributed to the removal of the Pongas Mission in Guinea-Conakry.[60]Regarding the British, it has also been noted that: "As soon as the First World War broke out the British quickly sent packing the German members of the Basel Mission and replaced them with Presbyterians from Calabar in Nigeria."[61] Church-state relationship in southern Nigeria, as suggested by all of the evidence discussed, was overwhelmingly influenced by one common interest: loyalty to the British Empire.

Chapter Three

Catholicism, Protestantism, and Imperial Claims in Kabaka's Buganda, 1860–1907[1]

Raphael Chijioke Njoku

> "*Nwaṅgwi pụo eze ya tapu mkpịshịrịaka zụrụa*" (When an orphan attains success he bites off the fingers that fed him)
>
> —Igbo proverb

INTRODUCTION

Although the late nineteenth century Christian missionary evangelism in Buganda has attracted more than ordinary scholarly interests, few studies have seriously considered the idioms of indigenous invectiveness in the making of colonial Uganda. The same Ganda colonial educated elite who deserted their traditional values for the alien ones partly explains this shortfall in the historiography given that their writings, which are often tainted with Anglophile/Christian bias, remain as our major sources of information about precolonial society and events of this period.[2] Since the colonial archive was organized to produce the victors' version of history, African historical memory has become so skewed that certain ideas loaded with cultural prejudices are uncritically accepted. This is exemplified with the copious literature on mission activities in Uganda in particular and the rest of Africa in general.[3]

Some of these studies have explored the intersections between precolonial structures of power, statuses, and social mobility as important determinants of the late nineteenth century history of this African kingdom. Others, primarily focusing on the events leading to violence in the 1880s, have generally used the concept of "martyrdom" as if non-Christians and non-Muslims who died in the fighting should not be ascribed with such tribute.[4] Tarsis Kabwegyere has viewed the question of violence from the perspective of psychology, arguing that the inductive crisis of social change and adjustment marking the European presence has continued to hunt postcolonial Ugandan politics.[5] In a sharp disagreement with Kabwegyere, Michael Twaddle has cautioned against such inferences given the dissimilar and changing cultural orientations and contemporary situations in the postcolonial state of Uganda.[6] J. D. Y. Peel further introduces a comparative element in his examination of conversion and tradition in two African societies: Ijebu and Buganda, with the conclusion that "Buganda is the classic case of the Christianization of Africa, Ijebu of the Africanization of Christianity."[7] While these and other sources provide ample normative and theoretical ideas for a perceptive analysis on the intersection between missions, state, and imperial rule in Africa, more constructive analysis is desired in defense of the traditional institutions and values that were targeted for destruction by the Europeans and their African fanatical cohorts.

This chapter reexamines the state-church struggle in Uganda with a view to question the judgments inherent in the earlier studies.[8] This is important for a better understanding of the mindset of such African collaborators (in the imperial enterprise) as Apolo Kagwa who described African religious belief as "bad" and judged the gods of the land to be "evil spirits . . . used to deceive the people."[9] But as Mbonu Ojike, the popular firebrand Nigerian anti-colonial nationalist reminds us, "No Religion is superior to another."[10] In his "Week-end Catechism" of June 5, 1948, Ojike declared that "the truth is: all religion is superstitious."[11] This vintage point will help us put in perspective the politics of Christian conversion and colonial intrusion in Uganda. This chapter, therefore, emphasizes the crucial role of indigenous inventiveness in one of the most intriguing cases of collaboration between missions, state and colonial expansion in late nineteenth century Afro-European relations.

The Ganda rulers, who ironically invited the European (*Bazungu*) missionaries, neither bargained that this move would precipitate local revolt within the Kabaka's (King's) court nor their eventual subordination to alien control. The circumstances that led to the rebellion of African Christian converts against the traditional authority stemmed partly from a marked Ganda propensity to status culture and mobility in an age of rapid social alteration. This tendency towards status culture, more than anything else, explains the wholesome manner in which the young pages from humble backgrounds grabbed the inductive and overpowering alien value enculturation—particularly mission education—as a vehicle for social mobility. The enticing promises of Christian conversion and Western education undermined a process of invectiveness originally projected for the benefit of monarchical authority. The so-called "Christian Revolution" of the 1890s was actually a class struggle between the elite and a small group of opportune individuals who cashed in on the missions' presence for personal gains.

The wholesome cultural sale-out that made the Christian (*Bagungu*) chiefs co-inheritors of the colonial state calls for a rethink of our notions of martyrdom and sainthood ascribed to those among this group who lost their lives in the process of rebellion. The manner in which the dissidents took advantage of their king's patronage and benevolence reminds us about the Igbo saying: "when an orphan attains success he bites off the fingers that fed him."

PRECOLONIAL ORDER AND MUTESA'S INVENTIVE ENTERPRISE

Encouraged by the subtle flirtation of Kabaka Walugembe Muk bya Mutesa I (r. 1856–1884), the decade following the first arrival of British explorers John H. Speke and Captain James Grant in Buganda in 1862, saw European missionaries prying into the lives of the Africans.[12] Mutesa did not invite the Europeans out of a genuine desire to imbibe the alien faith and was never fully converted to the new faith till death. Rather, his interest in Christianity was borne out of two central pragmatic and politically motivated factors. First and foremost, Mutesa's invitation of the missionaries was part of a calculation to use the European presence to ward off a military threat posed by Egyptian forces approaching the shores of Uganda to the North from Sudan. Second, and perhaps more intriguing, Mutesa's overture was part of a secret plot to gain an unparalleled absolute powers in Buganda.

In precolonial Uganda, the Kabaka exercised monarchical powers through a complex hierarchy of his appointed chiefs, who served as both administrators and judges. The king resided at the capital in a huge royal palace where he ruled the various thirty clans (*bataka*) that made up the kingdom. The Kabaka lived in the royal palace with his prime minister (*Katikkiro*) and a parliament (*Lukiiko*)—formed by the county (*ssaza*) chiefs whose houses surrounded the royal complex. A well-organized military and tax administration supported the governmental machinery.[13] This political structure that had evolved over the centuries placed the king in a position of first among equals. The Kabaka was revered as the embodiment of the Buganda, who has "eaten" the nation.[14] Yet, Ganda historian, M. S. M. Kiwanuka, explains that as powerful as the Kabaka was, he "learned to consult his chiefs on questions of great national importance such as war and peace and which religion to adopt."[15] More notably, the authority of the Kabaka could not transcend that of the major gods of the land. In an indigenous polity where only the peasant intellectuals—elders, clan chiefs, mediums, priests, and diviners understood the language of the gods—who as held in the cosmology wielded a peculiar form of influence akin to a theocracy—Mutesa had secretly began to scheme for a way to sidestep the influence of both the gods and their agents. If successful, Mutesa would have an unprecedented freedom to shape Buganda after his own image. On this ground, one would argue that political modernization was part of the original intent for inviting the missionaries.

D. A. Low, has correctly noted that for their power and success, the precolonial generations of Ganda kings had relied on "a pantheon of instrumental gods—of war, of health, of thunder and so on."[16] By implication, the Kabaka would hardly embark on any serious undertaking without seeking the approval of the oracles. In a twist of analysis, H. P. Gale contends that the Kabakas had always been the most powerful "god" of the land. At "any given time," Gale argues, "there was in Buganda but one God and one King, the reigning Kabaka . . . he was the God of Providence, since he alone controlled all that *Katonda* (Supreme God) created."[17] Gale's view appears slightly over-exaggerated for Low's analysis agrees with Kiwanuka's contention that, the kings of Buganda were no more than "political and military leaders of their people."[18] Other studies, including that by Steve Feierman, have concurred the critical role played by religion in indigenous African political systems.[19] These studies maintain that although autocratic structures existed here and there, the indigenous belief system provided astute checks and balances that made absolutism, as practiced in eighteenth century France, for instance, nearly impossible in Africa.

Generally the notion held about divine kingship implies that the human and natural worlds are dependent for their continued existence on the person and ritual activities of the king. According to Michael Kenny, the king in this type of political system,

> Iconistically represents the total society over which he presides; his physical and political fortunes reveal the quality of his relationship to the forces on which his people depend. If this relationship is cast in doubt—whether through personal illness, natural or political disaster—then the continuance of his tenure in office is threatened by rising pressure in favor of his replacement.[20]

Among the Yoruba of southwestern Nigeria for example, while the Alafin (king) of the Old Oyo Empire enjoyed "absolute" powers, he was at the same time vulnerable to the *Oyomesi* (a council of senior hereditary chiefs) who adjudicated suicide for the king should he breach the laws of the gods of the land.[21] Randall Packard's study of chiefly power among the Bashu people of eastern Zaire further reveals that pre-colonial African politics is only comprehensive when basic constitutional and cosmological ideas that motivate and legitimate power and exercise of authority are also comprehended.[22] This tells us that royal power, though substantial, was still subject to limitation. The indigenous belief system played a crucial role in the unity of Buganda. It also provided legitimacy to the position of the Kabaka while serving as a mechanism for checks and balances.

One may quickly add that this structure of authority and power was not cast on a rigid and unchanging context. In peculiar circumstances, the king and the local priests may disagree. Such disagreements usually led to changes in the existing structures of authority, as well as to reinvention and reinterpretation of relationships between the deities and man. For example in the Autumn of 1856, Rev. John Roscoe reports that the war-like Kabaka Suna II (r. 1832–1856), who was incapacitated by a deadly smallpox ailment during a dangerous expedition in Busongora, had the priests of the deity *Lubare* slain for their inability to either foresee or cure his sufferings. Soon after coming to power, his son and successor Mutesa, therefore, began to reinvent the status of the gods in a way that tended to cut the power of the priests.[23] According to Rev. Ashe, Mutesa also placed restrictions on royal princes, especially banning them from holding high chieftainships throughout the country.[24] These changes elevated monarchical authority and made Mutesa's position better secured that he "felt himself strong enough to permit foreign religions to enter his country."[25] In this context, Twaddle aptly observes that generally the "conflicts between kings and representatives of non-royal cults have been interpreted as a product of tension between the expansionist tendencies of kings at the expense of the peasantry and their indigenous religious practices."[26]

In nurturing the ambitious quest in the early 1860s to further elevate his powers above all in the entire kingdom, Mutesa may have come to regard religion as an instrument of power and control. Therefore, he could further elevate his position by simply offering the people an alternative source of spiritual authority. Meanwhile Mutesa alone had no power to transform the indigenous religion or even concoct an entirely new cult. The tradition of the people has it that "the great god Mukasa is lord of *Sesses* [the center of Mukasa cult], and will kill any person intruding on his dominions. He calls the king of Uganda his slave and the king when he sends to perform religious rites, must do so through his chiefs."[27] Conscious of this tradition and the dangers it portends, one would argue that in his flirtations with the alien religions (Islam and Christianity) Mutesa appears as a self-confident gambler who staked his life with the self-assurance that he would win.

UNDERGROUND SPIRITUAL GAME: THE KORAN VERSUS THE BIBLE

A few years before the appearance of the European missionaries in East Africa, Mutesa had begun his ego trip with Islam as an instrumental for political gamble. Early on in the 1840s, his father and predecessor, Kabaka Suna II had encountered the Arab and Zanzibari Muslim traders who came to trade gunpowder, firearms and other European goods for Ganda ivory and slaves, but he never accepted conversion to Islam before his death. According to Apolo Kagwa, Mutesa I persuaded some of his courtiers and palace servants to accept conversion to Islam and the new converts were circumcised in accordance with the Islamic practices. The king also adopted the Islamic calendar, and to demonstrate his seriousness, ordered the execution of twelve of his subjects for failing to greet him in the Muslim manner. From 1867, Mutesa took more serious steps in observing the Ramadan (or month of fasting), one of the five pillars of the Islamic faith. Mutesa also studied the Quran in order to be personally involved in promoting the new faith in Buganda. Kagwa adds that "all the chiefs" at the court were compelled to learn "that faith."[28] Gale asserts that such demands brought on the chiefs were unavoidable since "Everything which comes from royalty, whether by accident or design has to be adored."[29]

In the decade Mutesa experimented with Islam he was to learn the hard way that imperial religions are slippery and often despoil their prophets and patron saints. Unlike in the African traditional religious systems in which the priests own the mouth and ears of their deities, Islam and Christianity are open to discordant interpretations given that their sources of knowledge, the Holy Books, are easily accessibly to anyone. Therefore, converts to the world (imperialistic) religions are easily inspired by their convictions to oppose anything and anybody in the name of God or Allah.

In this context lies the explanation as to why the king's court was soon beleaguered with seditions as Islam made its way into the people's heads and minds. The new converts began to place Islam first before respect for their king and old values. Somewhere between July 1874 and April 1875 (the actual date of this incident is not available), a report came to a disenchanted Mutesa that some of his courtiers had despised the beef prepared from a bullock by his uncircumcised royal butcher. The anger of Mutesa was not simply because the pages refused the meat as being misinterpreted in certain quarters. According to Ashe, the boys dismissed the beef as "food only fit for dogs." On hearing these insulting words, a troubled Mutesa has asked in disbelief: "Is my meat only fit for dogs?"[30] As Gale aptly puts it, "To follow Kabaka was loyalty: to exceed him was 'insolence' and merited death."[31] Predictably, Mutesa's response to such forms of disloyalty was passed through his chief executioner, *Mukajangwa*, who brought death to a hundred of the uncouth young men. For a religion that promises paradise for martyrs, it was most disquieting for Mutesa to observe that some of these "disloyal" servants bravely accepted death with convictions about reward of paradise as commonly held in Islam. This fanatical act of defiance was not part of the expectations of the king for bringing Islam to his court. The underlying spiritual game was for Mutesa to "exchange" the Koran for the Bible.

THE BIBLE AND A "NEW" IDEOLOGY

All these transpiring within the same period that Speke and Grant arrived in Buganda, helped Mutesa welcome the Europeans as the dominant powers of the emergent world order. This perception follows his recognition of the superiority of European guns, which Mutesa supposed as the same with the Bible. Therefore, the religion of the Europeans should be more superior to Islam, hence after an audience with explorer Henry Morton Stanley (1841–1904) in April 1875, the British explorer had recorded in his memoir that a seemingly delighted Mutesa had declared to his court that "the white men are greatly superior to the Arabs, and I think, therefore, that their book must be a better book than Mohammed's."[32] During their meeting, Stanley had spoken about "the simple story of creation . . . the revelation of God's power to Israelites . . . the appearance of prophets at various times, foretelling the coming of Christ: the humble birth of the Messiah, his wonderful life, woeful death, and triumphant resurrection."[33]

This supposedly "new" ideology brought by the Europeans was not entirely new to the Africans. The Ganda had, before the Europeans, professed concepts of one God or Creator (*Katonda*) or Lord of Heaven (*Gulu*) or Master (*Mukama*) who had brought life to humans. The Africans also believed in the survival and immortality of the human soul, hence a French priest, Rev. Julien Gorju, wrote in 1920 that "the Buganda were Christians in origin."[34] Recent studies by Brierley and Spear, and C. C. Wrigley agree that "The Muslim Allah, Christian God (in both of his manifestations), and Kiganda were all omnipotent and supreme creator gods."[35] Since the times were not ideal for doctrinal contestations, Mutesa had simply pretended ignorance before the Europeans. Ever cunning and diplomatic, the king and his chiefs simply gave their promise to accept the Christians' Bible— even though this obviously meant that Mutesa hoped the goals he failed to accomplish with his espousal of Islam might still be attained with the white man's religion. More importantly, Mutesa held the hope that European guns and technology would flow into Buganda with the mission presence.

Edward Steinhart who studied conflict and collaboration in the age of Christian evangelism aptly notes that the missions' presence in East Africa coincided with a period when Uganda struggled with a serious problem of spiritual crisis. While this observation sums up the foregoing, it is important to stress that the Kabaka remained in control of the situation—or at least so he thought. Given his position, as the physical symbol of Ganda society and culture, his acceptance of any of the alien religions would have caused an irreparable damage to his status—an unpardonable weakness in the king. Samwiri Karugire's authoritative study, *A Political History of Uganda*, upholds this view with the assertion that the Kabaka was the symbolic as well as the active embodiment of the society and its cohesion.[36]

Also crucial in underpinning the dynamics of resistance and collaboration is class struggle, which defines the expectations of the various actors within the collaborative framework. While Mutesa's interest in a new religion was motivated by his uncanny obsession for survival, it was not lost to the indigenous religious elite—the oracular agents, priests and diviners—those that his maneuvers endangered their powers, and by implication, the very foundation of society. Besides these conservatives, the other formidable group comprised the chiefs and courtiers who had gone deep in their convictions on Islam. This group was strongly opposed to the mere presence of the Christian missionaries in Buganda.

In this polarized and ambiguous order, Mutesa continued to push the dangerous gamble of using Christianity to build a cult closely identified with the throne and his person. The end result of his imagination calls to mind King Alfonso I (r. 1509–43) of the Kongo kingdom, who had embraced Portuguese Catholicism in the late fifteenth century with the hope to ensure a better life for his kingdom.[37] Just as the very Europeans who introduced the Kongo to Christianity were responsible for its colonial subjugation, so did Buganda crack under Christian mission/colonial intrusion.

"COME OVER TO 'MACEDONIA' AND HELP US"

After his contact with Mutesa, Stanley appealed to the English public to make haste in cultivating Christianity in what he perceived as the fertile field for missionary endeavor among the Baganda. In 1876 the Church of Missionary Society (CMS), a Protestant mission, responded by dispatching their vanguard duo Lt. Shergold Smith and Reverend C. T. Wilson to Uganda. Two years later, a more ambitious team arrived with a key figure named Alexander Murdoch Mackay (1849–1890). In February 1879, the French Catholic mission led by the Holy Ghost Fathers Siméon Lourdel and Brother Amans arrived as the forerunners of the Roman Catholic mission in Buganda.

Intense rivalry marked the activities of French White Fathers and the British CMS in Uganda. In this light, one would agree with Karugira's apt observation that "in Uganda, unlike in any of her mainland neighbors, the missionaries were [to become] the most effective agents of colonialism."[38] What is particularly out of ordinary about the missionary presence and eventual colonization of Uganda is that the course of events could have turned out different without the uncommon attitude of complacency demonstrated by the local rulers. Mutesa housed the missionaries at the court and supplied them with an enthusiastic young boys brought over from different parts of the kingdom to serve as pages in facilitating the missionary works.

Most, if not all of the "mission boys" were conscripted from people of low estate—former slaves, outcasts, and poor people. For a society that was highly hierarchical, and the culture encouraged individuals to aspire for success, the stage was set for these young men to make the most out of the available opportunities. Like in other parts of Africa in the late nineteenth century, the missions' presence was a momentous transforming event as new belief system began to gain precedence among the young people. In what later become modern Uganda, Buganda became the launching grounds for the new order—religion, colonialism, cash economy, Western education and the making of a new dominant elite, missionary rivalry and doctrinal confusion, colonial violence, and so on. Incidentally, the respective missions and their leaders Mackay (for the CMS) and Lourdel (for the Catholics) were engrossed in doctrinal rift. While the Catholics claimed that they came to teach the Africans original version of Christianity, the Protestants attacked Catholic theology for making Mary, the mother of Jesus, and the Saints the center of their worship instead of the point of God. Meanwhile the Muslim chiefs at the *Kabaka*'s court have not given up on Islam. They responded to the ideological struggle with a determined campaign to discredit their Christian rivals. Mutesa manipulated the three religions in order to ascertain the secret of their powers and at times, when the pressure they brought became unbearable, he simply became evasive.

In May 1878, it was disclosed that Mutesa had taken ill and his ailment drew spiritual and political idioms. The process of search for a cure was a contested arena for politics and ideological competition among the diverse religious leaders. The CMS missionary Alexander Mackay, Muslim imams, and local Ganda healers—all congregated at the court seeking to do Mutesa a favor. Although the sickness that afflicted Mutesa was never officially made public, the missionary sources claimed that Mutesa had contracted a chronic gonorrhea through homosexual practices purportedly introduced to the court by Zanzibari Arab traders.[39] Whereas the Muslims invoked powers of the Quranic charms and prayers, the Christians applied mild antiseptics and prayed for divine intervention.[40] Meanwhile, Mugema, the medium of Mukasa, the god of Lake Victoria, pronounced that the "king became ill because he attempted to misappropriate" his position by flirting with alien religions.[41] Kenny who has made an in-depth study of this issue concludes:

> The judgment of Mukasa's oracle was therefore an expression of public opinion or faction about Mutesa's pretensions, phrased in such a way to appear the deliverance of transcendental authority and quite possibly in terms of the precedents of oral tradition, which recounted other similar visitations.[42]

Among the several gods of Buganda, Mackay had particularly been worried about Mukasa (the tutelary divinity of the Nyanza) and his female medium Mugema. In 1879, Mackay had reported in his memoir that "the name Mukasa is in the mouth of everyone. This morning I met scores of plantains sent to him by the king. Cattle, hens, etc, and women have also been sent him by Mutesa."[43] In an audience with Mutesa on December 11, 1879, Mackay tried to impress upon the king to ignore the oracle, which he dismissed as nothing but a "practice of witchcraft."[44] Such common European attitude towards indigenous institutions and practices remains one of the greatest problems of contemporary African knowledge system. European cultural imperialism planted an attitude of negativity in the minds of Africans towards indigenous religion and health care systems. Yet, the same Mackay had grudgingly acknowledged what he described as "a pervasive unwillingness" among the European missionaries in Africa "to attempt an understanding of the societies that they were attempting to convert."[45] On the strength of this evidence, one must stress the imperative of looking beyond the 'Westernized' accounts of what transpired at the *Kabaka*'s court in the late nineteenth century.

In response to Mackay's denunciation of Mukasa, Mutesa posed him a rhetorical question as to why the missionaries "came here and what [they] came to do," adding that it was to his understanding that they came "to make powder and guns." He therefore demanded that "what he wanted were men who could do so."[46] On that note, Mutesa passed his verdict that he would now "leave both the Arab's religion and Muzungu's [white man's] religion," and from that point, Mackay was largely an undesirable visitor to the king's court. In view that the tradition of the Ganda considered Kabaka's eldest sister the wife of Mukasa and that the king was Mukasa's "son-in-law," it is expected that Mutesa would feel greatly offended at each time the missionaries tried to sway his old belief system.[47] For self-preservation, in November 1882, the Catholics withdrew to a station at Kagei, south of Lake Victoria, leaving the CMS mission to contend with Mutesa's distrust and anger. The temporary retreat of the Catholics was followed by a revival of the traditional religion. The local priests who had been administering a series of human sacrifice (or *Kiwendo*) on Mutesa became more prominent at the court.[48] Between 1883 and 1884 when the Mutesa's illness entered its terminal stage, the remaining missionaries had completely lost their influence at the court.

THE REVOLUTIONARY YEARS, 1884–1902

In October 1884, the great Mutesa died and was succeeded to the throne by his son Basammula Ekkere Mwanga II (r. 1884–1897) at the age of sixteen. Under Mwanga, the simmering forces of social transformation became more prominent and profoundly disruptive.[49] The new ideologies professed by both the pages and some chiefs sowed the seed of discord among royal loyalists, Muslim adherents and the Christian pretenders. Over the years, the Christian missions had been busy grooming their converts for public leadership with new values and literary skills. Prominent figures among this new generation of schooled believers were Apolo Kagwa (later Sir), Solomon Kakungulu, a die-hard nonconformist, and J. K. Miti, among others. The reformist and rebellious opposition mounted by these restless individuals to the old order constituted the most disintegrating factor in the outcome of events of the coming years.[50] As Brierley and Spear aptly put it, for them:

> Although success might mean the acquisition of high office, failure could bring disgrace or even death, especially in such troubled times. Pages were not members of the ranking hierarchy and had to compete with each other to distinguish themselves before the great chiefs and the king in the hopes of gaining a patron for their own tumultuous climb to power.[51]

In essence, Mwanga was entrusted with the leadership of a kingdom threatened by a group of treacherous Don Quixotes whose ultimate hunger for power was masked under the guise of Christianity.

Apprehensive of the dangers the Christian elements posed to his authority, Mwanga ordered the death, on October 29, 1885, of the first Anglican Bishop of Eastern Equatorial Africa James Hannington who had just arrived Busoga, a town outside the state capital. Given the intense rivalry among the Europeans for territorial claims in Africa, Mwanga had perceived Bishop Hannington as an empire builder.[52] The killing of Hannington was subsequently followed up with a series of actions against all Christian converts. As a climax on June 3, 1886, thirty-two suspected rebels, most of them young pages, were openly cooked alive at Namugongo, a few miles outside the modern capital city Kampala. Some of those who escaped the pyre were later apprehended and punished with castration and their bodies were dumped at crossroads as a warning to the Ganda to keep their distance from the alien religion. To conceive this incidence simply as martyrdom is right or wrong depending on how the Spanish Inquisition of 1834 should be viewed.

In response to a question from Father Lourdel in 1886 as to why the *Katikkiro* would rather not ask the European missions to leave than wasting the lives of the young converts, the traditional priminister responded with the statement "it is our children that we are killing, not yours. As for you people, you are our guests; we will not drive you away, but as many of you teach we shall kill."[53] J. A. Rowe has rightly observed that the *Katikkiro*'s response sounded more like "a dramatic rejoinder than an accurate statement of policy," for the execution of Bishop Hannington had occurred some weeks earlier.[54]

The 'Ganda Inquisition' of 1866 did not very much succeed in dissuading the new Christian converts from disrespecting Mwanga's authority. Pioneer social anthropologists have studied the epistemological connection between power, politics, and rituals through which they are articulated. Max Gluckman for example, building on Edward Evans-Pritchard's study of ritual and regicide among Sudanese Shilluk, suggests that forms of ritual aggression directed at the king—in which the king is publicly insulted and even degraded by commoners—may express political tensions only barely restrained by the powers of his insecure office yet still strong enough to maintain the kingship as the symbolic focus of political competition.[55] This theory best captures the shaky position of Mwanga *vis-a-vis* the continuing daily incidents of insult from his pages that were now interpreted as common reaction to the old ways. In 1888, Mwanga hatched out a plot to rid his country of all foreign missions and their African followers. The plan was to get the entire group on canoes and maroon them at a remote Island off the coast of Lake Victoria.[56]

As the events turned out, Mwanga had far underestimated the resolve of his opponents, the Christian elements, who now regarded themselves as the arbiters of the kingdom. With the support of the Muslims under the leadership of Chief Mujasi, the Catholic Honarat Nyonnyintono, captain of the guards, and Protestant Apolo Kagwa, captain of the royal storekeepers, Mwanga was deposed in September 1888. Ronald Kassimir has aptly argued that the 1866 killings was rather complex. He contends that "the martyrdom event as represented in Catholic writings was an important (although not the only one) around which Catholic clergy and lay elites attempted to construct a religious institution and a religious community—first within Buganda, and then within Uganda as a whole."[57] The common notion held by theologians and historians in depicting the accounts of the killings as martyrdom were part of the colonial discourse aimed at discrediting the local traditional authority and in order to establish a new hegemonic leadership hierarchy built on Christian/Western ideals. This view has been corroborated by Holger Hansen whose study on the "Church and State in Early Colonial Uganda" reveals that part of the CMS core goals in African was to establish a hegemonic order that will make the church "independent" and "superfluous."[58] In pursuit of this goal, missionaries were glad to have found among their African converts, an ideal group of collaborators.[59]

Against the commonly held idea, Twaddle's 1972 revisionist essay credits the Ganda Muslim chiefs, rather than the Christian elements, with initiating the revolution that drove Mwanga from the throne.[60] If accepted, it becomes clear that Muslim chiefs decided to control Uganda by stopping the aggressive push made by the Christian party for power and control. In October 1888, barely a month after Mwanga's dethronement, the Muslims drew swords against their Christian competitors and chased them out of the capital. The Muslims had watched in frustration as Kiwewa, successor to Mwanga, failed to fully support the consolidation of Islam in Buganda.[61] In his place was Kalema (a prince and a felon already convicted for his recklessness), who was promptly circumcised according to Muslim rites.[62]

The war against Muslims united the Catholic and Protestant parties. After his dethronement, Mwanga joined the Catholics at their hideout in Buddu, and from here, they established a liaison with the Protestants at Ankole (or Nkore). By October 5, 1889, the Christian forces had defeated the Muslims at Mengo, thus, clearing the way for Mwanga to temporarily return to his throne. A month later, with the help of Kabarega, chief of Bunyoro, the Muslims once again chased Mwanga out of power. It was not until February 1890 that the Christians decisively defeated their Muslim foes.

Historians may highlight some key outcomes of these wars. First, having lost control of the politics of missionary conversion and resistance in his kingdom, Mwanga was turned into a hapless instrument of collaboration by the Catholics. This was a paradoxical twist in view that his father, Mutesa I, had originally planned to use the presence of the missions to save his kingdom from outside aggression, while also hoping to develop a new cult of power. Ironically absolutism, as desired by Mutesa, was nowhere close to reality. Second, emerging from the wars, the African Christian elite claimed rights as kingmakers, client-chiefs and co-owners of the colonial order. Henceforth Christianity would be the basis for political mobilization and power legitimacy. This raises questions as to whether the so-called Christian martyrs were truly martyrs or sinners. They remind us about the actors E. A. Ayandele, in a similar study on Nigerian colonial elite, condemned as:

> A new species of African—hybridized, transmogrified, and passionate borrowers of Western values, ideas, norms, mores, thought-patterns, religion, and cosmology; deserters of their fatherland's cultural heritage; revellers in the white man's mental world; worshippers of white man's education; apostles of political, social, and cultural aspirations completely at variance with the aspirations of the rest of the continent.[63]

Although the present writer does not buy, wholesome, Ayandele's sharp views, there is no other fair justification for ascribing sainthood to religious fanatics who took up arms against their fatherland than a historical judgment lost to Christian bias.[64] The rebels grossly abused the trust reposed in them by their indigenous rulers. Twaddle who shares a similar view argues that the Christians won the power struggles only "by being less 'Christian' in their political behaviour."[65] This further calls into question the problem of sources; for much is known about those who were killed, little is known about those Christians who escaped or even those who were not marked for elimination.

J. A Rowe, who has tackled this question, points out that only a few Christians were actually killed and not even all of them were converts. In fact, a number of issues remain inconsistent with the notion that Mwanga was out to eliminate all Christians in the wake of the 1886 crisis. For instance, soon after the purge, Mwanga not only retained a number of Christian officials, but also bestowed them with even greater powers. Two individual examples include Apolo Kagwa (Kabaka's *Ggwanika* or storekeeper) the Protestant leader, and Honorat Nyonyintono, the first Roman Catholic convert. Mwanga promoted these men as commanders of two powerful regiments.[66] Obviously, it was not merely the act of accepting Christianity that infuriated the Ganda leaders. Rather, one would suppose that the acts of disobedience, provocation, lawlessness and an unbridled ambition of these new converts invoked the fire that consumed them. Writing in 1890, Reverend Robert Ashe grudgingly acknowledged that the Christians were suspected of disloyalty and sedition.[67] Ashe wrote that "the Christians were accused of becoming insolent and disobedient," but then quickly adds that "the fact was that they [the pages] had begun to set themselves against the evil practices of Mwanga's shameful court."[68] Contrary to Ashe's perception, open disobedience to monarchical authority was a reality and not just a mere suspicion. Even Apolo Kagwa, a leading actor among the dissidents, noted that prior to the 1866 incident,

> The whole land was in disorder, for the [page] boys were looting goats and cattle wholesale . . . and they were killing people in the highway without cause, the king was paying no heed whatever to his country, but only the boys whom he favored at the expense of the *bakunga*."[69]

Thus, what appeared to Ashe as "shameful practices" of Mwanga were viewed differently by the old chiefs who remained loyal to the traditions of their ancestors. One of these royal loyalists urged on Mwanga to "kill them all [the pages] and we will give you better ones."[70]

THE FINAL CONFLICT AND THE UGANDAN AGREEMENT OF 1900

Since the missionaries controlled access to education, the power of the new African converts grew stronger, even as the Catholics versus Protestants antipathy deepened. In Mwanga's symbolic return to the throne, the Catholics appeared to have gained victory over their Protestant rivals who perceived Mwanga as leader of the Catholics and not of all Buganda. This is where political opportunism took precedence over religious pretensions in a period of intense drama following the scramble for and partition of Africa by the various European powers from 1884. The tensed situation in the capital of Buganda, Rubaga, boiled over on January 24, 1892 when a Catholic convert shot dead a Protestant in a personal altercation that should not have otherwise resulted in a civil war. Against the jurisdiction of Mwanga, Captain Frederick Lugard (later lord), who had arrived in 1890 to secure control of Uganda for her Majesty's Imperial British East African Company (IBEA), demanded a retrial and execution of the culprit. Mwanga, who is now widely seen as a Catholic, immediately rejected Lugard's pro-Protestant demand.[71]

Actually, the isolated incidence of murder was only pretence for Lugard to dramatize Her Majesty's claim to the East African territory.[72] In the ensuing confrontation Lugard, with the power of his maxim guns, forced victory for his English Protestants party. In a tactful move, Lugard decided to retain Mwanga as the traditional ruler of Buganda.[73] But Mwanga, more or less, remained a puppet in the hands of those who had restored him to power. His exile to Seychelles in 1897 and subsequent replacement by his two-year old son, Daudi Chwa (d. 1940), betrays the ulterior aims of the Europeans and their local collaborators to appropriate unhindered control of Uganda.[74] Writing in his personal diary on December 19 1890, a corpus of his *The Rise of Our East African Empire*, Lugard expressed surprise that Mwanga, was a murderer of Hannington, "I thought it was his father Mutesa."[75]

Meanwhile the decision to reinstate Mwanga on the throne was part of an elaborate and collective set of concessions leading to the Ugandan Agreement of 1900. Parties to the Agreement included the victorious groups of 'Christian' client-chiefs acting on behalf of the minor Kabaka Daudi Chwa and Sir Harry Johnston, Special Commissioner for Her Britannic Majesty's Government. The Agreement formally placed the region known today as Uganda under British control. It further confirmed Buganda a Westernized constitutional monarchy under British protection and rule. Meanwhile actual local powers lied in the hands of the African Christian nobility.[76] Apolo Kagwa, the Protestant leader, Zakariya Kinsingriiri, another prominent Protestant leader, and Stanislas Mugwanya, the Catholic leader, were appointed Regents over Buganda.[77] Among the trio, most power resided with Kagwa. Summing up his career, Wrigley stated that

> Sir Apolo, who had begun his career as the leader of a band of teenage ruffians in the service of the king, grew into a highly respected Christian statesman, Regent of Buganda for seventeen years and Prime Minister (*Katikkiro*) for thirty-seven, recipient of an order of knighthood normally reserved for ambassadors and colonial governors.[78]

The 1890s trend conforms to the deliberate colonial policy aimed at the erosion of monarchical authority and restructuring the chiefly hierarchy in favor of the *Bakungu* client-chiefs, whose powers were enhanced with freehold land tenures, entitling them to rents as well as chiefly tributes.[79] In the midst of the ongoing changes, the greater majority of Ganda commoners who remained attached to the traditional values were largely marginalized. Also the terms of the 1900 document established a pattern for the practice of colonial rule in which the Ganda became the most favored group among its neighbors. Buganda enjoyed special status and rights as co-inheritors of the colonial state of Uganda.

With the Christian chiefs in strategic positions, the church in Uganda demanded and was granted a degree of autonomy that was supposed to make it independent of any political/secular control in church matters. The church also demanded economic privileges like exemption from taxation and import duties, while recognizing the supremacy of the secular authority.[80] This recognition came after Tucker, the Anglican Bishop of Uganda, had succeeded in making client-chiefs subordinate to the prominent laymen in the government of the church. For long-term plans, Tucker also insisted on expanding mission education to ensure future leaders in both church and state.[81]

In the mainstream historiography, different aspects of the transformative period of the 1890s have been given a fair amount of scholarly attention. However, much is still desired as to why it mattered much for individuals to either be identified a Catholic or Protestant in this period of Ugandan history. This question draws attention to the crosscutting points of contact between church, state and local initiatives in constructing new and compositing forms of identities.

CONTESTING THE BOUNDARIES OF IDENTITY: CATHOLICISM VERSUS PROTESTANTISM

In resolving the war between the rival missions in Uganda, Lugard had tried to impress on the adherents that it was irrelevant if one were a Protestant or Catholic. This logic helped in restoring civil order, but did not reconcile entrenched competing ideologies held by the various parties. Steinhart's *Conflict and Collaboration* explains that often the various parties took a name and identity provided not by a set of policies, but by the religion and language of the missionaries who mentored them. Indeed,

> The progressive party in the administrator's terminology came to be synonymous with the 'English' Protestant party of the CMS missionaries and their African adherents. The conservatives accepted the designation and the practice of 'French' Roman Catholicism during the first years of contact with the religion of the French-speaking White Fathers Mission.[82]

Mwanga and his group aligned with the Catholics because they resented the English Protestant ideology, which they associated with erosion of monarchical traditions. These ideas mirrored the existing notions in Europe where the Catholic Church is closely associated with conservative politics and Protestantism with reform and liberalism.

In this dualism, the African actors constructed local networks and alliances in conformity with their individual and group interests. By implication, political mobilization along party lines "had little to do with the programs or ideology of the opposing parties. Rather bipolarity derived from a structural tendency of political competition under colonialism to channel itself into a relatively stable system of binary divisions."[83] Bipolar politics translates the structures of relationship with imperialism, which under the system of indirect rule was operated as a winner-takes-all game. As a result, the precolonial culture of chiefly competition was converted into what Steinhart describes as a "persisting opposition of named blocs under leaders of great stature"[84] This political culture became firmly entrenched in the body politics as each party accumulated distinct cultural symbols and by the late colonial era, these differences had assumed fundamental import in the political life of the entire Uganda protectorate.

More intriguing is the fact that the religious bigotry seemed to have masked the more fundamental problem of collaboration. Engrossed in their deadly struggle for power under the cover of Christian piety, the Africans (whether Catholic conservatives or Protestant progressives) abandoned themselves to the general condition of alien subordination.[85] Twaddle captures how the client-chiefs struggled among them themselves, especially in the 1890s, to please the European in order to maintain their "good boys" image in the face of Lugard's excessive demands for food:

> At first the *Bakungu* chiefs concerned thought of refusing to assist Lugard.
> But then they conferred at home of Apolo Kagwa 'and decided that they
> should humble themselves, remembering the Luganda proverb which says
> "Your superior may use your own stick to beat you . . . we were also
> aware that as subordinates of a ruler we should be wise.[86]

CONCLUSION

A number of ideas follow this analysis of mission, state, and colonization of Uganda. First is the model of indirect rule system, which was based on a hegemonic program of resource sharing between the imperialists, the church, and their African agents.[87] The elaborate linkage between the Africans, the church and the colonial state was sustained with the spoils of colonial rule.

Second, the collaborative project in Uganda may be regarded as yet another successful operation of the divide-and-rule strategy. Mahmood Mamdani has stressed the point that divide-and-rule was an official magic policy of colonial control.[88] This conclusion is supported by less generous treaties the British concluded with the other kingdoms in Uganda (Toro in 1900, Ankole in 1901, and Bunyoro in 1933)—all of whom were denied the favor of large-scale private land tenure. The smaller chiefdoms of Busoga were totally considered as inconsequential. Indeed, the preferential treatment reinforced the resolve of Buganda Christianized elite to participate actively as beneficiaries in the colonial system.

However, the context in which this divide-and-rule policy was implemented in Uganda defiles any simplistic notion of a pre-planned, deliberate and conscious application of the policy. The European colonialists preyed upon the indigenous forms of political culture and class structures. For the Africans, the tendency towards identification with either the Catholic or Protestant doctrines, and the alignments and realignments that characterized such associations underlined African response to the stimulus for social mobility. F. B. Welbourn argues that the failure of the Ganda elite to arrest the forces altering their society was symbolically translated into the terminal disease that afflicted Mutesa. Welbourn concludes that "What the Ganda needed was a new mythology which would enable them to come to terms with the outside world."[89] In extension to that, the Ganda also needed new skills and ideas to make meaning out of the various forces of modernity—Christianity, Western education, medicine, technology, new administration and cash economy that had evaded their world. Although colonial expansion of the late nineteenth-century was unstoppable, the Africans seized the available sociopolitical space, to pursue divergent goals within the limits of imperial control. Indeed, as Brierley and Spear argued, the Ganda who became Christians sought ways "to control the forces of threatening Buganda and themselves ideologically through syntheses of Kiganda and Christian beliefs and politically through the religious parties and their tactical alliance with the British."[90]

Additionally, colonial rule in Uganda in the first three decades was partly an implementation of Ganda imperialism to the neighboring territories. Ganda client-chiefs were tax-collectors, and labor administrators in the neighboring Bunyoro, Kigezi and Mbale. In these and other areas, the Ganda arrogantly offered their Luganda language, banana crop, and their traditional dress (*kanza*) as symbols of progress and civilization. With the-all-powerful Apolo Kagwa in power, also, Protestantism in Uganda was offered as the perfect religion. The *Bagandization* of Uganda was seriously resented by its neighbors and the Catholic Church exploited the situation to expand its sphere of popularity in Uganda.

Overall, the Buganda client-chiefs came to see the colonial order as designed for them to impose their culture and influence across the entire region of the Great Lakes of Africa. In the context of decolonization, David Apter argues that unlike their peers in West Africa, for instance, the Ugandan colonial leaders were less concerned with hastening the departure of the colonialists than with continuing with the local regime of collaboration.[91]

Chapter Four

Threatening Gestures, Immoral Bodies: The Intersection of Church, State, and Kongo Performance in the Belgian Congo

Yolanda Covington-Ward

> *Nsinsa wa ngoma wusobele, soba makinu maku.*
> (When the rhythm of the ngoma changes, change your dance)
>
> —Kongo proverb

INTRODUCTION

The above proverb is often used to remind people that when they find themselves in a different situation or place, they should also change their comportment to match their circumstances. This proverb captures the shifting nature of the uses and meanings of Kongo embodied practices in the context of the many socio-cultural transformations that defined the colonial period.[1] In colonial contexts, embodied practices such as dance were also likely to be altered by the dominating power in much the same way that the economy, social and political structures, language, and ways of dress of indigenous populations were subject to change. Susan Reed notes:

> The suppression, prohibition and regulation of indigenous dances under colonial rule is an index of the significance of dance as a site of considerable political and moral anxiety. Colonial administrations often perceived indigenous dance practices as both a political and moral threat to colonial regimes. Local dances were often viewed as excessively erotic, and colonial agents and missionaries encouraged and sometimes enforced the ban or reform of dance practices.[2]

This essay examines performances of the BaKongo[3] as sites of moral and political contestation between the church, colonial state, and the indigenous population in the Lower Congo of the former Belgian colony from 1885 to 1960. Kongo secular performances, *makinu*—that incorporate dance, traditional instruments, and song—were seen as "indecent" threats to public morality, and thus were persecuted and prohibited by both Protestant and Catholic missionaries, and were the subject of fervent debate amongst colonial administrators. Kongo non-secular performances in the context of independent *ngunza* churches—including practices such as trembling, jumping, and using traditional instruments—were seen as subversive movements that menaced the smooth running of the colony and the hegemony of the European-led missions. However, attitudes towards these practices and the manner in which they were used for different purposes changed over time and in varying contexts. Using historical documentation and personal interviews, this essay reveals that the realities of collaboration, conflict and accommodation amongst the colonial administration, missionaries, and the indigenous population were complicated and ever-shifting in regards to Kongo embodied practices in the Belgian Congo.

PART I: NGUNZA

Dancing with God: An Ethnographic Memory

May 22, 2005. Today we went to one of the independent *ngunza*[4] churches for service. When we arrived, you could hear the music from outside. The church itself was a small one room white washed building with a cement floor . . . The pastors were wearing all white robes, with white hats. Most of the women had their heads covered in white scarves . . . There were also several women dressed in all white dresses. The entire church danced quite a lot. The dancing was done to the rhythm of three smaller drums . . . called *bibandi*. . . . After this, there was the collection, and then a healing session, which was a sight to behold . . . Four men in the white robes lined up in front of the sick. . . . Each man had a white towel which they would utilize in the healing process, waving them over their patients. The healers began to shake and tremble and lay their hands on the sick, shouting out stuff, and massaging and touching different parts of their bodies; first their heads, then their abdomens and backs simultaneously, then their legs and arms. They kept on trembling, and all the while the drums are playing and everyone is singing and dancing again.[5]

This ethnographic story describes some of the embodied practices witnessed in 2005 that also characterized worship and devotion in the prophetic movements that rocked the Lower Congo from the 1920's to independence in 1960. The first part of this analysis seeks to describe the impact of colonialism and missionary societies in the Lower Congo during the late nineteenth century, the rise of the prophetic movement led by Simon Kimbangu, and shifts in the uses and interpretations of the embodied practices that characterized this movement.

A Brief History of Christian Missions in the Lower Congo

The history of Christian evangelization on the Lower Congo is a long one. The first wave of missionary activity dates back to the baptism of Nzinga-Nkuwu (Joao I), the sovereign of the Kongo Kingdom by Portuguese missionaries in May of 1491. Contacts were established between the Kongo Kingdom, Portugal, and Rome, and the Kongo received European Catholic missionaries of different nationalities up until the mid 1800's.[6] The BaKongo were soon to see major transformations in their lives with the arrival of colonialism and the second wave of Christian evangelization, which actually began before the arrival of H. M. Stanley.[7]

The opening of the Lower Congo to colonial exploitation began with H. M. Stanley's travels there starting in 1877, which led to the establishment of the Congo Independent State as the personal fiefdom of King Leopold II of Belgium from 1885 to 1908 (Congo Independent State), and a colony of the Belgian government from 1908—1960. During the years of the Congo Independent State, King Leopold of Belgium, a Catholic himself, fervently lobbied Belgian Catholic missionaries to come to the Congo, and this commitment was first officially recognized in a concordat signed between the Congo Independent State and the Holy See in Rome in 1906.[8] "They (Catholics) were freely given large concessions of land, while their personnel and goods were often transported in the state steamers. So much state favor was shown to the Catholic missions that the Protestants began to feel themselves at a considerable disadvantage."[9] However, the relationship between the missions and the colonial authorities wasn't unidirectional; missionaries were also engaging in activities that would aid the colonial government.

The Belgian colonial system operated on the basis of an interdependent triumvirate of missionary, administration, and commercial interests. The missions provided the government with a measure of social and territorial control, and they educated and trained Africans for work on the plantations and in the mines. In return they received subsidies, protection, and land. At their behest, the state would at times introduce laws that the missions felt they needed to further evangelization, for example, a law designed to discourage polygamous marriage by taxing surplus wives. The collaboration between the missions, especially the Catholic missions, and the administration was mutually satisfactory. [10]

For much of the early period of the Congo Independent State, Protestant missionaries had a very good working relationship with colonial authorities as well. This perhaps explains why one of the first people to publicly condemn the numerous atrocities that were being committed against the native population in the Congo Independent State (especially as a result of the forced collection of rubber) was not associated with a mission at all. George Washington Williams, an African-American pastor, civil leader, historian, and journalist was one of the first to do this in 1890, in his public document "An Open Letter to his Serene Majesty Leopold II," [11] based on his own travels in the Congo Free State. The first public expression of discontent with the policies and actions of the state by a missionary was by Augouard, a French priest based in French Equatorial Africa in 1894, in a Catholic newspaper printed in Paris. [12] This was followed by numerous public writings and speeches by Protestant missionaries condemning the atrocities from 1895 to the annexation of the Congo Independent State by Belgium in 1908. The ill treatment of the indigenous population overall was one among several key factors that spurred the arrival of the prophetic movement in the Lower Congo.

Conditions Leading to the Prophetic Movement

Traditionally, when there were disastrous situations and general social discord in Kongo communities, in order for a sense of balance and harmony to prevail, reconciliation had to be made with the ancestral and spiritual world through religious leaders. [13] Thus, when the BaKongo faced increasing stress and anxiety in dealing with the colonial situation, the end result was the development of prophetic movements.

The nascent colonial state sought to control the indigenous population, and as a result of many of the brutal policies that were enacted, the

Lower Congo suffered a period of depopulation. The devastating conditions that the BaKongo faced were multifold.

> As activities of the state's agents continuously increased in Lower
> Congo, the way of life of the Kongo came into more frequent conflict
> with European interests. The state government continuously sent
> expeditions into the villages to recruit labor for portage, railroad
> construction, the Force Publique, and for the collection of taxes and
> food, as well as for punitive expeditions.[14]

The Congo River wasn't navigable inland after a certain point,
and thus most goods and supplies were carried on the heads and backs
of Congolese porters, as pack animals couldn't survive in the area and
the railroad had yet to be constructed. In 1889, a decree was released
regarding the porterage system, and later in 1891, another was issued
establishing a labor tax system that compelled Africans to work for their
colonizers. The reaction of many Kongo to these changing conditions
was simply to move away from the caravan routes, and later, the rail
road, leading to a depopulation of certain areas of the Lower Congo.[15]
    Another situation that the Lower Congo frequently experienced
between 1872 and 1921 was that of famine, often caused by military
expeditions into villages, and further exacerbated by a growing "immi-
grant non-producing population."[16]
    Yet another factor that increased the general stress of the indig-
enous population was the large number of epidemics that devastated
the area. Between 1890 and 1913, sleeping sickness ravished the Lower
Congo, causing many deaths and migrations from plateaus to valleys.
Spanish influenza was to add to the destruction in 1918, part of a world
wide medical crisis that lasted until 1920.[17] As a result of all of these
reasons, there are estimates that the population declined by as much as
75 percent between 1885 and 1921.[18] All of these factors contributed to
an enormous sense of crisis for the Kongo, and thus, by 1921, conditions
were favorable for the development of a prophetic movement, which was
to be led by a prophet named Simon Kimbangu.

Kingunza and the Movement of Simon Kimbangu

Simon Kimbangu was born in 1889 in the village of Nkamba in the
Lower Congo, to a mother named Lwezi, and his father Kuyela. Unfortunately, his mother died when he was young, as did his father later on,
but apparently not before Kimbangu witnessed his father working as an

nganga-ngombo, or diviner.[19] Kimbangu became a Christian and a member of the Baptist church (of the B. M. S) as a young man. He worked as a catechist and a teacher in the mission for a short time. In 1918, during the devastating world wide flu epidemic, he heard a spiritual voice calling him, but refused to answer. He tried to escape the voice by going to Kinshasa, where he worked as a domestic servant and as a worker at a British owned oil refinery. It was there that he was exposed to Garveyist[20] ideas and readings by Black Americans and other Africans working there. The voice continued to call him, and eventually he returned to his village. On April 6, 1921, while walking through the neighboring village of Ngombe-Kinsuka, he heard the cry of a sick woman and was compelled to go and heal her. He laid his hands on her in the name of Jesus Christ and began to pray, and tremble. Miraculously, she recovered.[21] This monumental event was followed by other healings, and soon people came in droves to Nkamba to be healed by the prophet Simon Kimbangu.[22]

One of the most fascinating things about the prophet Simon Kimbangu is that, while praying and healing in the name of Jesus Christ, using the bible faithfully, and upholding the doctrine and moral rules of the Protestant church, he also incorporated many ritual practices that came from his cultural background.

This is most clearly shown in the eyewitness account of Leon Morel, a district administrator who went to Nkamba on May 11, 1921 to witness events for himself.

The report of Morel is five pages long, and describes the embodied practices of Kimbangu and his adepts. On the road into the town, Morel encountered Kimbangu, who " . . . was shaken by a general trembling of the body . . . Next to him, were two native men and two young girls, all shaken by the same trembling and all giving bizarre shouts. They erratically whirled around me, lacking self control. I tried vainly to speak with them . . ."[23] After failing to communicate with the group, Morel enters Nkamba and sets up his tent near Kimbangu's home, where he sees a huge crowd of people gathered. Kimbangu came to shake his hand:

> I took advantage of this period of calm to ask Kimbangu the reason for this not very suitable and grotesque manner of receiving me. He responded that: 'It's God that ordered him to come to meet me in that way and that the bizarre shouts are nothing but his conversation with God. It's God that orders him and his apostles to tremble in this way.[24]

Other European accounts of Kimbangu's practices and those of *ngunza* movements in general were similar. One person described them as "somewhat violent . . . He tossed his head, rolled his eyes, and jumped into the air, while his body often twitched all over."[25] In reporting to the procurer general in Boma the results of his investigation of the movement in August of 1921, N. Cornet reported witnessing "at Matadi, especially in interrogating the blacks, all the trembling N'Gunza."[26] Moreover, L. Cartiaux, in an encounter in June of 1921 with several leaders of the *ngunza* movement in the village of Mayombe in Luozi territory, recounted, "I ordered all my soldiers to tightly tie up the three n'Gunza . . . all three were making movements with the arms, the head, the body, the eyes rolling up to the sky . . ."[27] Missionaries at Kibunzi, in another part of Lower Congo, witnessed a man possessed by the spirit whose body shook continuously for three days, and saw other people who trembled, leapt, or danced when in a condition of ecstasy.[28]

Music and dancing played an important role in healing and evoking the spirit, which would possess one's body and lead to a condition of ecstasy.

> Kimbangu had already said that the hymns must be sung loudly and enthusiastically, for then he would be given the power of healing. The louder the song, the stronger became the spirit. The prophets therefore tried to get men with good voices to be their assistants most of whom also experienced ecstasy, so that the singing was accompanied by dancing movements. Loud instrumental music was used in addition to the singing and dancing in order to produce the desired condition.[29]

All of these elements were mentioned in a letter to the procurer general in Boma from the vice-governor general in July of 1921: "The visionary and his disciples read the bible, sang protestant hymns, danced, and engaged in grotesque contortions."[30]

Interestingly enough, although dancing within the context of worship was allowed, dancing in secular contexts was prohibited by Kimbangu, along with polygamy, use of fetishes, and the drinking of alcoholic beverages, among other things.[31] It is thus noteworthy that Kimbangu adopted many of the rules that already existed in the Protestant churches at the time.

Although Kimbangu was the impetus for the movement, many other prophets came to the forefront, both associated and unassociated with Kimbangu. The movements overall can be called *ngunza*, or prophetism, and the terms Kimbanguism and Ngunzism were often used interchangeably, and later variations such as Salutism (Salvation Army), Mpadism, and Dieudonne arose from the mid 1930's up until independence in 1960. Many of the same practices described above prevailed in all of these groups and movements, and some still exist today in churches of *ngunza*, as the ethnographic story demonstrates.

Reactions of the Colonial Administration and Missionaries

At first, the Belgian administration regarded the movement of Kimbangu as a purely religious matter, and until the end of May in 1921 saw it as an affair of churches and priests in which they had no reason to intervene. However, as more and more people left to visit Nkamba and witness the miracles of the prophet Kimbangu, businesses began to be affected, as workers were absent.[32] Thus, the business owners began to pressure the administration for action. Morel's report that he filed on May 17 is worth quoting at length to demonstrate his ideas about Kimbangu and his practices:

> I learned after from the mouths of the Protestant missionaries of Gombe-Matadi, that these expressions . . . are the exact reproduction of the manner of behaving of native witch-doctors of the past . . . I have noticed that the current that reigns at Kamba [sic] isn't sympathetic to us: the natives know very well that we can never approve of these grotesque and insane manifestations that accompany the religion of Kimbangu . . . the goal of the latter is to create a religion that corresponds with the mentality of the natives, a religion that contains the elements of Protestantism, which adds to itself external practices bordering on fetishism . . . Everyone can readily see that our religions of Europe are all filled with abstractions, not responding to the mentality of the African, who longs for concrete facts and protection. The teachings of Kimbangu please the natives because they are allegedly accompanied by palpable facts: healings, protection against sickness . . . It is therefore necessary to oppose Kimbangu because the tendency of his movement is pan-African. . . . The natives will say that they've found the God of the blacks.[33]

Thus, we can see that the practices of Kimbangu (trembling, jumping, etc.) that Morel witnessed at Nkamba (cited above) and saw as "fetishist" are what led him to distinguish the movement as different from Protestantism, and conclude that its goal of founding an African religion is in fact pan-Africanist and thus a threat to the colonial regime.

This lack of understanding, and even hostility that Morel showed in regards to Kongo traditional culture was repeated by the majority of both Protestant and Catholic missionaries, although not all. For example, one Protestant missionary wrote,

> Our village chapels filled whilst the Catholic chapels emptied. From everywhere requests came for teachers and school materials; in three months we sold about five hundred hymnbooks . . . So it seems to me that this is the most remarkable movement which the country has ever seen. The prophets only seem to have one goal—the proclamation of the Gospel.[34]

However, there were many more missionaries who weren't as pleased with the movement, and who doubted Kimbangu's abilities. Jennings, the district head of the Baptist mission under which Nkamba fell, wrote to other missions that he and a colleague went to Nkamba and were "unable to observe a single miracle . . . keep your folks away from there!"[35] In regards to the practices of the movement, many Protestant missionaries saw them as a revival of traditional African religion. Palmaer, a Swedish medical missionary said Kimbangu's practices resembled those of "heathen banganga"[36] John Geil, a missionary with the A. B. F. M. S. in Mbanza Manteke, wrote in a letter to headquarters dated June 20, 1921 that,

> Like all mission work on the Lower Congo our work has been affected by the prophet movement. A prophet has arisen here who claims power from God to heal the sick and restore the dead to life . . . Others say that the 'movement' is a repetition of the witch doctor who was possessed with so much power.[37]

The Catholic missionaries seem to have been more unified in their displeasure with the movement. Morel attested to getting letters from the Tumba Catholic mission demanding that the "agitation of the prophets" be put to an end.[38] They were likely letters from Father Van Cleemput, the vice-provincial of the Redemptorists, and the superior father at the Tumba Mission, who in a commentary on the movement wrote, "the immediate goal, if one can say: that of founding a religion of a prophet, a Negro religion, must lead to a goal . . . to get rid of the whites, to expel them, to become independent, in a word 'Africa to the blacks."[39] In the August 1921 issue of *La Voix du Rédempteur*, the journal of the Catholic Redemptorist Fathers, Monsignor Van Rosle threatened excommunication of all Christians who affiliated themselves with the church of Simon Kimbangu. In the same issue, other missionaries noted that the movement was a political problem, as "these individuals could provoke an insurrection"[40]

Taking Action: Collaboration and Discord

As both the majority of the missionaries and the colonials saw the *ngunza* movement as a threat to European religious hegemony, business interests, and colonial authority, collaboration took shape. On June 1, 1921, Morel, the administrator of the territory arranged a meeting with heads of both the Protestant and Catholic churches in the area. According to Morel, during this meeting, Father Van Cleemput, representing the Catholic missions "energetically demanded, and I support his view, that there must be an immediate end everywhere to the unrest of prophets," while on the contrary R. Jennings, representing the Protestants, opted for a more "prudent" solution.[41] In the end, the Belgian administrators went along with the plan of the Catholics since "they were afraid that Kimbanguism could turn into a political movement"[42] The district commissioner ordered Kimbangu arrested, and on June 6, Morel returned to Nkamba with soldiers to do just that. However, Kimbangu escaped and was hidden by his adepts for several months. During this time, businesses such as the railroad company were threatened by worker strikes and thus insisted that the government show the native populations that it was "their master,"[43] while the movement continued to spread all throughout the Lower Congo. The sub-district of Zundu, where Nkamba was located, was occupied militarily on June 14, and on June 20, Morel ordered that all native people owning guns turn them in to the local administration, prohibited "the usage of gongs, drums, or other means of communicating by signals of all kinds," outlawed all gatherings, and restricted people's movement.[44] On September 12, 1921, Simon Kimbangu willingly gave himself up to the administration, and was arrested, along with a number of his disciples.

During the trial, Kimbangu's embodied practices came into direct conflict with the colonial administration, whose reaction demonstrates how threatened they were by these gestures. Mandombe, a young female disciple of Kimbangu, was being questioned, when suddenly, Kimbangu went into a trance and began to tremble. M. de Rossi, the presiding judge over the case, threatened Kimbangu with a whipping and then when he didn't stop, called a recess. The doctor called to the scene to examine Kimbangu prescribed a cold shower and "12 blows of the whip."[45]

The day before Kimbangu was sentenced, it was noted in *L'Avenir Colonial Belge*, the colonial newspaper, that a meeting had been held between the territorial administrator Morel, Reverend Jennings of the B.M.S and Father Van Cleemput of the Redemptorists, from which nothing definitive emerged. This was followed by another meeting with only Morel and Van Cleemput, whose spokesperson told the paper that "the menace and influence of Kimbangu and his adepts are harmful for all of the country" and that Morel and Van Cleemput "estimate that an immediate and severe intervention is essential"[46] At the sentencing of October 3, 1921, Kimbangu was accused of a number of things including sedition and hostility towards the white population. The actual text of the sentencing reveals some very compelling fears of the colonial administration:

> Whereas Kibangu [sic] was recognized by the doctors as sound of body and spirit and by consequence responsible for all his acts, that his fits of nerves are nothing but shamming, that it might be that some cases of nervous sickness were healed by suggestion but that the accused profited by deceiving the good faith of the mass destined to serve as an unconscious instrument to his ends, that the goal pursued was that of destroying the authority of the state. Whereas it remain established that by his acts, remarks, schemes, writings, songs, and his history dictated by himself, Simon Kibangu [sic] has set himself up as a redemptor and savior of the black race in indicating the white [race] as the enemy . . . the sect of prophets must be considered organized in order to bear attacks on the security of the state, [a] sect hidden under the veil of a new religion . . . it is true that the hostility against the established powers was manifested up until the present by seditious songs, insults, outrages, and some isolated rebellions, yet it is true that the march of events could have fatally led to a big revolt.[47]

This selection from the text of the sentencing reveals that the colonial administration saw the prophetic movement as more of a political rather than a religious threat. Moreover, Kimbangu's bodily practices of trembling, unknown in the Belgian cultural context but understood in that of Kongo traditional religion, were seen by the colonials as false and were stopped with force as demonstrated in the account of the trial. After Kimbangu was sentenced to 120 strokes of the whip and then death, several Baptist missionaries (including Ross Phillips of the B.M.S and Joseph Clark of the A. B. F. M. S),[48] as well as the substitute public prosecutor[49] appealed to the governor-general in Boma, and King Albert in Belgium (Martin, 62), to change the sentence. King Albert did this on November 15, to life imprisonment.[50]

After Kimbangu's imprisonment, the movement continued without him as other prophets continued to appear, and tragically, continued to be prosecuted. Membership dropped in both missions. At a missionary conference of Protestant churches in November 1921, missionaries decided to ask

> [T]he native congregations to abstain from participation in a movement
> harmful to the progress of Christianity and the normal development of
> the native population . . . we believe that the authorities had to take
> severe and immediate measures to check the Prophet Movement which
> rapidly became favorable soil for propaganda hostile to all white men,
> endangering civilization itself.[51]

A report released in 1924 by a Catholic priest, Father Dufonteny, claiming that the movement sought to unseat the white administration and was all inspired by Protestant missions, led to an investigation[52] and even more severe repression of the movement by the colonial administration. It was officially forbidden to have anything to do with the movement on February 6, 1925, all Kimbanguist institutions were closed, and all religious meetings outside of those directed by missionaries "of the white race" were prohibited.[53] The governor asked the Catholic and Protestant missions to help suppress the movement in a circular of the same year.[54]

The persecution of the prophet movements continued until independence. For example, in 1944 in Manianga[55] territory in Mbanza Mona sector, a sergeant in the Force Publique was imprisoned by the local chief for organizing a "kibanguist" [sic] cell.[56] Similarly, in Mayumbe territory, the annual report noted "a regain of prophetic activity . . . in the 'Eastern' region of the territory near the frontier of A.E.F . . . Two catechists . . . (had) the view of carrying out proselytizing in favor of the Mission of the Blacks. This movement was quickly put down."[57] In Manianga territory in the same year a "cell" of ngunzists was discovered in Mbanza Ngoyo sector and its leader was imprisoned in Luozi. The annual report notes that, "This territory was repeatedly the theater of violent prophetic surges of a more or less subversive character."[58] In 1950, a "cell" of the Salvation Army was discovered and 65 people imprisoned in Luozi territory.[59] People arrested by the colonial administration were often deported to penal labor camps in other parts of the colony to serve long sentences. Kimbangu himself died in one of these camps in Katanga province, on October 12, 1951. Marie-Louise Martin, who likens these places to colonial concentration camps, estimates that approximately 100,000 people were sent into exile, when heads of family and their family members who accompanied them are counted together.[60]

An important issue that cannot be overlooked is varied reaction of the Kongo people. Although the vast majority seemed to at least sympathize with the movement, if not outright participation, there were people on both sides of the conflict. For example, some colonial native chiefs, on the one hand, assisted in suppressing the prophetic movements. A 1955 annual report gives credit to the prudence and vigilance of "notables" in avoiding many prophetic manifestations in the area that year.[61] Similarly, the authors of the 1957 report for Luozi territory seemed content to announce that "the attitude of all of the chiefs, vis-à-vis the subversive movements, was firm. The chief Makuala David of Kinkenge sector was particularly distinguished in this domain."[62] On the other hand, some refused to participate in the movements' suppression. Vuti, the chief of the sub-district of Zundu, was removed from his position on August 8, 1921 because he had "observed an absolutely passive attitude, not cooperating in any of the efforts of the authorities taken to seize . . . the said Kimbangu."[63] In short, BaKongo reactions to the prophetic movements were varied, sometimes collaborating with the colonial administration and antagonistic missionaries, sometimes passively resisting, and at other times openly defying them, often resulting in arrest and imprisonment.

The Prophetic Movement and Nsikumusu

During the explosion of prophetic movements in the Lower Congo, both Catholic and Protestant missions lost many members of their churches who were disappointed in what they saw as the collaboration of the European-led missions with the colonial administration in the persecution of the prophetic movements and their leaders. This reaction, ironically enough, led to a transformation of practices in the Protestant church. According to Tata Mukiese,[64] an older, long-standing member of the *kilombo*,[65] traditional instruments were allowed at one time, but starting in the late 1930's, all traditional instruments were prohibited in the Protestant church as a result of their association with worship in the prophetic movements.[66] One could only sing in a classical manner, using European instruments. He recounted the story of a conflict in the town of Kingoyi in Luozi territory over this very issue. In a Protestant church there, a missionary named Mr. Alden banned the use of traditional instruments in his church in 1934. Kalebi Muzita, a Kongo leader in the church, disagreed with him and challenged his policy. Kongo catechists, teachers, and pastors split into two groups, some siding with Alden and others with Muzita. Kalebi and his group decided to leave the church and he reportedly told Alden, "Since you have prohibited playing these instruments, you will see what will happen." Apparently, Alden and his followers became sick after this proclamation, and were healed only when Kalebi returned and prayed for them. This narrative demonstrates not only conflict and clashes over embodied practices in the use of traditional instruments, but also the importance of continuing this practice in worship for certain Kongo people, even to the point of revoking one's membership in a particular church.

As they lost more and more people to the various prophetic movements, the missionaries finally decided on a plan of action. This plan was touched upon in the 1956 annual governmental report for the territory:

> Since the month of June a new wave of mysticism colored by ngunzism has again swept a big part of the territory. This movement was provoked by a circular sent by the Protestant missionaries of Sundi-Lutete and Kinkenge, inviting their adepts to a moral and spiritual reawakening. Unfortunately, the text of this circular was ambiguous for the natives and was misinterpreted by them. The old ngunzist leaders took up again their subversive activity justifying it by the context of the circular. At a given moment the rumor spread that ngunzism was no longer prohibited by the government. Four big ngunzist manifestations took place in the territory.[67]

This spiritual reawakening was called *nsikumusu* by the Protestant S.M.F. churches in the Lower Congo. In this effort to bring people back to the Protestant church, many of the practices of the prophetic movements were to be incorporated into the S.M.F. churches. For example, traditional instruments could now be played in the church again, and speaking in tongues and trembling were no longer strictly prohibited. This led to a disapproving report by the colonial administration the following year:

> The movement *"nsikumusu"* or spiritual awakening, launched by the Svenska Missions Förbundet of Sundi-Lutete in 1956 didn't have much success at the beginning. The propaganda of opposition made by the territory against trembling made the Reverend Missionaries think, who finished by admitting that in the Territory of Luozi these phenomena are a characteristic expression of *ngunzism*.[68]

Therefore, the spiritual awakening of *nsikumusu* was a case in which missionaries, this time Protestant S.M.F. missionaries in particular, and colonial administrators, disagreed on the meaning and usefulness of Kongo embodied practices. Once again both groups had the same interest of curbing the *ngunza* movement, however colonial administrators did not approve of the S.M.F. churches' method of welcoming some of the same practices, such as trembling, which typified the prophetic move-ment, and were persecuted by the state. Although the S.M.F. churches did this in order to attract people back into their churches, the colonial administration saw it as encouraging the prophetic movements and thus increasing the threat to state security and their own authority.

PART II: MAKINU: KONGO SECULAR DANCE TRADITIONS

Rolling Hips: An Ethnographic Memory

> August 16, 2005. The light of the full moon clearly illuminated the way as we walked towards the large crowd of people haphazardly stand-ing in a circle, laughing, singing, drinking, and dancing . . . People looked at me quizzically as I politely wiggled my way to the front of the circle of onlookers to get a closer look. There were three long, thick drums [ngoma] being played, and the one with a circle in the middle of its drum head had the deepest sound and led the other two. In the cen-ter of the circle of spectators, there seemed to be two lines, one of men, and another of women. Two men or boys left their line and, following the rhythm, walked across the center of the circle to the other line, and stopped in front of two women or girls, effectively choosing them. The women then followed them to the center of the circle, and danced with them, rotating and shaking their hips and posteriors, while the tops of their bodies barely moved . . . The men, however, shifted from one foot to the other, following another cross-rhythm, and their own hip movements were emphasized by long lengths of cloth laid vertically from their waists to the ground, making a type of skirt.[69] The men jumped towards and danced around their partners, while the women remained in place, calm and collected, hips moving continuously, and feet shuffling slightly. At a particular drum signal, the couples stopped dancing, genuflected towards each other, and left the circle, to be replaced by another set of men coming in to begin the cycle again[70].

This ethnographic story introduces us to *makinu*. *Makinu* is a broad term to describe traditional secular dances among the BaKongo. The second part of the chapter will examine the interpretations of the meaning and uses of *makinu* by colonial agents, missionaries, and Kongo people themselves, and how all of these have changed over time and in different circum-stances, particularly in relation to the *ngunza* movements.

Moral Legislation and Ambivalent Action

The first official act of the colonial administration regarding traditional dances in general was on July 17, 1900, under the title of "indigenous dances." It basically said that in places to be determined by the administrative authority of the district or zone, indigenous dances could not be held publicly except on certain days, in certain locations, at specific times, and under conditions determined by the administrative authority. If these rules were broken, the punishment would be arrest and seven days of penal servitude, and/or a fine of 200 francs. Over the next several decades, a debate over indigenous dances emerged that is visible in the *Receuil Mensuel*, a circular of laws, ordinances, and general concerns distributed for the "exclusive use of functionaries and agents of the colony."[71] It is in this publication that we can see some of the opinions concerning indigenous dances. Although these circulars were couched in general terms without discussing particular cultural or ethnic groups, the capital of the Congo Independent State and then the Belgian Congo was Boma (in the Lower Congo) from 1886—1929, and thus the majority of the indigenous people with whom authorities in Boma had contact were most likely BaKongo. It is within this context that we can examine the assessments of indigenous dances made by colonial administrators. On January 16, 1912, there was an interpretive circular commenting on the above law of indigenous dances of 1900, written by the vice-governor general Louis F. Ghislain. In this publication, he addresses his main issue of concern:

> . . . it was brought to my knowledge, that in our posts, customary dances take place of a clearly lascivious or obscene character. On the part of the territorial authorities, charged with being the agents of civilization to the indigenous populations, to tolerate these practices and not to suppress them, could be with just cause considered by them as a sign of approval.[72]

He reminds them of the decree of 1900, and offers a specific definition of the word locality in the decree as including all the posts of the colony. He continues: "It is superfluous to add, that the regulations ordered by the decree of 17 July 1900, can't bear upon the customary dances that don't offer any danger to order or public tranquility, or that don't take on any character neither lascivious nor obscene."

Thus, in this first circular, we find evidence of a concern for the morality of the public, in that Ghislain wanted to prohibit traditional dances that he saw as obscene. He also makes it clear that it is part of the civilizing mission of the colonial agents to suppress such dances. However, Ghislain did not want to forbid all traditional dances in that he left room for traditional dances that weren't a threat to the public morale, excluding them from being regulated by the decree of 1900.

The next year, another vice-governor general, E. Henry, wrote a circular pertaining to indigenous dances that showed that "obscene" dances were still a problem:

> . . . in a number of posts of the colony and in proximity to them dances of a clearly obscene character take place. I remind territorial functionaries of circular no°14, of 16 January 1912, prescribing the prohibiting of dances of this type in all of the stations of the colony. The first of their duties is combating energetically the practices that constitute a permanent obstacle to all the civilizing efforts and that oppose themselves to the attainment of indigenous populations to an intellectual and moral level to which we have undertaken to raise them.[73]

In this circular, a similar pattern is evident. Dances that the colonial administrators deem to be obscene are seen as a threat to the civilization that the Europeans believed they were bringing to their African colonial subjects. They undermined the level of intellectual growth and moral turpitude to which the colonizers once again saw themselves as elevating the colonized. The morality of the public is again menaced by these indigenous dances. E. Henry continued by writing that if obscene dances were taking place, the functionaries must immediately put an end to them, and " . . . write a report to the chief of violations of morals and to defer the guilty to court." Thus, he insists on the persecution of transgressors of the 1900 decree regarding indigenous dances.

Two years later, in January of 1915, yet another circular appeared in the *Receuil Mensuel* regarding indigenous dances. Written by the governor general Félix Fuchs, it takes a more tentative approach to the control of indigenous dances, yet at the same time maintains ideas of European superiority and ethnocentrism that were part and parcel of the colonial endeavor.

> I have the honor to attract the very serious attention of the territorial authorities on the precise interpretation that it is important to give to the circular of the 1st October 1913, relating to native dances and to warn them against a too severe application of the prescriptions that this circular contains. If it is urgently incumbent upon us to prohibit practices of a clearly obscene tendency, it is also our duty to respect the traditional dances of the populations, when these demonstrations aren't at all in opposition to our conceptions of morality. The usual dances

constitute for the blacks a recreation, I will say almost the unique recreation that their primitive mentality and the environmental conditions
that surround them, allow them to appreciate. They are to them also
a beneficial exercise, the only effort of physical limbering up. . . . It
would not be a question of forbidding them excessively; one would
thus risk provoking very legitimate discontent. I invite the authorities
of the districts to communicate the present directives to their territorial
administrators.[74]

In this circular, F. Fuchs argues that native dances have a purpose in that
they are often the only form of recreation and exercise for the indigenous
population. He warns that being too strict in the rules regarding these
dances will lead to legitimate complaints and discontent among the Congolese, and he echoes the sentiment expressed by Ghislain in the circular
of 1912 in which non-obscene dances are excluded from being regulated.
Moreover, the theme of morality emerges once again in this circular, in that
Fuchs does encourage the prohibition of dances that are against "our conceptions of morality," in which "our" can be read as early twentieth century Belgian Catholic colonials.

   The hostility and general disdain towards indigenous dances that was
noticeable in the colonial administration was even more pronounced in the
European led missions. In the Protestant churches, dancing in general was
discouraged. For example, since the early establishment of the missions
of the SMF, dancing was strictly forbidden. At a missionary conference
in 1894, a resolution was passed that "old customs, habits and conceptions, such as dance, all forms of idolater feasts, hair cutting feasts, funeral
feasts, gun-salutes and wailing for the deceased, together with the drinking
of palm-wine at such feasts, and at palavers, should be vigorously opposed
and exterminated."[75] This policy persisted in later years as well.

The position of the Swedish Baptist Society on Kongo customs such
as funeral rites was articulated by K.E. Laman in a speech made at a
missionary conference in 1906. The Swedish missionary said that when
an individual was in the process of conversion, he had to separate himself from all dealings with the unbelievers and from worship or curing
by "idols." He had to stop dancing, drinking palm wine and all other
strong drink and to "cast off several bad customs of the Kongo" which
were specified in the church rules. A man who had more than one wife
had to separate from all but one . . . When a member of the church
returned to drinking of palm wine, marrying other wives or dancing,
the member was expelled.[76]

Moreover, the constitution of SMF in 1907 forbade "dance . . . (and) drumming at palm wine feasts and dance . . ."[77]

How did Kongo people react to these rules prohibiting dance? In some cases, people who were loyal members of the Protestant church upheld the rules and may have internalized the point of view of the missionaries, as exemplified by the following selections taken from *Au Pays des Palmiers*, a compilation of the recollections of Kongo instructors in the Protestant churches of SMF, originally published in 1928. Yoane Nlamba, a teacher at the Protestant mission at Mukimbungu, in describing some of the older traditions of the area, wrote that, "Dance was extremely appreciated by the ancestors. One would dance in all the villages; each village had their own drums. The dance took place during the evening and the night . . . and it was accompanied by immoral orgies."[78] Similarly, Lebeka Kiniongono, a teacher at the Protestant mission in Kingoyi wrote, "The women of long ago really loved dancing. But certain dances were very much shameful."[79] In both of these quotes, the moral interpretation of these embodied practices is very much a negative one.[80] In addition, in several interviews, people stated that there were some Kongo dances that they considered to be immoral.[81] When pressed for specificity, one interviewee, Mama Londa, a prominent leader in the Protestant church, explained:

> There is perhaps a dance of the man and the woman where they approach each other very very closely, or there is perhaps excitement . . . one can qualify that directly, that it is immoral, That, it is not for the church . . . if it is a dance which shows an odd manner, one where the people can be described as bad, one must not continue, and . . . we don't permit that.[82]

However, not all Kongo people agreed with the point of view. Ne Nkamu Luyindula,[83] recounting the story of his grandmother's position on dance and the Protestant church, explained that someone asked her,

> Ma Batikita, were you baptized? She said, 'Baptized? Why become baptized? To whom will I leave the dancing to? That's to say, me, I don't accept to be baptized at the Protestant mission. If I do, I will leave behind my dancing,' and she was baptized really very late (in life), very late.[84]

The point of the story, as he explained to me, was that there were many people who didn't accept the rules and policies of the different missions, and resisted them by continuing to dance. The fact that his grandmother became baptized only when she was too old to dance testifies to the importance of *makinu* as embodied practice to some BaKongo. Yet another interviewee supported this view when he said, "Dances of the BaKongo are a part of the process of education . . . dance is also for correcting behavior . . . I don't think that they [dances] were immoral . . . the adults, the people dance without a lot of negative ideas . . ."[85]

Protestant missions were not the only places where concerns and conflicts over traditional secular dances emerged. Catholic missionaries as well were generally against traditional dancing and music during the 1930s, in particular, although this came to change later. Dances of the BaKongo became a major point of concern for the Catholic missions in the Lower Congo, as revealed by several detailed studies of BaKongo dances written in 1937, 1938, and 1939 by three Belgian Catholic priests. These studies provide the details of the dances that were alluded to in the administrative circulars, and demonstrate that certain dances were a concern for the clergy as well, who sought methods to actively combat them.

In "Les Danses BaKongo," published in *Congo*, an academic review of the Belgian colony, Jesuit Catholic priest J. Van Wing begins the article by providing a stereotypical assessment of the genetic ability of people of African descent in regards to dance: "If there is an art in which blacks excel, it is the dance. It is the only one (art) that they practice universally. It is innate to them . . ."[86] Later in the article, the general form of BaKongo dances is described:

> When the drums are ready they are put in the middle of the space, the dancers come to arrange themselves in front of them: one side of men, the chest bare . . . the other side of women, covered in a small cloth of dance. The main drum gives the first measures . . . the *mvudi-toko* (dance master) places himself at the head of the two lines and strikes up the song . . . the choir picks up the song and the dance begins. It consists of a shaking, to make wriggle in a certain way the *luketo* [hips], that is to say the lower stomach, in the same rhythmical movement, the speed and the intensity of movement is regulated by the rhythm of the drums . . . two male dancers move themselves forward in front of two female dancers . . . and the two couples dance watched by the crowd who mark the tempo of hands and feet. At the signal of the *mvudi-toko*, the two couples withdraw themselves and two others come forward and do the same, and so on for all the couples. Then . . . [the female dancers] move forward near the men, and each of them grabs hold of a partner, and the two embrace chest to chest, and remain like this stuck [together], all while shaking the hips,

until the *mvudi-ntoko* gives the signal of separation. . . . There is the ordinary dance of eastern BaKongo.[87]

Similar descriptions abound for almost all parts of the Lower Congo, dating to even before the colonial period.[88] In addition, there was also another type of dance that had become popular by the 1930's called *maringa*. The *maringa* dance was a partnered dance with hip movement[89] that was performed to the accompaniment of European instruments, and was said to imitate certain dances of Europe and the Caribbean. Van Wing wrote of the maringa:

> Since some time the maringa has spread itself, imitating the whites, and takes place not in the public space but in the interior of huts of palm branches to the sound of an accordion. The couples embrace and wriggle in a so disorderly fashion that nothing remains in regards to the aesthetic. It all turns into shamelessness and obscenity.[90]

After describing these dances that were popular at the time (*makinu ma luketo* and *maringa*), Van Wing laments, "There is the brutal fact . . . our people have lost the sense of honest dancing." He then goes on to elucidate the numerous primary reactions provoked by BaKongo dances. He explains that certain traditional chiefs regulated dances, while others were more lax. He seems less than content with the reactions of the colonial administration which "hardly has intervened. Faced with certain excesses of public obscenities, it applies sanctions."[91] The reactions of the Christian missions, both Catholic and Protestant, and the leader of the kingunza movement, Simon Kimbangu, seem to be similar:

> The missions, the Catholics as much as the Protestants, maintained the severity of their disciplines. At the Protestant missions the dancer of ngoma was excluded from the Holy Communion. At the Catholic missions he was deprived of the sacraments and must do a required penance, if he wanted to return to the Christian practice. Kibangu [sic] came in 1921. With one word, he did away with the ngoma. Throughout all the country they were broken and burned . . . [92]

Finally, the opinion of Van Wing clearly emerges towards the end of the article:

> It is evident that the people need distractions and diversions . . . But it is also evident that no people need stupid diversions. Now the dance

of the *ngoma* is only a direct preparation, public and collective, for the sexual act. . . . It destroys the physical vigor, and the sense of morality.[93]

He goes on to suggest that the BaKongo either return to other traditional dances that are moral, or adopt appropriate dances from other Bantu groups around them. He then suggests that *ngoma* dances can become fertile ground for other "kibanguisms" [sic] or prophetic movements. He continues by saying that modern BaKongo dances can't be called diversions, strictly traditional, or vital, and thus the BaKongo are not being deprived of these things if the dances are prohibited. He closes the article by saying: " . . . If someone wants to participate in the life of Christ, he must refrain from immoral dances. And thus it is no longer a question of indigenous politics . . . it is an essential principle of Christian morality that coincides with morality and nothing else."[94]

Thus, "Les Danses BaKongo" pleads for the prohibition of modern dances of the BaKongo, almost all of which Van Wing sees as immoral. Upon examining the various reasons he gave for this opinion, from saying that the dances destroyed the physical vigor of the people to them being a possible threat to the security of the colony, he seems to be addressing the colonial administrators in particular. However, the prevailing justification for the prohibition of the said dances is once again a moral one. Van Wing sees them as being against a sense of Christian morality, which he then says corresponds to morality writ large.

The next year, at a seminar for Catholic priests held in Louvain, Belgium, the dances of the BaKongo came up again as the subject of a presentation and then discussion. P. Decapmaker, a priest in the Matadi area of Bas-Congo, was the presenter in this case. He starts by explaining that the Congregation for the Propagation of the Faith in Rome didn't recommend the modification of practices that are not positively against the religion or morality, and he explains that the missionaries were not condemning all the dances indistinctly, since to do so would cause many problems.[95] He goes on to say that morals of theology make it possible to distinguish three types of dances:

1. The honest dances, inspired by absolutely honest motives . . . in this category we can place all the BaKongo dances that are not mixed. They are rather games of dexterity . . . 2. The dangerous dances: that in themselves are not improper, but often end up in licentiousness, as a result of the circumstances that ordinarily accompany them: songs, excessive drinking, unhealthy exaltation produced by the frenetic

repetition of the same rhythm, perverse tendencies of dancers, drums, darkness. . . . These dangerous dances are condemned by morality because they constitute occasions close to sin . . . 3. The obscene dances: are those in which the gestures, the movements, the touching are shameless, licentious, and against morality.[96]

He then discusses dangerous and obscene dances in Matadi amongst the BaKongo, quoting the descriptions and opinions of missionaries from the seventeenth century to the present in regards to BaKongo dances, as well as descriptions of colonial agents, many of which correspond to those already given by Van Wing. He discourages acts of violence in the suppression of native dances (forcibly breaking drums, etc.), and suggests the use of missionary influence to pressure native chiefs to prevent obscene dances, as well as the creation of "honest" diversions such as football and other sports, and other past-times such as drama. He then closes his presentation by demanding suggestions for filling this moral gap, and ends with the following conviction: " . . . We are convinced that it is above all by-and at the occasions of dances-that Satan takes his revenge on our savior Jesus Christ and his missionaries."[97] This is a telling comment, because it reveals that in his opinion many dances of the Kongo people were the work of the devil himself, and can thus be seen, by extension, as the enemy of the Christian civilizing mission. After Decapmaker's presentation, an exchange of views took place among the Catholic priests present, which for the most part echoed Decapmaker's sentiments. Father Aupiais agreed that the corruption of dances was introduced by Europeans. Monsignor Van den Bosch also suggested the promotion of games. Father de Pélichy pointed out that although the more ancient dances of the Kongo had been morally acceptable, if they were encouraged, it could be seen as an invitation to return to traditional customs. Father Cooreman proposed the introduction of scouts groups to distract people from the dancing, while Father Van Hoof advocated the collaboration of the church and state with native tribunals and chiefs to regulate dances. M.G. Beken suggested the surveillance of dances rather than their absolute prohibition. Then, a remarkable exchange took place when Father Van Hoof was asked his point of view:

> The conclusions of the missionaries of the vicariate of Kisantu are in complete agreement with that of the missionaries of Matadi presented by P. Decapmaker. In fact, at the present time all the dances of the BaKongo are bad in [their] nature, or indifferent in themselves degenerating into bad in fact. Father Secretary: Then all the dances are bad?

Father Van Hoof: Certainly all those with the "ngoma," and all those with whatever instrument which are mixed [in sex].[98]

After this, the secretary then asked if all the dances as a whole were condemnable, and Father Van Hoof ended by saying, " . . . one will not condemn the good dances, but one has the hope that the bad conceptions give away little by little." Thus, the exchange of ideas at this seminar of Catholic priests reveals that BaKongo dances were seen by these missionaries in the Belgian Congo as a direct threat to not only a general idea of morality, but also the ideology of Christianity in particular.

BaKongo dances worried Catholic priests so much that Monsignor Cuvelier initiated an investigation of all of the Kongo dances throughout the Lower Congo. He sent a list of questions to all of the Catholic mission posts in this area, and compiled the answers.[99] Some of the responses he also used for the creation of the last article of interest, "Les Missions Catholiques en face des danses des Bakongo," published in Rome in 1939. In this article, Cuvelier presents historical and current descriptions of dances, makes distinctions between different types, and includes some discussion of the dances of *banganga*, which he describes as dances in which "all the devils of hell dance alongside them."[100] He sees these dances of the *banganga*, along with funeral dances and dances of mixed sex with hip movements as essentially bad dances that needed to be stopped. He ends the article by saying, "There's a lot left to do. The improvement of moral and civil life will allow the hope of better and lasting results."[101] Once again, concerns for morality appear.

Some of the actual actions undertaken by the Catholics in regards to BaKongo dances emerge in interviews and written texts. For example, in a document explaining the regulations necessary for the running of a Redemptorist mission in the Congo, Catholic catechists are described as having to be "model Christians," and some of their principal functions include ". . . to prevent prudently evil, above all the fetishism and the obscene dances . . ."[102] In an interview, Tata Tuzolana, a traditional drummer near Mayidi in Bas-Congo recounted an incident in which Father Masamba, a Congolese Jesuit priest, broke the skin of his drum to prevent him from playing.[103] Similarly, Tata Mbumba, a Kongo catholic, remembered that as a student he was threatened with expulsion from the mission school when he was caught dancing a secular dance.[104] These are just a few of the examples of Catholic intolerance towards dancing during the colonial period.

Overall, there appears to have been a conflict of cultural beliefs between European colonizers and BaKongo dancers in the Belgian Congo. As most Kongo secular *makinu* were mixed in sex, involved at least brief physical contact (often of pelvises or stomachs), took place at night, were associated with the drinking of alcohol, and incorporated movements which many Europeans interpreted as mimicking sexual copulation, these dances were often judged as immoral and dangerous. The overarching fear seems to have been the connection of these dances with sexual activity that was not sanctioned by the mission churches. The *ngoma*, the drum of choice for these dances, then became demonized by association. Thus, both colonial administrators and missionaries were overtly opposed to the majority of the *makinu* of the BaKongo, seeking to reform and replace them with other diversions, or just to eliminate them altogether.

The Influence of the Prophetic Movement on Attitudes towards Makinu

Regardless of the violence, arrests, and punishments meted out by the colonial authorities, the prophetic movements continued unabated in many different forms. Thus, other solutions began to be sought by the administration, resulting in a change in attitude towards secular *makinu* in relation to the prophetic movements. In 1924, an administrator wrote the following in a letter to the governor concerning the prophetic movements, "The natives who practice the Protestant religion can't drink palm wine, or dance. It is true that dances are also prohibited by the catholic missionaries. Why prohibit to man the distractions that entertain the spirit and the senses?"[105] This type of thinking wasn't put into practice until more than a decade later. In 1936, J. Maillet, the territorial administrator of Luozi, called together many of the chiefs and notables of the area for a meeting in the village of Kimbulu. According to Father Gotink:

> He made it known that the villagers must begin again to dance and must make an *ngoma*. The chiefs had noticed that the pastors and the priests were opposed to dance with the *ngoma* and had prohibited it to their followers. The administrator told them that the priest and he each had their own activities but that he, chief of the region, wanted that this order be executed. The chiefs didn't hide their repugnance and said that many of the dances were frankly immoral. The administrator invited the chiefs to come and celebrate at Luozi the national celebration with a group of young men and women.[106]

In addition, Maillet wanted to make dancing obligatory in the villages between 4 and 5 o'clock, and ordered that when he stopped in a village for the night, he would be welcomed by people dancing. What was the impetus behind this shift in policy from a negative view and ambivalent approach of earlier colonial policies regarding traditional dances, to policies forcing performances upon the Kongo people? Apparently, several months before the meeting there had been incidents of prophetism that required military occupation in Sundi

Mamba and Kivunda in Luozi territory. This and other outbreaks of prophetism had been discussed during the annual meeting of the territorial administrators of Lower Congo in February of 1936. In the minutes of this meeting, one of the suggested means of preventing outbreaks of prophetic movements is dance. "In the regions contaminated by prophetism the native doesn't drink palm wine anymore; dances are abolished . . . Dances constituent a public repudiation of the doctrine of prophetism. A propaganda for the encouragement of dances must be made by the members of the territorial service."[107] It was then noted that J. Maillet in particular had asked for the state to provide funding for organized dances in Luozi. Thus, Maillet thought to use secular, traditional dance to distract people from prophetism.

In regards to this issue, the opinion of missionaries was very clearly a disapproving one. Two Belgian Catholic priests expressed their discontent with Maillet in a letter written from one to the other: "Prophetism is a politico-religious movement. . . . It is a very naïve and dangerous illusion to think that one could fight it or even end it by an attempt of returning to paganism, like the . . . official obligation of the dance of the ngoma."[108] In this situation, the colonial administrator and the Protestant and Catholic missionaries, although they had the same goal of eliminating the movement, were not in agreement in regards to this particular method.

This case of using traditional secular dances to combat prophetism is clearly one in which the collaboration between the missions, both Catholic and Protestant, and the Belgian colonial administration was disrupted. Although all of the parties in question had the same goal of suppressing the prophet movements, they differed considerably in their opinions of using traditional secular dance to distract people from the prophetic movements. The missionaries saw the return to this particular form of traditional practice as a step backwards in their civilizing mission because of the supposedly "immoral" influence *ngoma* dances would have on Christian villagers. However, J. Maillet, the colonial administrator, seemed to prioritize the issue of the security of the state over concerns about avoiding the proliferation of "immoral" dances. Thus, the case of Luozi territory in 1936 can be seen as one in which missionaries and colonial authorities bumped heads, rather than worked together. This approach of the administration was noted in other cases as well, such as Van Wing's article, in which he wrote that the administration had reversed their position so that "the highest authority in the province encourages and makes his subordinates encourage the dances of the *ngoma*; because they say, the people need relaxation, and the *ngoma* is an excellent means of combating Kibanguism. [sic]."[109] This also resurfaced in interviews.

When asked about the regulation of secular dances during the colonial period, Tata Mukiese replied:

> The colonizer never prohibited dancing. On the other hand, they wished that people continue to take a lot of leisure time. Because that gave them the possibility moreover of keeping them [the colonized] in a state where they didn't want to bother them [colonizers] . . . It wasn't with the popular dances that the people were having revelations but rather with the *kingunza* . . . The colonizers weren't against the dances; they encouraged them; he [the colonized] could dance like he wanted without a problem. That doesn't bother him [the colonizer]. The thing that bothers him is the *kingunza*.

CONCLUSION

In closing, the examination of bodily practices in both religious and secular contexts during the colonial period in the Belgian Congo reveals the shifting meanings and uses of embodied practices so aptly captured in the proverb *Nsinsa wa ngoma wusobele, soba makinu maku*. Before the prophetic movement began in 1921, there were secular dances called *makinu* that existed amongst the Kongo people, many of which were persecuted as immoral by both the colonial administration and missionaries. With the arrival of the prophetic movements, or *ngunza*, leaders and adherents used practices such as trembling, jumping, singing, and the use of traditional instruments to worship a Christian God, heal the sick, and demonstrate their willingness to lead their own churches, while condemning secular dances such as *makinu*. Yet, their actions were interpreted by the colonial administration for the most part as a political threat to the state, undermining the success of European owned businesses, and menacing the religious hegemony of European missionaries. Most of these parties then worked together to combat the prophetic movements. However, there were also many instances of disagreement on the methods to do so. When Protestant missions in Manianga territory began to incorporate some of the practices of the movement into their own worship in order to attract people to return to their churches, the colonial agents saw this as encouraging the subversive movements. Conversely, when the administration began to practice a policy of promoting secular *makinu* to distract people from the prophetic movements, the European clergy were against this approach for what they understood as moral reasons. Throughout all of these conflicts, there were Kongo people on many sides; resisting as the actors and leaders of the prophetic movement, collaborating as the priests who broke drums or chiefs who arrested followers of *kingunza*, and accommodating by obeying the established rules and regulations of the administration and missionary-led churches, for example. Thus, a focus on Kongo performance reveals the complexities in shifting alliances and antagonisms, and completing claims in defining these performances, between missionaries, the colonial state, and the indigenous population in the Belgian Congo.

Chapter Five

To Hang a Ladder in the Air: Talking about African Education in Edinburgh in 1910

Ogbu U. Kalu

INTRODUCTION

The conference in Edinburgh in 1910 was the most important European gathering of missionaries in the twentieth century. Among its significance is the birthing of the World Council of Churches; its impact on missionary thought remained strong in the future that appeared scorched by the violence of the First World War and its untoward aftermath. The text generated by its nine committees constitutes a significant perspective into the missionary's mind. The effort here is to read the report of Committee Three on education from the African's lens because education was the instrument for colonizing the Africans' mind. The text could best be read in two ways: as the role of Christianity in the colonization enterprise, colluding with the racist imperial mental structures of colonialism, and acting out the script designed to transform the African's mind and worldview into Western molds. It could also be read from the African perspective, as an example of Africans' encounter with the rain of the gospel and agency in the appropriation, gestation, and responses to the missionary strategies by the end of the first millennium. It has been the contention of cultural anthropologists that culture encounters are complex because actors reconfigure the context in a variety of ways; victims write hidden anti-structural scripts at the level of infra-politics, and essay to maintain their worldview against the cultural invaders. This challenges hegemonic readings that are not attentive to the nuances.

To underscore the racist, evolutionary ideology that under-propped Christian presence in Africa under the colonial canopy, there was no African present at the conference, white missionaries spoke for them. My people are very concerned about the prospects of a discussion where those concerned were absent or whose "mouths" were literally not there. The verdict runs the risk of being so prejudicial that the conversation could be presumed to be a hostile gossip. Happily, the voices that spoke for Africa were so discordant that the conferees soon realized the vastness of the neglected continent, the complexity and incomprehensible depths of the problems, and the challenges that Africa posed for the integrity and future of the missionary enterprise. In spite of the high ideals about education, the Commissioners felt like people trying to hang a ladder in the air and concluded that "so varied are the conditions with which missionary workers are confronted in different parts of Africa that only a few conclusions apply to the whole region which is dealt with in this chapter. But these conclusions are concerned with matters of outstanding importance."[1]

The task assigned to Commission Three at Edinburgh was global though limited to China, India, Japan, and Africa. Latin America was imaged as a preserve of the Roman Catholics. Its focus was on education. The reflection here revisits the deliberations about Africa, the voiceless continent. It examines how the West talked about African education during the Edinburgh Conference of 1910. The reason is that the indigenous folks from the other nations participated. Some, like Reverend V.S Azariah from India, made stirring speeches. His plea for friendship that was more than condescending love struck at the heart of the racism, cultural hubris and disparity of wealth that distorted missionary relationship with host communities. Besides, much has been written about these places that constituted the focus of missionary enterprise. Europeans were intrigued by China, Japan, and India. Indeed, the Commissioners observed that, "more than one of our correspondents in China emphasizes the marvelous power possessed by Chinese civilization of influencing those who came in contact with it."[2] They acknowledged the power of Confucian thought and the need to approach "the Chinese mind along the lines of deeply laid convictions of truth which we need not disturb otherwise than to set them in their places as related to the higher truths of Christianity."[3] As J. R. Mott confessed in *Decisive Hour of Mission*, "The great and highly organized religions present a stronger resistance than the simpler nature-worship of barbarous tribes, and they would therefore require a larger and better-equipped staff of workers."[4] Later, when the Continuing Committee, the International Missionary Council, could not meet in China, it met in India.

On Japan, the Commissioners acknowledged that their education system was advanced, the literacy level was high, and "the percentage of children without schooling is far less than in Great Britain;"[5] that many Japanese Christians are superior in culture, native ability and education to the missionaries. "Thirty years ago, the missionary was first, today he is influential only when he is ready to co-operate with the Japanese and to give them initiative."[6] It would, therefore, require missionaries of the highest ability and training to function in such an environment.

The Indian context should have resembled the African in its complexity and in the depth of loathing that the conquering British had for the indigenous religions. But the Commissioners pointed to the allure of India beyond the opportunity for manifesting the arrogance of power as depicted in E. M. Forster's *A Passage to India*. Two dimensions mattered: The first was "the deep and subtle powers of the Indian mind bent continuously towards the fundamental problems of religion, the unequalled capacity of the Indians for meditation and inwardness, their wonderful devotion to the ascetic discipline-the qualities which have made men call the Indian thinkers 'God-intoxicated.'"[7]

The second was ironically the success of "Christian colleges (that) have in a wonderful way been assimilated by the people themselves and become in a sense indigenous."[8] The Asian countries possessed enough to invite attention and dialogue. Africa was truly at the periphery and its conditions conjured an image that was exotic, at the lowest rung of the evolutionary process of both religion and civilization, and as if from the penumbra of the missionary zone. After listening to twenty-eight correspondents that included some prestigious veteran missionaries, the Commissioners were dumbfounded and concluded that it appeared that the core elements of a meaningful education did not exist, especially in the development of industrial skills, training of girls, higher education and evangelization of the culture (or national life).

It should, therefore, be germane to reconstruct the profile of African Christianity through the nineteenth century to the end of the first millennium in 1900. This may aid our understanding and re-evaluation of what they were talking about in Edinburgh in 1910. Second, a short comment on the significance of the conference in missionary discourse provides another introductory background. Here, we are confronted with the problem of images and lenses. The image of African education could be explained by the lens through which the conferees *read* the African cultural landscape, the responses to the presence of the gospel and their needs. There is little doubt that the core of the conference was the problem of *legibility*, the way people read other people. As the Commissioners observed, "It is only of recent years that we have been learning to look with sympathy on forms of religion which are strange to us. We are an insular race."[9] Quite important in this regard is Mott's account of the conference in 1912 based on the documents generated by the conference. He reviewed the profiles of the mission fields, articulated the strategies, and recommended the directions for the future in bold terms. Reading non-Western contexts with Western lenses has remained an enduring aspect of the ecumenical relationship with non-Western world and a source of the ambiguity, paradoxes and complexities in their relationship especially as the center of gravity of Christianity has shifted to the southern hemisphere.

Third, on the specific matter of education, three dimensions would be privileged: the ideology—broad aims and specific goals—of missionary education; the interior of the educational process and its enemies; and ecumenism as an antidote. Since some of these are complex, they may not receive the adequate treatment that they deserve.

CHRISTIANITY IN AFRICA IN 1900

Perhaps to understand the import of the neglect of Africans at the conference, we could analyze the shape of Christianity in Africa at the turn of that century. The story of Christianity in Africa took a specific, enduring turn in the 1880s as a reflection of currents in European geopolitics. After the British trade fair in the 1850's that exhibited the inventions and glory of industrialization; after the German invasion of France in the 1870's and the Paris commune that fought it to a standstill, competing nationalism consumed Europe and this was played out in the acquisition of colonies. Arguments abound whether colonies were acquired in a fit of absent-mindedness; whims and caprices of officials in the Colonial Office; spurred by men-on–the field; the urging of missionaries; an effort to protect the natives or paltry returns in commerce. The literature has attempted to debunk the economic arguments for colonization. But all agree that the Berlin conferences of 1884/5 to partition Africa among competing nations dramatically changed the geopolitical terrain and the relationship between Europeans and the rest of the world.

The effects were in the mindset and attitudes; at once hegemonic, filled with hubris and salted with a conquering spirit. Jingoism filled the air to drown the protests of the enemies to the imperial idea. It also had much to do with space, expansionism and enlargement of European space, and migration to non-Western world. Without this, one may not appreciate either the popularity of Rudyard Kipling or the children stories of G. A. Henty and the attraction of Romantic poets as Coleridge. Armchair theorists such as Frazier wove the myth of *The Golden Bough*. One of the provisions of the Berlin treaty included the need to demonstrate actual presence instead of mere claims of areas of influence. European interest in Africa and the non-Western world increased and its presence opened the innards of communities to foreign gaze. Chiefs were now treated in a cavalier, imperial manner; middlemen were brushed aside; maxim guns became important in the pacification projects. Even the romantic notion of savages turned into pejorative insistence of African lack of capacity and the need to control and tutor the half-man, half child. Trusteeship replaced the vision of using indigenous agents to evangelize. There was an enlargement of scale in missions: number of missionaries, number of participating nations; areas evangelized; level of participation by females and amount of funds raised for the enterprise.

Competing interests bred virulent rivalry that spurred the pace, direction, strategies and. Right up to Edinburgh Conference in 1910, the European missiologists remained hostile to the new spirit in the nineteenth century missionary enterprise. Race and control dominated missionary encounter in Africa resonating from the mood in the secular imperial age. Often ignored is the African story in the encounter.

Missionary message, presence and attitudes determined some aspects of the patterns of African responses. The power of the Word and the translation into indigenous languages determined the charismatic elements. Some scholars have emphasized control and hegemony in the relationship; that racism generated counter racism; European nationalism bred imitation. Others have argued that in culture contact, all parties are agents who give, take, negotiate and appropriate according to basic needs; that even when the playing ground appears unequal, translation goes on; the vulnerable party always has command of the infra-political zone to articulate feelings and that Africans were not passive proselytes; indigenous religions remained resilient, birthing the new. In spite of the control system that essayed to make the victims legible, Africans wrote their own hidden scripts. Still others argue that it was a contest between rival narratives; each party engaged in universe maintenance. In the moral economy designed by the intimate enemies (missionaries and colonial order), Africans responded variously by loyalty/collaboration, voice and exit.

Yet the story of missionary enterprise is characterized by its varieties and fluidity; and missionary presence was always vulnerable though the control system bred dependency and disunity in many communities. Yet the exigencies of the mission field continuously compelled modifications of missionary hardware. Therefore, its story is a fragmentary one precisely because the size of the continent, number of players and vested interests proved so daunting that they took opposing positions on socio-economic, political and cultural themes. Some have argued that the contributions in education, medicine and translation of the Bible into indigenous languages catalyzed the changes in African Christianity. The point has often been made that when people read the word in their languages, the power catalyzed tremendous changes. Each regional context presented its own challenges as culture became the contested ground. The argument here is that both education and the effects of translation became more apparent after the First World War when the character and provenance of education changed, and when the flares of revivalism grew more intense. In 1900, the Commissioners would have been confronted with a rudimentary education system that was operated haphazardly.

Periodization is important in the reconstruction of Christian presence in Africa. The missionary enterprise was unsuccessful in many parts of Africa till the second half of the century. This may explain why African Christianity was not central in missionary discourse when they met in the Edinburgh Conference of 1910. J. R. Mott enthused about changes in education and socio-economic development in the continent that he described as "the most plastic part of the world."[10] But in 1900, African Christianity was like the tender offshoot of an emergent non-Western plant. The maturity and galloping changes would occur later in the 20th century. The argument here is that those changes benefited from these forces of regeneration that started during the 19th century. In the Horn of Africa, indigenous agency struggled to maintain the independence and orthodoxy in Ethiopia, confronted by Jewish, Protestant and Catholic efforts to "clean" up Ethiopian Christianity. The return of court Christianity by 1856 and the victory at Adwa in 1896 sealed the nationalist rebuttal. In southern and Central Africa, missionary villages as enclaves served as the means of evangelization and encrusted a certain ideology of education that concentrated on primary level education. Its ideological contradictions became apparent with the years. Venn's indigenous ideal in West Africa, that produced the novelty of Adjai Crowther's bishopric in 1864, collapsed by 1891 betraying the rising tide of "scientific" racism that thwarted the evangelical spirituality of yesteryears. White settler Christianity dominated in Eastern Africa, escalating a diatribe against indigenous culture to a breaking point. Metropolitan Christianity in Belgian Congo rivaled Portuguese underdevelopment of Angola and Mozambique through religious instruments. French secularism and British protection of Islamic emirates would arouse missionary outcry.

The Africans responded to missionary structures through *loyalty* and collaboration in certain places, serving as native agents. Critical *voices* were heard in other places while some would *exit* either out of cultural nationalism or through charismatic and prophetic initiatives that appropriated the pneumatic elements of the gospel. Sometimes, these manifested in curious ways as Nxele and Ntsikana did among the Xhosa; or when Shembe saw transforming visions in 'Boss' Conrad's barn. Others joined the early Pentecostal movements that came from the West, especially between 1906 and 1910. When racism snuffed off the Spirit, the Africans built their own "Zions" on the smoky ashes. At other times, anti-structural rebuttal appeared in cultural, religious and political protests and even exit as in the foundation of "African Churches" that seceded from mainline churches from the 1880's. In all cases, the forces that catalyzed the first phase of growth of Christianity in the period, 1914–45, had appeared in nascent forms by 1900. Unfortunately, their salience was unrecognized when whites talked about Africans in Edinburgh in 1910.

Wade Harris typifies the African Road to Edinburgh. In the year that whites met to talk about Africa, a bearded man, decked in a long white *soutan*, walked from his native Grebo Island across Liberian coast, through Ivory Coast to the Gold Coast. He carried a long staff, a Bible and a bowl of holy water. He preached; he created choruses and taught these to large crowds. He baptized, healed and performed other miracles. He was very ecumenical; he founded no churches but convinced many to burn their idols and go to the nearest churches. The Methodist Church in the Gold Coast exploded numerically because they took the old man seriously. The Roman Catholics in Francophone colonies also benefited. Others engineered problems for him using the colonial governments. On his return through Ivory Coast, he found that shipmasters had not stopped the practice of using Kru men to offload their ships on Sundays. He had warned them; and now, decided to punish their recalcitrance. He threw his holy water at some ships and these caught fire. The French authorities put him under house arrest. Undoubtedly, his missionary journey achieved more within months than the labors of many expatriate missionaries through many years.[11]

IMAGES AND LENSES: THE SIGNIFICANCE AND STRUCTURE OF EDINBURGH CONFERENCE

Edinburgh Conference in 1910 has become the referent point in missionary discourse because of a variety of reasons. It was not the first attempt by those engaged in the massive missionary resurgence of the period to meet and compare notes. The conference in New York in 1900 touched on a number of similar issues. It was simply the largest and best organized of such conferences. Twelve hundred delegates from over one hundred and fifty missionary organizations participated. The combined genius of two people whose personalities complemented each other produced an efficient administrative structure: John Mott enjoyed the glare while J. H. Oldham, who had some hearing difficulty, preferred to stay in the background. In constituting the eight commissions, they deployed people from academia, church leadership, administrators of missionary organizations and people with missionary experience. They paid attention to geographical and denominational spread, gender and participation by indigenous people from the key areas of the mission field.

For instance, on Commission III on Education in Relation to the Christianization of National Life, the Right Rev. Dr C. Gore, the Bishop of Birmingham, a High Church Anglican, chaired while Rev. Professor Edward Caldwell Moore of Harvard University served as his Vice-Chairman. Out of twenty members in the Commission, twelve came from Britain, six from the United States, one from Canada, Professor R. A. Falconer, President of the University of Toronto, and one from India, a Scot, Reverend Dr. John Morrison who was formerly the Principal of the Church of Scotland College, Calcutta. In fact, twelve of them were leaders of Western academic institutions including Universities of Oxford, London, Manchester, Harvard, Chicago, Columbia, Toronto, and Rutgers, and four others were connected with colleges. Two were administrative secretaries of key missionary societies. The membership deliberately excluded missionaries.

The strategy for gathering data privileged active participants in the mission field. They sent out questionnaires to about 223 correspondents whose names were submitted by missionary societies from Europe and North America: 69 in China, 62 in India and Ceylon, 33 in Japan and Korea, 28 in Africa, 14 in Mohammedan lands in the Near East, and 17 special interest groups that included 8 from Dutch East Indies, Sumatra and Java. This last category included Dr. T. J. Jones of Hampton Institute, Virginia, who was an expert in Industrial Training, and would later become very important in designing the plan for African education in the mid-1920s. The size and distribution of correspondents may indicate the priority and perception of the size of the mission field. However, in China, the correspondents included only one indigenous person, Cheung wan Man, a medical doctor with the Southern Baptist Convention at Shiuhing. India had five, Japan and Korea, five and Africa, none.

In Africa, the regional distribution of correspondents created a lens that could distort the image: twelve came from South Africa, seven from Nyasaland, five from the whole of West Africa, two from East Africa and one each from Madagscar and Mozambique. Within West Africa, three came from Nigeria and one each from Sierra Leone and Liberia. Within Nigeria, one came from the northern region, the intrepid medical doctor, Dr. Miller, who confronted the exclusion of missionaries from the Moslem emirates, and two came from Calabar: one Presbyterian and one Primitive Methodist, ignoring the vast south-western region where the educated, religious nationalists were very strong.[12] From hindsight, the strategy of using participant observers served better than arm-chair theorists but the distribution flawed the results. It is argued that the distortion in sampling factored the distortion of the image of Africa and African Christianity in the conference.

The Commission received replies from over 200 and distributed these by regions to separate sub-committees. "The English members of the Commission met in London for a week (November 1–6, 1909), discussed these reports, and determined the lines to be taken by the report as a whole."[13] They submitted their work for the input from the American members, who suggested changes. At a meeting between the British members and a representative of the American members in London on April 22nd, 1910, the report, conclusions and recommendations were harmonized to be presented with the assent of the entire commission. One approach to the document is to examine the roles of individuals behind the scene and trace how disagreements were ironed out. Another approach, as adopted here, analyzes the document in the spirit and words of the protagonists, that "the conclusions or recommendations represent the deliberate opinion of the whole Commission." There is every indication of a high level of responsibility, attention to the data and a certain level of frankness in dealing with the role of education in the missionary enterprise. It was the lens that distorted the image!

The fourteen questions administered were exhaustive and shall be considered along with other aspects of the interior of missionary education. Suffice it to say that the Commission was sensitive to the pioneering hardship of missionary work, and endeavored to balance the achievements with new theories of education. As the Report put it:

> It has seemed to us that we should probably best assist those who are actually engaged in the educational work of missions by formulating such a series of conclusions or recommendations . . . not to make final pronouncements or to arrogate authority to ourselves in any sense, but rather to stimulate thought and to provide a basis for discussion.[14]

The significance of Edinburgh 1910 in missionary discourse is the astonishing level of self-criticism that made the movement resilient. The Conference espoused high ideals. Having acknowledged the achievements by missionaries, it moved quickly to observe that "Education, as pursued under missionary auspices, has exhibited certain *weaknesses in its methods*, and is exposed to certain *perils*, which make it necessary to review its *principles and its processes*."[15] This startling acknowledgment opens up the discussion on the gap between the ideal that the Commission perceived and the practice that the missionaries pursued. The very title of the Unit was theologically loaded as it proposed to examine how education could be used as an instrument to engage in mission to culture, baptizing the nations or Christianizing the national life. In re-imagining the conference, it is argued that the Commissioners started a conversation on African education that combined with geopolitical realities to nudge missionary practices in new directions.

THE IDEOLOGY OF EDUCATION IN EDINBURGH

The Commission espoused an ideal of education that resonated with Roman Catholic ideals and practices. In spite of the collapse of their early mission to China, their indigenizing principles remained classic. In many parts of Africa, Roman Catholic education enterprise outpaced the Protestant. In southern Nigeria, Bishop Shanahan boasted that if he captured the hearts of the children, the heart of the country would be safe in Roman Catholic hands. He prosecuted the education apostolate with such vigor that inspectors from Lyon in 1929 wondered whether the Holy Ghost Fathers had not deserted evangelism. The absence of their input in the conversation in Edinburgh was regretted. But apparently, Protestants at Edinburgh arrived at the same conclusions. As Mott put it, a German proverb says that, "What you would put into the life of a nation, put into its schools."[16] Education was the instrument that mediated the missionary message.

Imagining the Educational Process

First, the Commission delineated the contexts or types of education that are required: primary, higher education, teacher training, ministerial formation, industrial, education of girls, and education for Muslim evangelism because Islam is reaching out and Christians must penetrate its hearts. Second, it derived the rationale for missionary education by exploring the lessons from the early church. The early church recognized the *pilgrim/universal* and *indigenous/local* principles in Christianity. It sought to be universal and catholic without becoming exotic or foreign. In the early church,

> Christianity became indigenous in each race and place from the first, because it was entrusted to native teachers and rulers almost at once. There was somewhat later accommodation to such national religious customs as were thought to admit of a Christian interpretation and use. The result was the diffusion of a Catholic religion exhibiting local variations of customs and presentation.[17]

Education was crucial to Christianity for several reasons: a commonly shared elementary education saved the catholicity of the Christianity from becoming exotic or representing a foreign influence. Christianity was a religion of ideas and institutions that could only be maintained through teaching. It inherited from Judaism a profound respect for teachers and special instructions in catechism that were designed as a process of training and initiation into the religion. When the center of gravity shifted from Palestinian roots into the Graeco-Roman world, it came into an empire well furnished with schools that it utilized. People were versed in both secular and Christian literature. Some leaders were wary about the idolatrous dimensions to secular education but recognized the utility for Christian evangelism. Those who engaged in "spoiling the Egyptians" in their apologetics, demonstrated the usefulness of secular education. The implication is that the goal of education is evangelization and the method or process utilized cultural pathways.

The Commission recognized the changed environment. In some places, there is no commonly shared public education that could serve as a framework; so, each mission designs its process. The Commissioners may have been blind to indigenous models of education and socialization that could serve as acculturating pathways; they ignored the voices of educated Africans crying for indigenization of the gospel; but conceded that the ideal method of propagating Christianity in the contemporary period is that,

> The Gospel should be received by each race through the ministry of evangelists from nations already Christian but that the church should pass as rapidly as possible under the control of native pastors and teachers, so that while all churches hold the same faith, use the same Scriptures, celebrate the same sacraments, and inhere in the same universal religion, each local church should from the first have the opportunity of developing a local character and colour. [18]

Converts, they argued should, with their children, continue to share the education and social life of their own races and nations; and bring the distinctive genius and its products within the circle of the Holy Spirit, to the glory and honor of all nations. They not only promoted the Venn policy shared with Rufus Anderson but moved towards a compromise with the German *volkskirche* principle that Gustav Warneck and other German missiologists urged. It was an espousal of a brand of ecumenism in which all nations and cultures stood equidistant to the kingdom of God. But one suspects that they proffered this idea for Japan and China and hardly for Africa.

The Ecology of Learning

Third, they explored the counteracting forces in the ecology of learning, for instance, the tendency of Western people to reproduce "strongly defined and intensely western forms of Christianity." This creates a gulf between the mental equipment of missionaries and that of the indigenous people. Missionaries pay little attention to presenting the gospel in the form best suited to the context and spirit of the people. This tendency to plant "the religion of conquerors or foreign devils and unwelcome intruders" betrays a lack of the wisdom of the apostles, especially when conquest, perception of the other, insularity, lack of sympathy for and study of other religions may have caused alienation.[19] This has created the peril that the replacement of the indigenous vernacular and culture may create an exotic religion and promote false ethics that replace communal ethics with western individualism.

They pointed to the teaching-learning environment that privileges imparting ideas and exercising the memory and intelligence of the student. The Commissioners observed that the missionaries "did not estimate how little the imparting of information, with the appeal to only the too facile memory to receive and repeat it, would really do in the way of reforming the fundamental habits of thought or instinct in their pupils."[20] It is exciting to find that the Commissioners said in 1910 what made Paulo Freire famous in 1970. Here is the banking model described by Paulo Freire. The banking model is built on a jaundiced image of the host community, perceiving it as a "pathology of the healthy society" represented by the home of the missionary. The teacher "mythicizes" the indigenous social structure and creates a platform for causing division, manipulation, cultural invasion, alienation, conquest and all manners of induced actions. The teacher's high profile is that he knows all things, thinks, teaches, talks, disciplines, enforces, chooses the program, confuses authority of knowledge with professional authority and deposits knowledge that the students bank by memorizing mechanically. The teacher withdraws from the bank when he chooses. The teacher is the subject and the learners are mere objects. The goal of the teacher is to change the consciousness of the students to ensure that the students internalize the teacher and his world.[21] Using India as an example, the Commissioners argued that the product contents of missionary education are imitative, dependent, weak native Christianity, lacking initiative.[22] Paulo Freire dubs this model as "cultural invasion" in which "the actors draw thematic content of their action from their own values and ideology; their starting point is their own world, from which they enter the world of those they invade.[23] The opposite is "cultural synthesis" in which "the actors who come from another world to the world of the people, do so not as invaders. They do not come to teach or to transmit or to give anything, but to learn, with the people, about the people's world." The actors integrate with the people and become co-authors of the action that both perform upon the world. For him, this model of transformation, dialogue and liberation does not deny the encounter of two different worldviews, but argues that each can affirm the other in a process of "mutual humanization;" that knowledge of the indigenous culture frees it from alienation and enables it to be transformed in a creative manner. [24]

The Commissioners did not go this far but called for a reversal of the contemporary trend. Education should be a social process that trains students for social functions. It should train the whole being-body, soul and spirit- through music, poetry and dance. It should engage and develop the psychological roots of the child such as the instincts of one's nature or the subconscious nature. Education should train the individual into conscious and intelligent participation in the great social movements and challenges of one's environment. As the South African educationist, Bongani Mazibuko said, "It is stressing the affective and experiential, rather than the narrowing rational and academic, that students are affirmed and empowered."[25] As a practical measure, the Commission urged missions to train native Christian leaders as teachers and church officers as people who will bear the responsibility of building the church, produce the indigenous literature and use the vernacular in instruction in the elementary schools because "a man's mother tongue is that which reaches his heart, and always offers the best approach to the deepest subjects."[26] Simply put, foreign language makes Christianity a foreign production.

Fearing that the divisions and rivalry among western Christianities may confuse the non-western world, they suggested that the best approach is to teach the original and fundamental elements of Christianity, using the vernacular. The challenges in Japan brought this matter home because the Japanese feelings for the ancestors, patriotism and their assertion for leadership in the church not only compelled the need for highly educated missionaries but people who were open for dialogue in the vernacular. Even in India where the religious base was heavily pantheistic, there was still the possibility of a dialogue that sifts the best values such as the peaceful or passive ethics of the Hindu as a pathway to the character of Jesus, a critique of western aggressive culture and ethics and the representation of "a full-orbed type of Christian life, embracing the eastern and western emphases."[27]

The undergirding ideology of education was based on the reading of the peoples, the times and conditions in the various mission fields. The geopolitical environment was suffused with intense nationalism all over Asia: Japan emerged as a major power player in 1905; China showed an astonishing awakening of national consciousness, enormous changes in the social infrastructure, and rapid proliferation of education; Indian Christians brought the political nationalism into the church. R. Suntharalingham has traced the politics of national awakening in South India in the prelude to the conference.[28] For instance, in 1888 the Madras Native Christian Association was founded and two years later, their newspaper, *Christian Patriot* appeared. Edwin James Palmer, the Bishop of Bombay, confirmed in 1909, a report that "the modern young man wants a national church, first and foremost, to attain independence from all foreign sway and its concomitants . . . There is a sort of idea floating around that India could start with a clean state and evolve something wholly new and Indian, based as some of its advocates openly say, on the 'religious treasure' of non-Christian India."[29] The Christians were pressurized by the temper of Hindu nationalism that stereotyped Christians as unpatriotic, denationalized people who pandered to foreign churches that bore such names as the *Church of England* or *Lutheran Church*. In Africa, Ethiopianism continued to garner strength in western and southern Africa. In 1891, the firebrand, Wilmot Blyden, gave a lecture in Lagos entitled, *The Return of the Exiles* in which he intoned that "*Africans must evangelize Africa*" or, as Mojola Agbebi would say, the sphinx must solve its own riddle! The Niger Delta pastorate had split from the Church Missionary Society in that year. A young Ghanaian Methodist lawyer, J. Casely-Hayford wrote his play, *Ethiopia Unbound* in the year that white people met to talk about Africans in Edinburgh. There was ferment in the young mission fields but the din did not interrupt the discussions.[30]

As J. R. Mott read the signs: beyond the strategic position of Japan, there was an openness to receive the gospel in Africa and a significant conversion rate occurred in Korea and Manchuria. China remained attractive to missionaries because of its population density. The challenge from Islam in both Moslem countries and Equatorial Africa contested the enterprise. Moreover, Christianity needed to deal with certain neglected regions as Sudan and the Pacific Islands, and buffer the marginalized caste groups in India.[31] In this task, education was a core instrument and the distribution of Christian literature was imperative. This included devotional materials, apologetics, literature for moral formation and general, scientific materials that would provide information and aid reading abilities.

But there appears to be three different perceptions of the goal of education among the conferees in Edinburgh 1910. The first was the *assimilationist* that argued that the African indigenous civilization was low; education could be deployed to uplift the culture to the European level. By the mid-1880s this benign view suffered a defeat. Mott may represent a second posture held by the "*cultural invaders*" when he enthused that, "As already seen, the influence of western learning has been in the direction of undermining the faith of the student class in the non-Christian religions and of breaking up the social and ethical restraints of the old civilizations."[32] As Jacob Ade Ajayi would argue in 1965, the goal of missionary education was "the making of an elite" class of detribalized, educated people who will interpret Christianity to their people. [33]The Commissioners may not have been averse to the civilizing project of the missionary enterprise but nuanced their *indigenizing* position differently. The task was to explore how to Christianize the national life through education or how to respond to the challenging social and economic structures that would determine the fate of Christianity. The handwriting on the wall was boldly nationalistic and suggested the need for a native agency trained to shoulder the burdens of self-governing, self-funding, self-propagating churches. Education should be "an instrument for raising native Christian Churches, which shall be in the fullest sense national, and capable of a growing independence of foreign influence and support."[34] To achieve this, they recommended changes in the content and method of education, with emphasis on agricultural and industrial training. This should culturally and economically equip people who will lead the churches and the nations, and respond to challenges of their ecosystems.

The problem of industrial education emanated from three sources: there was a concern about the effect of "book-learning" that did not enhance the full productive capacity of the person; the second was a racial commentary on the pretensions of educated Africans who served as clerks and imitated white people. The third was related to western enthusiasm with industrialized economy. In 1900, a conference in New York had insisted that the industrial spirit, when properly directed, would champion liberty, serve as handmaid of education, and an auxiliary to the gospel and aid missions. [35] The problem was how to ensure that the indigenous people participated in its benefits and avoided its vicious effects. The Commissioners suggested a gender sensitive model of education to mobilize the women and girls. However, they merely envisaged "raising up a pure girlhood and womanhood such as is only possible in truly Christian home." This wove the traditional community's goals to new white needs for domestic servants, nurses and teachers. The curriculum consisted of domestic science, hygiene, cooking, laundry, sewing, cleaning, spinning, lace-making, basket weaving, and dispensary assistance.[36] The only missing subject was hewing wood.

The education ideology in response to Islam was more creative than the confrontational habits of evangelical Sudan parties. They urged for special education facilities in Moslem countries manned by evangelists trained on how to witness without injury to the sensibilities of the Muslims. The strategy would privilege edification, leavening and living the faith without preaching it.[37] Behind the contrasting ideologies of the "cultural invaders" and the "indigenizers" was a certain reading of the contentious matters of race, indigenous cultures, mission and the future of Christianity. Racism so vitiated the force of the missionary enterprise that J.H. Oldham wrote a book, *Christianity and the Race Problem* in 1926 and many imaged him as a friend of Africa.[38]

The Commissioners, however, privileged a technical or professional view of education as an instrument and avoided the larger issues. In their view, contemporary missionary education suffered from a wrong method, wrong subject matter, wrong articulation of goals, and a challenging environment. That environment consisted of imploding materialism introduced from the West, destruction of old values that had not been adequately replaced by a new moral system; vagaries of official policies and practices, symbolized by Education Codes that could harm education; insurgent nationalism; and inadequately trained teachers.

Returning to the old premise that teachers constituted the point men in the enterprise, they asserted that "Nowhere has experience more conclusively shown that the essential thing in education is the personality of the teacher. The clearness of his moral convictions, his unselfishness in the sphere of his duty, his personal example, are the character-forming influences which make education a living thing."[39] They paid close attention to the training, requiring that it should become more professional than based on spiritual fitness. Thus, the training of the missionary became a major consideration in reforming and revitalizing missionary education. This broad ideology determined the contours of the questions sent to respondents in Africa.

THE INTERIOR OF MISSIONARY EDUCATION IN AFRICA IN 1910

The Questions of Education

Using the social science model of the shape and flow of Christian education, the fourteen categories of questions could be schematized under four headings: the purpose (broad aims and specific goals) of education; the teaching-learning process focused on the facilitator/teacher, the learner/student, and the environment. On the teacher, they queried about the technical training and moral quality. On the learner, they identified the various contexts of education and rehearsed the same questions for various contexts of the process (elementary, higher, teacher training, education of girls, industrial and Muslim contexts of education). They sought to assess the product-content or result of the process: whether it had caused Christian conviction, permeated indigenous thought, feelings and outlook and whether it had percolated a certain influence directly, indirectly or by general diffusion on the learner's community; whether "the course of education is being gradually brought into more vital relation to the real needs of the different categories of native pupils"? [40] Specifically on the learner, the Commissioners wanted to know whether the process has catalyzed a higher ideal in life, equipped the learner for leadership roles and enhanced physical development. Most of the questions focused on the environment of learning: on curricula, especially use of indigenous and other Christian literature; on the mode of communication, either English or vernacular; and the social ecology of learning characterized by competing power nodes, Government policies and actions, the white settler communities and their racism, indigenous nationalism, and dysfunctional missionary rivalry.

The Answers from the Fields

The discussion of the responses of protagonists in the mission fields could start with J. R. Mott's typical hyperbole that galled the Germans. He intoned:

> It is not necessary to call attention to the economic, social and educational development of the natives races of South Africa, which development, along with the political evolution, has advanced steadily through the past two or three generations. Suffice it to say that in no period has the progress been more marked, judged by every test, than during the last two decades. This progress is observable in almost every part of what is known as the Sub-Continent, the parts of Africa lying south of the Zambesi.[41]

In reality, 1910 was a dark year for the black population of South Africa as the Afrikaans declared a political status that denied the indigenous people of their political and socio-economic status. They were compelled to appeal for Britain's intervention in 1912, the year that Mott's book came out. So, what was the advancement catalyzed by missionary education?

The correspondents showed that missionary education in 1910 was prominently at the elementary level, with little effort at the higher or secondary school level and a few Teachers' Colleges. Industrial education was either non-existent or rudimentary and girls' education remained at the lowest priority. The correspondents usually skipped the opportunity to dialogue on broad ideology of missionary education. They were more interested on the specific goals of education. These focused on enabling the pupils to read the Bible and devotional literature; moral re-orientation that would subvert the traditional worldview and culture, imaged as the bondage of superstition, and victory for the civilizing mission. This would, in turn, foster a closer dependency on the gospel bearers, broaden the vistas of Western civilization and produce interpreters or native agents and teachers. The intellectual and moral equipping of the native agents was the missionaries' contribution to the leadership of native churches. It was also hoped that technical education would attach a breed of intelligent natives to the periphery of the new capitalist society, engage them in "useful living" and improve their earning power. The brass ceiling of missionary education was moral formation, skill acquisition, and production of native teachers.

The reasons were not hard to find. As Reverend D. D. Stormont, Principal of Blythswood Institution, Butterworth, insisted: education in the Cape Colony certainly has taught the people to improve their hygiene, physical surroundings, acquire higher ideals in life and capacity to dissent from tribal ties and family control. But the unintended consequence has intensified individualistic ethos, assertion of independence often amounting to license, and opposition to Europeans. Admittedly, this last fact is linked to wider socio-economic factors such as erosion of "tribal life" or social control system, effects of alienation of land, and urban morality. Stormont basically admitted that missionary education did not provide an adequate coping mechanism in the face of dire socio-economic changes in the lives of the indigenous people. The product-content left much to be desired because the key component in the teachin–learning process was faulty. The native teacher, he wrote, is unchastely, conceited, and lover of ease and money, unless he apprentices for a very long time under the European who could provide him with money and morals.[42] Stormont did not comment on the European teacher as the Commissioners would have liked; but he was impressed by the effect of missionary education that has liberated the impulse of individualism in the "native" by crushing by tribal norms. There is little of industrial training in the Cape Colony but it must be seen in perspective. Industrial education is no prophylactic against moral weakness because those who show less capacity for academics turn to industrial education; these function as second rate people with lower moral quality of life.

Interestingly, the other leaders of institutions in the southern African region echoed Stormont. Henderson of Lovedale repeated the goals of moral regeneration and character formation, confessed the little engagement in higher education, unfocussed goal of generating Christian influence in the communities, and low priority of industrial education because the youth find it unattractive. Even less attention was paid to girls' education because they would rather stay at home. Blame polygamy, early marriage and love of ease.

Reverend J. D. Taylor of Adams Mission Station, Natal, devoted immense effort in answering the questionnaire. He perceived the moral dimension of missionary education as access to the Bible, arousal of interest in higher education, and spread of Christian influence. But he rated the enterprise as a failure because of poorly trained native teachers, who despoil primary schools and lack earnestness in giving religious education. Blames go to parents who use child labor and encourage indolence and absenteeism as well as the Government that under-funds education. He explained missionary reluctance to engage in higher education precisely because the products so far are "leavening the native population with new ideas and ambitions-a process which is at the present stage unsatisfactory in many of its results, and is causing a ferment of half-comprehended ideas."[43]

The teaching-learning environment, observed Taylor, is vitiated by an over-emphasis on academics, undue attention to examination results by government inspectors, lack of textbooks suitable for local conditions, and multiplication of low quality schools by competing societies. Industrial education has low priority because the Government plays to the gallery of white labor organizations who resent the skill acquisition by blacks. The dark picture in South Africa is completed by Rev L. Fuller of Johannesburg who saw less of the academic emphasis and more of a religious emphasis in primary education, and would not encourage higher education for natives because it will afflict them "with a horror of hard work, either mental or physical," and make them "rather immoral and very far from religious."[44]

In Nyasaland, the chorus continued as if orchestrated or reflected the editorial agenda behind the records. Dr. Robert Laws of Livingstonia appeared to be the most optimistic about missionary education that has widened the horizon of those who have learnt to read, enculturated higher ideals and standard of life, and created a fruitful evangelistic agency. Miss M. W. Bulley of the Universities Missions to Central Africa, Likoma, explained the catch phrase, 'higher ideals.' It means "bringing the natives in touch with European ideas," building a disciplined character, and breaking ties with traditional norms. Or, as Dr. Hetherwick of Blantyre Mission put it, it means "gradual purifying of the atmosphere of native thought and morality, and imparting a higher ideal of life to the native and his race."[45] All agreed that higher education was practically non-existent and industrial education was confined to producing artisans who work for the mission stations. According to Reverend H. H. Weatherhead of King's School, Buddu, Uganda, the training of indigenous teachers remains unorganized and on small scale because the salaries are low and young people would prefer other occupations. The Native Church apparently paid low wages to the clergy in Uganda as in the Sierra Leone. In 1950, the World Council of Christian Education, in New York, conducted a very elaborate global survey of the practice of Christian Education, and produced a source book for the convention in Toronto. Virtually all respondents linked evangelism to Christian education and stressed moral formation and destruction of indigenous religions as their aims.

INTERNAL DIAGNOSIS: PROBLEMS AND PROSPECTS

The missionaries pointed to some of the problems and possible solutions. On the social environment, they pointed to the political resurgence, Ethiopianism, that spread throughout the Zambezi, Cape Province, Natal and Nyasaland; the effect of increased demand for labor in the mines and its attendant moral consequences; growth of Islam; the spread of materialism and urbanization; and the competition by governments, some of whom were hostile as the French in Madagascar, or suspicious of missionaries as the Portuguese in Mozambique. Besides, Africa suffered from conflicting policies by the British, French, Portuguese and Belgians.

The missionaries did not always agree on how to improve the results of missionary education. J. K. McGregor, United Free Church, Calabar, blamed the lazy 'natives,' their distaste for manual labor, and preference for high salaries as interpreters and civil servants. Others wanted a review of the teaching-learning environment. Dr. Weatherhead raised the question "whether (missionaries) may not have laid too much stress on Bible teaching in the past to the exclusion of the practical side of education."[46] Reverend W. T. Balmer of the Wesleyan Methodist Missionary Society, Freetown, Sierra Leone concurred, adding that Sierra Leone was now educating the fourth generation of Africans; that the Native Pastorate handled much of the Christian work while missionaries served as supervisors. However,

> the weakness of the system of education which followed the British models too closely is now apparent . . . Education has been too much confined to instruction in the art of reading and writing, with the tacit assumption that manual labor is of less dignity and worth than the exercise of those accomplishment . . . Mere book knowledge is compatible with the retention of the corrupting notions of the natural world, and is even capable of aggravation of the corrupt ideas which prevail. Hence in the educational policy of Missionary Societies, emphasis should now be laid upon the giving of instruction in manual arts and upon the systematic study of nature.[47]

Beyond content, the use of vernacular as a means of instruction and the use of indigenous literature became contentious. The Commissioners had been scandalized by the fact that,

> So little has as yet been done in this direction that there is not even a school history of South Africa dealing with the subject in any way suitable for natives or from the native point of view. The musical gift of many of the African native tribes is remarkable. As at Hampton and Tuskegee in the United States, vocal music may be made a great factor in this connection. Much good is done by the introduction of hymns in the vernacular as an alternative to such of the native songs as are low and indecent.[48]

The debate on the use of English squared off Dr. Stormont against M. Junod of Lourenco Marquez who had delivered a very thoughtful paper entitled, *Native education and native literature* at Bloemfontein Missionary Conference in 1909. Stormont had delivered his counter view on *Literature for native Christians* at a conference in Johannesburg in 1906.Three issues were raised: use of English as a branch of study; use of English as a means of instruction; and at what level of education. The protagonists said little about the translation of the Bible or catechisms into indigenous languages. Yet, this was the primary literature for learning to read; except in Francophone colonies where people were designated as illiterates if they could not read in French, and even if they could read in Bambara or any other indigenous language. The debate turned into the contest between a monocultural and a multicultural approach to education.

Arguing for the former, Stormont insisted on the use of English as a branch of study and means of instruction at all levels, because it will help the blacks in their relationship with whites; it is necessary for commerce and civilized life; good government and public morality; and it will be economical as students could acquire cheap literature from Europe. He represented those who fought against vernacularization because "there is no native literature in Africa. Tradition is largely based on myths and vague ideas. Thus, there is practically no stock on which to graft Christian ideas."[49] The Nigerian representatives disputed this because enormous translation work had been a part of the missionary task in West Africa. As W. H. Mobley has shown, the indigenous educated elite in the Gold Coast had graduated by 1900 from producing literature of tutelage to critical literature. P.E.H. Hair has studied the enormous translation work in West Africa and commended the high quality of the Efik Bible translated by the Presbyterians, thirty odd years before Edinburgh conference. Translation work was a priority for Adjai Crowther who co-operated with Schon to publish a number of such translations; he also encouraged missionaries on the Niger to do so. J. D.Y. Peel has argued that the Yoruba Bible created the identity of the Yoruba. The ingenious capacity of T. J. Dennis who gathered a group of indigenes to produce the Ibo Bible (1907–1911) has been celebrated as the achievement of the Church Missionary Society in Nigeria. John S. Mbiti, therefore, explored the translations and impact of the Bible on Africa in 1987. Three years later, Lamin Sanneh reinterpreted the African church historiography on the touchstone of translation.[50] Educationists recognize that first grounding in the vernacular is essential for transmitting and preserving indigenous knowledge and for developing mental and communication skills. The irony was that many communities wanted to learn English. When the CMS insisted on using vernacular as a means of instruction, village chiefs chose to patronize the Roman Catholics who easily obliged to teach in English. Pundits wager that this fact explains the pre-eminence of the Roman Catholics in education and numbers of votaries in civil service and professions. But all these appear as historical hindsight.

Among the protagonists of this era, William Beck of the American Lutheran Church, Monrovia, Liberia, concurred with Stormont that he "finds native tongues barren of words to express Christian thought."[51] Dr. Laws added his weighty voice to urge that the vernacular suffered from an imprecise interior and encouraged tribalism. Those who deploy the political theory of mobilization in nation building, always look for a *lingua franca* that would wipe away competing power nodes and the differences of "tribes and tongues." Missionary ideology in the settler communities was a mobilizing concept. Vernacularization was not one of its ideals. The total rejection of the resources of indigenous knowledge destroyed the potential of a liberating education.

H. A. Junod (Mission Romande, Switzerland/Rikatla, and Mozambique) countered that the mother tongue must be retained because it is the medium of thought and emotion; for producing native teachers who will teach their compatriots because English is as foreign to them as Latin was to Europeans; their vernacular is composite and contains all that is necessary for communication. J. E. Hamshere (CMS, Freetown) opined that Swahili was sufficient for those in British East Africa. At this point, P. S. Kirkwood of Livingstonia beat his chest in guilt and picked up enough courage to disagree with the venerable Dr. Laws:

> Let us remember how much our own national growth in Christianity
> was hastened by translation of the Scriptures into our mother tongue.

> We must get at the hearts as well as the heads of the natives. For that
> we need the vernacular . . . our students when they pass to the village
> schools as teachers are apt to attach an altogether exaggerated impor-
> tance to English, both as a medium of instruction and as a branch of
> study.[52]

Vernacular, some argued, could be the needed antidote to the nagging problem of "narrow ignorance and overweening self-conceit" among educated
Africans. Europeans found their insolence to be insufferable and carica-
tured them as "Black Englishmen." In Joyce Cary's novel, *Mister Johnson*,
the Europeans deserted the African who dared to dress in white and inch
his way into the charmed circle.

However, many missionaries conceded that translating the Bible
into indigenous languages was one kettle of fish, using the vernacular as a
medium of instruction was another. The myriads of languages and dialects
may necessitate the use of English at the higher levels of education while
vernacular could be used to teach at the lowest grades. Reverend W. T.
Balmer of Sierra Leone had the brilliant idea that the best means of cleans-
ing the impurities of the vernacular was "having it used properly and vigorously in schools and colleges, where its use can be brought under direct
Christian oversight."[53] Few were prepared to engage in such sanitary work.
Some looked into the seeds of time and predicted that the future belonged
to western civilization; the blacks cannot do without European supervision;
and the appropriate language of the future should be English. The debate
among the correspondents said more about the minds of missionaries and
the temper of the era than the subject matter.

CONCLUSION: ECUMENISM AS AN ANTIDOTE

The Commissioners were overwhelmed by the discordant voices emanating
from the mission fields, impressed by the breadth of the continent and complexities of its problems, and filled with "anxieties as to the present results
of some of the educational work upon which men and women are unself-
ishly spending themselves in many regions of the African mission field."[54]
Scholars, therefore, speak about African Christianities that grew out of
these realities as well as the patterns of appropriation of the gospel from
many cultural contexts. Edinburgh Conference proffered few solutions: it
sought to bring modern educational theories into missionary practice. In
considering the immense challenges, it suggested an ecumenical endeavor
as antidote, urging missionaries to co-operate in building inspectorate divisions in the system, operating joint training of teachers so as to harmonize

the instructional methods, intensifying the care of alumni, improving the education of the girl child, and especially emphasizing handwork, manual labor, sports, industrial skill acquisition and agricultural education. The North American ideals of Hampton and Tuskegee Institute would continue to beckon throughout the colonial period. But the Commissioners were aware of the need to review the education ideology at the home base of mission and the training of those who will go out as teachers. Many missionary societies did not differentiate between gospel bearers and teachers, or provided them with the requisite skills. A study of ministerial formation institutions that prepared missionaries in various parts of Europe and America will be quite instructive. Government inspectors complained about the rapid opening of schools in the heat of rivalry without adequately trained teachers. Missionary co-operation would, by delimiting areas of operation, diminish competition; by bonding save resources and avoid duplication; and by dialogue engage the colonial governments' policies, and harmonize cultural policy in response to the tensile strength of indigenous religions and cultures. Examples abound that from 1911, the conference inspired many co-operative efforts.[55]

But Christian missionary enterprise remained unsuccessful till after the First World War because its cultural hardware and dark image of the African hosts restrained its capacity to exploit the enculturating pathways. Ironically, education and translation would fuel both charismatic spirituality and nationalism and change the character of Christianity in the aftermath of the conference. The gospel would expand under the indigenous bearers just as it did in the early church. All these lay in the future. The challenge of re-imagining the Edinburgh Conference is to reconstruct it with a keen eye to context. It was 1910 and hindsight does no justice to the protagonists. Christianity had not encountered many African communities in the hinterland of the coastal regions. The European mind gloried in the Enlightenment worldview and Social Darwinism. The missionary was a child of his age and struggled to balance an evangelical spirituality with the racism of the age and the challenge of a civilizing mission. The exigencies of the mission field, the compelling desire to work with the colonial governments, and the resilience of indigenous structures complicated the scene. Indeed, some of their strategies were sourced from the model employed in dealing with delinquent children in 19th century Europe. A missionary would often adapt the familiar principles of education. William H. Taylor's study of the Scottish Presbyterian Mission to eastern Nigeria, argued that, "the first Calabar mission schools were to borrow many of their practices from the Ragged Schools that had been started in Edinburgh by philanthropist and theologian Thomas Guthrie and from the Scottish

Sunday School movement."[56]Africans were read as "docile bodies," to borrow from Michel Foucault. A body is docile that may be subjected, used, transformed and improved; or plastic according to Mott. Chosen young, three factors, time, space and the constitution of a new individuality, contributed directly to the culmination of this African docile body.[57]

This makes the conference significant in revealing the strength of the missionary enterprise as its capacity for self-criticism. The Commissioners and the men-on–the–spot differed over the ideals, content and method of education. The Commissioners set out to revamp the entire educational apparatus of evangelism by indigenizing it. That was a tall order. Yet on closer look, the Commissioners did not go far enough in distinguishing *training* from *education*. They diagnosed that the primary pedagogy for learning did little to impress upon the learner the importance of knowing self. It was directed more toward a formation that promotes social maintenance instead of promoting a liberating agenda that reveals the divinity of the human spirit. It fitted individuals into the colonial caste system maintained by the pedagogical approach termed as "action-reaction." Most often this is manifest in "presentation of information-information regurgitation" or banking model. It did not encourage reflection and analysis as much as it promoted singularity of thought, uniformity of ideas, and monolithic universality of response. It privileged training over against education. Training is skill based, whereas education is identity based. Training focuses on learning mechanics; education focuses on learning one's place in the world through an emphasis on one's history or high culture. Education nurtures the human being and expands the person's understanding of the self through the identification of a cultural-social location.

The historian must, however, put their ideals in the context of the period. What is the significance of reconstructing this era? The result provides an interesting cameo of an era, an insight into the adventurous western imagination at the turn of the century, and the backdrop to what happened later. Indeed, the revolution in education in the aftermath of the Conference becomes more significant. As education exploded, it became clear that it was the African who initiated the modern face of Christianity. Mary Slessor wrote soon after the Edinburgh Conference that the chiefs at Itu "want their boys educated and they want someone to guide them safely through the new world in which they are being enclosed by the white man of whom they know so little and whom they fear."[58]

This is more astonishing because Edinburgh Conference did not represent the actual face of Christianity in Africa because of the lenses used in reading the people and their responses to the presence of the kingdom of God in their midst. By focusing on the settler communities of southern and central Africa, it missed the ferment in the western theatre and the signals of transcendence all over the continent. It ignored the key players in the indigenizing movement, misrepresented Ethiopianism and paid scant attention to the rising tide of charismatic revivals. Finally, education became the strongest weapon in western underdevelopment of Africa because of its power of eradication. It is intriguing to note how some of the missionary ideas of the early period survived till the decolonization period and served as the backdrop of the hostility to missionary control of education. The study of the past always has meaning for the present and future. It is always useful to know where the rain met us.

Chapter Six
Mission, Colonialism, and the Supplanting of African Religious and Medical Practices

Jude C. Aguwa

INTRODUCTION

Africa's religious and medical traditions offer fascinating insights into the world view of its varied cultures. They provide important perceptions about a world that was challenged as Europeans encroached into the continent from the middle of the nineteenth century. As a result of their centrality in African conceptualization of their world, they faced the most visible objects of European attack during the colonial period. Despite the huge amount of work done on European attempt to supplant African religion, a lot of attention has not been paid to the interconnectedness between these two aspects of African life and the attempt made by both colonial officials and missionaries to supplant them. In reality, both missionaries and colonialists shared a common conviction about their divine mandate to evangelize and to civilize. While such mandate was obvious with regard to Christian evangelical work, the architects of colonialism claimed it, even when their task essentially was secular. Yet, they believed that God was using them to extend civilization and salvation to the barbarous savages that inhabited remote parts of the earth.[1] No where was this belief clearly expressed than their attitude towards African religion and medical practices.

The purpose of this chapter, therefore, is to examine the impact of missionary and colonial enterprises on African culture, specifically, African religious and medical practices. Religion and medicine are chosen as special areas for discussion because they are perhaps the more mutually interwoven parts of the African culture. Indeed, the epistemological foundation of African indigenous medicine was rooted in the idea that the gods superintend the medical practice. Besides, religion and medicine preeminently embody the key elements of the African worldview. Thus, European discourses around Christianity and medicine can be seen as an attempt to control the African body as well as mind. The perspectives around these two integral elements of African culture also called for a high degree of collaboration among Europeans—based on a common worldview or association of Africa with primitivism, disease, and death. Such imaginations gave rise to the dominant discourse in the nineteenth century that described Africa as the "Whiteman's grave." For Giuliana Lund, the civilizing mission was "thus conceived, from the first, as a healing mission."[2] But it must be understood as one in which European medical practices, in particular was for the protection of Europeans in Africa and much less the protection of the African population from disease and death.

The first part this chapter focuses on missionary and colonial attitudes towards African religion and the conversion agenda; the second part examines Western attitudes towards African traditional medicine. The experience of change in the areas of religion and medicine offer opportunity a critical understanding of issues of cultural change in Africa during the colonial period as much as areas of agreement and disagreement between two important elements of European influence: missionaries and colonial officials.

INDIGENOUS RELIGION AND MEDICINE IN WESTERN PERSPECTIVE

The conquest of African societies by Europeans—missionaries and colonialists—was accompanied by unprecedented attempt to transform African societies to achieve the object of the "mission to civilize." Indeed civilizing Africans entailed an extensive enculturation process that portrayed all aspects of African culture as inferior. Support for this view came from both missionaries and colonial officials alike. Reports by European travelers and missionaries, who had visited Africa before the colonial period, have been criticized for being abysmally negative. Buhlmann recalls that Africans were depicted as idolaters, ignorant of God, savages and descendants of Ham.[3] However this negative attitude continued during the colonial missionary periods. It reflected prevalent Western prejudices and feeling of superiority, and above all shows Western ignorance of African value systems.

Religion was important in the African indigenous society. Its force permeated every aspect of life and institutions. Individuals became religious merely by being born into such religious milieu. Religious ideas are evident in the native myths, folklores, traditions, beliefs, institutions and relationships in such ways that no sharp division could be made between the sacred and the secular. The traditional religion informed and regulated individual and communal ethics as well as the entire social values system.

African indigenous religious tradition affirms a Supreme Being who is a creator and benevolent god, and who exercises control over minor deities. This Supreme Being, for example, is known as *Chukwu* and *Olodumare* respectively among the Igbo and the Yoruba peoples of Nigeria. This benevolent ruler of the earth is often associated with the sky. His presence in the sky and relative absence from the earth is the cause of the various local stories of divine migration and absence. Yet, his presence in the world and in the lives of individuals is strongly acknowledged in the many divine honorific titles given to individuals as personal names. This practice among other purposes, points to the deep religious attitude of Africans.

Other deities are recognized as personifications of different aspects of nature and superintendents of human activities. Among the Igbo, the earth goddess (*Ala*) guarantees fertility of humans, fauna, and flora. The earth goddess plays the role of defining individual and social identities in relation to community. In doing so, she defines and guards communal unity and ethics. *Agwu* patronizes traditional medicine and divination. Among the Yoruba, he is known as *Ifa*. The many *arusi* (deities in Igbo religion) and *orisha* (deities in Yoruba religion) and the pantheons of other ethnic traditions, patronize farm work, carving, war, rainmaking and other human occupations and skills. Thus, achievement, success, and the overcoming of misfortunes, were primarily attributed to divine initiative and benevolences. In the same way, failure and misfortunes were blamed on the gods. While the gods bring blessings to reward human fidelity, they punish transgressions and infringements of their laws and prohibitions.

Rituals and worship are the ways to maintain contact with the deities. These activities are particularly important when divine taboos are broken. Such infringement affects cosmic harmony and the purity of land and society. In such cases, rituals of purification are required to restore cosmic equilibrium and harmony. Prayers are a very essential part of ritual and worship. They were the first activities of each day. It is the duty of the head of a family to pray regularly for the welfare of its members. The prayers come in a diversity of forms, such as begging, thanksgiving, conversing, telling, petition, reporting, unburdening the heart, consulting with God, calling God, or crying to God.[4] The head prays for protection against subversive forces which can stand in the way of progress and good life.[5]

Indigenous African religion is also founded on the belief that ancestors maintain active presence in their earthly families. Their progenies observe ritual services in their honor and they reciprocate by protecting, healing and prospering their endeavors.[6] The role of ancestors is crucial especially in protecting their earthly families against the intrigues of evil spirits and their agents who always attempt to ensnare and harm them.[7] In most African cultures, ancestors are recognized for playing a vital role of repopulating their earthly families through their reincarnation. This is perceived as an act of love and solidarity. The descendants reciprocate by venerating their memory and observing festivals in their honor.

African religion inspired and nurtured several rites of passage. These rites mark the various stages of development which an individual passes through as a member of the community. They celebrate birth, naming, puberty, marriage and funerals. They unveil and affirm the responsibilities as well as the privileges associated with the evolving stages in the individual's relationships with other people and with the society. Thus, from birth until death, the individual is immersed in religious ceremonies, making religion a chief determinant of choices and a life-long engagement.

Despite the centrality of African religion to every aspect of the African world, European perceptions were very negative. Early missionaries were influenced in their perception of African religion by the prevailing racism of the time.[8] The typical missionary possessed an unflinching conviction about Christianity as the universal truth which would leave no room for any compromises. Malinowski thus described the apparent lack of doubts in the mind of the missionary:

> [He] would not be true to his vocation if he ever agreed to act on the principle that Christianity is as "any other form of cult." As a matter of fact, his brief is to regard all the other forms of religion as misguided, fit only for destruction, and to regard Christianity as entirely different, and the only true religion to be implanted. Far from leaving other cults side by side in juxtaposition with the message of the gospel, the missionary is actively engaged in superseding them.[9]

Okot P'Bitek maintained that colonial anthropologists and missionaries intentionally favored derogatory or disparaging terms to support prevailing theories of Western superiority.[10] Hence in word and deed, missionaries characterized African indigenous religions as primitivism, fetishism, idolatry, heathenism, paganism, or jujuism.[11] Such negative characterizations denied validity to African indigenous religion, and as John Peel clearly pointed out, led the missionaries to justify its replacement with the missionaries' own religion.[12]

To this end, Christian missions and the colonial state mounted relentless attacks on the indigenous religion and other cultural practices. It was common knowledge, as Kirby has pointed out that, "as a general principle . . . before 1960 all missionary-founded churches insisted that their converts abandon all contact with African traditional religions and cultures."[13] The cost of civilization and of Christianization was expected to be the loss of African religion and culture. Since the indigenous religion and culture intertwine, almost in the same way that Christianity and European culture do, mission work necessarily involved the European cultural values. Missionaries, as is well known among historians, presented Christianity, "as part and parcel of their own European cultural values . . . even to the extent of insisting that African converts adopt European clothing."[14] Early Christian converts were thus led to confuse European cultural values with gospel values to such an extent that the good Christian was one who imitated European practices.

MISSIONIZING IN THE COLONIAL SETTING: MISSION-STATE COLLABORATION

The missionary and colonial enterprises were intended to transform African society and culture. The missionary efforts, which were carried out through preaching the gospel and other activities, focused on undermining the indigenous religion. The colonial agents, on the other hand, imposed a new socio-political order intended to suppress the indigenous institutions. Yet, colonial agents and missionaries mutually exchanged *avant-garde* roles, and they collaborated in other ways in the pursuit of their respective aims. There are reasons for this collaboration. First, their respective goals sometimes traversed each other. Second, they shared a common religious and cultural background. Third, they shared the same ideologies about racial differences, as well as stereotyping. Both considered their subjects and potential converts barbaric, and so it was justified to use any means available, to subdue them into accepting Western notions of civilization along with the Christian faith. Fourth, in the mission and colonial lands, missionaries and colonial agents faced common traits of resistance and physical dangers.

Reports abound on missionary activities which promoted the interest of their national governments in exchange for the military or political protection their home governments gave them. According to Hastings, the missionary, especially among the Protestants, "seemed to be in open league with the new colonial government, and at times acted as if he shared in some general authority for the running of African society."[15]

Missionaries in various parts of Africa, in the late nineteenth century, usually appealed to their home governments for protection and assistance in opening the frontier for the gospel.[16] There were instances when particular missionaries seem to have exploited the ignorance of their African friends, by misleading them into writing agreements that cheated them of their lands and authority. The well known case of Reverend Helm and King Lobengular of Ndebele in 1888 was a typical example.[17]

In West Africa it seemed to have been common knowledge that missionaries and colonialists collaborated. Ayandele notes that "traditional rulers . . . were not unaware of the relations between the missionaries and the imperial-minded secular agents on the coast. In fact, the missionaries never scrupled to impress it upon the rulers that they had a common identity with their secular countrymen."[18] As a result, European colonizers were sometimes confused with missionaries and while there were obvious advantages for the mission, there was often a price to be paid. Ayandele explained that "whenever the secular agents offended the chiefs, the onus of responsibility was placed on the missionaries."[19] Among the Catholic missionary the case of collaboration was the same. In his Apostolic Letter, Maximum Illud of 1919, Pope Benedict XV had denounced such a practice and wrote:

> Some of the mission accounts published recently make very painful reading for us, as we find therein an anxiety not so much to extend the Kingdom of God as to increase the power of the missionary's own country. We are surprised that it does not occur to the writers to what extent the mind of the heathen is in danger of being thus repelled from religion.[20]

The postcolonial criticisms of Christianity, as an arm of imperialism, seem to justify the pope's fears. The pope genuinely believed that collaboration based on securing personal gains was the goal of evangelization.

The mission enterprise involved different types of activities: humanitarian work, preaching, establishment of schools and hospitals. Each activity constituted a different approach to the goal of planting Christianity. But in conjunction, they acted as tools for supplanting African cultures and identity and opportunity for collaboration between missionaries and colonial officials. For example, humanitarian work focused on alleviating poverty; preaching focused on expounding Christian doctrines; education was concerned with imparting Western cultural values, and hospitals provide new ways of dealing with health issues. Some of these activities according Adrian Hasting "provided an almost incontestable authority to those who brought them, once Africans began to appreciate them."[21] In the following section, these activities are further elaborated.

From the inception of Atlantic slave trade in the fifteenth century to its abolition in the nineteenth century, Africa suffered unprecedented loss both in human life and labor. The practice had severely undermined the indigenous socio-ethical system by exacerbating warfare and kidnappings, which were the means of obtaining captives. The practice distorted age-old values of human worth, dignity, and respect. In the words of Senghor, the slave trade "had ravaged black Africa like a bush fire, wiping out images and values in one vast carnage . . ."[22] In some places, greater value came to be accorded animals than human beings. Elizabeth Isichei noted of these practices in some parts of Nigeria:

> In the years of the slave trade, the practice of human sacrifice expanded vastly . . . In the Nsukka area, the going rate was ten slaves for a horse . . . At Uburu, in the 1880s, a horse was exchanged for four to six adult slaves. The practice of human sacrifice came to be a way of disposing of sick and disabled slaves . . ."[23]

It is into this environment that the early missionary stepped in and began their work. The CMS mission was the pioneer in West Africa. Its European founders, Wilberforce and his associates, had conceived of mission as the means of spreading both the gospel and 'civilization.' Taking into account the humanitarian situation in West Africa, Rweyemamu described the missionary effort as "humanitarian movement whose chief agents were those coming to Africa for the purpose of evangelization and civilization."[24]

Humanitarian work was the response to the immense human suffering caused by the slave trade. Its immediate good was to assuage sufferings of all kinds and to promote the quality of life of the people. In undertaking humanitarian work missionaries preached the gospel of Jesus for the same purpose of liberating the people from suffering and pain. At this time in the history of Africa, the need for liberation was urgent and required massive and compassionate efforts. Hence, humanitarian work was a challenging undertaking of the missions.

The alternative to slave trade was trade in agricultural produce. Both colonial agents and the missions were quick to recognize its preeminent importance. Fowell Buxton, a renowned abolitionist of the time, had thus conceptualized the conjunction of gospel, education and commerce: "Let missionaries and schoolmasters, the plough and the spade, go together, and agriculture will flourish; the avenues to legitimate commerce will be opened;

confidence between man and man will be inspired; whilst civilization will advance as natural effect, and Christianity operate as the proximate cause of this happy change."[25] Missionaries saw that economic undertaking was necessary for promoting and sustaining their humanitarian work and its goals. Hence, they encouraged agricultural development as soon as they established their presence in a locality, by starting farms and encouraging agriculture. The missionaries hoped that legitimate trade with the West would permit the introduction of other western institutions. The goal was to alleviate the sufferings of the people and to bring due attention to legitimate and viable occupations.

The CMS movement had an important resource in the group of ex-slaves, who had resettled in Freetown, present Sierra Leon, and who were educated and had converted to Christianity. These missionaries, as July has noted, were eager "to encourage the spread of Christian European ideal and institutions among neighbors and relatives and thereby, to introduce revolutionary social and economic concepts, which would bring about the modernization of West Africa."[26] Some from this group embarked on missions to other parts of the West African Coast in the early nineteenth century. Bishop Crowther, a Yoruba ex-slave, was among this group of African pioneer missionaries of the CMS who came from Freetown. He was able to employ his knowledge of his native heritage to great use in the establishment and growth of protestant missions. Equally, other missionary groups, the French Society of African Mission, the Society of African Mission, and the Holy Ghost Missionaries, made the abolition of slavery and introduction of Western institutions their priorities. On the whole, the humanitarian spirit and work created a favorable milieu for preaching the gospel, because it portrayed a humane and compassionate image of the missions. It was therefore, a necessary foothold for preaching evangelization.

Preaching was perhaps the most important tool of mission and a key stipulation of the biblical mandate. The majority of converts were those who listened to the gospel of salvation as interpreted by the missionaries. Peel has pointed out the following stages as early missionaries commenced their work in the Yoruba territory. First, the early missionaries preached on the streets and market places; second, they preached to people who gathered at various compounds; third, they toured towns and villages and would stay in the place for a few days; fourth, chiefs offered them hospitality and protection, and they would stay and preach to the crowds.[27] This pattern was more or less followed by missionaries of the various organizations. In their preaching and teaching missionaries condemned the indigenous religion and all practices associated with it. They denounced polygamy, the native healing practices, divination, rainmaking, rites of passage, festivals, and several others religious and cultural practices. Nevertheless, quite slowly, people responded to the initiative of the missionaries by accepting their invitations to their Church.

Evangelists of the Freetown missionaries of the CMS had some advantage over their competitors because of their knowledge of the Yoruba languages. They could preach without interpreters unlike their expatriate colleagues. But before long, other missionary groups had the assistance of catechists and teachers who were trained in their schools. These catechist and teachers understood the native religious practices much better than expatriate missionaries. As a result, their preaching was more penetrating.

Conversion and the presence of missionaries had serious socio-cultural consequences. As Peel has pointed out, "The mission was bound to some degree to challenge the normative order of the community and (to the extent that it succeeded in making converts) to create a degree of alienation in a section of the population from its institutions."[28] As more people converted to Christianity, the fabrics of the indigenous religion all the more weakened.

Both missionaries and colonialists pioneered the establishment of schools. Both were in need of educated assistants. It was necessary, that many people should acquire knowledge of English and other skills in a short period of time. Missionaries needed local catechists, interpreters, and teachers. Colonial institutions, such as trading companies, hospitals, courts, the police, and the army, needed clerks and well trained workers.

Missionary schools served two major functions: to educate young people in the secular subjects and to convert them to Christianity. Most of the school children embraced the Christian faith, which was nurtured with regular and intensive doctrines and rituals. From the beginning, the missionaries seemed convinced that the school would be an astounding tool of mission. Jehu Hanciles had thus described missionary Crowther's enthusiasm for schools: "The school was Crowther's primary tool of mission. He was a firm believer in the evangelical mantra of his day, that civilization and Christianity went together. Moreover, the widespread desire for Western education meant that the establishment of a school easily provided the first foothold for evangelization . . ."[29] Similar optimistic views and motives also characterized the early Catholic missionaries. Jordan reported, that Bishop Shanahan, the Prefect of Igbo land, had chosen the school as "the spearhead of his attack on I[g]bo paganism . . ." [30] The school, as Shanahan hoped, "would open wide its portal to all children of the town whether rich or poor, slave or free, by far the greatest proportion would be free."[31] Furthermore, it would present "a Christian outlook on what constituted the essence of I[g]bo paganism—juju worship, cannibalism, slavery,

[and] polygamy."[32] The school held such great appeal that before long, the initiative to build schools was taken over by local communities. In these schools, young minds continued to be formed in ways that gradually alienated them from the indigenous religion and culture.

AFRICAN EVANGELISTS: INTOLERANCE TOWARD INDIGENOUS RELIGION

Both Christianity and other western influences were significant in transforming African societies and their identity. Indeed, these changes did not occur easily or unproblematically, as the contestation between African values and European values left the African in a dilemma.

Africans were actively involved in the Christian missionary enterprise from the beginning. The case of Freetown missionaries is a good example. The role of African evangelists easily came to the center stage of mission development. Among some church organizations, their response focused on satisfying the huge demands for schools and health institutions. However, many of the native evangelists concentrated on a quick eradication of the native religion and culture. Perhaps this is direct result of less available resources with which to undertake elaborate school and health programs. An outstanding example was the *Kwa-Iboe* missions in Nigeria, which tended to become fanatically antagonistic to indigenous religious practices. According to colonial government reports, the *Kwa-Iboe* missions engaged in activates against the indigenous religion, which are reminiscent of the iconoclastic movements of medieval Europe. These reports, dating back to 1927, stated that "a large band of men and women all adherents of the *Kwa-Iboe* Mission went round in Ikot-Ekpene District destroying objects sacred to the pagans."[33] The ensuing investigation by the Colonial Resident pointed to the following causes: incitement through reading American Revivalist literature; encouragement by the missions with the hope of advancing their cause; and activists who claimed to possess supernatural powers.[34] The report described the activities of adherents of these Christian missions as atrocities. It further explained that the other Christian missions also complained against *Ekpo* and other pagan institutions.[35] The reports, among other things, show that missions complained to government agencies against the practices of the native religion, when they should be content with preaching against them. Such proactive steps certainly were intended to solicit government support toward their suppression.

The effort by government to protect pagans and their religious symbols against the intolerant and Puritanistic attacks of some fanatical Christian converts tended to legitimize government intervention in religious matters, including those that did not embody any negative elements of the culture. Colonial courts intervened in conflicts relating to Christian and so-callled pagan customs. A colonial official in Onitsha, Nigeria, wrote in 1925 regarding possible conflicts between native law and custom and Christian principles: "I have found a tolerance toward Christians by pagans much greater than one might expect. I am of the opinion that any difficulties that arise are more frequently due to high handedness on the part of native church committee and individual Christians."[36]

Burning of effigies, icons, ritual plants, and other symbols of the indigenous religion were common during parish missions or retreats, especially among Catholics. In these instances, new converts surrendered their protective charms and other religious symbols, as the condition for full admission into the Church. Christians were forbidden to become members of socio-cultural institutions such as *Ozo, ekpo, odo, ogboni*. However, latter generations Christians have continued to be interested in these institutions. This interest has given rise to syncretistic practices and subsequent controversies. The staying power of the controversies shows that the supplanting of indigenous religion and culture may have succeeded to a great extent, but not fully. As Father Mullan, a contemporary of colonial time said of the African Christianity: "Its roots in its new soil are not strong."[37] He argued that Christianity radically alienated the Africans from the securities they had enjoyed within their cultural pattern of life and so when crises arose the converts fell back on their familiar securities.[38]

Concurrently, Anglican and Catholic missions flourished and nurtured the gradual emergence of indigenous clergy. Humanitarian work, education and preaching of the gospel continued with increasing involvement of local people. All through, these developments were revolutionary especially, with regard to their impact on African culture and religion. Many governments, fearing total loss of national cultural identities, quickly adopted national, cultural policies, aimed at critical cultural revival, whereby positive values of the culture are upheld and promoted. This was a way to restore cultural pride and to give some official direction to cultural change in their areas.

Although change was significant, the goal of both Western colonial and missionary enterprises had only been partially attained with regard to supplanting of African religion. This limited success shows that cultural change is a gradual process that is subject to human and social variables. Evidence is noted in the official declaration by the bishops of Onitsha Ecclesiastical province (Eastern Nigeria) in 1980, during the centenary celebration of the history of the Catholic Church in Eastern Nigeria. The bishops acknowledged the reality of progress made by the Churches, as well as the immense task ahead, in the following comments: "There is abundant evidence to show the prevalence of superstitious native customs and beliefs as well as materialism under a thin veneer of Christianity among many of our Christians."[39]

A new model for change has emerged, arising from several factors, including: the fervor for the use of vernacular among protestant Churches; the spread of African independent Churches; as well as the publication of *Gaudium et Spes* (Second Vatican Council). This model encourages dialogue between Christianity and African culture and religion. Unlike the approach, it does not advocate cultural and religious imposition. It requires that agents of Christianity show respect for and sensitivity to African culture. What this means for both parties is constant shifting of positions in this dialogue and continuing critical reappraisal of related issues. This dialogue has borne visible fruit among some independent Christian churches. One example is that some Churches have moved toward the incorporation of African religious and healing ideas into their faith healing practices.

AFRICAN TRADITIONAL MEDICINE: WESTERN PERCEPTIONS

African ethnomedical systems and religious belief and practices, as visible elements of African cultural landscape, were under severe attack. The lack of knowledge about African realities notwithstanding, Europeans rejected African healing systems, although plants and herbal remedies were part of European medical system in the nineteenth and beyond. Indeed, while Europeans rejected African ethnomedical practices as superstitious beliefs, these stereotypes ignored that European practices were still very rudimentary in the nineteenth century. Robert Voeks argues in the case of colonial America that "Colonial physicians, few in number and often self-trained, doled out the medical care then known to late medieval and Renaissance Europe." Like their African counterparts, the views of many European about causation "ranged from astrological imbalances to the effects of evil spirit and bad air . . ."[40] The persistence of African religious and medical practices, however, has to be understood in the context of the deeply-rooted link between religion, ethnomedical practice, and African cosmology.

Moses Ochonu has noted that "Colonial medical officers were not purely scientific personnel who happened to be serving in the tropics; they were self-consciously involved in the pursuit of the goals of Empire. . . . British medical personnel came . . . first as colonial agents, saddled with the medical challenges of "the White Man's Burden." Like their missionary counterparts their every effort, medical, religious, political and economic were made to convert "natives" to the "ideals and practices of Western culture."[41] In his work on colonial Northern Nigeria, Ochonu argues:

> The correlation of culture with susceptibility to diseases on the basis of ethno-religious inclination in Northern Nigeria illustrates and implicates the extent to which the divide and rule ideology of British colonialism found expression in the protectorate. The deployment of this principle in the British colonial discourse on sanitation is only a strand in a broader British colonial scheme of manipulating ethnic and cultural differences among its subject population in order to strengthen its rule.[42]

Thus, a Eurocentric view of medical knowledge and perceptions of African societies defined Western ideas about cure and disease in the colonial context. Indeed, early colonial officials "formed protopsychiatric ideas of a distinct African mind and personality," largely based on "pejorative ideas."[43] The resulting stereotypes, "were increasingly rationalized by the impress of science; in keeping with a growing organic bias in psychology, the "African mind" came to be a reflection of the African body—in particular, the brain."[44]

From their Western medical point of view, missionaries believed that traditional African therapeutic practices were not only ineffective but also undermined essential Christian tenets. Charles Good has pointed out that Europeans saw African medicine as irrational and superstitious witchcraft or magic.[45] Good explained that the attitude of missionaries, colonial administrators, and European medical workers derived from the assumption that Western cultural and medical practices were superior. Missionaries consistently mounted vigorous campaigns aimed at discouraging consultation of healers and diviners, and the use of icons and other symbols of healing. The missionaries discouraged converts to use African medicine or to consult any of its specialists. Converts, who consulted African medical practitioners or used their advice or prescriptions, were often reported to the missionaries. Such converts were required to denounce the traditional practice. In the Belgian Congo, the colonial governments in some parts of Africa proscribed indigenous healing practices.[46]

Christian missionary discourses around health were rooted in the larger European debates about diseases in the nineteenth century. Lund argues that the advent of germ theory in the latter part of the nineteenth century increased public interest in hygiene. This perhaps explains the adage—"cleanliness in next to Godliness,"—"cleanliness of mind and body were increasingly inseparable in public discourse, and dirt of any kind was thought to be morally as well as physically corrupting."[47] Africa was an experimental lab for these discourses. According to Lund, John Ross, the son of a Scottish missionary, "exemplified the attitude that cleanliness was next to godliness when he wrote the following in a pamphlet of 1887" It was his view that "People must be taught that attention to public health is a moral duty, that cleanliness, avoidance of excess, and health preservation go hand in hand with mental and moral training, and that morality consists as much in a hearty submission to the precepts of health as to the observations of creed."[48]

Early European explorers who laid the groundwork for imperialist expansion included numerous doctors. David Livingstone's early work in African missionary field remains legendary. But they did not just seek the African's soul; as healers, "missionaries in Africa viewed themselves as the harbingers not only of spiritual enlightenment, but also of material progress. Medicine was thought to serve both goals because in addition to saving lives and alleviating suffering, it would attract followers to the missions and contribute to the prestige of Western culture at the expense of local culture."[49] Such hegemonies were expressed by several European missionaries. James Stewart, a typical disciple of Livingstone, used this "union of medical and spiritual work" to combat indigenous healing practice, "one of the mightiest and most malignant of influences in Africa."[50] And for Jean Comaroff, "medicine became a means of controlling African bodies and minds and thus an instrument of imperialism."[51]

African medical practices and Western practice shared common ideas about the control of infectious diseases. Quarantining the sick to prevent infection was evident on both medical traditions. However, African practices in this regard conjured up images of strange primitive practices. A *New York Times* report commentary in its January 16, 1921 issue confirms these inventions of the European mind:

> When there is illness or an epidemic in darkest Africa, the medicine man sets up a roughly cut image of Buiti to warm of the danger lurking near the scene of the disease. A Buiti with a cavity in the middle signifies that a serious stomach *malady, perhaps cholera,* is afflicting the community. . . . The missionaries forbid the carving and setting up of a Buiti, but his mandates are of avail only upon missionary property.[52]

Although this attitude has its roots in late eighteenth century European pseudo-scientific theories, there were some Europeans who rejected such simplistic explanations or outright dismissal of African medical practices as witchcraft. Dr. Michael Gelfand, special physician to the Central African Federal Government in a paper entitled "The African in the Medical Field" deplores the use of the word "witchcraft" in reference to African herbal practitioners. The African traditional medical practitioners is a priest or minister of the individual and "His real strength lies in the psychosomatic field," stated Dr. Gelfand.[53]

Elspeth Huxley confirms: "African witch doctors, like herbalists and old wives everywhere, certainly knew of plants containing drugs in use today by American and European doctors. They could and did treat some troubles pre-scientifically. They could set broken limbs, for instance, with success and dress wounds so effectively that they seldom festered or turned gangrenous." Still, the psychological tools in use today in modern medicine were applied effectively by traditional African healers. Huxley notes that "the witch doctor's real power was psychological. . . . He was in some respects the forerunner of today's psychiatrist."[54] These examples illustrate the ambiguous Western attitude towards African culture and practices.

The negative attitude portrayed by missionaries and colonial agents toward African medicine easily affected African Christian converts and those educated in colonial and missionary schools. Some authors have referred to this development as "colonization of the mind"[55] In other words, it was a process of indoctrination based on the notion that Western culture and Christianity were superior rather than on evidence of the ineffectiveness of the indigenous medicinal system. Yet colonial governments allowed indigenous medical practice to flourish, where the latter was the only available healthcare for the native population. Indeed Dr Gelfand cautioned in the case of Southern Rhodesia in the late 1950s: "Until there are more physicians, especially African doctors as well as nurses and clinics in the territory, there should be as little interference as possible with the only medical aid within reach of the African."[56]

The uncritical approach, which was characteristic of early African and Western encounter, changed to the more critical approach, as anthropological studies of African systems commenced. The initial anthropological studies, which were sponsored by colonial governments, examined traditional healing systems and practices to determine how they had served Africans over the course of several centuries. They used the fieldwork method and closely examined the work of ritual agents. The studies identified cultural paradigms and expressions characteristic of therapeutic practices. They discovered that the healing systems were complex, had long history of spread beyond ethnic boundaries, and generally had earned the confidence of the

African people.[57] Further more, latter studies discovered that African concepts of disease are in some ways similar to Post-enlightenment concept of disease in Europe.[58] The result of these anthropological studies among others was that a more objective discussion of the validity of African therapeutic systems would continue. It borders on the clearer isolation of the two essential components of traditional healing methods, namely, the use of herbal medicine and religious rituals. It meant that the blanket condemnation of African medicine based on European prejudices would cease.

Africa's *materia medica* has become an object of scientific study in recent times. In the colleges of medicine and pharmacy, as well as in government sponsored research centers, scholarly interest in the different ethno-botanies is generated and nurtured. Impressive results include works that identify and classify various national or regional medical plants. In *Medical Plants of West Africa,* Edward Ayensu identified the local names of 187 medicinal plants of the region, evaluated their uses and the binomials. *Medicinal Plants of North Africa* by Loutfy Boulos' also has examined over 500 species of medicinal plants. Maurice Iwu's *A Handbook of African Medicinal Plants* is a study on the ethno-botany, chemical constituents, and probable therapeutic applications of several medicinal plants of Africa. Many African medicinal plants from the various regions have been identified and documented.[59] The level of recognition has encouraged a more objective and perhaps fruitful employment of the pharmacopoeia.

One of the important directions, which herbal medicinal research has taken, is that of the scientific screening of traditional medicinal plants to determine their curative qualities. Many herbs with important antibacterial, anti-inflammatory, anticonvulsant and antiparasitic activities have been identified and classified. In confirming the traditionally held knowledge about their therapeutic use through scientific screening, protagonists of traditionalism and reform find their meeting point. Effort in another line of research consists in the testing of traditional herbal drugs for their chemical contents, toxicity and their unknown potencies. Case studies of herbal drug medication show the validity of their traditional applications. The cases include studies of medicines used in the following cases: during pregnancy, to achieve sexual arousal, to treat maladies of the eye, ear or liver.

Another important direction in scientific study seeks to determine the inappropriate use of certain herbal medicines.[60] What has been accomplished through research into African medicinal systems has significantly transformed indigenous medicine. In other words, the tradition of education, which started with missionary and colonial schools, has in the course of time generated enormous power over the traditional medicine. Its limitations have become more obvious and its continued existence rendered more precarious.

AFRICAN MEDICINE AND CHRISTIAN HEALING MISSIONS

Like other aspects of African life in the encounter with Europe, African appropriated Christianity and incorporated same into indigenous healing practices. The Pentecostal churches, charismatic movements, evangelical and other forms of Christian faith healing Churches, have created a new facet of experience for African healing ideas. This is because these Christian missions espouse spiritual healing, which has parallels in the African traditional practices. Consequently, some African healing ideas have found strong legitimacy arising from this syncretistic situation. The reason behind the fast proliferation of Christian healing missions, is to a large extent, the fact that Christian healing ideas strongly resonate through the spiritualism of the African traditional therapeutic practices. Christian faith healers have continued to explore ways to integrate such common elements.

One outstanding similarity between African and Christian healing is that both groups admit that illness has probable spiritual dimension. African medicine affirms that physical sickness could be caused by adversarial spirits as a result of the individual's moral flaws or witchcraft. Similarly, Christian Charismatic healers see evil as a "real malevolent personal spiritual force"[61] They espouse demonology in order to explain various types of illness, misfortune and negative human experiences and in so doing, as Hunt has pointed out, they expound "a dualistic perception of the world: good and evil, the divine and the demonic, in very stark terms."[62]

The Christian healing missions have therefore employed various aspects of African culture. J. E. Kunnie has referred to "the utilization of song, spirit evocation, spirit possession, musical improvisation, polyrhythmic harmonization, hand-clapping, foot stamping and singing, water baptism and even drumming."[63] The fight against illness in the African Zionist and Prophetic churches required the power of superior good spiritual forces which is cultivated through prayer and other rituals. Prophet Mokaleng, for example, exercised divinatory powers including interpreting dreams and visions among the Matsiloje of Botswana in early twentieth century through these means. He also sought to bring healing through prayer to a wide range of human personal issues including physical deformities and impairments, infertility and psychotic illness.[64] People came to such healers to seek a variety of answers pertaining to protection, security, prosperity, family and marriage disputes, barrenness, and success in general success[65] Prior to the advent of Christianity, related problems were believed to result from the anger and attacks of spirits, witches, sorcerers, ancestors. In both African medicine and faith healing, recourse was made to benevolent spiritual powers.

The Aladura Churches, which has grown in great numbers in Nigeria, especially among the Yoruba, espouses Pentecostal beliefs in faith healing. Historians link the origin of the Aladura Churches to the worldwide influenza of 1918. When the influenza defied known remedies, including those offered by Western medicine, resort to faith healing became the only option. In Aladura churches holiness of life is projected as the foremost goal. There is the espousal of a dualism in illness etiology, namely physical and spiritual and which is also the approach in African medicine. Aladura Churches explain that spiritual battles are waged to overcome demonic incursions in individual lives which cause illness and misfortune of all forms. Material prosperity is explained as a sign of authentic divine favor and if this prosperity gospel is easily acceptable among Africans, it is above all because the African worldview underscores wealth and health as divine blessings.

The African worldview has parallels in the Bible, such as in the belief that divine intervention in healing is possible. The bible has many accounts of such miracles. Modern scientists have also expressed interest in determining any relationship between a patient's religious faith and recovery. Are people who have deep religious beliefs likely to recover more quickly than others who do not have, or who have no belief in God at all? To even consider the legitimacy of this question might indicate that although modern science does not embrace the religious worldview about healing, it nonetheless discovers some underlying concurrences.

The development of African medicine and the role of Christian missions, even if unintended shows a set of different dynamics in cultural change. Over issues of religious beliefs the missionary would be far more uncompromising than when the issue deals with the more personal issues of life and health. This goes to agree with the verity that medicine is about healing people and not ideas.

CONCLUSION

The religious and cultural change, which was sparked off by the encroachments of the combined forces of missionaries and colonialists in Africa, has remained unabated. It is part of the history of the development of Christianity, from virtually, being a Middle-Eastern and European religion to becoming a world religion. Through this development, Christianity has extended its influences far beyond the boundaries of its origins. Western ideas and institutions have also engendered preponderant ideological and socio-cultural changes. The African experience of these changes, as has been explored in this chapter, was radical and revolutionary at the beginning of missionary and colonial enterprises. This chapter also established that the Christianization of Africans and modernization of African health services is determined by the spiritual and economic circumstances in Africa. These circumstances sometimes have slowed the rate and manner by which Africans embrace Christianity and their response to Western medicine. In some instances, the spiritual and economic situations have encouraged the revitalization of traditional practices and the persistence of others. Through these influences, they have inspired efforts at dialogue and integrations of some African cultural values with those of Christianity and modern healthcare.

Chapter Seven

Conflict and Compromise: Christian Missions and New Formations in Colonial Nigeria

Chima J. Korieh

> It must be recognized that conflict between native law and custom and Christian principles is inevitable as Christianity spreads into pagan areas.[1]

INTRODUCTION

Colonialism and Christianity still bear the most significant influences in the construction of African societies since the nineteenth century. Christianity was less popular than Islam in Africa until the mid-nineteenth century when a significant number of African societies south of the Sahara were influenced by Christian missionary evangelism. Since then the number of Africans that profess the Christian faith has doubled every two decades and is estimated at over 350 million today.[2] This phenomenal increase has led to unprecedented social and cultural change in sub-Saharan Africa, where Christianity rather than Islam, has made the greatest impact. Yet, Christianity made its most significant inroad in the late nineteenth century, a period that coincided with European imperial expansion in Africa. The historical coincidence, and peculiar worldview of both European agents (missions and imperialists), became important in shaping the African world from the late nineteenth century. That both missionary endeavor and colonial expansion occurred during the same period, was a significant factor in the forms of compromise and contestations that occurred between the two.

Missionaries, for a variety of reasons and factors, advocated colonial expansion although they also criticized some imperial policies. In their mission to civilize, however, both the imperial and missionary agents exerted social and political influences on the African population. The notion of the "Bible and the Gun" is used to illustrate the dual approach and influence of administrators and missionaries on African societies. As "civilizing" agents, they sought to reconstruct African societies by imposing Western cultural values, while simultaneously attempting to supplant African indigenous cultures and identities. The central aim of this chapter is to provide some perspectives on the contested nature of these formations as Nigerian peoples encountered Christianity and colonialism from the early period of the twentieth century.

Indeed scholars have examined the relationship among missions, empire, and African receptivity, yet how indigenous people selectively appropriated Christianity and Western values, as well as the conflicts that emerged between missions and imperial agents on one hand, and between them and Africans, on the other have not been fully examined. How did local groups respond to these external factors, particularly, Christianity and a new emerging identity as it evolved in the twentieth century? How did Africans appropriate aspects of missionary and imperialist culture in the colonial context? How did Christian missions and their adherents re-define or re-create a new identity for non-Christians and vice versa? What role did colonial authorities play in negotiating these encounters? This paper analyzes the contrasting views expressed by missionaries, colonial officials, and Africans, and the contested and polarized identity formations associated with the introduction of Western influences on the African population. It argues that what emerged from conversion to Christianity and the impact of colonial rule on the African population was a hybrid identity, and one, in which Africans continuously faced a dilemma as they straddled two worlds—indigenous and Western. However, the collaboration between the Bible and the Gun was not always smooth in the attempt to impose hegemony on African societies. Indeed, the ambiguous relationship between mission and Empire, which were at times cooperative and collaborative and at other times, antagonistic and ambivalent, elicited varying degrees of acceptance or resistance on the part of Africans. Still, significant as these Western forces were, African societies proved resilient as they traversed the cultural boundaries of their new and indigenous world views.

MISSIONS, EVANGELISM, COLONIALISM

Nineteenth century European missionary enterprise in Africa was not unrelated to the political, economic, and social developments in Europe at the time. For most of the nineteenth century, the image of Africa in Western World was that of the "Dark Continent."[3] Although Europeans knew little about Africa, yet, many carried an image of Africa defined by a very strong stereotypical mental image of the continent.[4] Any exploration of the question of African identity, therefore, should necessarily begin by exploring European ideas about Africa, the imperial agenda of

Christian missionaries and European colonizing agents, the concept of Africa at all levels of interpretation in relation to what Mudimbe defined as "their roots in and reference to the Western tradition . . . their past and present constellations."[5] Writing in 1897, the *New York Times* summarized what was the prevailing view in the West:

> It is not unlikely that the most momentous change on the face of the earth in the next century will occur on the continent of Africa. Civilized nations are getting out of patience with its obstinate barbarism and making preliminary assaults on all sides that must sooner or later break down the barrier, that has from the beginning of time guarded the mysteries of the interiors and kept out the regenerating influence of civilization. Science is eager to know the secrets of its geography, its geology, its zoology, its ethnology, and governments and learned societies are ready to promote and push on its investigation. Trade is importunate for new realms to open up, and anxious to get at the unexplored treasures of the vast tropical regions in which intelligence and enterprise are yet to begin their work. Christian zeal is ready to lend its powerful aid in behalf of the salvation of those dusky millions that still bow down to wood and stone.[6]

This image of Africa obviously informed subsequent missionary, commercial, and colonial endeavors in Africa.

Throughout the period of European domination in Africa, the attempt to elevate this degraded portion of the human race remained firmly embedded in the minds of these European groups, but more prominently in missionary circles. The contact between African societies and Europeans in the nineteenth century was based on this mission to civilize—a process that aimed to the transform African societies and the identities of Africans. The preoccupation with this civilizing mission was expressed among different elements in European society. For the European missionaries and colonial officials, given the objectives of civilizing their African subjects, the formation of new identities was essential in this mission. The next two hundred years witnessed a rapid expansion of Christianity in Africa.

Scholars have used a wide range of perspectives to address the intersection between missions, evangelism, and colonial expansion in Africa. Richard Gray argues that Christianity "made its rapid advances precisely because its emissaries, the missionaries, were so closely linked with the whole apparatus of colonial rule."[7] John Du Plessis argued in the first quarter of the twentieth century that "missionary enterprise is so intimately related to the political movement on the one hand and to the commercial undertaking on the other that its history cannot be accurately traced without continued reference to both."[8] For Kenneth Dike, both economic and non-economic motives helped to make discordant elements in British society "into one channel and provided a common ground for unity and alliance among such strange bedfellows."[9] Felix Ekechi has noted that the Church Missionary Society (CMS) missionaries, following the discovery of the course and mouth of the River Niger in 1830 by the Lander brothers, were already seeking a form of collaboration and attempt to penetrate the Niger territory.[10] The expeditions of the 1841 and 1854 were significant in what was to become the triumvirate of the so-called legitimate commerce, Christian evangelism, and British imperialism on the Niger. The Expedition of 1854, sponsored by the businessman McGregor Laird, with a modest grant from the British government, was very significant in European attempt to penetrate the interior of southern Nigeria from the coast. The expedition was very successful in penetrating the River far into the Hausaland. While the objectives of the expedition was primarily commercial, it was also made up of some British government officials, and some CMS African missionaries under the leadership of Reverend Samuel Crowther, thus, fulfilling Fowell Boxton's claim that the "Bible and Plough" would serve the cause of civilization and Christianity.[11] This doctrinal stance led to intricate and complex relationships between the elements of European civilization in their encounter with African societies.

While colonial powers provided a supportive environment for missionary enterprises, missionaries were also often vocal critiques of the commercial and political tactics of other Europeans. For instance, while the missionaries had worked closely with the European trading firms in establishing posts on the Niger, in using the trading firms to facilitate transportation and communication along the Niger, and in inviting the British naval bombardments of the various Niger communities. The same missionaries were also some of the most vocal critics of the unruly behaviors and excessive exploitations of the African communities by the European traders, especially, by the Royal Niger Company.[12] These ambivalences were influenced by the larger ideological issues of imperialism, mission to civilize, and race.

The ambivalent nature of these relationships was reflected in how African converts perceived themselves in relation to other Africans and different elements of European institutions in Africa as much as how different facets of the European encounter perceived their mission. These contesting dynamics were not a nineteenth century phenomena;

they had an earlier root in the fifteenth century European commercial explorations.

EARLY ENCOUNTERS AND FORMS OF COLLABORATION

Missionaries were closely aligned to European commercial and coloniz- ing powers and their identification with the colonizing mission often resulted in both alliances and opposition in the attempt to construct new African identities. This notion was not a nineteenth or twentieth century phenomenon. It goes back to the earlier periods of European contact with Africa. In the fifteenth century, for example, Portugal's crusading spirit focused on Africa south of the Sahara. As European countries began to search for a new sea route to Asia, Papal Bulls "offered the *padroado* rights to the Portuguese monarch to appoint clerical orders for evangeli- zation and to ferd off competing European interests."[13] The Portuguese supported Roman Catholic missionary priests who first attempted to work with the rulers of some African kingdoms. Thus the Iberian Catho- lic presence in Africa was characterized by court-alliance and the use of religion as an instrument of diplomatic and commercial relationship. There was the hope that court conversion would lead to the mass con- version of the people. They established contact in the Canary Islands, Cape Verde Islands, along the Guinea coast, the Kongo, Angola, Mozam- bique, and Kenya. The early Portuguese built prototypes of Lisbon and established churches and cathedrals in the islands of Cape Verde and Sao Tome. They built trading forts in the Gold Coast on the Atlantic Ocean and at Kilwa on the Indian Ocean. The evangelization effort, however, concentrated on the *mestizo* population.

Conversion among Africans met mixed success. While the com- bined motives of gold, glory, and God, fitted into the rhetoric and the "Christian motif of the period," the commercial interest remained privi- leged, perhaps explaining why there was little success in mass conversion between the sixteenth and eighteenth centuries.[14] Some African rulers rejected Christianity because it threatened the basis of their spiritual and temporal authority. Attempts at Christian conversions in the kingdoms of Benin and Warri soon failed as the Portuguese focused their search for pepper in India.

The Portuguese missionaries had their greatest success in the Kongo and Soyo Kingdoms. The Portuguese came into contact with the Kongo kingdom in 1483 and by 1491, missionaries were sent to the Kongo and soon afterwards King Nzinga was baptized as a Christian. His son Nzinga Mbembe was sent to Portugal where he received a Catholic education.

On his returned to the Kongo, he replaced his father as king and changed his name to King Afonso I. The role of Afonso in the Kongo illuminates an early example of state-church relations. After his coronation as king of Kongo in 1506, Afonso used the planting of Christianity as an instrument of diplomatic relations between the Congo and Portugal. According to Paul H. Gundani, Afonso "persistently made pleas for more priests and teachers from Portugal with an idea of making his kingdom a leading African Christian state."[15] Missionaries opened schools across the kingdom, and many Kongolese were converted to Christianity. Among the Soyo, Capuchin missionaries from Portugal established themselves as crucial intermediaries between the kingdom and Europe, relying on the assistance of local interpreters, who translated during confession, prepared the altar, and taught converts. The ruler of Soyo was attending mass three times a week and wearing a cross of solid gold by the late seventeenth century.

The Portuguese missionary effort in inner Africa faced challenges from within and without. The evangelical movement often took the back-burner in relation to commercial interest, particularly after the expansion of the slave trade in the seventeenth century. Over time, the commercial interest compromised the missionary zeal. As with the Kongo, conflict developed between the Capuchins and the Soyo over the issue of monog-amous marriage and traditional religious practices and over the slave trade. The Capuchins did not want the Soyo to sell baptized slaves to the English or other non-Catholic traders. They insisted that baptized slaves could only be sold to the Portuguese. As in the Kongo, the commercial motivations compromised the evangelical goal. In Mashonaland, Central Africa, missionaries were expelled for meddling into local politics and commerce. On the East African Coast, missionaries faced increased com-petition from Indians and Arabs and relentless conflicts with the indig-enous groups of Madagascar while Omani empire re-established control over the northern sector of the eastern coast. Competition from other European countries challenged Portuguese dominance of the lucrative trade in slaves, ivory, and other goods. Overall, the fleeting encounter with Christian presence collapsed as the missionaries concentrated on enslaving prospective converts. Missionary revival and mass conversion had to wait the nineteenth century enterprise.

Many factors contributed to the growth of Christianity in Africa in this period, but the most important historical factors were undoubtedly the abolition of the Atlantic slave trade and evangelical revival in Europe. Spiritual awakenings occurred in many Europeans nations between the mid-eighteenth and nineteenth centuries. The revival in Europe included an emphasis on the Bible, the conversion experience, and evangelism. A central message of the revivalist movement was a call on Christians to proselytize and spread the Christian message to all parts of the world, including Africa. Thus, European and North American missionary endeavors were directly tied to a Christian revivalist movement that occurred in the nineteenth century. Many Christian missionaries from Europe, North America, and the West Indies worked throughout the African continent to spread Christianity. A network of philanthropists and religious groups pushed the abolitionist agenda within and outside Europe. British philanthropists were concerned about the poor conditions of liberated slave. It was hoped that the mission to civilize could be achieved by introducing Christianity and commerce.

Large-scale conversation occurred throughout most of sub-Saharan Africa due to Christian evangelization works. Missionaries learnt Africa languages and often translated portions of the Bible into local languages in order to facilitate conversion. They opened schools, which focused reading and religious instruction as tools for conversion. Missionaries believed that the ability to read the Bible was vital in the conversion process. As colonialism became entrenched, mission education expanded as the colonial governments spent money to support education. Many African accepted conversion and missionary education for utilitarian purposes.

Missions were established by different Christian denominations, including a variety of Roman Catholic orders and Protestant denominations. Missionaries did not only come from predominantly White churches. They came from different races and backgrounds. Liberated African formed the core of Sierra Leone mission in 1792, with a clear vision to build a new society under the mandate of the gospel. The liberated slaves linked the Enlightenment ideas and Christianity to individual liberty and freedom and set the cultural tone of industry and religion that nurtured thousands of recaptives in Sierra Leone between 1807 and 1864.Some became agents of missionary enterprise throughout the West coast of Africa. The liberated slaves served as educators, interpreters, counselors to indigenous communities, negotiators with the new change agents, preachers, traders, and leaders of public opinion in many West African communities. Perhaps Ajayi Crowther, who was made a bishop in 1864, signified the epitome of their achievement.

The founding of Liberia in 1822 by the Colonization Society and the recruitment of African American missionaries marked a significant factor in the missionary enterprise to Africa. The African Episcopal Methodists and National Baptist Convention, among other African

American churches "created a form of appropriation of the gospel that endured."[16]

Developments in the nineteenth century and the expansion of European interest in Africa introduced new dimensions to missionary enterprise. The colonization of Africa in the nineteenth century and the expansion of Christian missionary enterprises were undoubtedly the most important monumental events that shaped contemporary African societies. While the colonial enterprise focused on the economic and political restructuring of Africa, missionary influence impacted heavily on the social and cultural life of Africans. The rapid expansion of Christianity in Africa owned much to the support of colonial governments. As the Berlin Conference sorted the geographical boundaries in the interior of the continent, missionaries followed Imperial powers and haggled for souls along imperial lines and in the spirit of the scramble and partition.[17] Thus, missionaries in different parts of Africa reflect the European origins of the colonizing power. Chukwudi Njoku argued:

> The underlying logic of this matching of the colonial powers to 'fitting' missionary groups lay in the need for a stable framework for the work of the missionaries. The colonial framework therefore created for the Christian missionaries in Africa a powerful sense of security and protection and a psychological sense of at-homeness. The very aura of power which the colonial machine established through its ruthless campaigns in the *mission-colonial*territory was capital for the missionaries.[18]

Colonialists and missionaries established a hegemonic relationship that used Christianity as a civilizing agent. Colonial rule provided a politically peaceful and supportive environment for the work of Christian missionaries with the hope that Christianity would provide support for colonial rule as African converts see the value of colonial rule. But the relationship between colonial authorities and missionaries were ambivalent and often ran counter to the Enlightenment ideas of both missionary and colonial forces. Missionaries often became part of colonial exploitation and expropriations as was the case with the Holy Ghost fathers that turned their plantation into a lucrative exploitation of young people at Bagamoyo, off the coast of Zanzibar. The Dutch Reformed Church provided the grounding in formulating the ideology of apartheid in South Africa. Belgian Catholic missionaries in the Congo were complacent with the brutality meted to the local people by Leopold II's Congo Free State employees until he relinquished the colony to Belgium in 1908. It was the international outcry about the brutality of Leopold' Congo and not the Enlightenment ideal of Belgian missionaries that ameliorated the "slavery" of the Congolese. Thus, "collusion with the civilizing project diminished the spiritual vigor of missionary presence and turned it into cultural and power encounters."[19]

Both Christian missionaries and colonial authorities professed love for Africans in the context of the assumed inferiority of African cultures. The nature of this relationship created a crisis of identity that dominated most of the colonial period and beyond. Both missionary and colonial agenda often acted in collaborative and hegemonic fashion—to achieve the goal of colonizing the African—economically, politically, and socially. The Christian missionaries were crucial to the course of history as their activities molded colonial projects and directed imperial activities, determining where and how people lived their lives. Because they were incapable of seeing the African landscape as anything but pristine or wilderness, both mission and imperial officials wanted "their" African subjects to construct a new society, a society based on European models or notions of civility and modernism. V. Y. Mudimbe's novel *Between Tides*, highlights the psychological processes involved in the conversion process. Mudimbe wrote:

> Christianity is skillful, Pierre. It is the depository of a truth not more true than any other, but its strength is that it levels all men to its own condition. They submit. It is powerful, disciplined, and dictatorial, and it knows wonderfully well how to exercise both rifle and benediction; as it also knows how to modify a policy just in time. Look at Teilhard de Chardin, and the cult of tolerance so fashionable these days.[20]

For many Africans, selective appropriation of European ideas in both the missionary and colonial system was commonly employed as a means of getting the best of both worlds. This raises important questions about the ways in which African and European views on a number of issues that defined the formation of colonial societies may have interacted. Indeed, missionary reports and dialogues can be read as colonizing texts, in which missionaries used language, imagery, and Eurocentric centered epistemologies to legitimize relations of inequality with Africans. Strategic alliances with European trading and colonizing powers were necessary to control the African population. Several analyses that transcend the narrow boundaries that often separate the role of these two elements of European encounter present missionary endeavors and official colonial actions as hegemonic encounter in which both pursued the same goal, at least at the ideological level even if they adopted different strategies. Such collaborations effected the colonization of African societies, the formation of new African elite, and defined their new identity. But it was one also in which Africans attempted

to develop a new, modern African identity with its own values and its own
validity in a colonizing context that sought to destabilize African identity.

The selective appropriation of European culture and values was
expressed in no better place than the attempt to acquire Western education—
a project that was initially the product of missionary encounter. Schools
offered missionaries, and later colonial governments an important tool for
the constitution and construction of African identities, but the literacy and
schooling offered unexpected tools for self-empowerment. For the African
population, education had what Michael Echeruo referred to as a "tangible
attraction" because it "opened up opportunities for work with the missions;
it made it possible to secure appointments with the expanding British administration."[21] By the mid-nineteenth century the Church Missionary Society
has established educational institutions at Abeokuta—the Christian Institute
(founded 1852), which trained young people for work with the European
missionaries in the interior, and the Abeokuta Industrial Institution (1856)
which "concentrated on the trades, on giving the students some basic training in a technical subject, such as cotton curing, simple accounting, carpentry
and joinery."[22] Such immediate and practical needs paved the way for rapid
Christianization in several parts of Africa. For example, Meredith McKittrick
has shown that the violence of raiding and warfare and the powerlessness
of "traditional" political and spiritual leadership and structures in the face
of drought and disease paved the way for rapid Christianization among the
inhabitants of the Cuvelai floodplain of Namibia.[23]

Yet the growth of education in the colonies had implications for the
colonial project. Until the early twentieth century, in most cases, colonial
government abandoned the task of educating the population to the Christian
Missions. In the colony of Lagos, the growth of education "was also ham-
pered by a second factor—the attitude of the Lagos Government, which had
more or less, abandoned the task of educating the population to the Christian Missions. Even after the 1882 Ordinance and the appointment of an
inspector of Schools, considerable apathy persisted in the administration and
supervision of schools."[24] As late as 1898, the missionaries who controlled
secondary education in Lagos "fought hard to retain this control by opposing
Government sponsorship of secondary education just as they had opposed
the Education Ordinance of 1882."[25]

The view of missionary educators and the colonial government differed
considerably, especially regarding religious education. The Education Code
promulgated in 1882 was essentially a regulatory ordinance that aimed
to provide machinery for the disbursement of government aid to schools
and for the regulation of standards and methods in such schools. For the
primary schools, the Code merely states that the "subjects of teaching

shall be reading and writing in English, with Arithmetic, and with plain needlework to females. English Grammar, History, and Geography, may also be taught or not at the option of the teacher."[26] An important step was taken towards the secularization of schools by the provisions (reported in the *Observer*, July 20, 1882) that "direct religious teaching" should not be given 'in Government schools' and that no child should:

> Receive religious instruction to which his parents or guardians object or be present whilst such religious instruction is given . . . [but] every minister of religion, or person appointed by him, shall have, at appointed time, free access to Government schools for imparting religious instruction to children of his own religious denomination.[27]

While Christianity was not the only external influence on African societies from the nineteenth century, its extraordinary application and exploitation of African's need for social services such as education and health care ensured the missionary engagement with African societies was unique in terms of its attractiveness. The interconnectedness of these two dominant influences were often seen in their broader context and from diverse perspectives by local peoples, hence the selective appropriation of these competing influences on the part of the African population.

CONFLICTS AND COMPROMISE: A NIGERIAN PERSPECTIVE

The early periods of the twentieth century witnessed fundamental changes in the scale and nature of the interaction between Christian missions, colonial authorities, and Nigerian peoples. Both of these European institutions—Christianity and colonialism—were important in the process of new social and political formations. This phenomenon, witnessed throughout sub-Saharan African, foreshadowed the birth of new identities as much as crisis as the contestations for the soul and the body of the African population intensified between missions and colonial powers. While the impacts of these interactions, within the larger nexus of Western hegemonic influences, were turbulent, yet, African societies were not disintegrating in the wake of these influences. But how to transform African life and resolve conflict between Christian converts and non-converts preoccupied Christian missions and colonial officials who sought to settle these conflicts as best as they could.

In Nigeria, such challenges were witnessed in the areas of marriage and inheritance rights, cultural practices, community life, and social obligations. Some examples of these conflicts and compromise, as they occurred in Nigeria, will suffice. In a memorandum to the Honorable Chief Secretary of colonial Nigeria, in February 25, 1925, Donald Kingdom, Attorney-General of colonial Nigeria noted the inevitable conflict "between Christian and pagan customs when Christianity is first introduced into a pagan area." The question, he noted was "what is the attitude of the administration towards the problems that arise from such conflicts?"[28] This memo was the result of a meeting with the Bishop of Lagos whom he noted was "fully alive to the danger of undermining the influence of native authorities, if those over whom they should rightly exercise jurisdiction can easily avoid their obligation by professing to embrace Christianity. But at the same time a case such as that quoted must inevitably give cause for protest."[29]

The difficulties expressed in this memo arose from a specific case, which happened at Oban Aiyobaju in Oshogbo, as the Bishop explained it. Joshua Fasipe (male, aged 15) and Comfort Ayo (female, aged 8) are the children of the late Nichodemus Mabayoje by his wife Ruth Oyeleye. After the death of her husband, Ruth married again in church and the second husband paid the dowry to the first husband's (pagan) family. When the issue of the custody of the children from the previous marriage arose, the District Officer, Osogbo, ruled in court that the children must be returned to the pagan relations of the first husband, though they and their mother desire that they should continue to live with the mother and attend church and school.[30]

As this case indicates, the colonial government understood the importance of supporting missionary effort as part of the overall civilizing mission, but its ambivalent attitude is also a reflection of the attempt to retain the good will of the indigenous authorities under the British Indirect Rule system. The case also clearly shows that African converts lived in both worlds. Christianity offered opportunity to enter into the white world and to the Western way of life. At the same time, retaining aspects of African culture was valued because it offered full integration into their African world. How to balance these competing ideologies often left the African in a dilemma and generated identity conflict that reflected in the larger society.

Well into the 1950s, the question of African identity within Nigerian society, as in other colonized territories, remained contested as the African population struggled to create a niche for themselves within the colonial society. Such contestations were reflected in the struggle between African converts and non-converts in issues of marriage, inheritance, and child custody. The District Officer, Agwu wrote to the Resident, Onitsha in the Eastern Region of Nigeria Province on April 4, 1925 regarding the custody of children involving widows. According to the District Officers in the Onitsha, Owerri, and Calabar Provinces, the first husband's heir is entitled to the custody of the children; whether marriage was conducted under native customs or under the marriage Ordinance introduced by the British. Throughout the colonial period, this problem remained evident but the rhetoric clearly shows that neither colonial officials nor missionary had a clear legal strategy to resolve these contestations: "I doubt whether in any of these provinces the first husband's heir would place obstacle in the way of such children continuing as Christians or attending Christian churches or schools," a district officer wrote. "In fact parental authority in these areas is so small that the children having once embraced Christian ideas of Church and school would probably ignore any opposition to their continuing in such way of life. In the rare events of the heir attempting to enforce his or his families' wishes in opposition I feel sure that any native court to which the children appealed would advise the family to cease from such opposition."[31] Indeed, the Bishop of Lagos "cautioned and recognized the necessity of "going slow" and avoiding any upheaval of native institutions.[32]

Indeed some colonial officials recognized that African converts lived in both worlds. "The majority of marriages in Christian churches are not full Christian marriages, but merely a short service, with dowry paid as in native custom," the colonial Resident for Calabar wrote in 1925. A large number of converted natives he noted "do not wish the full Christian service, as it is too binding for their natures—if the parties to the marriage feel they cannot accept the limitations of a Christian marriage, they must reap the disadvantages in Native Customs of an elastic marriage,"[33] he concluded. The ambiguity of these expressed and imposed identities—in which the African population, missions, and European administrators protected to certain degrees, both worlds, reflected on European attitudes towards child custody, marriage, and inheritance. On the broad question of custody involving a Christian woman and non-Christian kins, the colonial officials did not interfere with native law and customs, but instructed district officers to "endeavor to arrange a compromise" when the issue is the custody of the children, that the children should remain with their mother; provided that, in the case of female children, dowry on marriage was paid to the family of the deceased father and not to the mother, and in the case of boys, compensation was paid by the mother to the deceased father's family for loss of services."[34]

Both the missionary and the civilizing mission of colonialism were imbued with the values and attitudes that reflected their understanding of Christianity and their view of African religions and cultures. For many missionaries, part of the Christianization and civilization effort included assimilation of Euro-American culture and the shedding of African beliefs and cultures. The arrogant belief in the superiority of European culture provided a lens through which many missionaries interpreted their experiences in Nigeria, as elsewhere. On their part, some Africans responded by going back to their roots through the formation of African-centered churches—a process and means through which they expressed their African identity and incorporated African elements to Christian religious worship to the discomfort of many European missionaries and some African converts. The Africanization of Christianity was also a response to several issues associated with the attack on African identity and the racist ideologies of mainline churches.

Although this was a process that has been going on for centuries in Egypt and Ethiopia, African initiated churches became an important force in colonial Nigeria from the 1920s onwards. African Initiated Churches (AICs) arose for clearly peculiar reasons, including the socio-economic, political, and religious factors of colonial Africa.[35] These movements became an important part of African expressions as reflected in Ethiopianism in West Africa, the Bwiti in Gabon and the *Eglise de deu Nos Ancestres* in south Zaire.[36] For many African converts to Christianity, the AICs were an African reaction against the impositions of Western culture and an attempt to adapt Christianity to the local traditions.[37] Mudimbe's *Between Tides*, captures the ambiguous project of Africanizing Christianity.

> The Church submits too. That's what Vatican II was all about. A tactical revision. The world was slipping away. The Church led us by a different path to unfamiliar nourishment. The liturgy is translated into African languages, disclosing the secret of divine communications. The sense of magic dissipates. And the mystery. Christ, our supreme strength, revealed in stark unceremonious words, will soon bore us and then disgust us. Unless the revision cancels itself by fully embracing African modes of thought.[38]

In other words:

> A complete break with occidental Christianity in favor of the seasonal rhythms and esoteric observances of Bantu witch doctors. The rites of hunting and healing, fishing and building would be reborn then, perhaps transformed. Otherwise the present modifications will deaden the magical powers that Africans responded to. Will platitudinize the message. My colleagues worry about it. They fret and toil so that Christianity will not be reduced to the familiar taste of sweet-potatoes-beans. But do they know that taste?[39]

It is not clear, according to Ralph Dumain "whether this represents a stratagem of the imperialist Church or a victory for Africa."[40] But the issues that led to the schism which started in the nineteenth century metamorphosed in other forms during the colonial period. The underlying factors of African identity, the issue of faith and tradition, leadership structures and principles, and doctrinal dogmatism doctrines, led to large-scale emergence of AICs. During much of the African contact with Europe, racism and exploitation of African was accepted by a large portion of European population.

Although missionaries did not embark on colonial exploitation for purely economic reasons, their paternalism did colonize Africans on matters of faith, methods of evangelism, and education. African response in the light of the degradation of African culture led to the emergence of syncretism movements, by individuals brought up within the mainline missions, whose vision "differed with the missionaries, and so became leaders of the African masses who found a better placed allegiance."[41] AICs employed African institutions and cultural expression, including African music, songs, and liturgy and defied "formal theological education in homiletics and unintimidated by the threat of heresy." Godfrey Ngumi notes that "The personal testimonies that characterize the worship ceremonies have an African aspect related to communality of guilt and forgiveness, and are both cathartic and pastoral. The individual feels forgiven by the whole cosmos, including God, the community, and the ancestors. This is based on the African concept of sin, guilt, and affliction—that no one's sin results in individual guilt. Church is a place to feel at home and wholly welcome."[42]

In colonial Nigeria, such movements emerged as spirituous movements, including the Christ Army Church (CAC), Samuel Spiritual Church, Spiritual Holiness, and Pentecostal Assembly.[43] Like many such African Initiated Churches, CAC practiced faith healing and guidance of the Spirit in addition to African ritual practices such as sacrifice and divination."[44] In a letter to the Senior District Officer, Opobo, U. U. Usen described the CAC as a church that engages in divination "in the same way as IDIONG members." CAC orders their adherents, he wrote to "sacrifice goats, fowls, eggs etc, and the village paths witness sacrifices prescribed by a set of Christian elements. . . . 'How many Gods are there?" he asked?[45] By this letter, Mr. Usen was calling on the colonial authority to stop what he believed was a combination of African 'pagan rituals' with Christian worship. One can interpret this duality as part of the dilemma faced by Africans as they immersed themselves in a new religion but one which did not always provide answers to all life's spiritual problems.

The attempts to wipe out native religious practices and related cultures were backfiring on the Christian missions in the 1960s.[46] A return to native religion in Africa has put Christianity in "serious trouble" a Unitarian minister, Reverend Jack Mendelsohn, told a New York congregation in September 1960.[47] Reverend Mendelsohn, who had returned from an eight African countries tour noted that "From high ranking officials to native villager Christianity is identified with colonialism."[48] Christianity refused to deal realistically with African social and cultural practices such as polygamy and was reluctant to "transfer church leadership to trained Africans" Missionaries tolerated racial discrimination and were indifferent towards African nationalism.[49] B. A. Oji, general president of the Natural Religion of Africa Mission in Aba, Eastern Nigeria had told Rev. Mendelsohn that "goodwill to men was meaningless because Christianity 'has proved itself to be a quarrelsome religion, each denomination attacking the other.'"[50] Consequently, more Africans turned back to forms of African-centered churches, forcing some missionary to adopt policies of constructive engagement.

Conflicts between African converts and non-converts extended to cultural practices rooted in earlier European contact during the Atlantic slave trade. Pre-colonial societies in Nigeria were influenced by several forces beginning with the Portuguese contact in the fifteenth century and the subsequent development of the slave trade. The slave trade led to the formation of new social systems, a mixture of peoples and cultures, and the emergence of a trading/merchant class who, in the process of protecting their trading interest, began to form new secret societies, such as the *Ekpe* and *Okonko* societies. As contractual relations became increasingly more important than kinship, new forms of identity, as an ongoing process in the expanding mercantile economy, emerged. These societies remained important as new and very important elements were introduced with the transition from slavery to commodity trade—the missionary expansion in the late nineteenth century and colonization.

In Eastern region of Nigeria, the contestation between indigenous culture, identity, and political authority was evident in the crisis between several oracular priests and secret societies, such as the *Okonko* society on the one hand, and between missionaries, African converts, and colonial authority, on the other. The ethnographic literature describes *Okonko* as a secret society whose members are sworn not to disclose the secrets of the society "excepting at the formation of a Branch Society in some other countries for the purpose of money making."[51] From the era of the slave trade, *Okonko* houses proliferated throughout the interior of Igboland in the Umuahia, Ngwa, Ohuhu, and Nkwerre regions. Understanding the dynamics of power and identity in Southeastern Nigeria, for example requires an important analytical shift, away from imposed Eurocentric categories and toward locally situated basis of power, identity and authority. The *Ekpe* secret society, like its *Okonko* counterpart in the Bight of Biafra hinterland "aided in the creation of a Cross River trading network by facilitating trade along and away from the river." [52] with its strict hierarchies and important religious and judicial roles. Membership in *Ekpe* helped cement relationships of trust and offered opportunity for commercial credit in the Cross trade network.[53] *Okonko* played some religious and judicial roles, but it also provided entertainment at communal festivals.

With the elimination of the slave trade, the emergence of the missionaries, and colonial authorities, *Okonko* slowly lost its important judicopolitical and commercial role in the region. At the same time, African converts to Christianity were attempting to eliminate the powers of these traditional institutions. Perhaps this was because Christian converts were in the struggle for power and relevance in a rapidly transforming society, where the old political elite, still to the displeasure of many Christians, were part of the new political dispensation under the Native Authority system of colonial administration.

The 1950s witnessed the intensification of this rivalry between *Okonko* members, members of the Faith Tabernacle Gospel, and the Faith Tabernacle Congregation. In March 1951, for example, the Eastern Regional Public Relations Office sent out a press release titled: "Religious Sects Class in Owerri Province." The press release stated that 100 arrests have been made in a clash between adherents of the Faith Tabernacle Mission and members of the *Okonko* Secret Society. *Okonko* members were enraged. During the clashes, several churches of the Faith Tabernacle Mission and houses belonging to members of the mission were destroyed. In retaliation, the Faith Tabernacle Mission members burnt several *Okonko* meeting houses.[54] The clash occurred after it was alleged that the secrets of the Okonko society were divulged to certain women by a pastor of the Faith Tabernacle Mission. In a letter to the Secretary of the Eastern Provinces, the colonial resident for Owerri Province noted that "the effects of the statement that the secrets had been shown was very widespread and reached as far as Mbawsi, in Aba Division and Uzuakoli in the Bende Division."[55] The secrets had never been known to non-members, an *Okonko* spokesman, Johnson Onwukamuche told an assistant superintendent of Police at a meeting with *Okonko* members. If such an incident occurred, the person was forced to become a member, and if women learnt the secret "they would be killed."[56] *Okonko* members had demanded that such women should be "either hanged or banished from Nigeria.

The responses of *Okonko members* and African resistance to colonial and missionary discourse must be understood as oppositional as much as a protectionist acts. Indeed, what are African in local resistance to the dominant ideology are not simply the people, but the ways in which African resistance to the dominant ideology was framed and contextualized as a part and process of living.

With the gradual elimination of traditional authority in the early years of the twentieth century, new coverts and Western educated elite had slowly established new identities that continued to challenge the indigenous elite. At the same time members of the old elite were resisting this transformation through the control of marriage, inheritance, and traditional judicial authority. It is clear from the accounts of missionaries, converts, and colonial officials that traditional structures were in decay but their ambivalent attitude in dealing with them also reflected the tenacity of the old order to give way to new. They seemed to have held on. One can, therefore, note the role which old traditions have played in building new identities despite the overwhelming portrayal of Christianity and colonialism as the most important forces of change in African in the twentieth century.

CONCLUSION

The forces of Christianity and colonialism were problematic for a colonized societies. Although the new contacts had an uneven impact, they nevertheless activated new discourses on issues of identity. The formation of new identities was evidently critical to the construction of new societies as envisioned by Europeans, as much as African response in the colonial context. The representation of African identity in colonial Nigeria, as was the case in other colonized territories in Africa, unconsciously-replayed the images embedded in European sub-consciousness. Stereotype of Africa and Africans as reflected in missionary and colonial writings points to the more crucial psychic division that positions black and white cultures in polarities of worth and value.

An examination of the dialogue between Africans and Europeans in the colonial context portrays them as an interpretations of African culture as inferior and European culture as superior. A major obstacle emerged from the imperialist informed distinction between European cultures, based upon modernity, and the attempt to replicate them in African Societies. In the mission cum colonial context, major changes where not achieved by dominance alone but often by the use of material resources, such as education, and non-material resources such as values, law, ideologies, to influence local perceptions and desires to convert. Yet understanding colonial and missionary encounter as hegemonic—dominance—in which African identities were transformed only from without, despite the exertion of a dominating influence, is problematic. African attitude towards Westernization were therefore also achieved through a coincidence of interests, and willingness on the part of African societies to accept the dominant values of the West.

Yet, many Africans lived in a dual world in which the new structures combined with the old forms of ideology. At the political and social levels, the new emerging African elite and converts constituted a treat to the traditional elite, whose power diminished as a result of the corroding influence of Christianity and colonialism. Such conflicts exacerbated as African converts attempted to challenge so-called "pagan" practices or impose their power on local societies.

Overall, the dialogues between European missionaries and African peoples on the one hand and between missionaries and imperial officials on the other, provide a historical anthropology of two cultures attempting to understand, contend with, and accommodate each other. This interaction occurred within a context in which African cultures were confronted by an externally imposed/dominant/hegemonic cultures, but one in which such hegemonic impositions were often influenced by African initiatives. As such, these hegemonic attempts can also be broadly seen as negotiations between African identity and the imposed identity of Christian and colonial forces. But it was one also in which African groups were trying to understand and re-evaluate themselves from within, a process in which both missionary and colonial forces responded in very ambivalent ways.

Indeed, the formation of identity remains a potentially powerful conceptual framework for analyzing the outcome of African-European interactions in the colonial context. Yet, its fluidity in the colonial and missionary context, calls for a reassessment of African reactions and the problematics of essentializing African responses. Understanding African responses to Western influences from the colonial period should, therefore, interrogate the histories, cultures, and other interlocking variables about African societies. Such an analytical framework will deemphasize the privileging of European factors over the responses and dynamics of their African hosts at the political, social, and cultural levels. Indeed, the idea about African identity needs to be situated squarely within African responses to the imperialist views of Christianity and colonialism and "filtered out" from the dominant Eurocentric ideas about Africans and their identity in the contemporary era.

Chapter Eight

West Indian Church in West Africa: The Pongas Mission among the Susus and Its Portrayal of Blackness, 1851–1935

Waibinte Wariboko

INTRODUCTION

European and American Missions desirous to Christianize and civilize the benighted populations of West Africa, enlisted many West Indians of African ancestry in the nineteenth and early twentieth centuries. Some of these, among others, were: the National Baptist Convention of America in Liberia; the Church Missionary Society Niger Mission in Southern Nigeria; the Baptist Mission in Cameroon; the Presbyterian Mission to Calabar in Southeastern Nigeria; and the Basel Mission to Akropong in the former Gold Coast—now Ghana.[1] For West Indians of African ancestry in the evolving New World diaspora, the desire and preparedness to participate in the European and American civilizing missions was prompted, among other reasons, by a sense of racial empathy and affinity, including humanitarianism. Evangelizing West Africa was also perceived as a sociopolitical project intended to redeem the image of the motherland as a "dark" and "barbarous" continent. With education and conversion to Christianity, black scholars, publicists and activists in the New World—for example, W. E. Blyden, Albert Thorne, Alexander Crummel, Henry Turner, Sylvester Williams and Marcus Garvey—believed that the motherland and its inhabitants could gain the respect of the civilized world. Earning the respect of the civilized world, they also believed, would enhance the overall image of black people in the New World diaspora. In other words, for these New World black scholars, publicists and activists, the respect and recognition of black personhood could not be dissociated from the image of Africa— hence they campaigned vigorously and relentlessly for the cultural regeneration of the continent through the efforts of its sons and daughters in the

New World.[2]"Blacks [in the New World] felt compelled," as E. P. Skinner puts it, "to rehabilitate Africa and African peoples in their own eyes and in the eyes of the world so that by extension both they and that continent would be saved."[3]

The overall aim of this essay is to critically assess how Caribbean black missionaries pursued the above objectives under the auspices of "The Mission from the Sons and Daughters of Africa in the Diaspora to Africa"—another name for the Pongas Mission. This evaluation is critically necessary for two reasons. In 1933 L. E. P. Erith, a member of the Church of England in Jamaica and an ardent supporter of the outreach program to West Africa, made the following comments about the Pongas Mission.

> The history of the [Pongas] Mission illustrates the danger of acting in a hurry, of letting zeal dominate caution, without taking time to consider conditions in the proposed mission field and to organize against obstacles. For years the Mission has languished for lack of proper organization, especially Episcopal direction.[4]

Despite this kind of biting criticism, however, there is to date no adequate discussion in the existing published materials[5] of the difficulties and challenges encountered by the Mission, including the factors responsible for its inability to achieve its goals and objectives, particularly the establishment of a West Indian Church in West Africa.

In addition to filling this yawning gap, this paper intends to argue that, as an evangelical project designed to implant the "West Indian Church" in West Africa, the Pongas Mission fell short of achieving its target because it could neither raise nor foster a self-propagating, self-supporting, and self-governing church in West Africa. These, for example, were the comments of the missionary bishop of Gambia in 1949.

> The old Pongas Mission did not succeed in establishing a truly indigenous church; the opportunity was there but the Church in the West Indies was unable to send sufficient money or men to grasp it.[6]

The Church Missionary Society under Henry Venn as secretary, including the Church of England by extension, had endorsed this "three-self formula"—otherwise called "the euthanasia of the Mission"[7]—as the basis for encouraging Africans to develop their own church during the nineteenth century. In the United States this mission principle was introduced and made popular by Rufus Anderson, a Congregationalist from Boston.[8]

The paper also argues that, as a sociopolitical project, the Pongas Mission undermined blackness and the black personhood wittingly or unwittingly in the Caribbean. In order to evoke and sustain the interest of philanthropists, whose financial contributions sustained the missionaries, distorted and sensationalized accounts of West Africa's indigenous socio-cultural and religious heritage that emphasized the myth of African savagery were bandied through the Caribbean media- especially the *Jamaica Times*. Here is one example published in 1932 by the *Jamaica Diocesan Magazine*–an official magazine of the Church of England in Jamaica.

> A plaintive wail, and lo! Another little life has been launched into this world. But alas! What is this? No smuggling of the little child into nice warm clothing, but instead something stands ready with a sharp razor! Not indeed to end the infant's life by violence but to do something which often results in death all the same. For that tender little body just born *is shaved all over and then the little one is placed for hours in cold water to shiver and to wail!* Sometimes pneumonia follows this terrible exposure and the frail little life is ended almost as soon as it has begun.

> Where is it that such a barbarous thing can be, you ask? It is happening today in West Africa. . . . *Remember every penny you collect . . . will ensure some precious babe a better chance to live,* a better opportunity to learn of God, and best of all to know the love of the Lord Jesus for every little child.[9] [my emphasis]

To discuss these related evangelical and sociopolitical issues and their implications for perceiving blackness in the Caribbean, including the implantation of the West Indian Church among the Susus of West Africa, the rest of the paper will be divided into four parts: The Pongas Mission: its conception and birth, 1851–1855; Barbados and the construction of the Pongas Mission before formal colonialism in West Africa, 1855–1896; Jamaica and the Pongas Mission during Colonialism, 1896–1935; and the impact of the Mission.

THE PONGAS MISSION: ITS CONCEPTION AND BIRTH, 1851–1855

A number of interrelated remote and immediate factors led to the conception and birth of the Pongas Mission between 1851 and 1855. Persons of African decent in Barbados, inspired and motivated by the mutually reinforcing factors of Africa consciousness, the ideal of Pan-African unity, including humanitarianism, founded the Fatherland Union Society and the Colonization Society "for assisting in the suppression of the slave trade, and the introduction of civilization into Africa"[10] in 1847–the year Liberia became a sovereign state in West Africa. In 1851, the year the Society for the Propagation of the Gospel [SPG] celebrated its third jubilee, the Church in the West Indies commemorated this auspicious landmark event in the history of Christianity by deciding to inaugurate a mission to Africa.[11] As a result of this resolve, the West Indian Church Association was formed in June 1851 to put in place the necessary mechanism for sending a mission from "the Church of the West Indies to Western Africa."[12] This Association, a large body by all standards, also constituted the Mission Board; and its membership consisted of persons of African descent who belonged to the Fatherland Union Society, including Europeans, headed by Reverend R. Rawle—the man who later became the principal of Codrington College where the missionaries for the Pongas Mission were trained.

The West Indian Mission, as distinct and different from those initiated and sponsored by European and American organizations, was perceived from the very outset as a mission to be manned and funded by the Anglican Communions or Churches in the English-speaking Caribbean–Jamaica, Trinidad and Tobago, Antigua, and Guyana. In the words of Rawle:

> Let it be well understood that it is to be a West Indian work in respect of origin, motive, and machinery; whatever help may be obtained from other quarters, the main labour and cost will rest with the colonial branch of our Church [The Church of England]. It must be the joint act of all our congregations there; it must be planned and appointed by the West Indian Bishops and carried on [independently of Societies in England] on a system and by instruments on which they shall agree.[13]

The West Indian Church, as the above excerpt suggests, generally perceived the Caribbean as a "mission frontier;" and, under the auspices of its bishops, for example, Enos Nuttall of the Church of England in Jamaica,[14] it often expressed its preparedness to assist the mother country, Britain, in carrying the torch of civilization and Christianity to West Africa. These bishops also endorsed the idea of using the peoples of African descent for the regeneration of their ancestral homeland, because they believed that black West Indians would be more resistant to the abiding ailments associated with the West African environment than Europeans.

As it will be shown later, despite the popular sentiment that this was an endeavor from the sons and daughters of Africa in the diaspora to

Africa, actually, Europeans initially led the Pongas Mission between 1855 and 1863. Under its European managers, recruits of African descent such as John Duport and Moses Morris were meant to play subordinate roles in the Pongas Mission. In that regard the Pongas Mission was not different from the 1846 mission sponsored by the Church of Scotland to Old Calabar, Southern Nigeria. The Afro-Jamaicans who accompanied Hope Waddell on that mission were recruited on the reasoning that: "[The European leaders of the Mission] see plainly that the fittest men for the evangelization of Africa are the native Christians of the West Indies, headed, in the first instance at least, by Europeans inured to the tropics."[15] In the words of N. Titus the Pongas Mission between 1855 and 1863 was dominated and led by "West Indian [gentlemen] of English descent."[16] These comments beg for one question. In terms of its leadership and personnel before 1863 how truly was this mission from the sons and daughters of Africa in the diaspora to Africa?

In 1848 the Church Missionary Society (CMS) folded up its proselytizing activities in Jamaica, Trinidad, and Demerara due in part to financial difficulties.[17] Aubrey George Spencer [1843–1854], the second bishop of Jamaica, later appealed, but without success, for the CMS to renew its work in the Caribbean generally, and Jamaica in particular.[18] Before leaving Jamaica, however, the CMS had expressed "the hope that among the converts in the West Indies many would be found who would be willing to go to West Africa as teachers [and evangelists]."[19] Seen from this standpoint the Pongas Mission represented, like the CMS Niger Mission in Southern Nigeria that utilized black West Indians from 1895 to 1925, a fulfillment of that hope expressed in 1848.

Another critical point needs to be made in relation to the sentiment expressed by Rawle. Although the Pongas Mission was presented as "a West Indian work" to be supported jointly by the Anglican Communions in all the English-speaking Caribbean Islands, it "was regarded," according to Ellis, "as a Barbados movement with Codrington College as its bases of operation and Mr. Rawle as its leader."[20] This begs for two related questions. How truly committed initially were the other islands in supporting the project financially? How did the lack of financial support affect the capacity of the Mission to pursue its mandate in West Africa? It has been said, for example, that the Church in Jamaica "looked on rather coldly and unsympathetically"[21] at the beginning; and only started to support the Mission financially from 1861–six years after the first set of missionaries had departed Barbados for West Africa. In 1870, as a result of the disestablishment of the Church of England in Jamaica, the finances of the Church fell drastically and Jamaica discontinued its contribution to the Pongas Mission until 1896.[22] This left Barbados, among the Anglican Communions in the English-speaking Caribbean islands, to finance the initial cost of preparing and educating the pioneer missionaries recruited for the Pongas Mission.

THE RECRUITMENT AND PREPARATION OF MISSIONARIES FOR THE PONGAS MISSION

On September 1851, three months after the formation of the West Indian Church Association, Archdeacon Brathwaite of St. Kitts recommended two candidates of African descent–Moses Morris and John Duport—for training in the Codrington College under the auspices of Rawle as principal. The subjects taught at the College, which consisted of Bible Knowledge, History, Geography, Grammar and Music, lasted from November 1851 to June 1855. According to one critic of the program:

> There was no indication . . . as to the duration of the course before the candidates were admitted for training and considered ready for the mission field. This means that the decision lay entirely in the hands of the Principal of the College. Equally, it means that one cannot say, with any degree of certainty, that the candidates had completed their training. Quite apart from all this, there seems not to have been any reports as to their progress.[23]

Judged by the number, quality and variety of theoretical and practical courses—for example, Book Keeping with special emphasis on the keeping of Church Accounts, basic practical courses in carpentering, including elementary medicine—given to trainee missionaries intended for Africa at the Church Missionary Society's Training College at Islington in England,[24] it could be argued that the program at the Codrington College was defective in many ways despite its protracted duration. Some of the difficulties, as I will be arguing later, that were encountered in the mission fields by the missionaries of the Pongas Mission were directly traceable to the inadequacies in their preparation. In addition to the specific shortcomings in the Codrington study program, Waddell has made the following general comments about West Indian Churches and their capacity to prepare missionaries for overseas mission work.

> The missionary service, like every other, needs training in its practical working, as well as mental preparation; classes need experience as well as individuals; and our coloured West Indian Churches were in that respect very deficient. The British Churches have now had sixty

or seventy years disciplinary practice in the mission work, and are the better at it; and we must not expect from the raw recruits of our Jamaican mission churches the conduct of veterans.[25]

Codrington College, like the one at Islington, emphasized the nineteenth-century mission ideology that influenced and underpinned proselytizing in Africa. Waddell has aptly summarized that principle: "[You] need never attempt to propagate the Gospel by putting new wine into old bottles, building the temple of God on heathen foundations, or going halves with the devil to win him over to our side."[26] Put differently, all missionaries in the nineteenth century, including those under review, were trained to believe that what was Christian could not abide with what was African. Black West Indian missionaries of the Pongas Mission, like those under the auspices of the CMS Niger Mission in Southern Nigeria, were determined to impose European church-culture on West African societies. The concept of church-culture was predicated, according to J. Kirby, on the notion that " . . . a new social order, a new political economy and a new culture must accompany the change to a new moral order. Proper European civilization was Christianity, and the only way to bring about conversion was to establish this cultural framework."[27] This ideology influenced and reinforced the way the Mission perceived, discussed and portrayed Africa and its blackness to the sons and daughters of Africa in the Caribbean.

BARBADOS AND THE CONSTRUCTION OF THE PONGAS MISSION BEFORE FORMAL COLONIALISM IN WEST AFRICA, 1855–1895

Officials of the colonial state, as it evolved in West Africa, generally perceived and portrayed all missionary organizations as essential partners in the onerous task of civilizing Africans. Vice-Consul Harry Johnston, for example, portrayed that perception to the British Foreign Office while discussing the activities of the CMS Niger Mission in the Oil Rivers Protectorate of Southern Nigeria in 1888: "We [Britain] must be content to let missionaries dogmatize and indoctrinate, without let or hindrance, on account of the education and civilization which they literally introduce."[28] On the other hand missionary organizations, as the following excerpt from Bishop S. A. Crowther of the Niger Mission indicates, were prepared and willing to collaborate with the colonial state for one principal reason: to secure protection against hostile African potentates who perceived them as cultural invaders of society.

Since the treaties for the abolition of the slave trade and the introduction of legitimate commerce were made with the kings and chiefs in the
Bights of Benin and Biafra, Old and New Calabar Rivers, Cameroons,
Bonny, Brass have become easily accessible to Christian missionaries,
and a visit now and then from the Consul in a gunboat has served to
keep the people quiet from molesting the missionaries and their establishments.[29]

The history of the Pongas Mission illustrates that, in the decades leading
up to the foundation of the colonial state among the Susu of West Africa,
the missionaries had to put up with some of the difficulties and challenges
described by Crowther in 1876.

In July 1855 the pioneering team of Morris and Duport led by Reverend
James Hamble Leacock, a West Indian gentleman of English descent left Barbados for West Africa. After a brief stay in England, they eventually arrived
in Freetown, Sierra Leone, in December 1855. With the initial support and
advice of their host in West Africa, the Bishop of Sierra Leone, negotiations
began with Tintima—one of the Susu-speaking chiefdoms located about one
hundred and fifteen miles to the north west of Sierra Leone—in order to
secure a site for the construction of the proposed mission. In terms of sociopolitical organization and settlement pattern the Susu lived in village communities headed by chiefs along the navigable river systems of Rio Pongo,
Dubrika, Bramaca, and Nunez. Economically, like their Fulani-speaking
neighbors in the interior, they were active participants in the internal long-distance trading activities within West Africa, including the external commerce
across the Sahara and the Atlantic. The socio-cultural effects of their participation in these long-distance trading activities were far reaching. In terms
of religion the Susu became thoroughly exposed to Islamic influences from
North Africa, although many of them still held on to the values of the indigenous heritage and cosmology. Secondly, as a result of the marriages between
Susu-speaking women and European slavers, small groups of politically and
economically powerful mulatto families, exposed to Christianity and Western
education, emerged in the coastal communities along the river systems of Rio
Pongo, Dubrika, Bramaca and Nunez before the beginning of the nineteenth
century.[30]Bearing in mind this socio-cultural background and the proximity
of the Susu settlements to Sierra Leone, Leacock felt that Tintima was an
ideal place to establish the West Indian Church in West Africa.

Discussion between the rulers of Tintima and the West Indian Mission
got off to a difficult start and eventually collapsed. Leacock, probably perceiving matters from the standpoint of Christian moral ethics, refused to offer
the customary "mouth-opening" gifts[31] to the sovereign of Tintima. Among

the Mende generally, including the Susu, it was not unusual for strangers to express loyalty through gifts to the potentates of their host communities. Such gifts, it should be noted, also readily secured the potentate's support and protection for strangers who were otherwise defenseless against the whims and caprices of hostile indigenes within the host community. Having failed to secure Tintima, Leacock approached Chief Richard Wilkinson—the son of an English man and an African woman—to donate land for the construction of the West Indian Mission in Fallangia. Wilkinson and his two sons, Charles and Lewis, were educated and Christianized by missionaries working for the Church Missionary Society in Sierra Leone. Given their social background and orientation, they readily welcomed the West Indian Mission and also provided land for the construction of the requisite infrastructural facilities: school, church and houses for the missionaries. However, Leacock died from fever before any constructions could begin. For his courage and modest achievement, he is fondly remembered in the history of the West Indian Mission to West Africa as "The martyr of the Pongas."[32]

Duport and Morris, described by the source just cited as "subordinate teachers" and "industrial helps" were ill-equipped to lead the nascent Mission. However, before a replacement—Reverend W. L. Neville—could be sent from Barbados in 1858 by the West Indian Mission Board, Duport was able to successfully supervise the construction of those facilities required for the commencement of the Mission. For reasons that are not unrelated to the training program at Codrington, he was not so successful in the administration of the Mission before the arrival of Neville. "When Leacock died," according to Titus, "the missionary [Duport] inherited practical problems attached to the administration of the mission."[33] These practical problems ranged from the management of church accounts to the administration of the Church congregation. Regarding the first problem, for example, Duport "seemed not to know" that he was required to forward the financial statements of the nascent Mission to Barbados for scrutiny. Duport, without any training in Church administration and African history, could not deal with certain socio-cultural matters satisfactorily. Some polygynous converts and supporters of the nascent Mission, including members of the politically powerful elitist mulatto families, had expressed their preparedness to be baptized. Without prior instructions on these matters, Duport referred the matter of their baptism to the Mission Board in Barbados. The Board, also unprepared for such theologically and socio-culturally controversial matters, merely referred Duport to the Bishop of Sierra Leone. But the Bishop of Sierra Leone, already overburdened with work within his own unwieldy diocese, was not able to provide the needed Episcopal advice regularly and timely. In the event Duport was left to his own inefficient administrative devices and skills before the arrival of Neville. These and other matters affected the growth of the nascent Mission in Fallangia.

Three other European missionaries—Reverend John Dean, Reverend Abel Phillips, and John Maurice—sponsored by the Society for the Propagation of the Gospel were sent to Fallangia to assist Neville with the organization and development of the nascent Mission between 1858 and 1861. But, owing to incessant ill-health, they were not usually in the mission-field; as a result, their contributions to the growth and development of the Mission were very minimal indeed. Between July and December 1861, Neville and Dean died; and in May 1862, on the advice of the SPG, Bishop Parry of Barbados appointed Abel Phillips to succeed Neville as the superintendent of the West Indian Mission. Phillips, after frequent attacks of fever, returned to Barbados at the end of 1862; and in February 1863 he finally resigned from the Mission. As a result of these circumstances, the SPG recommended to the West Indian Mission Board to appoint Duport as the superintendent for the Pongas Mission after his ordination on 24 February 1861.

The appointment of Duport as superintendent on 18 September, 1863, marked a new beginning in the West Indian Mission to West Africa for one ideological reason: after an abysmal record of performance under Europeans, who were very vulnerable to diseases associated with the tropical West African environment, the mantle of leadership was finally given to someone of African descent. With this appointment, the Mission Board increased Duport's annual stipend from two hundred to two hundred and fifty pounds. This amount, however, was less than fifty pounds when compared with the stipends of his European predecessors: Leacock, Neville, and Phillips. The foregoing narrative lends itself to one conclusion, among others: missionaries of African descent were being marginalized even in a mission ideologically construed as coming from the sons and daughters of Africa in the diaspora to Africa. It was this unacceptable hypocrisy that engendered the following critical comments from Titus: "Despite the flood of words about the mission being led by Africans, the actual organization of it shows that European leadership had always been intended. Such Africans as they had hoped to attract were intended for an inferior role in the Mission."[34]

FROM A "SUBORDINATE TEACHER" TO MISSION SUPERINTENDENT: THE ACTIVITIES AND ACCOMPLISHMENTS OF DUPORT

It may be recalled that the pioneer mission-station at Fallangia was established in 1855. Thereafter, it took about six years before the second mission-station was established at Domingia in 1861. The slow expansion rate of the Mission could be attributed to many factors, including the loss of its European staff in quick succession and the inability of the missionaries, particularly the European missionaries, to proselytize in the Susu language. Unlike the CMS Niger Mission in Southern Nigeria,[35] the West Indian Mission between 1855 and 1861 did not insist on the acquisition of the Susu language by its missionaries before embarking on the difficult task of proselytizing in the mission fields. Again, unlike the CMS Niger Mission, the acquisition and mastery of the indigenous language was neither a requirement nor a precondition for the promotion of missionaries in the West Indian Mission. Duport, like the European superintendents before him, had no language training; and there was no pressure or incentive for them to acquire the Susu language. However, through diligence, hard work and determination, including the realization that effective proselytizing and church expansion could not be achieved rapidly without acquiring the local language, Duport learnt and acquired mastery of the Susu language between 1855 and 1860. Having sufficiently mastered the language, he successfully translated the *Prayer Book* into Susu and also prepared a Susu *Primer* for the schools at Fallangia and Domingia. This pioneering work provided the foundation and inspiration for Douglin, one of the black West Indians working under his superintendence, to "compile a Susu reading book with native folklore and proverbs,"[36] including translating the *New Testament* into Susu. With these literary accomplishments, Duport began a program of instruction for teachers and catechists with a view to expanding the Mission. They were taught English, History, Church History, Grammar, Geography and Arithmetic twice a week. Some of the beneficiaries of this program, Thomas Morgan and his sister Sarah Morgan, for example, were subsequently employed at different times to teach in the schools established by the West Indian Mission. Through the combined activities of these persons and the West Indian missionaries, according to McEwen, "there was expansion northwards and southwards" to incorporate Boke in the Nunez, Conakry, and a group of islets just off the coast of Conakry called Isles de Los.[37]There is, however, no record at present to indicate the population of the evolving Christian community in these areas in the mid-nineteenth century. Titus has given an account of the pastoral work of the missionaries and the difficulties that confronted them in the process of winning converts for the mission.

> The pastoral work of the missionaries was rendered more difficult by their inability to admit their converts to the sacrament of communion. The regulations and discipline of the Church required

that such persons should be first confirmed by the Bishop. But the Bishop, under whose jurisdiction the mission was placed, failed to visit. Duport lamented this lack of Episcopal care. So that it was a source of joy when, near the middle of 1865, the Bishop visited Fallangia [and] confirmed eighty-seven candidates. He was unable to visit any other station.[38]

By 1865, the source just cited further reveals that there were only nine Christian marriages in all of the communities under the evangelical sway of Duport and his missionary colleagues—Douglin and Turpin—from the Caribbean.

Between 1868 and 1873 the West Indian Mission went through a turbulent and scandalous phase that culminated in the removal of Duport as the superintendent of the Mission. Duport, it was alleged, had lived with his fiancée for a short while before they got "regularly married by a clergyman." This was proven when his wife gave birth to a child just after five months of their marriage. Prior to this particular case of moral impropriety Duport's critics, including members of Wilkinson's family in Fallangia, had in 1857 accused him of misappropriating funds, engaging in an unlawful relationship with a young woman called Jane, over-indulging in alcohol, and participating in commercial activities at the expense of his missionary duties. As a result of these charges, some of which were unproven, the Mission Board, acting on the advice of the Bishop of Barbados, decided "That the connection of Mr. Duport with the Mission must cease." Following this development, the Mission Board appointed Reverend J. B. Williams, a missionary from Antigua working with the Sierra Leone Mission, as the interim superintendent of the Mission in 1874. William's stewardship as superintendent, which spanned from 1874 to 1896, could be described as a period of stagnation before the arrival of W. A. Burris from Jamaica. L.E.P. Erith has summarized the factors responsible for that stagnation.

[The Mission during this period] was no body's child. The great Societies [the SPG and the CMS, among others] left it to the West Indies to finance; it was extra-diocesan, depending for Episcopal ministrations on the slight help and infrequent visits which the Bishop of Sierra Leone, already overburdened with an unwieldy diocese, was able to afford; while it has been a hard struggle in the West Indies to maintain interest in a mission for which we with our slender resources have been left solely responsible.[39]

These comments could suggest, among other things, that the West Indian Association—the main sponsor of the Pongas Mission in Barbados—was no longer taking its parental responsibilities very seriously around the end of the nineteenth century. It was at this juncture that Jamaica came to the rescue of the Mission.

JAMAICA AND THE PONGAS MISSION DURING THE PERIOD OF COLONIALISM, 1896–1935

Jamaica's overall support, particularly its financial support, for the Pongas Mission between 1855 and 1896 undulated; and, as noted at the beginning, Jamaica "looked on rather coldly and unsympathetically" when the Mission was launched in 1855. This situation changed at the turn of the nineteenth century when the Church of England in Jamaica under Enos Nuttall, who was appointed the Bishop of Jamaica in 1880, expressed preparedness to resume its support for the Pongas Mission. According to P. Bryan, Nuttall was a believer in Anglo-Saxon civilization and a "keen imperialist" who "spoke of the promotion of the 'mental and moral elevation' of the African, by those who had an interest in their welfare."[40] Nuttall encouraged and prepared Jamaicans of African descent for missionary work in the Pongas Mission. In 1896, a period roughly coinciding with the inauguration of the CMS Niger Mission scheme that engaged many black West Indians for the evangelization of Southern Nigeria between 1895 and 1925,[41] Nuttall sent three black Jamaicans to the Pongas Mission as missionaries of the Church of England in Jamaica: Mr. March, Mr. W. A. Burris, and Miss Brown who later got married to Burris.[42]

Jamaica's expression of support seemed to have rejuvenated the sagging interest in the Mission. Between 1896 and 1901 Farquhar joined the Mission from Antigua; while Barbados sent D.J. McEwen to replace Duport, who died in England en route to the West Indies after his disconnection from the Mission in 1873. The Table below shows the various mission-stations where these new recruits served in West Africa at the beginning of the twentieth century. These missionaries, according to the *Jamaica Times* just cited, were assisted by six indigenous catechists and an unspecified number of lay readers in the respective mission-stations. March joined the Sierra Leone Mission on getting to West Africa. In keeping with the arrangements forged between the Mission Board in Barbados and the CMS in Sierra Leone, the Bishop of Sierra Leone at the beginning of the twentieth century, Rt. Reverend E. H. Elwin, was approached by

Table I. West Indian Missionaries in the Pongas Mission at the Beginning of the Twentieth Century

Names of Missionaries	Origin in the Caribbean	Mission- Stations
Reverend W.A. Burris and Mrs. Burris	Clarendon–Jamaica	Dominga, Fallangia and Farringia
Archdeacon Farquhar	Antigua	Conakry
Reverend D.J. Mc Ewen	Barbados	Isles de Los
Reverend J.B. Williams	Antigua	Dubrica

Source: *Jamaica Times* 30 April 1910.

Nuttall to provide the necessary Episcopal oversight and supervision of the above mission-stations. In 1908, as an expression of their renewed common interest for the Pongas Mission, "the Bishops of the West Indies decided that this Mission should be the official mission of the Province."[43] With these auspicious developments, the missionaries were reinvigorated to pursue the goals and objectives of the Pongas Mission–the socio-cultural transformation of an estimated 33,000 Susu-speaking population in the aforementioned mission-fields.[44]

For the Pongas Mission in the twentieth century, a movement conceived within the historical womb of the Church of England and informed by the Victorian values of the nineteenth century, the French colonization of Guinea-Conakry posed an ideological obstacle to the realization of its cultural mandate. According to Erith: [T]he French colonial government, if not actively hostile has always been passively unsympathetic towards missionaries of another nation."[45] The Pongas Mission, in effect, neither enjoyed the patronage nor goodwill of the French colonial administration in Guinea-Conakry as compared, for example, with the goodwill and patronage the CMS Niger Mission[46] enjoyed in the Eastern Niger Delta under British overrule. The reasons for the "unsympathetic" attitude towards the Pongas Mission might not be unconnected with the ideological issues reflected in these comments from one of the missionaries.

> The country [Guinea-Conakry] in the scramble for Africa, which took place some years ago, now came under the French flag; and this meant gradually the loss of our schools. Our greatest need is for teachers–teachers of French–so that our schools may be reopened in the Rio Pongas district. For many years past we have been faced by the gradual absorption of our school children into the Roman

Catholic schools. This can only be checked by having our own French schools.[47]

Let me put the matter more clearly. The inability of the Pongas Mission to establish French schools, as the comments indicate, did not promote one of the cardinal aims of French imperialism in West Africa: the promotion of French cultural values through the teaching of the French language. Hence the French administration was "unsympathetic."

In addition to the ideological problem French colonization of the Susu posed for the Pongas Mission, its inability to establish French schools to compete with the Roman Catholic Mission was largely due to inadequate funding. The loss of pupils to the Roman Catholic Mission also meant a decline in the Church population because, throughout West Africa during the colonial period, the school was the most potent instrument for the propagation of Christianity. By 1910, for example, there were only 600 genuine Christians among the Susu in all of the mission-stations under the evangelical sway of the West Indian Mission.[48] The cost of operating the secular and evangelical activities of the Mission, at the beginning of the twentieth century, was estimated at 1,000 pounds per annum.[49] Out of this amount about 200 pounds was expected to be raised in the mission-fields of West Africa; while the remainder was to be donated by the sponsors of the scheme in the Caribbean and the Society for the Propagation of the Gospel in England.

In order to secure funds for the provision of schools and the training of French teachers, extensive fundraising activities were often undertaken in the Caribbean. In 1908 Reverend A. H. Barrow—the rector of St. Paul's Vicarage in London—undertook fundraising campaigns in Jamaica for the Mission without much success. It should be noted that the Caribbean, as a result of the depression in the sugar industry, was going through economic difficulties. In 1910, according to the *Jamaica Times*, Reverend and Mrs. Burris went from parish to parish in Jamaica giving public lectures on aspects of the indigenous socio-religious heritage of the Susu. Here is an account of their activities at Bull-Bay, Jamaica, in July 1910: "Last month they were at Bull-Bay mission station where Mr. Burris spoke as interestingly as ever, while for fifteen minutes Mrs. Burris held the attention of the children enchained. An idol, *Nyamba*, from West Africa was exhibited." The idea of these lectures, in the words of Burris, was to "bring conviction to the minds of many as to their obligations and responsibilities *in assisting* to make disciples of the nations" [my emphasis].[50] On 10 September 1910 the same newspaper reported thus: "It is gratifying to note that Mr. Burris has through his efforts realized 130 pounds on behalf of his mission."[51]

Without the contributions from the principal sponsors in the West Indies—the dioceses of Barbados and Jamaica—the fundraising activities of individual missionaries alone could not sustain the missionaries and their operations in West Africa. Up until 1925, according to Major W. H. Plant, Burris and the other missionaries were financially supported by Barbados and Jamaica. This support, as this story about Burris indicates, was withdrawn in 1926.

> In 1926 he [Burris] was so broken down in health that he had to get long leave to return to his native land where he regained his health. To his great surprise and disappointment he has since been retired and without any previous notice. Expecting to return he left all his personal effects in Africa; these will be lost; he can neither sell them nor transfer them to Jamaica. Seeing that he has returned to settle in Jamaica I am [W. H. Plant] of the opinion that the Synod of the Church through the Missionary Committee should take some official notice of Mr. Burris' long and faithful service in the mission field and give him, if not a grant or gratuity, some form of recognition.[52]

It appears that the overall financial support for the Pongas Mission did not significantly improve despite its adoption in 1908 by the bishops of the West Indies as "the official mission of the Province." In fact, as these comments from McEwen show, the bishops could not effectively deliver on their promise.

> The supply of men from the West Indies appears to have ceased, for during the 25 years [1904–1929] service in the mission over which the present writer can look back, not a single recruit has come from the province to which the mission looks for its staff.[53]

By implication Jamaica, following the return of Burris in 1926, did not send out new missionaries to administer the mission-fields previously under his superintendence—Dominga, Fallangia and Farringa. Barbados did not also send any new missionary after McEwen.

With all of these problems—personnel shortage, the inability of the West Indian Church to sustain the Mission financially, and the "unsympathetic" attitude of the French colonial administration—the Bishop of Sierra Leone in 1933 advised the Archbishop of the West Indies to consider integration between the Pongas Mission and the diocese of Gambia with headquarters in Bathurst. Archdeacon Jullion of St. Kitts was thereafter sent out "by the province of the West Indies to examine on the spot the work of the Rio Pongos Mission." In his report Jullion concluded that, in view of the "unsympathetic" attitude of the French colonial administration, "the obvious place for the headquarters of the [Mission] was the English crown colony of Gambia."[54] With this and other recommendations, the Pongas Mission was formally amalgamated with the diocese of Gambia under the Episcopal ministration of Reverend John C.G. Daley—the vicar of Holy Cross in Yorkshire, England.[55]

CONCLUSION: THE IMPACT OF THE PONGAS MISSION

As an evangelical project the Pongas Mission fell short of achieving its cardinal objective: the establishment of a viable West Indian Church in West Africa. From its inception in 1855 through to its demise in 1935, there was no carefully conceived and articulated program to establish and foster a self-supporting, self-propagating and self-governing West Indian Church in West Africa. As early as 1861 Abel Phillips, one of the European superintendents, had warned that the Mission will not flourish without indigenous Susus being trained as clergymen and schoolmasters. The Mission Board in Barbados, perhaps handicapped by finances, ignored this warning. In January 1862, the failure of the Board to react to William's warning notwithstanding, Duport recommended two boys for missionary training; but, once more, the Board did nothing. In 1865, still undeterred, "he sought boys from local chiefs" for training as teachers and catechists; thereafter, he wrote a strongly worded letter to the Board in which he argued that "they [the indigenes] would have been better than the strangers," including West Indians of African extraction, to disseminate the gospel in West Africa.[56] In a way Duport was arguing, like Bishop S. A. Crowther in the mid-nineteenth century, that the future of Christianity in Africa was more secure in the hands of the indigenous population than black West Indians and Europeans.[57]

The attempt at persuading the Christian community in the West Indies, and the West Indian Church in particular, to raise the necessary funds for the training and development of an indigenous African agency continued, but without success, in the twentieth century. In 1933, the following appeal for assistance was made by one of the missionaries before the Pongas Mission got amalgamated with the diocese of Gambia: "More than two million souls in Lower and Upper Guinea are waiting for the Gospel, and the Roman Catholic and the Anglican are the only Christian bodies in the field. With splendid opportunities for advance, the Pongas Mission is anxious to train six of its boys who have vocations as teachers-catechists. But in order to do this it needs an additional 300 pounds."[58] This was what in 1949 led the Bishop of the diocese of Gambia to the conclusion that, although the opportunity was there to establish "a truly indigenous church" in the Upper Guinea Coast, the Church in the West Indies could not grasp it.[59]

There was, as shown in the body of the essay, a link between the ugly press publicity given to Africa and the fundraising endeavors of the West Indian Church to evangelize the continent. This was, in a sense, the continuation of a tradition that started at the beginning of the nineteenth century among European missionaries.[60] That tradition presented black communities, black families, and black bodies as the bearers of diseases, danger and violence. Blackness, associated with savagery, ignorance and crime, was thus perceived as a humiliating and problematic stigma or identity. Elizabethan Englishmen, according to W. D. Jordan "found in the idea of blackness a way of expressing some of their most ingrained values."[61] Seen through their own racialized eyes, Jordon continues, "White and black connoted purity and filthiness, virginity and sin, virtue and baseness, beauty and ugliness, beneficence and evil, God and the devil." "The Mission from the Sons and Daughters of Africa to Africa," under the auspices of the West Indian Church, perpetuated and reinforced this repressive notion of blackness in their fundraising endeavors between 1855 and 1935. According to Charles Mills: "The exposure of the misrepresentations of Eurocentrisms, not-so-innocent 'white lies' and 'white mythologies,' is part of the political project of reclaiming personhood."[62]

Seen in the context of that "political project," the Pongas Mission was counterproductive. By facilitating the process whereby things European gained ascriptive status while things African were correspondingly devalued in the evolution of a Creole culture in the Caribbean, the Pongas Mission could be described as one of the instruments that severely tarnished the black personhood and the "African Presence" in the New World during the period of colonialism. Rex Nettleford, among other scholars, has commented on the incalculable damage done to the "African Presence" and its implications for harmonious coexistence among the ethnically heterogeneous populations of the Caribbean islands.

> As far as Caribbean society itself is concerned, our current cultural fiction of multiracial harmony will become social fact only when the historic denigration of the African Presence disappears, *and disappears as a result of the demonstrated efforts of the Blacks themselves* who, after all, are principal "insiders" in the Plantation struggle of the region.[63] [my emphasis].

Nettleford has also noted elsewhere that: "while in Malaya the Malays are the accepted indigenous sons of the soil and the foundation of the Malayan image," in postcolonial Jamaica "the blacks are not regarded as the desirable symbol for national identity."[64] The rejection of blackness as part of Jamaica's national heritage is, arguably, the most lamentable net result of several decades of indiscrete reporting about Africa in the Caribbean.

Chapter Nine

Collaborative Landscape: Missions, States, and Their Subjects in the Making of Northeastern Tanzania's Terrain, 1870–1914

Michael McInneshin

INTRODUCTION

Among the prerequisites—both ideological and material—for the colonial occupations of East Africa, were the records and descriptions of the land itself. The perceptions of travelers, missionaries, and resident officials were crucial to the course of the area's history, as their reports molded colonial projects and directed imperial activity, determining where and how people of subsequent generations lived and worked. By examining European productions of knowledge about the land, and peeling back the tropes and preconceptions of the creators of this knowledge, this chapter will reveal the collaborative processes that drove the creation of Northeastern Tanzania's cultural landscape. Understanding how the African population generated and re-generated this actual terrain will provide insight into the lives of the colonial subjects and rehabilitate their historical contributions to the East African landscape.

This chapter centers on the Pangani River valley, a fairly populous region in the northeastern corner of German East Africa, currently located in the Tanga district in the country of Tanzania. The population in the valley and the highlands flanking it spoke mostly Zigua, Shambaa, and Bonde, a set of closely related languages. This area and its inhabitants became the focus of a number of external imperial interests in the last quarter of the nineteenth century, drawing an influx of missionaries, scientists, merchants, and eventually, planters and officials from the Germany.[1] Northeastern German East Africa featured a situation common to Africa during the period of high imperialism: it witnessed overlapping colonization by two European powers, a German state and English missionaries. Early German rule was under the management of the German East Africa Company (DOAG), but when the company was unable to afford the local resistance their rule engendered in the late 1880s, Berlin itself took over the colony. The missionaries hailed from the Anglican Universities' Mission to Central Africa (UMCA), and had begun their efforts in East Africa two decades prior to the partition of Africa in the mid-1880s.

This chapter will describe how the colony's British missionaries and German officials found themselves competing in their claims over the colony and its subjects, yet how they ultimately collaborated in their treatment of the territory's subjects, due to shared ideologies about the landscape. First, the largely superficial quarrels between the colonizers will be examined. Second, the analysis will show how the colonials' discourse was dominated with discussions of an "untapped" or "untouched" landscape—in both the spiritual and economic realm—and this, in part, functioned as justification for overrule. Because they were unable to see the transformations that had been wrought on the land by East Africans, Europeans were able to validate their claims on the territory. European descriptions of and preconceptions about the land also informed their approaches to determining imperial subjects' labor. Because they were incapable of seeing the East African landscape as anything but a wilderness, both mission and company wanted "their" Africans to construct a fruitful landscape, a landscape based on European models. Whether in the service of Mammon or God, East Africans faced a very similar work regime, one based on how Europeans viewed the landscape. In closing, the discussion will show how the colonizing forces ultimately shaped African lives with their shared views of the landscape.

BACKGROUND

The first successful effort to establish a European presence in the Pangani River valley came from the Anglican Universities' Mission to Central Africa, the UMCA. This institution grew out of the evangelical sermons by Bishop Selwyn of Cambridge and the exhortations from Dr. Livingstone in the late 1850s. Both men had publicly championed carrying Christianity and commerce to central Africa, and Anglican leadership at both Cambridge and Oxford established committees to tackle this goal. The UMCA grew out of these meetings. After a disastrous start in southern Africa (in the Shiré River Valley in what would become Malawi), the UMCA established a foothold in Zanzibar in 1864. From Zanzibar they expanded their operations to the East African mainland, and by 1869, founded a station at Magila in the hills rising over the Pangani River valley. After an initial period of irregular occupation, Magila became a continuously operating station from 1875, and the UMCA subsequently founded a number of substations throughout the region.

This decade head start on the Scramble for Africa led the bulk of these British missionaries to be very unhappy with the way the imperial map shook out in East Africa.[2] The missionaries argued that their presence had staked a claim to British overrule. However, the local treaties obtained by German adventurer Carl Peters in 1884, constituted enough of a claim that the Berlin Conference (1884–85) allocated the territory to the German sphere of control. Virtually all British observers deemed these documents dubious in nature, disputing the legitimacy of the chiefs who had signed with Peters. The missionaries had at that point already worked out a number of verbal agreements with village headmen in proximity of Magila, and had working relationships with some of the heirs to the Shambaa throne, whose kingdom ruled most of the highlands along the Pangani River.

The UMCA missionaries resented their own government for not staking a stronger claim to the region, and generally reviled the Germans who became their rulers and neighbors in the latter half of the 1880s. The Archdeacon of Magila declared publicly that the Germans wantonly shot, chained, beat, and raped ("forced") their new African subjects,[3] all the while expecting the English missionaries to have prepped their converts as laborers for the colonial machine.[4] In 1888, nearly all the coastal towns claimed by the Germans rose in revolt against DOAG practices and policies. During this violence—known variously as the "Arab Revolt," the "Abushiri Rebellion," or the "Mrima Uprising,"—one missionary argued that the German savagery excelled that of the rebels, their warships "throwing shells promiscuously onto the land. . . . The natives talk of Bushiri's barbarism. This is much worse."[5] Following the opening events of the Maji-Maji revolt in 1905, the partly religious crusade by the majority of German East African subjects to rid themselves of German rule and labor conditions, the current UMCA Bishop found his competitors to be: "the most detestable race in Europe—I would rather be a Turk and as unspeakable as you like than a German. Their brutal cruelty to the people in this country has for ever made me hate the sight and sound of a German . . ."[6]

A handful of UMCA missionaries openly collaborated with the German occupation, offering the new colonizers access to the mission's information about their surroundings, to mission beds and foodstuffs, and to the labor of their converts. These men were disdained by their peers: "Magila is suffering from a German invasion which riddle in great simplicity welcomed, found porters to assist them in their annexing projects, and has given them the aegis of the mission, much to my disgust."[7] There was much animosity and suspicion from the missionaries towards all classes of the German arrivals. Others in the UMCA's employ wrote that "[T]he ordinary German planter or mechanic or trader out here[:] If he has any religion it certainly is not visible to the naked eye,"[8] and that "the middle class Germans, traders &c who seem to have a deep dislike and jealousy of England though pleasant as can be to us as individuals."[9] This enmity largely arose from the competition for African bodies, valuable containers of corporeal muscles or intangible souls.

The Germans in the colony often reciprocated this ill will from the beginning of their interaction. Karl Juhlke, one of the men in Carl Peters' group who participated in obtaining the treaties that formed the basis of German claims to East Africa, published a harshly critical account of the missions. Juhlke argued that the English were merely pawns of their national government (the missionaries, of course, would hotly dispute this claim), that they beat and otherwise mistreated their converts, and worst of all, educated them in ways that made Africans even more useless to Europeans.[10] 1903 saw a furious exchange of letters, when the expansion of the Lutheran Evangelical mission and the UMCA encroached on each other's claimed territory.[11] After the First World War broke out, German officials force-marched the missionaries and staff at Magila to a concentration camp for British nationals in the center of the colony.

Yet even when the British missionaries and German officials found themselves at odds in defining their "spheres" of control, both approached the description and cataloging of the landscape they sought to command with a shared set of assumptions. The European suppositions regarding the Pangani Valley's landscape can be described with three intrinsically contradictory tropes. The first described parts of the landscape as "wilderness," or even "uninhabited." Underlying these descriptions was the assumption that the inhabitants of Pangani valley had not transformed the terrain to their own ends. In other words, Africans were unable to conquer nature, and were part of the wilderness themselves. The second trope presupposed almost the opposite, that the land was "lush" and overflowing with potential. This way of viewing the landscape could explain away the seeming contradiction of successful indigenous horticulture and stereotypes of East African laziness. In addition, the apparent productivity of "wild" areas made even more egregious the East Africans' failures to exploit some of the East African land. The final trope envisioned a landscape "over-exploited" by East Africans—a "degraded" present. The Pangani valley needed to be saved from its own population, before they destroyed their own habitation.

All three of these tropes used to describe the landscape gave the imperial actors justification for their actions: the landscape was unoccupied and thus fair game for colonization; the landscape was under-utilized, and should be used fully by colonizers; or the land was over-exploited and needed proper management. Despite their contradictions, the three beliefs existed simultaneously and across nationality. The language used in descriptions of the land legitimized the inequality of racial relations and functioned as a means to control imperial subjects culturally, economically, or politically.

THE WILD LANDSCAPE

It is noteworthy that the sister of the first Bishop of the Universities' Mission to Central Africa, Anne MacKenzie, defined the goal of the mission with the phrase, "To subdue the earth" of East Africa.[12] A landscape described as wild functioned as an allegory for the condition of East African social mores and souls; the savage self-evidently resided in a savage landscape. J. P. Farler described the UMCA missionary's lot as one of living "year after year in this barbarous land, cut off by hundreds of miles of swamp and wilderness from all civilization,"[13] despite the fact that the head station at Magila lay only two day's march from the coast, mostly along roads well-traveled and surrounded by cultivation. The missionaries shared the ideology of a wild interior with nearby urban Swahili.[14] Farler's disdainful remarks provide evidence of numerous stockaded towns in the vicinity of Magila, half-a-dozen miles to the south.[15] Farler ignored the fact that this manipulation of the landscape meant that the "lonely villages" were anything but places in "primeval forests," that they were fully part of a cultural landscape, not a wilderness.[16] A number of the missionaries actually did adopt the local parlance for wilderness, *nyika*, a very specific reference to a landscape of scrubland (sometimes useful to cultivate more drought-resistant grains) between the coast and the low hills.[17]

German observers reiterated the claims of the English missionaries. Karl Juhlke even scoffed that they took "'old England' with them into the wilderness."[18] Carl Peters' early descriptions of the land to the south of the Pangani River stressed the vastness of the area's swamps, a hold-over from armchair geographic theories in the mid-century, rather than a portrayal of actual landscape that he had traversed.[19] Hans Meyer, working for a DOAG commission in 1888, trying to sharpen profits for the German East Africa Company, likewise grimly assessed a portion of the colony that he witnessed during his hike through the Pangani valley: "The greater part . . . of all Equatorial Africa, is a sterile, thinly-populated wilderness, which is barely capable of supplying the frugal wants of the Negro, and has no natural products of value to Europeans."[20]

The legends of the German colonial state's maps also demonstrate European preoccupations and preconceptions about the African wilderness.[21] The modifier *urwüchsig*, denoting a rugged or rough landscape, accompanied the terrain categorized as Grasslands (*Grasflächen*). The term also connoted (or claimed) an "elemental" or "untouched" nature of these prairies, as well as the implication that the landscape was "unsophisticated." This description functioned as a cognate to the standard German descriptions of the forests overlooking the Pangani valley as "*Urwald*": an un-cultured, ancient landscape, one that alleged the failure of its "primitive" inhabitants (or neighbors) to have changed over time or have been capable of altering their own habitat.

These representations of the landscape implicitly suggest that colonial control was justified and even a new phenomenon, since indigenous people purportedly never used the grasslands and forests. The imperial claim, however, neglected the fact that portions of these grasslands were periodically and purposefully fired to be locally useful (obvious from years of official and missionary complaints), and that the landscape was most decidedly a fairly recent production, a cultural landscape forged by humans.

Although they, too, indicated another form of wilderness, colonial map designations of forests had another purpose; they emphasized the woodlands' potential utility to the state. The symbols for both the bush (*Busch*) and tree-covered steppes (*Baumsteppe*) mimicked the density of the forestation with the concentration of the symbols. A "closed" forest (*geschlossene Wald*) marked a treescape with densities suitable for extraction and protection. Thusly, a portion of the "wilderness" became a landscape of great potential.

THE LUSH LANDSCAPE

Even though the idea seems at odds with the previous trope, the same observers who tagged the Pangani River valley and its environs as a wilderness also found it to be overflowing with potential, with commercial promise. Whether a UMCA missionary or a DOAG employee, the writer could represent the landscape as a site of unrelenting plenty. J. P. Farler, the Archdeacon who lamented the wild state of his station's environs, boasted that "Africans can produce enough food from their farms in three months to last them for a year . . ."[22] Implicit in this argument was that the colonial subjects were available for three-quarters of the year for other pursuits, namely labor for European ends. Charles Smith, a Lieutenant Vice Consul in the British consular corps in East Africa, journeyed from Mombasa to the Magila mission station during the first years of German rule. During his expedition Smith noted that: "The Shimba [sic] country easily grows all the usual products, that is to say, tobacco, maize, millet, rice, castor-oil plant, coco-nuts, bananas, mangoes, cassava, and ground nuts; and an excellent India [sic] rubber may be obtained. . . ."[23] Farler was even more exuberant about the landscape's potential:

> When we consider the wondrous fertility of this country, together with its vicinity to the coast, . . . [I]t is impossible to doubt but that it has a great future before it. . . . [W]ith a government that would develop [sic] its resources, it would quickly repay any money laid out upon it. . . . I should say no more fertile soil could be found in the world.[24]

On the German side, Hans Meyer wrote that the land his party had traversed—the same one he described as largely barren—was "eminently suited for cultivation."[25] This landscape was, of course, one already cultivated, with bananas, maize, millet, and rice. Carl Peters wrote in his biography "On December 14th 1884 I found myself . . . as the rightful owner of 2500 square miles of very *lush* [üppig] tropical land, located to the west of Zanzibar."[26] Herman von Wissman, German general and colonial administrator, wrote in 1895 of the "great magnificence and lushness [Üppigkeit] that covered the entire mount Handei."[27]

One further convention of landscape representation duplicated this function, a practice Russell Berman calls "Mulatto Geography": travel writers' comparisons of exotic terrain to familiar metropolitan landscapes.[28] This "naturalize[d] the colonial claim on African territory" and made a strange landscape familiar, serving as an evocation of an appealing overseas home.[29] Berman contends that German compilations of travel writing—spanning Asia, the Americas, and Africa—were the educational entertainment of the nineteenth century, and as "a literature poised ambiguously between popular science and colonial advocacy" laid the ideological groundwork for Germans to accept the establishment of colonies towards the end of that century, particularly through their descriptions of a familiar-exotic landscape.[30] Mary Louise Pratt includes this practice as a portion of "narrating the anti-conquest," one of a number of rhetorical means used to direct the reader away from the violence of the activities cf conquest.[31]

Both sets of European colonizers produced this "Mulatto geography." J. P. Farler wrote in the 1870s that the highlands ranging above the Pangani River had been dubbed the "Switzerland of Africa."[32] Farler also compared the lowlands to his own home, while moving across the portions described as wilderness by him elsewhere: "At times I have fancied myself in a well-kept park, and I have looked out for the mansion upon some knoll."[33] Other missionaries compared the banks of the Pangani to the banks of the Thames, walking along the main road like passing through an "English hay field," the flora reminiscent of English shrubberies, and a resemblance to the terrain of Devonshire.[34] Oscar Baumann, a gentleman scientist in the employ of the DOAG, rather generically described the grass flanking the Pangani River forests as "like European grass, with short ferns and heather poking through."[35] This practice of "Mulatto geography" was most likely done chiefly for the ease of description; the comparison provided a ready-made vision in the mind of the reader without much hard work on the part of the writer. But the "Mulatto geographies" also enticed settlers and perhaps made "natural" any sort of colonizing process.[36]

Comparisons to metropolitan landscapes were not the only conventions of international geographic comparison; others practiced what I am tempted to call "Zambo geography." Due to the institutional structure of colonial service, as well as the likelihood that travelers in East Africa had traveled elsewhere, it was quite probable that those who posted their observations were familiar with other non-European parts of the world. Alfred Bellville (a missionary for the English Church Missionary Society, and guest of the UMCA) compared the hills surrounding the Magila station to an existing colony where the British had already begun to incorporate African labor into their economic system, and his description hinted at a similar future:

> [T]he country became more undulating and the trees thinner, and it assumed a more park-like appearance—very like Natal in the first fifteen miles from the sea. The soil . . . appeared eminently suited for sugar and coffee.[37]

Oscar Baumann argued that the lopsided peaks in the German colony's northeastern quarters were a "perfect analogue" to the mountains in the German possessions in West Africa.[38] (Perhaps he was using the tautological argument that because one geography belonged to Germans so did a similar landscape?) Herman von Wissman, remarked that the slopes on the northern side of the Pangani River were "jungles" comparable to the forests on the foothills of the Himalayas.[39] It is not clear whether he meant this observation to refer to the eroded landscapes that had British Indian officials fretting about their own colony's future productivity, though his description of the trees' "lushness" suggests this was not so.

As Christopher Conte has suggested, the "Mulatto geographies" reveal something about the terrain that the Europeans were blind to: by suggesting the highland forests were like the Alps (or other places long-inhabited by Europeans), the observers reveal that the landscapes indeed were cultural landscapes, not untouched primeval forests. These highlands had been cleared and altered by their inhabitants for centuries, just as the Alps, Devonshire, or the Himalayan slopes had been.[40]

The descriptions of a lush and familiar landscape functioned to instill a colonial drive, whether assuring the reader that the area was worth retaining as a colony, or worth expending the effort to convert. A ripe landscape indicated ready souls. But this brings us to the conundrum that vexed most of the other observers in East Africa in the late nineteenth century: how could so valuable a land be so obviously impoverished at the present? The answer to this contradiction came in the form of the degraded landscape, the historical decline of East Africa, which European observers duly recorded.

THE DEGRADED LANDSCAPE

Even though Charles Smith (as described earlier) wrote that "the Shimba country easily grows all the usual products," he simultaneously contended that the "low undulating country, consisting of uncultivated land or of coco-nut plantations, [was] either already deserted or gradually *relapsing* into jungle."[41] Hans Meyer's observations of hunters (both African and European) foretold a future doom:

> If things are to continue as they have begun, it needs no seer to prophesy the ultimate result. The rich preserves of East Africa will share the fate of the vast hunting grounds of South Africa and North America, and in the not far distant future will utterly cease to exist.[42]

In 1904, Governor von Goetzen wrote worryingly to the Colonial Office about the "scarce forests of the protectorate . . . which are constantly subjected to damage and destruction by human interference, notably the detrimental habits of the local people."[43] These descriptions were the clichéd conception of the golden past written into the landscape, and this informed what the authors recorded. The Europeans in the Pangani River valley had encountered a landscape they had not foreseen; they expected far more tree cover in the tropics. The savanna woodlands and thin forests in most places were a disappointment.[44] The country seemed to be in the throes of an ecological crisis, and this was blamed on the indigenous population. The degradation narrative also validated the presence of missionaries:

> [S]et forth in their true light the moral misery and degradation to which the heathen nations of East Africa have fallen, and to point out the various routes by which these benighted populations may be approached, and the means for their elevation to Christian truth and Christian civilization conveyed to them.[45]

The degradation narrative helped the UMCA missionaries tautologically explain the existence of slaves, slave raids, and slave caravans in the Pangani River valley. A hostile environment produced slavery; slavery, in turn, led to an unconquered, and therefore uncontrolled landscape. The continued reality of enslavement also gave missions a solid argument (to their sponsors) for being in East Africa, as Christianization was the only means by which slavery could be completely suppressed, according to the Anglicans.[46]

The trope of degradation actually had its origins in the landscapes in crisis in metropolitan homelands, in both urbanization and the decline of metropolitan forests, and in colonial sites beyond the bounds of Africa. As Richard Grove has argued, observations by European officials of environmental destruction in profitable island colonies, combined with a growing international scientific information network, led to a widespread perception of a global climactic crisis.[47] This network of information dissemination, which included the Royal Geographic Society of London, was the same system that first inspired the efforts of the UMCA. The British and Germans also shared data: Station-head H. W. Woodward used German explorer Oscar Baumann's maps while drawing his own version of the hills adjacent to the Pangani River.[48] (Grove also attributes the growth in Christian environmental consciousness after 1860 to the ontological uncertainties facing the faithful in the wake of Darwinian science and the growing evidence that species might become extinct, namely the human species.[49])

From the German perspective, the existence of the phenomenon of *Waldsterben*, or "forest death," in Germany itself made German observers nervous about the future of Pangani valley forests. *Waldsterben* had been the result of German states' efforts to rationalize timber harvest by turning forests into predictable, orderly monocultural zones.[50] The weaknesses of monocultural practices—which would soon be imported to a number of African colonies with all too predictably disastrous effects—produced a massive die-off in various German forests.

The perception of a landscape in crisis, and the reports that accompanied such perceptions led to the implementation of purported scientific controls over the Pangani valley forests. The colonial state began establishing Forest Reserves at the end of the 1890s. The implementation of reserved forests led to cases of alienation and restrictions on local activities, although the weak state found these rules somewhat difficult to enforce. Despite the seeming conservationist bent of a Forest Reserve system, the process was actually tied closely to the idea of the landscape's potential; it was about extracting timber from the "lush" forests. One Pangani District Officer complained about the lack of proper forests that could be reserved along the Pangani River:

> Nowhere in the district of Pangani are their forests known to be worth protecting. . . . It is unknown even if these can still be classified as forests, as they consist of badly developed, bent trunks, which do not possess wood value. . . . Grassland gaps [between the trees] make large forest fires nearly inevitable.[51]

While searching for further expansion of forest reserves, Head Forester Eduard Deininger also found the woodlands lacking in character:

> I visited the country requested. . . . This land is not suitable for the mechanism of a forest reservation. The burgeoning vegetation carries essentially the character of an orchard steppe. [The useful species] all show terrible stature. Only in some places do the trees take on the character of rain forest, where a few individual camphor plants appear usable.[52]

The valleys and hills in the area were *not* limited to forests of weak and malformed trees, at least according to their fellow officials. (This discrepancy does not show rapid decline in the arboreal landscape, but rather different points of observation and the influence of the degradation discourse.) In 1903, one District Officer was writing about the formidable timber resources potentially available for the railroad's use: "Between the 17th and 19th kilometer lies the forest of Bassi, which, with its large number of strong trees, perhaps can be used by the railroad for the extraction of firewood, and it would be for this reason that the government would reserve the wood."[53]

The forestry officials ended up returning to the trope of wilderness to establish their claims. In 1911, when Lieutenant von Bieberstein claimed the "abandoned country," the forest along the Pangani River at Buiko, he "took possession of the land by declaring that it belonged to the Crown, for the treasury of *Deutsch Ost-Afrika*."[54] The phrase "*herrenloses*

Land" (abandoned country) was used repeatedly in descriptions of publicly announcing forest reserve land for the Crown.[55]

COLONIAL LABOR REGIMES

How did these European concepts of the East African landscape have an impact on the inhabitants of the Pangani River valley? How did these notions actually change East African lives? On the basis of their grasp of the East African terrain, the two colonial regimes decided when and where East Africans had to work, and where they were no longer allowed to work.

To the missionaries, the climate, the landscape of the tropics meant the people who lived there were different; their character was determined by their surroundings. Bishop Smythies, who assumed the post in October of 1883, argued that Africans should remain culturally mostly African:

> Our desire is to distinguish very clearly between Christianising and Europeanising. It is not our wish to make the Africans bad caricatures of the Englishmen. What we want is to Christianise them in their own civil and political conditions; to help them to develop a Christian civilisation, *suited to their own climate* and to their own circumstances. For instance, we do not allow any of the boys in our schools to wear any European clothing. . . . It is not our business to encourage the trade in boots by spoiling the feet of Africans for their own climate . . . [56]

Bishop Smythies continued, "I am certain that the people of Africa need not so much to be taught an emotional as a disciplining religion. It is not difficult to work upon the emotions of the inhabitants of a tropical country."[57] The missionaries read the "wild" landscape as a sign of ill discipline in the population of the landscape. The missionaries believed the solution to this problem was appropriate labor. This meant working the land within the mission's jurisdiction, putting the terrain in a proper European order. External order in the African landscape would produce internal order in African souls, "building up Christian characters within the limits of the African tribes themselves."[58]

The UMCA had success at drawing converts and political alliances to the Magila station in the late 1870s, as their resources offered some stability in a region facing insecurity in the wake of an extended war of succession and the recurring violence of a shifting slave trade (various British treaties imposed on the Sultan of Zanzibar altered the operations and goals of East African slavers). Magila's position of strength enabled the missionaries to begin an effort to make the mission station that much more permanent, reconfiguring the surrounding landscape and erecting a stone church building. This construction of course began and ended with African labor.

The missionaries continually required the felling of trees on the Magila hilltop: for building room and materials, to clear a square, for fuel.[59] Francis Mabruki, an African sub-deacon, and some of the town's other citizens were required to cut away groves of grass which had grown up during a missionary absence. This process "made the place homelike."[60] In 1881, when the resources of Magila drew a number of African settlers, these newcomers chopped down the trees on nearby hills and began new cultivation.[61] The mission continued to hire "natives" to cut wood in the surrounding forest into 1886.[62] The immediate vicinity of the Umba sub-station's mission house was clear cut, "which improves the place immensely," as well a wide road that opened a view to the sea.[63] The missionary in charge of Umba, H.A.B. Wilson, was "anxious to cut away more of the forest and improve the place," in 1881.[64]

The erection of the stone church building at Magila took years of work, from 1880 to 1886. The church's construction first drew negative attention from nearby chiefs' militias when it seemed to be the foundation for a stone fort. In 1881, the quarrying of limestone (as a construction material) near Magila created an even larger uproar. The mission's attempt to mine the limestone without paying for it drove nearby residents (from the villages of Mfunte, Mudili, kwa Magoda, and Lunguza) to demand compensation.[65] Archdeacon Farler demanded that the Bishop bring in soldiers from Zanzibar to defend the process and frighten the protesters, who had beaten and chased away the Africans actually mining and transporting the limestone back to Magila. Farler made the argument that since the land was uncultivated (even though the terrain could never produce agriculture), it was wilderness and owned by no one but God. [66] The Bishop Steere actually ruled against Farler, and eventually a church large enough to house seven hundred worshipers was completed.

Although the initial phase of German occupation was deadly and destructive only on a small scale, the 1890s saw the impact of colonization siphon away some of the bodies (and power) of the UMCA missions. Locusts destroyed most of the grain in the Pangani River valley of 1894, 1895, and 1896, and German colonial policy exacerbated the resulting famines. The UMCA solution was two-fold: they imported and gave away rice and employed local women to build roads around the station, paying them a tiny stipend for outside food purchases. This had the tripartite purpose of ordering the landscape, disciplining these women, and saving their bodies from malnutrition and starvation. Construction of the colony's railway began in 1895, and while this new transportation improved the mobility of the missionaries, it also sapped their congregations, for the labor it required, the official labor re-allocation it enabled, and the wages it could bring.

Like the UMCA missionaries, the Germans began re-ordering work in the Pangani River valley, in part based on their conceptions of how the landscape needed to be shaped. A Forest Assessor in the latter years of the colony, Theodor Siebenlist, combined the three conceptualizations of the landscape to argue that East Africa needed a managed nature:

> Left unattended, the [native] forest will renew by its own force, be it via seeds, coppices or root suckers. This new "urwald" with its mass of trees and bushes, vines, tree fern and other weeds allows for a pictorial image, but does not make any profit. The goal of forest administration must be to make profit out of existing woods and to increase it in the future; therefore this virgin forest, after using up all the usable old woods, has to make space for a planned, profitable artificial forest.[67]

His statement combines the presumptions of the wildness of the terrain, the potential of the land, and the degradation of the forest without European intervention. Who would do the work to salvage the land? It would be Africans, of course, under German supervision.

The fact that "planned . . . artificial forest[s]" had failed in Germany (the *Waldsterben* mentioned above) did not deter colonial Germans from their objective of creating forests with equilibrium and order. First, the colony's forests, in theory, would get neither over-crowded nor over-harvested. The second goal for the Germans was to create orderly forests: *Normalbäume* ("average" trees) of the same age growing largely in a grid. This would make forest income predictable and regular for the forestry bureaucrats. A standardized nature made it easier to train forest wardens and woodcutters. The process of making nature more legible to the state made it more manipulable, and thus more profitable to the state.[68] In German East Africa, the conventions of an untitled (J. No. 7033109), colored sketch map of the Msubugwe Reserve illustrate the German mindset.[69] Half the forests on the map appear as an orderly grid of trees; the German goal of sustained production and *normalbäume* meant to make the world resemble the map, rather than the other way around.

The Germans had trouble creating this landscape within East Africa. The labor to shape these forests was difficult to come by, as the officials were competing with the railroad, nearly one hundred plantations, caravans, and the missionaries for workers. Still, beginning in 1904, the state began creating forest reserves throughout the colony, including a number along the Pangani River and in the adjacent highlands. Four of these reserves, Marimba, Bwiti, Magogo, and Msimbazi, were created in the lowlands of the East Usambaras, on the north side of the Pangani.[70] To manage these reserves on the ground, the state hired Africans and Indians as wardens, paying as many as 127 in the peak year of 1910.[71] The main goal of these local officials was to prevent the inhabitants of the Pangani River valley from altering the forests they lived among, and some villages were forcibly resettled to remove them from reserved lands.

The Germans produced a series of decrees to preserve forests they found worth protecting. The colonial state's 1895 Usambara Ordinance, which was repealed in 1897, was a preservationist measure intended to control erosion and climate, and to sustain forest harvestability. The 1895 decree ordered that 150m of forest had to remain uncut on ridgetops, that timber on slopes greater than fifty degrees could not be harvested, and that 30–50m belts of forest had to be left standing every 600m along a valley or riverside; the ordinance also restricted other forest use.[72] The Forest Conservation ordinance of 1899, which regulated all forest lands adjacent to plantations, required similar measures and government approval for European timber-cutting. A final order, the Private Forest Conservation Ordinance of 1908, limited extraction to trees greater than 25cm in diameter, and required that one quarter of legal trees remain uncut.[73] An ordinance in 1909 expanded the number and expanse of the forest reserves, partly to create territorial stockpiles of safe water and soil zones in reaction to the Maji-Maji rebellion (1905–07) in the southern half of the protectorate. [74]

Along the northern banks of the Pangani, "Landwirt" (farmer) Eick wrote in 1899 that the previously "magnificent" forests on the hills of Eastern Usambara had "largely vanished."[75] Two decades later, while surveying their new Mandate, British forestry officials wrote almost precisely the same thing. Remarking that "squatters" lived in these same forests, their policy recommendation was a compensatory removal to save "rapidly disappearing" trees.[76] This scarcely had been enough time for reforestation and yet another decline, suggesting that the concept of "detrimental habits" dominated these officials' ways of seeing the landscape. These observers were unable to see any sort of sustained use by "non-rational" actors. In fact, the colony's population decline in the 1890s had in most places in the river valley reduced any sort of stress on the forests' sustainability. In a few places, the concentration of people, whether due to the recent famines or the colony's forced resettlements (to make the populace more legible or employable to the state and the settlers), may have created situations of over-exploitation of forest resources, namely firewood.

The truth, however, was that German plantation agriculture and, to a lesser extent, forestry science, had had disastrous impact on the hillsides of the Pangani Valley—indeed the major force behind the creation of "bald" hilltops.[77] Coffee crop plantations, which had been established by clearing forests beginning in 1891, were by the first decade of the twentieth century mostly abandoned, leaving scrubland and ruined soil in their wake.[78] Local Africans performed the labor of felling trees and tilling soil for these farms, but also some workers were drawn from the center of the colony ("Nyam-wezi," people from the west) and a few hundred indentured from Asia. The European origins of the disaster notwithstanding, Forestry officials used the degradation narrative to justify the control of forest resources. In 1909, Pangani District Officer Spieth wrote that, "The forest stands on the slopes and hills along the southern bank of the Pangani are not yet occupied," and he recommended hiring a "colored" watcher to establish a "sharp demar-cation" and keep the hill forests un-exploited.[79]

Pangani valley inhabitants were often forcibly drawn into the land-scape imagined by Germans. A sketch map of Herrn Kröger's property shows an *"Arbeiter Dorf,"* a worker's village built on the marginal terrain at the edge of his plantation. It should be noted that the state was often too weak to keep labor from fleeing the plantations in many cases, but that the flip-side of this "choice" was a self-removal forced by circumstance.[80]

CONCLUSION

The three standards through which the agents of imperialism represented the landscape of the Pangani River valley often had little to do with the actual terrain. Certain narratives dominated the way that European observ-ers saw and reported on the land, and they fit their descriptions into a worldview that necessitated colonial intervention of one sort or another. The discourses established in the nineteenth century continued to exert influence in the twentieth century as a number of scholars have shown. Notions about preservation and development had "major ramifications for the transformation of African land rights and land-use practices. . . . Both development and preservation were at heart attempts to recast society-nature relations in Africa to fulfill the commercial and aesthetic dreams of the European colonizers."[81] No matter what the metropolitan origins of the colonizers, or their stated imperial goals, the Europeans in the Pangani River valley collaborated to control the East African bodies situated in the East African landscape.

Chapter Ten

Anglo-American and European Missionary Encounters in Southern Sudan, 1898-Present

Gideon Mailer

INTRODUCTION

This chapter will focus on the encounters between American and British evangelical Christian missionaries and the indigenous communities of Southern Sudan in the last hundred years. It will draw continuities and differences between nineteenth and early twentieth century missionary activity in the region, and that which took place in the second half of the twentieth century. This will allow us to contextualize the more recent formation of evangelical Non-Governmental Agencies (NGOs), whose perceptions of earlier colonial encounters have been brought back to the lobbying halls of Washington in the postcolonial era. The extent to which the reintroduction of Christian influences around 1900 acted as a hegemonic or counter-hegemonic force, vis-à-vis Sudan's Northern ruling class, provides a central analytical focus. We will use this case study to modify certain existing assumptions regarding the role of missionary power in the development of African colonies and nations.

Ali Mazrui, for example, maintains that there was "profound incongruence" at the heart of the "imported educational system" of the colonial missionaries in Africa. Here resides a supposed paradox regarding the development of "Western" values on the one hand, and the kind of skills implanted by missionaries within the colonial order. Mazrui highlights Western civilization's growing secularism by the end of the nineteenth century, which was at odds with the colonial missionaries' propagation of a Christian religiosity already anachronistic in the West. To adopt his thesis for our study of Sudan, we might, therefore argue that missionary schools "taught the virtues of obedience instead of the ethos of the initiative: they taught the fear of God instead of the love of country; they taught the evils of acquisition instead of the strategy of reconciling personal ambition with social obligation."[1] It would be tempting to adopt such an analysis in order to argue that the American-European missionary presence in Anglo-Egyptian Sudan deployed a deliberate anachronism in this regard. This form of education would maintain distance between a "civilized" colonial order, and communities of indigenous Southern Sudanese who would be unable to speak its language, as it were, given their schooling in "anachronistic" religious ideas. The latter may have, therefore, served to bolster the ruling colonial hegemony.

It might be even more tempting to widen such a focus on the role of missionaries in colonial and postcolonial Sudan, through recourse to the kind of ideas inherent in studies of "Western Missiology" by sociologists and historians such as David Bosch. As with the Mazrui paradox, perhaps the following dichotomy outlined by Bosch ought to be borne in mind when we analyze the introduction of Christian missionaries into colonial and postcolonial Sudan. This may have represented a

> [D]ichotomy of two completely different and unrelated worlds. It is not that the new worldview publicly opposed religion or proscribed it, but rather, it fostered a private religion that had no real function in society as a whole. The underlying 'Christ against culture' stance in Protestantism meant, in practice, that religion was relegated to the private sector, to the world of values, where people are free to choose what they like. Thus, where religion did persist, it had to settle for a much reduced place in the sun.[2]

As with Mazrui's missionary anachronism, Bosch points here to a growing weakness of religious acculturation in a post-Enlightenment world. A partition between "facts" and religious "values" meant that these values were a matter of individual opinion. Given the separation between facts and values, claims that went beyond the individual were perhaps less appropriate when it came to missionizing in areas such as Sudan during the period in question. It "was not therefore surprising that individualism began to run rampant in Western Christianity and the saving of individual souls became increasingly apparent."[3]

Again, we might argue that this "dichotomy" was consciously harnessed, so that, to use Bosch's words in relation to our analysis of the indigenous communities of Southern Sudan, their contact with missionaries derived from the fact that the latter groups were a useful colonial conduit to reduce their "place in the sun." This gave them "no real function in society as a whole," both in relation to the British rulers, and the Sudanese Arab elites in the North, who these colonial rulers sought to keep separate from those black Southern Sudanese who were given the empty vehicle of religious choice. The Mazrui paradox connects missionary and colonial hegemony through "anachronistic" religious missions. The allied Bosch analysis highlights the "irrelevance" of religion as a tool of cultural growth, thereby suggesting that missionaries were more a part of secular ruling control.

Yet this chapter will modify such assumptions in relation to Sudan. It will be demonstrated that in late nineteenth and twentieth century Sudan, the kind of individual religious choice that Bosch and Mazrui, in their differing ways, link to a diminishment of individual agency in relation to ascendant power structures, led to anything but such a phenomenon. "Choice" encompassed agency, rather than simply representing a chimera constructed by agents of secular colonial hegemony. It was, to use Bosch's analytical framework, precisely a post-Enlightenment notion of individual choice that led to heightened anxiety by ruling British authorities regarding the missionary presence in the colonial state. Moreover, we will see that in the postcolonial order, the ruling Arab North maintained many elements of the previous British hegemony, so that a similar anxiety could come about on their part regarding the missionary influence and Southern Sudanese agency.

Of course, many elements of collaborative hegemony between missionaries and colonial officials existed. Yet after an initially ambiguous perception of Christian influence as an agency for colonial control, many came to believe that Christianity connected them to a world larger than their traditional ethnic communities and added strength in their struggle for political freedom, economic justice, and cultural survival. Moreover, it could also connect them to more "ancient" Christian African communities in the region's South. This could allow an important-and unstudied-positive re-conceptualization of the missionary presence in colonial Sudan during the postcolonial period. This will enable us to point to the kind of ambiguities regarding supposed colonial—missionary collaborative hegemony during the first part of the twentieth century. It will also allow us to move the analysis of missionary encounters away from missionaries themselves, and onto those whom they encountered, so that the views of the latter could come to utilize the position of missionaries for their own agency, even if the actual missionary groups, as well as the colonial order which allowed their introduction, did not necessarily intend this consequence. A new paradigm could develop within late twentieth century Southern Sudanese consciousness, thanks to a re-conceptualization of these previous encounters with the missionary "other." This paradigm could pave the way for new encounters between Southern Sudanese and largely American "evangelical NGOs."

ELEMENTS OF COLLABORATIVE HEGEMONY BETWEEN MISSIONS AND COLONIAL RULERS

It would be wrong to completely revise our historical understanding of the collaboration between missionaries and colonial administrators in an area such as Sudan during the period in question. We may, however, demonstrate that the nature of this collaboration was not always perceived in the same manner on both sides. In many ways, Anglo-Egyptian administrators discouraged missionaries from carrying out a religious form of education, thereby shattering previous missionary illusions regarding the ability of the colonial infrastructure to "resource" their religious mission. From initial missionary perspectives, the colonial establishment of law could be seen to have helped the missionaries in their task of propagating the Christian faith in the Sudan.[4] Here, Britain was a Christian power that would therefore guarantee their work both spiritually and logistically. Ironically, we may see, the opposite could take place: A lack of funds among ruling British forces necessitated a form of collaboration with missionaries whereby the latter were charged with imparting a form of quasi-secular education to those in the South amongst whom they were present. A new generation of indigenous administrators was needed, and it was missionary educators who were charged with fashioning them, and creating the kind of infrastructure that would allow colonial rule to be smoothly developed.

The reason British colonial forces opposed a religious underpinning to missionary education was a simple one: The growth of a specifically Christian identity might heighten Southern indigenous Sudanese agency, by creating a potentially new identity that would threaten the British policy of divide and rule, which centered on the maintenance of differences between North and South, rather than the transformation of identities in one region with respect to the other. For example, it is important to note that when Reginald Wingate became Governor General of the Sudan after Kitchener's departure in 1900, figures such as he could link the allowance of Christian missionaries into Southern Sudan, to their potential ability to "build a strong Christian counter-weight in the South to balance Muslim strength in the North."[5] Lord Cromer had previously reassured the Northern Sudanese Muslims that "there will be no interference whatever in your religion." After the conquest of the Sudan, Kitchener was appointed as Governor-General, and he, like Cromer, was concerned about the possibility of a conflict arising between Christian missionaries and the Muslim Arabs in the North. In November 1899, Kitchener gave permission to the Christian "missionaries to come [into the Sudan], so long as they did not speak to Moslems on religion."[6] Gywnne was urged by many British colonial representatives to move the Church Missionary Society (CMS) into Southern Sudan. Thus, in March 1900, the Deputy Governor-General, Colonel H.W. Jackson, requested "Gywnne to go south . . . go slowly Gywnne, it will be best for us all."[7] What is telling in such perceptions is that missionaries were to be employed as agents in bringing about a southern counterweight to the Arab North, rather than a necessarily stronger force. The colonial aim in this regard was to use missionaries to maintain stability and buttress a status quo that would make colonial rule as easy and inexpensive as possible, rather than risking the ire of Muslim elements in the North, and provoking a Mahdi-style uprising. In 1903 the expansion of Islamic schools in the district of Wau led to a British anxiety regarding an increased Islamic confidence in the Southern region of Sudan. It was this anxiety that led to the allowance of Roman Catholic missionaries in the region, making missionaries part of the colonial hegemonic order as it related to the political balance between North and South.[8]

Indeed, while the period 1912-1919 witnessed a reinforcement of the Christian faith through the replacement of Friday with Sunday as the day of rest, this change arguably derived much of its impetus from the secular colonial rhetoric of separation between North and South. Southern soldiers and British officers in the South were rested on this different day, meaning that the Arab and Muslim Northern soldiers who had maintained the Sudanese army in the South emptied from the Southern provinces.[9] The *Milner Memorandum* of 1920 advocated that:

> The Government policy has been to keep the Southern Sudan as free as possible of Mohammedan influences. Black Mamurs (administrative officers) are employed where it has been necessary to send Egyptian clerks, Copts are, if possible selected. Sunday is observed as a day of rest instead of Friday as in the north and missionary enterprises encouraged . . . .The possibility of the Southern (black) portion of the Sudan being eventually cut off from the northern (Arab) area and linked up with some Central African system is borne in mind.[10]

We may even be able to point to a certain colonial consciousness that religious missionaries were not fully able to educate in the vernacular languages of various Southern Sudanese communities, making them an unwittingly useful colonial mechanism: Southern Sudanese communities could not develop too much agency from education, owing to the language barrier. To the British administrators in the Southern Sudan, "education meant the Western concept of literacy in the language of the government, not the education customary and required by the African societies in the Southern

Sudan."[11] This could be carried out by Christian missionaries who were "anxious to teach English in order to facilitate the spread of the Word of God." Financial and administrative considerations thus underpinned the devolution of educational power to missionaries during the early colonial period in Sudan.[12]

This may explain a certain silence in those sources detailing British colonial ministers' perceptions of various missionary groups as they entered Sudan in the 1900s. This relates most particularly to initial references to the British Church Missionary Society, which, when it came to references by figures such as Lord Cromer, were conspicuous by their absence. When Lord Cromer visited Southern Sudan in January 1903, he made positive reference to the Roman Catholic Mission (RMC), and the American Presbyterian Church (APM), noting on his return to Khartoum, his commendation of "the medical, educational and general "civilizing" work of these missions . . ."[13] Lord Cromer's failure to mention the CMS arguably derived from the latter's more ambiguous relationship to the ruling colonial order, given the very real zeal that they derived from the martyrdom of their hero in the nineteenth century, General Gordon, at the hands of Mahdi Arab fighters. Soon after Gordon's death at the hands of Mahdist soldiers in 1885, "the Church Missionary Society met at Exeter Hall and established the Gordon Memorial Mission. A fund of £3,000 was subsequently raised to begin work in the Sudan as soon as the Mahdist state was overthrown and British order had been re-established. Gordon's martyrdom, as much as the call of Christ, propelled the Church Missionary Society up the Nile."[14] In this way, European Catholic and American Presbyterian missionaries were better able to carry out the kind of general "civilizing" work that their colonial agents sought from them. They thought that their religious mission could be put in place once this more infrastructural help had been given. The CMS, on the other hand, wanted an overtly religious role from the outset, and this may explain their absence in Cromer's initial statements.

In this light, it would be most appropriate to view the Condominium government's 1914 "grant-in-aid" mechanism for missionaries as a means of preventing their focus on a form of religious education that may have given too much individual agency to those in the Southern Sudan who were to receive this education. Vitally, British officials could use the aid as leverage in order to pressure missionaries to comply with more secular colonial educational measures, such as the formation of elementary and trade schools. In this regard, these schools were to act as "civilizing" centers.[15] Southern "natives" did not need to be turned away from their ancestral African traditional beliefs and converted to Christianity. This British perception, articulated most explicitly in a series of letters between Governor

Wingate and Gwynne, did not, however, derive from any innate respect for indigenous cultures. [16] Rather, they were to be exoticized, rather than missionized, because the latter risked creating a new identity, which had a potential to alter the status quo between North and South, if this new identity created any heightened agency among those indigenous Southerners in relation to both colonial and Northern elites. In this way, it was precisely because missionary groups were not allowed to follow up the initial religious impetus for their arrival in Southern Sudan, that they came to be connected to secular ruling colonial hegemony. Although the latter was collaborative, this was, therefore, an uneasy connection.

British District Commissioners sought a trained contingent of Southern Sudanese bureaucratic administrators as their movements in the South increased. In the Annual Report of 1925, the Governor-General, therefore, noted that increased "economic and administrative development in the Southern Sudan demands additional educational facilities."[17] In 1924, the Anglo-Egyptian administration outlined the apportionment of funds for the support of missionary educational development in the Southern Sudan. The Annual Report of the Sudan Government stated that the "happy combination of missionary enterprise and experience on the one hand, and of government aid, on the other, should afford sure ground and opportunity for the development of the negroid and pagan peoples."[18] That missionaries could be used for "civil" education, making them an adjunct for ruling power, is perhaps most ironically demonstrated by the fact that many Northern Sudanese, especially around Khartoum, Wad Medani, El Obeid, Atbara and Shendi, sought to send their children both to Christian schools run by the CMS, APM, and Roman Catholic missionaries. Even if they were careful not to publicize this phenomenon too widely, it aptly demonstrated that there was a real element of collaborative hegemony between missionary educators and colonial power elites, even if the former would have preferred a more religious rather than civil education.[19] Ironically, this particular example demonstrates that despite the colonial impetus behind missionary civil education deriving from the perceived need to cement the balance between North and South by moving the South up as an equal force, the nature of this "civil" missionary education meant that it was an attractive proposition for the children of many Northern elites.

The Nuban Mountain area provides a particularly valuable case study of these ambiguities regarding the role of missionary education in the colonial state order. On the one hand, missionary schools in this area did not teach in pure Arabic, as some colonial schools did in the North of Sudan. This may have been because many missionaries lacked expertise in this language. But it also seems to have derived from the fact that although they had previously been colonized by Arab forces, they were no longer deemed part of the Northern Sudan in particular. The Nuba region was located in Kordofan, and officially classified as northern, yet given that it was a predominantly non-Muslim region that had suffered slave raids in the nineteenth century, the province also resembled the south, and ought to have "kindred protectionist policies that promoted local vernaculars and English as educational languages."[20] It was this dilemma that arguably explained the use of a peculiar form of "Romanized Arabic" by the missionary schools in the area, which did not replicate Arabic script. While one could argue that this form of script was designed to enable missionaries to understand the language that they taught in (through its scriptural similarity to English), it could also be seen as a "linguistic device of underdevelopment, a dead-end endeavor that confirmed the marginalization of the Nubas relative to the Arabic-speaking peoples of the riverain north . . . that used language and writing to erect internal barriers."[21]

INITIAL MISSIONARY DIFFICULTIES ENHANCE BRITISH CONTROL

Within this context of uneasy collaborative hegemony between missionaries in the Southern Sudan, and the wider colonial state, we can find two further connected ironies. Both of them could provide the background for the colonial rhetoric of separate ethnic spheres, and "indirect rule," and the missionaries' uneasy role in its formation. First, although many missionary groups entered the Sudan on an anti-slavery mission, their physical appearance often led them to be associated by Southern Sudanese communities with the European slave-traders who had been in alliance with Arab traders in the nineteenth century. This association was exacerbated by the fact that missionaries had previously used Arab and European trade routes to carry out reconnaissance work for the potential expansion of their missions. It is important to note, for example, that in the nineteenth century, Catholic missionaries, met with various Dinka groups, as well as the Shilluk, Nuer and Bari peoples of Southern Sudan. Yet white missionaries were often associated with the "Turks" who came before them. A Catholic missionary report of 1850 stated: "We sailed along deserted banks, because the poor savages living near the river are in constant fear of the Turks, from whom they often receive cruel treatment, especially from the annual expedition."[22] Such associations, of course, would have made missionary attempts after 1900 initially very difficult. Most early missionary stations in this later period were set up amongst Nilotic communities in the Upper Nile Province. The indigenous communities here were "notoriously conservative- and hostile to strangers. The attitude of the Shilluk, for example, to the Americans, was one of superiors to inferiors."[23] The *Wingate Papers* similarly demonstrate that both Catholic and CMS missionary groups were distressed at their initial inability to make progress in the South in terms of religious acculturation.[24]

Second, a certain similarity between indigenous Southern beliefs and cosmologies, and missionary Christianity, actually prevented the acculturation of the former towards the latter. Why adopt a belief system, when one already adheres to a similar one? We may see that such a rhetorical question provided an easy answer for the Condominium government vis-à-vis the missionary capabilities in Southern Sudan. Many early twentieth century missionaries perceived Southern Sudanese society in the manner that they imagined Old Testament religious structures. Yet this perception ironically derived from a similarity, which initially maintained the gap between Southern communities, and the biblical word that the missionaries sought to impart. Evans-Pritchard, for example, has drawn attention to the supposed "biblical" similarities to pastoral Nilotic religion. It resembled "less other Negro religions than some of the historic religions. They have features which bring to mind the Hebrews of the Old Testament . . . Miss Ray Huffman, an American Presbyterian missionary who spend many years among the Nuer, remarks that 'the missionary feels as if he were living in Old Testament times, and in a way this is true.'"[25] The missionary word could, however, appear as an "alternative and foreign version of religious truths already familiar." Burton thus describes a conversation with Charles Manyang, a politically educated Bor Dinka man, who succinctly outlined this phenomenon: "Why should we say we are Christian when what we have is really our own?" Francis Deng's study of Dinka cosmology has also noted this idea.[26] Notions of a "high God, of sin, of sacrifice and redemption, as well as the possibility of divine forgiveness" were all present in indigenous practice and sentiment.[27] Nilotic communities even contained within them "diviners," who, like missionaries, were intermediary figures that could connect people to their spiritual hinterland.

Ironically, we will later see that during Sudan's postcolonial period, the outside force of Christianity could combine with, rather than rival, these structural similarities, as a response to the new hegemony of the Arab North. As evangelical groups discovered in later years, a concept similar to "grace" would already have existed during the period in the southern region.[28] Prior to this realization, however, many of the Presbyterian and Catholic missionaries acting among the Shilluk did not take into account their conception of divine kingship, which derived from their "incarnational" understanding of God's "recreating" presence in their creation narrative.[29] In the first decades of the twentieth century, initial missionary failures could justify the collaboration of missionaries with the secular colonial regime, from the latter's standpoint. Given their uneasiness regarding new religious developments among indigenous Southerners in relation to the Muslim North, British colonial agents thus sought to utilize missionaries as cost-effective civic educators. An initial lack of religious acculturation among the Southern Sudanese could, for colonial administrators, provide just the justification for the promotion of a quasi-secular form of missionary education, thereby forming an important component of Indirect Rule in southern Sudan.

It was this initial position of the missionary as "other" in Southern Sudan that, when viewed in the larger context of competing hegemonies between Northern Arab and British condominium rule, may be seen to have eased the way for the policy of British Indirect Rule. Owing to the initial failure of missionary religious acculturation, British colonial officials could pay specious lip-service to their "respect" for ancient ethnic cultures, rather than encouraging the development of any new identities through recourse to religious missionary education. During 1927 the Governor-General of the Sudan described the mission schools he had visited in the South as showing "bias against the social and matrimonial customs of the people."[30] The British High Commissioner in Cairo raised similar concerns regarding those missionaries charged with "educating the boys destined for government service."[31] Nonetheless, "an Educational Conference held in Juba in 1932 . . . confirmed that the government would not provide its own schools, but co-operate with the missions in providing an education which would . . . aim at guarding against the destruction of native social institutions and the diversion of the African from his natural background."[32] Contrary to received historiography, this use of missionaries as a paradoxically secular conduit for Indirect Rule meant that the genesis for this ruling policy appeared before the 1930s. We can only note this fact if we take into account the potentially destabilizing role of missionary Christianity, which could have given the Southern Sudanese a sense of agency, if their new identity led to a sense of collective renewal.

The missionaries' initial failures in this regard, (caused also by disease and lack of funds) therefore allowed their co-option towards more secular colonial ends, pivoting on the maintenance of a status quo between North and South. The latter was to be a counterweight, rather than a newly identified rival. In the 1930s, Indirect Rule became the hallmark of British colonial African policy. Yet the co-option of missionaries before this date into a colonial system designed to maintain decentralized secular rule towards the end of regional stability, ought to alter our conceptual time line. It also demonstrates once again that Southern "native" ancestral African traditional beliefs were to be "respected" not necessarily because of any innate colonial respect for indigenous cultures. Rather, respect for African traditions was a convenient rhetorical vehicle for the maintenance of a status quo, from within which missionaries would be allowed to carry out secular education to maintain the infrastructure of the ruling order.

Thus, in 1930, several years after their co-option into this role, the central government drafted "The Southern Policy," which stated that indigenous peoples were to be treated as "a series of self contained racial or tribal units with structure and organization based, to whatever extent the requirements of equity and good government permit, upon indigenous customs, traditional usage and beliefs."[33] The documents which articulated this policy also urged missionaries to send trained "boys" away from the missions, once they had acquired an adequate knowledge of English, in order to become administrative members of civil society. Burton argues that the British policy suggested that customs should be preserved so that they could then be transformed to meet the requirements of administration. Missionary education was not intended to develop the Southern Sudan per se, but was rather a money saving measure.

It is rather ironic that the specious British respect for indigenous African rights led to a criticism of missionaries as too reflective of the "Middle West." This criticism mirrors those of sociologists such as Mazrui, who highlight the "anachronism" and parochialism of missionary education in Africa. Using similar reasoning, the Governor of the Upper Nile Province accused missionaries of disrupting "tribal life and discipline," and in a similar manner the American Presbyterian Mission was denounced as "squalid and of low standard . . . too impregnated with the atmosphere of the Middle West,"[34] Another administrator attacked the missionaries even more strongly, stating that they "were out to break the indigenous customs, traditional usage and beliefs of the natives, and anyone passing through their hands became de-tribalized- they became either converts apeing Europeans, or...despising their own people."[35] As Sanderson argues, with the southern policy, "the government ruthlessly sacrificed genuine educational goals to administrative goals."[36] Americans missionaries continued to rationalize about the manner in which the Christian character could develop alongside the best of American Western civilization.[37] A paradox emerges here: Missionaries were employed to educate a minority of people towards the end of civil administration. Yet when their success in this regard was noted, they were tacitly blamed. This was surely because even their quasi-secular form of education could be indigenized by Southern Sudanese so that the latter could gain greater agency, or at least, a newly formed collective identity in contrast to the North, where missionary "others" were not present.

MISSIONARIES AND THE LEGACY OF ARAB SLAVEHOLDERS

A central question that has divided contemporaries and historians alike relates to the supposedly cynical impetus for the invocation of the Northern Arab legacy of slavery (during the Turco-Egyptian and the Mahdist regimes between 1821 and 1897) by missionaries in the Southern Sudan during the Condominium period. This connects to our previous discussion of the uneasy collaborative hegemony between missions and the colonial Sudanese state, given the ambiguity of the supposed moral nature of missionary references to slavery. Some argue that secular authorities could encourage this invocation of slavery as a means of maintaining animosity, and therefore, separation between North and South. For Besher Mohamed Said, this tendency "had left no stone unturned to intensify the feelings of Southerners against the North."[38] The Northern Sudanese elites at the time, and later historians, therefore charge Christian missionaries with the partial creation and fermentation of the chronic question of national unity, the so-called "Southern Problem."[39] Daly argues that the sense of Southern separateness in the provinces of Bahr al-Ghazal, Upper Nile, and Equatoria continued as an open sore because of the "constant reminders of the nineteenth century slave trade and by the facts of cultural, linguistic, and religious differences."[40]

Yet as with our previous examples, we can in fact see that secular colonial authorities tacitly discouraged a moral/religious approach to missionary education, and the depiction of Northern slavery that formed one of its more emotive components. Again, this arguably derived from a colonial anxiety that an increased perception of the slave legacy among Southern Sudanese communities would do anything but maintain the status quo between North and South, which it was within their interests to maintain. Rather, a heightened perception of their collective history might lead to an enhanced collective Southern identity, which, in relation to the competing hegemonies of colonial and Northern Arab elites, might rupture this status quo. In logistical terms, we have seen that the educational curricula used by the missionaries were prescribed by the Condominium colonial government. The Northern politicians knew what was being taught in the Southern mission schools. After the reversal of the "Closed District Ordinance" in 1946, Northern officials even served as junior education officers and teachers in the South. Even before this date, they were involved in the curricula of mission schools.[41] Thus, "teaching" the slave trade would not have formed a component of collaborative hegemony between missions and the state as it is usually defined, given the colonial wish to maintain the balance between the different sectional components within this state.[42]

Indeed, it seems rather myopic to argue that various communities in the Southern and Nuban region would somehow have forgotten their experiences of slavery by the British Condominium period: The destruction of the Nuba people through enslavement and violence, for example, had occurred particularly between 1850 and 1900, during the Ottoman and Mahdist rules. They, along with their more western neighbors in Southern Darfur and Western Bahr el Ghazal, were devastated by a Northern slave route that followed that of the ivory trade directly through their regions. Zubeir Pasha, a Northern slave lord, established a monopoly on the Nuban regions. Those who survived his campaigns mostly took refuge in the Nuban Mountains, and it would be disingenuous to state that it was only later missionaries who could make known the reason for their asylum in these mountains.[43]

The missionary invocation of the slave trade was anything but a component of collaborative hegemony. If anything, it represented one of the last moral components of missionary acculturation, which caused much anxiety amongst secular British governors. Indeed, some missionaries even managed to penetrate Northern Sudanese schools, and their educational approach further demonstrates the fact that their references to historical slavery put them at odds with colonial power elites, as well as the Northern Arab elites with whom they were in competition for hegemony. Although some Muslim Northerners attended missionary schools in Southern Sudan, the "region's future nationalists and power-brokers, all sons of Muslim landowners, merchants or scholars who represented an elite, [mostly] went to government, not missionary, schools, where the funding was better, the coursework more rigorous and access to government jobs guaranteed."[44] Yet Sharkey has demonstrated that missionary schools could enter the North through more unorthodox means, given the Condominium government's wish to restrict their movements among Muslim communities, for fear of provoking Mahdist style instability. These more unorthodox means often related to marginalized groups in the North, most notably the former descendents of slaves, who the CMS saw as a top priority. Again, the same anxiety among ruling elites would have been present, given the potential for enhanced collective identity among these marginalized groups, should their perceptions of historical injustice at the hands of former slave-holders have been enhanced. Despite the restrictions under which they worked,

CMS missionaries even played a pioneering role in formal schooling for girls, many of whom were slave descendents. The latter came across missionaries in a clinic the CMS opened a clinic in Omdurman in 1900. Similarly, American Presbyterian missionaries opened schools in Khartoum, populated mainly by Sudanese ex-slave boys. The CMS followed suit with a similar school in Khartoum in 1902, except this time, for girls. They could, therefore, use their experiences in Omdurman of more informal education of slave descendents in a more formal setting.[45]

MISSIONARY SPHERES AND ETHNIC IDENTITY

We have seen how the missionary position as "other" in the Southern Sudan allowed colonial authorities to utilize their networks towards more secular administrative ends, within the framework of an uneasy collaborative hegemony. They were employed in order to maintain a balance between sectional communities, rather than endow any one community with new identities or heightened religious agency, even if this had been their initial aim. Yet we may now see that the policy of Indirect Rule that missionaries were co-opted into in fact allowed a new paradigm to develop among many Southern Sudanese peoples, which could be utilized to their own ends.

In one important respect, missionaries were treated by the colonial administrators in the same way that they treated the various communities in the Southern Sudan. The latter were divided into "separate ethnic spheres" in order to allow a more efficient form of decentralized, indirect rule. It was also designed to prevent the alliance of different southern communities in a more pan-national framework, which could threaten stability. Different missionary denominations were also treated in this manner, and divided up so that different denominations could enter different ethnic spheres. For example, the CMS worked among the Dinka and Equatoria, and the Presbyterians were assigned to the Upper Nile. Duany also indicates that the Verona Fathers of the Roman Catholic Church were engaged in Western Upper Nile, but that the "American Presbyterians were given the largest part (3/4) of the Nuer population to proselytize."[46] Different missionary groups were to be divided and ruled, at the same time that they were to be part of the ruling infrastructure. This idea was tacitly expressed as early as 1905, when the British set up the *Missionary Regulations for the Southern provinces*: "In practise the country was divided into zones, one for each missionary body. One area, one mission . . . Poaching for converts over inter-confessional borders was forbidden. No missionary station was permitted to be established north of the 10th parallel." American Presbyterian missionaries even accused the government of "putting boundaries to the preaching of God's word."[47] They too, according to the colonial administrators, should not develop a collective position that was too strong.

Indeed, the 1905 colonial regulations for missionaries demonstrated a language of "omnipotence" that tacitly stressed the hegemony of their word, rather than the word of the missionaries as intermediaries to God. The "Regulations and Conditions under Which Missionary Work is Permitted in the Sudan, 1905" are detailed by Collins. For our discussion, it is telling to note that in the fourth clause restricting missionary activity relating to trade, it was stated that it was in Britain's interests not to obviate "any suggestion of trading on the part of missionaries in effect this would (a) advance the image of the government as 'omnipotent' in the eyes of local peoples."[48] Missionaries could be engaged in trade because the nature of trade was reciprocity, which had the potential to endow both sides of trade with agency and choice. The delineation of missionary spheres matched the grid patterns assigned to various ethnic groups in the Southern Sudan. Tellingly, in an analogy with these ethnic grids, particular missionary denominations were expected to produce sufficient goods for their own subsistence within their own missionary sphere. During times of particular scarcity, as with ethnic groups, they would turn to central colonial authorities for relief.

Burton's analysis of the "native courts" established by British officials provides another important parallel: "Appointed chiefs, or 'friendlies,' were granted limited authority under the general auspices of a resident secular official. Of special note here was stricture that missionaries could not act as intermediaries between 'the natives' and the local government."[49] Missionaries, as with the indigenous Southern Sudanese, had to rely on the colonial government for their ability to promote religion in times of need, just as they had to rely in resident secular officials-the local governors-for any extra-mission activities such as trade or free movement. Just as ethnic groups maintained some "internal" autonomy through appointed chiefs, so missionary groups were charged with their own subsistence. Yet when it came to any activity that may have gone beyond the bounds of their assigned sphere of influence, they were to report to wider authorities. The *Wingate Papers* thus demonstrate that the CMS under Bishop Gwynne expected the government publicly to support missionary work, even going as far as requesting them to encourage local chiefs to send their boys to their own missionary schools. Yet such collaboration was rejected on the grounds of indirect rule, and the supposed colonial respect for indigenous structures already outlined.[50]

That half the Dinka-speaking population should be exposed to Roman Catholic missionaries, while the other half to CMS groups, suggests that missionary spheres were haphazardly designed to correspond with often arbitrary administrative boundaries.[51] While F. R. Wingate, Governor-General of the Sudan, reasoned that separate missionary spheres would "prevent any likelihood of disagreement between the various mission bodies," government policy regarding their work would be the same as that relating to indigenous peoples: divide and rule was designed as much to prevent universal agreement between various groups, missionary or ethnic, as it was to prevent instability deriving from their potential disagreement.[52] In many ways, when one takes into account the delicate balance between competing British and Northern Arab hegemonies, the potential for a more universal missionary identity in the South would have caused far greater anxiety. Universal Southern missionary work could bring about greater connection between various Southern indigenous groups, in relation to Northern Arab elements, which would threaten the kind of balance that the British sought to maintain as part of their own ruling colonial hegemony.

In this way, we may understand the parallels regarding the treatment of separate missionary and separate ethnic spheres, which often corresponded. Once again, this ambiguity in the power structure related to the competing power emanating from Northern Sudan. This, therefore, makes any notion of collaborative hegemony between missionary and British colonial groups even more complex and multi-faceted. Something of a power conflict developed, in which British colonial leaders feared alternative power sources emanating from missionary headquarters. For example, Roman Catholic missionary proposals to move into the (less malaria prone) higher grounds near Kodok in 1901 were rejected because the British did not want the missionaries to be too close to the government administrative headquarters, as well as the residence of "Reth," the Shilluk divine king.[53] Alternative missionary power sources in Kodok would have led to potentially reciprocal relations between the Reth residence and Roman Catholic missionaries, and an alternative to the nearby colonial station. Presbyterian missionaries were only permitted to open their first mission in Southern Sudan at Doleib Hill, over sixty miles south of Kodok, for the same reason.[54] The CMS faced British colonial opposition in their endeavors to missionize the Bari communities of Mongalla. Tellingly, Mongalla contained within its "grid" boundary the colonial government administrative and military headquarters for the wider region. On the other hand, missionaries saw British intransigence as a sign of the corruption of their spiritual ideals in favor of Islam.[55] The potential for competing, rather than collaborative hegemony was often the order of the day.

We have seen that the colonial division of the Southern Sudan into parallel missionary and ethnic spheres also related to a lack of central colonial funds, and a wish to use missionaries as a conduit for a decentralized, and cheaper, form of governance. Yet it is also interesting to note the diverging manner in which different missionary denominations responded to this phenomenon. Tellingly, Roman Catholic missionaries were far more vocal in their opposition to the separate missionary spheres, than even groups such as APM and CMS. The Roman Catholic missionaries, unlike other Protestant groups, felt comfortable with a "free marketplace" concept of missionary competition over an unmarked geographical area, given their ability to access economic support and human capital from more abundant sources. They therefore demanded more vocally that they be allowed to evangelize anywhere in the Southern Sudan.[56] The CMS and APM missionaries were less confident about their abilities to compete with Roman Catholic missionaries because of their more limited sources of funds and missionary personnel. Thus, they viewed the "ethnic sphere" structure in a slightly more favorable light.

It is true that a main purpose of separate spheres centered on the wider curtailment of their movement and expansion. Yet the latter point could be placed on the backburner by Protestant missionaries, at least in the short term, given that from their viewpoint, the ethnic-missionary grid system protected the Southern community from being converted from their "African traditional heathenism to the Roman form of idolatry," given the greater funds to expand held by Catholic missionary groups.[57] In this way, not only can we analyze the division into separate spheres as a result of a British policy of maintaining an indirect form of decentralized rule designed to maintain a balance against a competing Northern hegemony. We can also note competition between missionaries with regards to the role of separate spheres in their expansion or consolidation. A lack of money among some denominational groups made them passive allies in this regional division, while deeper funding sources made others resent the curtailment of their expansion at the expense of other competing missions. Indeed, World War I complicated things even further in this regard. Many European Catholic missionaries were further restricted, or at least suspected, owing to their Italian, Austrian, and German nationalities.[58]

THE INDIGENIZATION OF RELIGION ACROSS COLONIAL BOUNDARIES

The ambiguous role of missionary power in relation to the secular colonial leadership could be noted by indigenous Southerners, in order to separate the missionaries from the colonial order, when an alliance with the former became appropriate in the mid-twentieth century. For our present analysis, this irony is all-important, as it paved the way for the kind of paradigms adopted by indigenous Southerners in the postcolonial period. Before we analyze that period, however, we need to trace the manner in which colonial restrictions on missionary group movements were overcome through the use of new indigenous missionaries, who did not face the same curtailment of movement between delineated boundaries. Ironically, we will see that this led to just the kind of heightened Southern collective identity that separate missionary spheres were designed to prevent.

The arbitrary nature of the "zonal" boundaries that marked out religious spheres of influence meant that many relatively homogenous southern ethnic groups were split in two, with different missionary denominations essentially vying for the same ethnic populations. This necessitated the creation of "free" or "neutral" zones, where two or more Christian denominations could operate together, but with different doctrinal contents. One might contend that within such zones, Southern communities could gain a certain agency from the competition for their attention, between various denominations within a single "neutral" area. They could demand services, such as education, rather than the latter being thrust upon them. This education could be indigenized, allowing them to traverse the regional boundaries that were forbidden to Anglo-American and European missionaries. For example, Allison has documented the many indigenous clergy who moved between different ethnic regions in the South.[59] A native clergy maintained linguistic and cultural advantage over Anglo-American and Roman Catholic missionaries in the area. Perhaps more importantly, they were not subject to the colonial regulations concerning zonal missionary boundaries.[60] Without these indigenous evangelists, the spread of Christianity would not have been as strong as contemporaries saw it to have become by the 1930s.[61]

Ironically, the formation of separate missionary-ethic spheres made the relationships which formed within their bounds more intimate; they were characterized by less suspicion because missionaries were perceived in more local terms, as opposed to answering to more central colonial authorities. In fact, the colonial policy of placing missionary centers away from secular governing headquarters simply served to widen the difference between the two, and make Southern Sudanese perceptions more amenable to specifically religious teaching. In this way, on this local and decentralized level, the use of catechists by new native missionaries could then come to break down precisely those regional boundaries that missionary spheres had been formed to buttress. Native missionaries could go where Americo-European missionaries could not go, having received religious education at these local levels. If these boundaries had not been there, ironically, western missionaries would more often than not have taken this very role, with probably less successful results in terms of religious acculturation. Secular colonial policy therefore backfired, so that more universal indigenous links could be formed between various southern social and ethnic groups.

Thus, between 1928 and 1947, missionaries trained many Southern Christian teachers and catechists, who came out from teachers' training centers or intermediate/normal schools, and elementary schools, respectively. These "native" missionaries went to more remote corners of Southern Sudan where Western missionaries could not reach, and even used Christian works translated into local languages. This would seem to corroborate the missiologist Lamin Sanneh, who argues that "by their root conviction that the gospel is transmissible in the mother tongue, I suggest, missionaries opened the way for the local idiom to gain the ascendancy over assertions of foreign policy."[62] Because the Condominium government wanted to separate Northern and Southern education even further, students from Southern Sudan who aspired to enter post-secondary education were sent to Kampala in Uganda rather than to Khartoum in the Northern Sudan. Yet this had the result of creating an educated elite that somehow transcended the various ethnic boundaries within the South. Moreover, the ascent of black Sudanese to the religious ranks of those who previously had been seen to have been connected to colonial hegemony, could give them, and those they represented, a new founded and potentially empowering agency. For example, in the 1930s, many of these new indigenous elites in areas such as Equatoria and Western Bahr el Ghazal, realized that power and stature were moving away from certain forms of traditional leadership, towards a new elite often mission-educated Southerners, or those who had returned from universities such as those in Kampala. By the mid-1930s, those who had received some education at the CMS, APM and Roman Catholic schools had entered the civil colonial infrastructure.[63]

It is only through an understanding of this unintended indigenization of missionary education that we can contextualize the changing attitudes of Southern Sudanese after 1930, when it was they who provided the impetus and call for Western missionary education. Some boys entered school out of choice, while other sources even demonstrate that some asked to transfer from their previous schools to one of another mission, in another missionary zone.[64] Choice, of course, meant agency, and this might explain why in the 1930s, the government further limited the growth of intermediate education, emphasizing instead the "growth of more local crafts".[65] Overly educated and underemployed southern boys posed a threat to the status quo. British administrators in this way actually counted up the number of posts likely to be available and allowed only that number to continue beyond elementary schooling.[66] The same even applied to girls in missionary education, which reflected anything but the kind of anachronism that Mazrui would interpret. A CMS authority in 1924 noted that the new vernacular schools in Mawrada and Abu Rawf were exemplary and should be "multiplied." He even went as far as arguing that CMS education was "of too advanced a type for most Sudanese girls." A mission report, issued soon afterwards, concurred. It noted approvingly the government's new training college for female teachers, where "everything is native" so that "the CMS Girls' School syllabus is 200 years ahead of the Sudan!"[67] One can see why secular colonial administrators felt some anxiety regarding the possible threat to their policy of stasis, and preferred instead to encourage a more simple form of education, employing the rhetoric of respect for tribal structures to support this simplicity.

NORTHERN RESPONSES TO SOUTHERN SUDANESE-MISSIONARY ACTIVITY

Of course, it was not only British colonial administrators who anxiously noted the growing role of Southern missionaries, in their Western and indigenous forms. Just as British colonial anxiety towards missionary education matched their gradually declining grip on power after the Second World War, Northern Arab elites saw the continued presence of missionaries in another light: They might prevent Northern Arab power from filling any gap left in the South by the imminent departure of secular colonial administrators. While both sides in the 1940s and early 1950s often separated missionaries from any collaborative role in colonial governance, we may see that the Northern Arab reasoning in this regard was all-important. The fact that they opposed missionaries as an extra-Sudanese element, while at the same time employing the rhetoric of religious pluralism, will show us that that missionary groups could by the 1960s find themselves in the middle of a conflict between North and South that was racial, rather than religious, in nature. This will modify those analysts who point to the reversal of the British Closed District Ordinance, in 1946-47, as setting "the Christian and Muslim forces on a collision course," while at the same time accelerating "the rate of the expansion of Christian evangelism in Southern Sudan."[68]

There is no doubt that many initial Northern Sudanese proclamations spoke positively about the missionaries still working in the South in the 1940s and 1950s. Perhaps they simply mirrored the departing British authorities in this respect, seeking to maintain missionaries as a useful plug for a potential Southern power vacuum, in order to allow the North to maintain the strongest voice nationally. At a conference in Juba from 19 to

22 October 1953, missionary education was praised by the Northern Sudanese Awad Satti, the first Sudanese Director of Education. While clearly pointing towards the imminent departure of the British secular ruling hegemony, he also sought to reassure the Southerners that the "Sudan would continue to rely on the help and co-operation of the missions and would continue to need the fruitful work carried out by them in the sphere of education."[69] On 11 April 1954, Sayed Alo Abdel Rahman, another education minister in what was now a transitional government, even explicitly sought to separate the missionaries from any supposed involvement in colonial collaborative hegemony: "The present imperialists were responsible for the bad state of affairs in the South and not the Missionaries . . ."[70]

But how much of all this was simply rhetoric? Were missionaries used as a kind of reassuring symbol for a status quo that would be maintained in the South, without any further Northern encroachment within a postcolonial framework? An analysis of many of the statements in the mid-1950s show that this may indeed have been the case. When Ziada Arbab, the Minister of Education, expressed his "gratitude" to missionaries, as opposed to the British colonial infrastructure, he employed a rhetorical device designed to placate Southern interests, while still encircling them: In a speech on 13th February 1957, it is no coincidence that this "gratitude" was nonetheless a precursor to increasing "nationalization" (read Northern expansion) measures in the Southern Sudanese mission schools:

> . . . I should like to take this opportunity to express, on behalf of the Government, our gratitude for the good and devoted work which you have done in the field of Southern education since the beginning of this century . . . I assure you that they new policy does not in any way imply that the mission system of education is under suspicion by the Government for being disruptive of our national harmony. On the contrary, the Government is fully appreciating the good work which you have done and for which it has expressed its gratitude and admiration on several occasions . . .[71]

Missionary schools, as they stood, could be curtailed by Northern Sudanese governors, just as British administrators had sought to do. Yet such a rhetoric of "gratitude" meant that their curtailment did not have to be presented as a sign of fear, but rather, as a necessary development towards the growing nationalism of a postcolonial Sudan. Paradoxically, missionaries could be separated from any supposed collaboration with previous colonial elements, precisely in order to placate the South while nationalization measures were being carried out. Northern Sudanese elites could, by stating their ostensible gratitude towards the missionary legacy, represent the replacement of the latter as a positive step towards nationalization, rather than what it may truly have represented: A fear that they would form a competing hegemony with regards to their interests in the South. The indigenous Southerners, of course, would not be amenable to such reasoning, and a placating gratitude to missionaries, whose influence had often been indigenized, was designed with this point in mind.

Just as Southern educated elites were starting to appear, Prime Minister Abdalla's ban on missionaries was partially a means of asserting Northern hegemony against what was now an indigenous phenomenon. Sure enough, even the surface gratitude towards missionaries started to disappear now that the transition phase of government was over. They were accused of seeking "to operate, through different means, open and disguished [sic], against the public policies of the national government."[72] The Northern Arab dominated newly independent Sudanese leadership increasingly accused missionaries as being part of same hegemonic project as previous British colonial governors: ". . . Adoption of the Christian Faith, to make English the language of letter and communication, Stir national aspiration and sentiments based on fear, hate, and distrust of the Northerners. Magnify the differences in characteristics between South and North in order to widen the gulf and crear [sic] a separate political character for a separate southern entity."[73] Tellingly, during the debate on the continuance of missionaries in the country, Northern Arab elites reversed the British policy of missionary education, but did so for same general ends. Now, some Northern elites were only willing to tolerate missionaries if they were purely religious in nature, as opposed to the previous British administrators who worried that this might endow indigenous Southerners with a new identity, and heightened agency. Ali Baldo, the new Governor of Equatoria province now replied in the following manner to a missionary placement application by the Catholic Bishop Mazzoldi: "The Ministry of Education do not support the initiation of educational institutions by other than itself . . ." but only for "purely religious institutions."[74] The Taposa ethnic group in Equatoria would, in these new Northern Arab perceptions, be given too much agency from a *civic* form of education, given that it was they who were seeking civic control of the South under the banner of "nationalization."

In this way, an inverse policy to that of the British nonetheless masked a similar wish to maintain and perpetuate a new ruling hegemony.[75] Skopas Poggo has in fact shown that Ali Baldo disagreed with his District Commissioner in the Eastern District regarding the religious nature of missionaries in the Boya region.[76] The reasoning behind this disagreement supports our wider argument. If the Christian missionaries were carrying out "purely religious" duties among "wild tribes" then they should not be curtailed, Ali argued: "Education is now, unlike the past, a Government and not a Missionary duty and it is for you to see that Missions confine themselves to purely religious teachings."[77] Here, in the mind of men like Baldo, missionaries could at least pacify groups who remained recalcitrant, and outside of their national control. As long as this remained a purely religious pacification, they could then move their national civic order onto this pacified population. This, after all, formed part of their policy in other areas of the Southern Sudan, where they had initially placated communities with their "gratitude" towards the missionary legacy, which had been partially indigenized. Indeed a growing national language policy, which emphasized the learning of Arabic, put members of the newly educated Southern elites some "50 years back since English would not help him [them] any longer."[78]

The growing importance of Arabic in government offices automatically barred most Southerners from nearly all departments. By the early 1960s, many Southerners viewed this language policy as a means of the military government of Abboud to reduce them to "political slavery" just at the point when (partially thanks to an indigenized missionary education), they had the potential for a greater voice, and greater agency in a postcolonial Sudan.[79] This point is made even clearer when we remember Sharkey's study of the use of "Romanized Arabic" by missionary groups, at the behest of secular colonial administrators. Now, Northern politicians in the 1950s and 1960s advocated the Arabic alphabet as a "national script for rendering southern vernaculars." Hence "they promoted experiments, for example, with Shilluk rendered in Arabic script within some Upper Nile province elementary schools instead of the Romanized Shilluk that Christian mission schools had used."[80] This was one more linguistic move to maintain enhance a form of hegemony that had previously been constructed by British colonial administrators.

Given their initial surface toleration for specifically *religious* missions, it is interesting to note the language used in these increasingly strident Northern Sudanese statements. Here, racial identities were often most important, which may explain why doctrinal specifics did not arouse as much anxiety among Northern Muslims as one would have thought. For example, the new Department of Religious Affairs in 1955 aimed, in its own words, to spread "Islam and Arab culture in the non-Arab and non-Islamic parts of the Sudan."[81] We should note carefully the coupling of the words "Islam" and "Arab culture." This already demonstrates that religion and race were becoming even more intertwined in this postcolonial setting, so that the departure of missionaries may have said more about racial identity, than any ongoing religious competition between Islam and Christianity. Such an interpretation is in accordance with the latest historiography of Sudan, which seeks to move our understanding away from any easy dichotomy between Northern Muslim and Southern Christian, in favor of more ambiguous ethno-racial tensions.[82] Ali Abdel Rahman, Minister of the Interior in the Peoples' Democratic Party (P.D.P.)—Umma Party coalition government of Abdalla Khalil stated in 1958 that "The Sudan is an integral part of the Arab world . . . Anybody dissenting from this view must quit the country."[83] Where the British Governor General's report of 1929 had stated that "Missions are our bulwark against Islam in the Sudan," Northern Sudanese elites now often saw Islam and Arabism as a mutually inclusive bulwark against any other elements in the country.[84] Dr. Kamal Baghir, the Northern Sudanese head of the Department of Religious Affairs further outlined a missionary policy that in fact demonstrated profoundly racial concerns vis-à-vis North and South. In the Arabic newspaper *Rai El Amm*, he wrote the following on September 30th, 1959: "The nationalization of the Mission schools was an important step in the direction which recognizes cultural unification...and we, of the Department of religious affairs are ready to do our duty. We have begun with the opening of Islamic centers in the Southern Provinces and we will not cease to work (and are still) in the direction until we have realized the *cultural Islamic unity* which we seek [italics added]."[85]

Phrases such as "Cultural Islamic Unity" arguably represented an ethno-cultural concern, rather than a specifically religious one. In a circular worldview that ended with a racial identity, "Islam" was conflated with a "culture" that was, by its Northern Islamic nature, "Arabic." Thus, while Governor Ali Baldo offered a withering critique against Catholic missionaries, he did so through reference to their supposed propensity to foment racial, rather than religious, differences, within the context of "our national feeling." He went on to add that "We note with certitude as clear as the sun that origins of all the misfortunes and contrarieties in our way is the Roman Catholic Church and that the greater part of these evils come from it . . . .They do not cease to instil their poison and create the *spirit of racial division* [italics added]."[86] Southern students admitted into government schools in the 1960s were "threatened with loss of education if they go [went] to church on Sunday."[87] An official of the Ministry of Education in Khartoum testified that children of Christian parents were usually told that no room existed for them. Abboud's policy of "One religion (Islam), one culture, and one language (Arabic)—one nation (Sudan)" was increasingly apparent.[88] A Southern Sudanese petition thus portrayed the "nationalization" of mission schools as an attempt "to use these schools as a vehicle for the spread of Islam, because education has become the refined method of effecting the cultural assimilation of the Negroes."[89] Southerners now also perceived a racial-religious link.

In this way, where Northern "Arab" elites were wary of remaining missionary groups filling any gap left in the South by the imminent departure of secular colonial administrators, many of the new Southern educated elites responded to increased Northern nationalization measures with a different form of anxiety. As we have seen, a certain part of the early postcolonial Northern Sudanese rhetoric expressed a "gratitude" towards the missionary presence in the South, in order to placate Southerners while they carried out encroaching nationalization measures. It is difficult to gauge the initial optimism regarding missionaries among the Southern educated elites in the early 1950s. It may on one level have reflected a genuinely growing belief that missionaries were not part of the same hegemonic project built by British colonial officials. Yet when Sayed Kosmas Rababa, a Southern Member of Parliament, stated on 26 April 1954 that "for fifty years the Southerners have got all their education from the Missions; and the Sudan Government should be grateful... had it not been for the Missionaries, there would be no Southerners in parliament now," he may have been aware of a further issue.[90] Such a statement may also have reflected an anxiety that such missionary groups would be removed by a Northern dominated legislative assembly, so that a case needed to be made that they supported the Southern infrastructure, and maintained national stability. Sayed Edward Odhok, another Southern politician added that "the Missionaries have educated . . . the southern clerks [,] Sub-Mamurs and Ministers. The Missionaries should be thanked for this work."[91] Such southern political elites partially owed their status to a missionary education, and any link that the latter may have had with the British colonial order had to be conceptually broken. Paradoxically, any missionary link to the ousted colonial order had to be blurred by a Southern intelligentsia precisely in order to maintain some of the stability that such a link had in fact engendered. If this stability in the South was significantly diminished, a power vacuum would emerge, which could lead to the Northern Sudanese offering themselves as a challenge to missionary groups who they could easily de-legitimize through any supposed connection to the old colonial regime. Between 1948 and 1957, Southern youth, had increasingly sought western, often missionary, education. This was particularly the case in Bahr el Ghazal and Equatoria. As they came to enter the public sphere, their prestige was often linked to a retroactive perception of missionaries as separate from a colonial entity that, if anything, had restricted their abilities.[92]

As it became clear that Northern "gratitude" was mostly just rhetoric, Southerners thus sought to de-couple missionaries from any previous collaborative hegemony with British administrators. Yet they did so in order to enhance their legitimacy, so as to maintain the missionary position in a gap that could otherwise be filled by Northern hegemony. This phenomenon came to represent a response to the assertion of Northern racial, as opposed to specifically religious, identities. For Southerners, the presence in their midst of the missionary "other" was ironically perceived in terms of the protection of their *own* ethnicity and culture. The years following the nationalization of mission schools in 1957 lead the *Voice of Southern Sudan* to link "the domination and economic exploitation of the African people" to the spread of "Islam" southwards.[93] Tellingly, in these statements, "Islam" was often dichotomized alongside the word "African" rather than any Southern religious identity. Indeed, references to racial slavery often accompanied the charge that neo-Mahdists and Islamists approached Christianity as "an obstacle which must be removed and fast," so that missionaries would have to be eliminated.[94] In fact, as missionaries suffered greater expulsions after 1958, they perceived a far greater need to deepen religious understanding among southern converts so that they could withstand any increasing pressure from Northern groups. At this time, leaders of the CMS, APM, and Roman Catholic churches devised unprecedented "pilot experimentation" programs for meaningful dialogue (as opposed to missionary-style instruction, among Southern representatives.[95]

The elimination of missionaries was perceived by Southerners not so much as an assertion of a purely Islamic religious identity, but rather, as a means by which racial hegemony could be reasserted. Indeed, one should note the language used by Southern Sudanese intellectuals regarding the increasingly belligerent attacks by Northern politicians on missionary groups. After the various southern student riots of 1962/3, the Sudan Government accused outside Christian missionary forces of stoking the troubles. Yet Southern spokespeople reacted to such accusations in an interesting manner: They were meant "solely to divert and mislead public opinion," making missionaries the "victims of Arab religious chauvinism . . . Arab propaganda and double talk." Religion was used by the Sudan government as a basis for "national unity," which in fact represented a Northern racial chauvinism over the black south, according to this statement.[96] Note the word "Islam" was not mentioned once by the Southern Sudanese authors of this lament. Rather, they painted themselves-and missionaries-as victims of "Arab religious" chauvinism. In a peculiar hybrid, race had become connected to religion, making the doctrinal content of the latter less important than its use as a means to assert the interests of Northern ethno-racial groups. Indeed, in a letter to *The Times*, John V. Taylor, the General Secretary of the Church Missionary Society (CMS) of England, warned the world media not "to mask the far more serious issue of the political clash between the Arab-North and the African-South," as opposed to any specifically religious tensions.[97]

MISSIONARIES, SOUTHERN ANCESTRAL REVERENCE, AND A NEW POSTCOLONIAL PARADIGM FOR "EVANGELICAL NGOS"

The stage was now set for a new paradigm to develop within late twentieth century Southern Sudanese consciousness, thanks to a re-conceptualization of these previous encounters with the missionary "other" during the colonial and immediate postcolonial period. The position of missionaries in their near history (the colonial period) could combine with Southern indigenous ancestral spirituality, in order to form a historical counterpoint to the destruction inflicted upon their communities from Khartoum, and Northern elites, during the later twentieth century. We may see that this entailed the further separation of missionaries from any collaborative colonial hegemony, so that they could be seen as precursors to the kind of outside religious groups that provided resources and support to war-torn southern communities during the late twentieth century, in the form of evangelical NGOs.

The missionary expulsions that followed the student strikes in 1962 were counterproductive with regards to the assertion of Northern hegemony in the South. Northern rhetoric portrayed missionaries as an "outside" force lacking any indigenous legitimacy. On November 15, 1962, Abboud's military government introduced yet another provision: the Regulations for Missionary Societies. This "imposed innumerable previous approvals for even the most necessary actions, including repairs in one's home."[98] The mass expulsion of missionaries from the Southern Sudan soon followed the implementation of these regulations. Yet Northern rhetoric could be inverted by some Southern ethnic groups, who could fuse a notion of "outside" Christian interests with their indigenous conception of the spiritual *jok*. The latter was also partially perceived as an entity that would enter their region from without.[99] Moreover, the indigenization of the missionary gospel among groups such as the Nuer meant that a level of syncretism could now come about between Christian and traditional spirituality, given the fact that the two were now deemed to be equally under threat from Northern Sudanese groups. The indigenization of church leadership had been intended by the government to stop Western Christian proselytization in the South, and to stop religious acculturation more generally in the region. Yet all this did was to indigenize, localize and make vernacular the missionary gospel.[100] Nuer living in ruling areas, for example "were now exposed to Christianity by other Nuer, and the Christian teachings so presented seemed less exotic than the teachings of the missionaries. Conversion to Christianity grew rapidly after 1972, both in the rural areas and among Nuer migrant workers in Khartoum."[101] Moreover, Wal Duany describes the ability to temporarily unite when Nuer groups faced a common threat from "outside" forces: "Successful use of force by a non-Nuer group against any one Nuer region is perceived to undermine the peace of God among the Nuer. The belief in a common Nuer destiny imposes, then, a normative requirement: loyalty to the Nuer commonwealth. The operation of the Nuer commonwealth requires cooperation. It is this cooperation that makes it possible to describe the operation of the Nuer militia as a system of teams of teams."[102] They could be united by a common threat which was also posed against missionary groups, whose beliefs had in many cases molded synchronically with their own indigenous ones. Missionaries had translated Christian scriptures into the Nuer vernacular, thereby creating a literate pool of Nuer who began to "gain access to a literary tradition somewhat more congenial with their own (Nuer) covenantal theology."[103] This idea was perhaps further strengthened by the fact that many of the reformed missionaries' theology, most notably the American Presbyterian missionaries, was covenantal in nature. Covenants were always to be tested, and this idea could be maintained-even strengthened-after the official expulsion of missionaries in the later postcolonial period.

Particular Southern ancestral cosmologies could unite different ethnic groups such as the Dinka and Nuer, who before had been separated into different ethnic spheres, along the lines of different missionary spheres. A new ruling Northern Sudanese hegemony partially and unwittingly erased these differences through its own rhetoric of generalized "outside" Christian missionary forces. Various Nuer communities, for example, could be united by the expulsion of the missionaries, which they somehow saw has an attack on their own agency. Representatives of the United Presbyterian and Reformed missionaries issued a joint statement to Abboud's government that in fact demonstrated that the Christian mission was not a "western" imposition, but a more "universal" phenomenon: "We hope that the fact that Christianity is not a Western religion will enable the Sudanese government to reconsider its action on the basis of the fact that in their service to the people of the Sudan the missionaries represent the worldwide Christian community."[104] Vitally, such a conception, when perceived by indigenous Southern Sudanese Christian and spiritual leaders, could tie in form of spiritual "grace" from outside, that historians and anthropologists such as Francis Deng have analyzed in relation to various Southern communities. The Bari people, named the minor spirits *ngunyon*, while Nilotic communities such as the Dinka, Nuer, and the Luo Shilluk, Anywak, Acholi, called the minor spirits names such as *juok* or *juoki* to distinguish them from God, the supreme Creator Spirit, who was called *Ngun, Nyalit, Kwoth*, or perhaps most commonly, *Jok*. The latter could be perceived as an outside force, while the former were often related to the spiritual presence of ancestors in contemporary life.

If missionaries could be de-coupled from collaborative hegemony with former British colonial leaders, then their position alongside such ancestors several generations previously could be similarly understood. Lowrey has demonstrated that among the Nuer, some Christians "saw a relationship between former Nuer prophets, especially Ngundeng, Nuer covenantal theology and the new Christian message [in the later twentieth century]."[105] Johnson has noted that Stephen Lam, a Lou politician, "would readily, and quite happily, quote from the Bible or the songs of Ngundeng to prove a point. A convinced rather than pious Christian, he did not reject the sacrifice of animals accompanying prayers, as many of his co-religionists, but he was no less certain that Ngundeng, Dual Diu, and others had pointed the way towards his own faith. It could not be said that he was typical in the way that he combined these religious traditions, but neither was he unique."[106] Johnson continues that he was often told by Lou in the 1970s that, "when we heard about Jesus we were surprised, because Ngundeng had said it all before."[107] With a unifying attack from a Northern Sudanese government, many Southern Sudanese could turn to an ancestral spirituality for comfort and solace. This could come about even as tens of thousands within their community were murdered by Northern Arab forces. When this same attack affected missionary groups, the first missionary communities in the Southern Sudan could be perceived in the same manner as these ancestors.

The latter could be present thanks to a conception of contemporary ancestral spirits, while at the same time, "outside" evangelical Christian groups could also provide solace. Pitya's analysis of the changing perceptions of the figures of Jesus and Mary among various ethnic groups in the South is particularly interesting in this respect: After the 1950s, Bari communities identified Jesus and Mary with their local and legendary ancestral heroes and heroines, "Konyi," and "Kiden," respectively. With growing assaults on their communities from Northern armed militias during the 1970s and 1980s, Pitya's identification of human salvation motifs that embedded Bari ancestry within Christian cosmology, is particularly relevant for our present discussion. Southern converts could come to believe that "Christianity and their traditional religious and ancestral beliefs derived from the same source."[108] For the Bari, Jesus was also identified with "Mor," an ancient "unifier" king.[109] For the Shilluk and Dinka communities, Jesus was identified with "Nyikan" and "Deng Dit," the ancestors believed to have founded the communities.[110]

Indeed, while largely American evangelical NGOs absorbed a notion of an "ancient" Sudanese Christianity that preceded Islam, this point could be promoted amongst decimated Southern communities in less polemical terms during the civil strife of the 1970s and 1980s. The existence of Christianity in the Sudan (Nubia) prior to the dominance of Islam in Northern Nubia in the thirteenth century and in Southern Nubia in the sixteenth century is relevant to our discussion of indigenous links between ancestors and Christian historical actors. Like the missionaries during the comparatively stable colonial period, these ancient communities could perhaps also be understood through the prism of contemporary ancestral reverence.[111]

CONCLUSION

The position of the missionary "other" in their near history (the colonial period) could combine with their indigenous ancestral spirituality, in order to form a historical counterpoint to the destruction inflicted upon Southern indigenous communities from Khartoum's Northern elites during the later twentieth century. We have seen that this re-conceptualization could only take place because of very real ambiguities regarding the nature of collaborative hegemony during the colonial period, and the manner in which these connections, or disconnects, between missionary and colonial rulers, related to the competing hegemony of Northern Sudanese groups. This formed a continuity between the colonial and postcolonial period in Sudan. The expulsion of missionary groups during the postcolonial era mirrored the increased persecution of Southern Sudanese ethnic groups at the hands of a Northern ruling class who increasingly substituted religious identity with an overarching racial one. Hundreds of thousands died and were displaced as result in the last three decades of the twentieth century. Yet the "jok," even with its many incarnations between different Southern ethnic groups, could be accessed for solace, support and identity in the light of this persecution. The manner, in which missionaries were re-understood, and connected to an indigenous religious cosmology as a result of their perception as similar "outside" religious force, has been the subject of this chapter. During the destruction of the last decades of the twentieth century, new evangelical groups could also enter the Southern Sudan.[112] A paradigm had been created to make Southern communities more receptive to their entry into the region. It is perhaps too early to create a historical analysis of these "evangelical NGOs" who have been able to achieve some success in the region as a result in the last few years.[113] This ought to be the subject of the next chapter in the complex history of religious acculturation in Southern Sudan. What is clear, however, is that this next chapter has only been able to begin, thanks to the sometimes unintended consequences heralded by more established missionary groups during the colonial and immediate postcolonial period in Southern Sudan.

Notes

NOTES TO THE INTRODUCTION

1. Ogbu U. Kalu, "Missionaries, Colonial Government and Secret Societies in South-eastern Igboland, 1920–1950," *Journal of the Historical Society of Nigeria* 9, no. 1 (Dec. 1977): 75; T. O. Beidelman, *Colonial Evangelism* (Bloomington: Indiana University Press, 1981); "The Anthropology of Colonialism: Culture, History and the Emergence of Western Governmentality," *Annual Review of Anthropology* 26 (1997): 163–83.
2. Perhaps, Chinua Achebe's maverick character Nweke Ukpaka summarizes it all in his comment that "the white man, his government, the new religion, the new road, they are part of the same thing"—political aggrandizement through oppression and exploitation that was colonialism. See Chinua Achebe, *Arrow of God* (London: Heinemann, 1975), 105.
3. Jeffrey Cox, *Imperial Fault Lines: Christianity and Colonial Power in India, 1818–1940* (Stanford, CA: Stanford University Press, 2002), 6.
4. Jean Comaroff and John Comaroff, *Of Revelation and Revolution Vol. II: The Dialectics of Modernity on a South African Frontier* (Chicago: University of Chicago Press, 1997), 411. See also "The Colonization of Consciousness in South Africa," *Economy and Society* 18, no. 3 (August 1989), 267–96.
5. Comaroff and Comaroff, *Of Revelation and Revolution*, xi.
6. Felix K. Ekechi, *Missionary Enterprise and Rivalry in Igboland, 1857–1914* (London: Frank Cass, 1972), 114; and also Ekechi, "Colonialism and Christianity in West Africa: The Igbo Case," *Journal of African History* 21, no. 1 (1971): 103–15.
7. See E. A. Ayandele, *The Missionary Impact on Modern Nigeria, 1842–1914* (London: Longmans, 1966), chap. 2.
8. For other studies that have made similar argument, see F. Bowie, D. Kirkwood, and S. Ardener (eds.), *Women and Missions: Past and Present, Anthropological and Historical Perceptions* (Oxford: Berg, 1993). See also Ikenga R. A. Ozigbo, "An Evaluation of Christian Pioneering Techniques

with particular reference to Nigeria," *Nigerian Journal of Theology* 8, no. 1 (1994): 43–62.

9. Carol Summers, "Tickets, Concerts, and School Fees: Money and New Christian Communities in Colonial Zimbabwe, 1900–1940," in Kenneth Mills and Anthony Grafton (eds.), *Conversion: Old Worlds and New. Studies in Comparative History Series* (Rochester: University of Rochester Press, 2003), 254.

10. This was the same in many colonial societies. See for example, Peter Gose, "Converting the Ancestors: Indirect Rule, Settlement Consolidation, and the Struggle over Burial in Colonial Peru, 1532–1614," in Mills and Grafton (eds.), *Conversion*, 140.

11. Chukwudi A. Njoku, "The Missionary Factor in African Christianity, 1884–1914," in Ogbu U. Kalu (ed), *African Christianity: An African Story* (Pretoria: University of Pretoria Press, 2005), 241, (218–257).

12. Waibinte Wariboko, *Ruined by "Race": Afro-Caribbean Missionaries and the Evangelization of Southern Nigeria, 1895–1925* (Trenton, NJ: African World Press, 2006).

13. Ogbu U. Kalu, "African Christianity: An Overview," in Ogbu U. Kalu (ed), *African Christianity: An African Story* (Pretoria: University of Pretoria Press, 2005), 38.

14. See for instance Toyin Falola, *Violence in Nigeria: The Crisis of Religious Politics and Secular Ideologies* (Rochester, NY: University of Rochester Press, 2001), esp. 37–9.

15. Comaroff and Comaroff, *Of Revelation and Revolution*, 28.

16. Lamin Sanneh, *Translating the Message: The Missionary Impact on Culture* (Maryknoll, NY: Orbis Books, 1989), 5.

NOTES TO CHAPTER ONE

1. Jeffrey Cox, *Imperial Fault Lines: Christianity and Colonial Power in India, 1818–1940* (Stanford, CA.: Stanford University Press, 2002), 6.

2. The monographic literature on missionaries and British imperialism is voluminous and the range of topics beyond the scope of a single paper, particularly relating to South Africa. The most recent, excellent survey of the topic is Andrew Porter, *Religion versus empire? British Protestant missionaries and overseas expansion, 1700–1914* (Manchester, England: Manchester University Press, 2004). See also Brian Stanley, *The Bible and the Flag. Protestant missions & British imperialism in the nineteenth and twentieth centuries* (Leicester, England: Apollos, 1990); John de Gruchy, ed., *The London Missionary Society in Southern Africa, 1799–1999* (Athens, OH.: Ohio University Press, 2000); Leon de Kock, *Civilizing Barbarians: Missionary Narrative and African Textual Response in Nineteenth-Century South Africa* (Johannesburg: Witwatersrand University Press, 1996); Richard Elphick and Rodney Davenport, eds., *Christianity in South Africa: A Political, Social & Cultural History* (Berkeley Way, CA: University of California Press, 1997); Holger Bernt Hansen and Michael Twaddle, eds., *Christian Missionaries and the State in the Third World* (Athens, OH.: Ohio University Press, 2002).

3. Porter, *Religion versus Empire?*, 76.

4. John L. and Jean Comaroff, "Cultivation, Christianity and Colonialism: Towards a New African Genesis," in John De Gruchy, *The London Missionary Society in Southern Africa, 1799–1999* (Athens, OH: Ohio University Press, 2000), 55. For further discussion of the relationship between commerce and Christianity see Brian Stanley, "'Commerce and Christianity': Providence Theory, the Missionary Movement, and the Imperialism of Free Trade, 1842–1860," in *The Historical Journal* 26(1—March 1983): 71–94; and Andrew Porter, "'Commerce and Christianity': The Rise and Fall of a Nineteenth-Century Missionary Slogan," in *The Historical Journal* 28 (3—Sept. 1985): 597–621.

5. Or, as John Comaroff notes, the "dominated fraction of the dominant class," as described by Bourdieu. See John L. Comaroff, "Images of Empire, Contests of Conscience: Models of Colonial Domination in South Africa," in *American Ethnologist* 16 (4–1989): 663; and Pierre Bourdieu, *Distinction* (Cambridge: Harvard University Press, 1984), 421.

6. Richard Elphick, "Africans and the Christian Campaign in Southern Africa," in H. Lamar and L. Thompson, *The Frontier in History: North America and Southern Africa Compared* (New Haven, CT.: Yale University Press, 1981), 279.

7. Freund, "Cape under the Transitional Governments," in Richard Elphick and Hermann Giliomee, *The Shaping of South African Society, 1652-1840*, 2 ed. (Middletown, CT: Wesleyan University Press, 1988), 352; Elphick. "Africans," 282.

8. Christopher Saunders and Nicholas Southey, *A Dictionary of South African History* (Claremont, SA.: David Philip, 1998), 127.

9. J. S. Marais, *The Cape Coloured People, 1652–1937* (London: 1939; reprint ed., Johannesburg: Witwatersrand University Press, 1962), 33, 43–44.

10. Martin Legassick, "The Northern Frontier to 1840," in Elphick and Giliomee, *The Shaping, 1652–1840*, 2nd ed. (Middletown, CT.: Wesleyan University Press, 1988), 363–64. The most comprehensive study of the Griqua remains Martin Legassick, "The Griqua, the Sotho-Tswana, and the Missionaries, 1780–1840: the Politics of a Frontier Zone," (Ph.D.; University of California, 1969). See also Legassick, "Northern Frontier," 358–420; and Robert Ross, *Adam Kok's Griquas: A study in the development of stratification in South Africa* (Cambridge: Cambridge University Press, 1976). For a view of the Griqua as the "voortrekkers of civilization on the northern frontier," see Marais, *Cape Coloured People*, 32–108.

11. Legassick, "Northern Frontier," 370; Legassick, "Griqua," 176–77; Monica Wilson, "The Hunters and Herders," in Monica Wilson and Leonard Thompson (eds.), *The Oxford History of South Africa* (Oxford: Oxford University Press: 1969, 1971), 70; Ross, *Adam Kok's Griquas*, 1, 13–15.

12. A recent study by Nigel Penn, *The Forgotten Frontier: Colonial & Khoisan on the Cape's Northern Frontier in the 18th Century* (Athens, Ohio: Ohio University Press, 2005), although focusing on an earlier period, does

provide some very useful background and context for this paper. See particularly pages 268–87.

13. Legassick, "Northern Frontier," 376–7, 383.
14. Ibid., 276; Legassick, "Griqua," 146–51; Ross, *Adam Kok's Griquas*, 14–15.
15. Legassick, "Griqua," 174–75. See also Hermann Giliomee, *The Afrikaners. Biography of a People* (Charlottesville: University of Virginia Press, 2003), 41; and Elizabeth Isichei, *A History of Christianity in Africa. From Antiquity to the Present* (Grand Rapids, MI.: Eerdmans, 1995), 106.
16. Porter, *Religion versus Empire?*, 79.
17. Legassick, "Griqua," 195; Legassick, "Northern Frontier," 379.
18. Legassick, "Griqua," 196–200.
19. Ibid., 182–85; Legassick, "Northern Frontier," 377; Ross, *Adam Kok's Griquas*, 17–19; Karel Schoeman, ed., *The Mission at Griquatown, 1801–1821: An Anthology* (Griquatown: Griquatown Tourism Bureau, 1997), 14.
20. Legassick, "Northern Frontier," 377–78.
21. Ibid., 378–79.
22. Some of these points are briefly discussed in Marais, *Cape Coloured People*, 39; and Legassick, "Griqua," 200–1.
23. Legassick, "Northern Frontier," 387.
24. Ibid.
25. For a discussion of the problems associated with the identification of these and other societies on the northern frontier see Legassick, "Northern Frontier," 363–8.
26. Legassick, "Griqua," 177–9.
27. Ross, *Adam Kok's Griquas*, 15–20; Legassick, "Griqua," 195–200; Legassick, "Northern Frontier," 391.
28. Legassick, "Griqua," 226–38; Legassick, "Northern Frontier," 371–2; Ross, *Adam Kok's Griquas*, 16.
29. H. M. Robertson, "150 Years of Economic Contact between White and Black," in *South African Journal of Economics* III (1935): 403–407. For two examples of these *placaaten*, one for 12 April 1677 and another for 13 February 1770, see Donald Moodie, *The Record*, 1st ed. (Cape Town: 1838; reprint ed., Cape Town: A. A. Balkema, 1960), pt. I, 349–50 and pt. III, 5–6.
30. Hermann Giliomee, *Die Kaap tydens die Eerste Britse Bewind, 1795–1803* (Cape Town: Hollandsch Afrikaansche Uitgevers, 1975), 75, 200–5; R. F. M. Immelman, *Men of Good Hope: The Romantic Story of the Cape Town Chamber of Commerce 1804–1954* (Cape Town: Cape Town Chamber of Commerce, 1955), 14–17.
31. Somerset awaits a scholarly, fully-documented, objective biography. The Somerset biography by Anthony Millar meets none of these criteria. See Anthony Kendall Millar, *Plantagenet in South Africa. Lord Charles Somerset* (Cape Town: Oxford University Press, 1965).
32. Legassick, "Northern Frontier," 377; William M. Freund, "The Cape under the transitional governments, 1795–1814," in Elphick and Giliomee, *Shaping*, 340–343; Legassick, "Griqua," 153–65.

33. S. D. Neumark, *Economic Influences on the South African Frontier, 1652–1836* (Stanford, CA.: Stanford University Press, 1957): 117–23, 145–51.

34. Roger B. Beck, "Bibles and Beads: Missionaries as Traders in Southern Africa in the Early Nineteenth Century," *The Journal of African History* 30, no. 2 (1989): 214–5 and *passim*.

35. For a discussion of the trade, illegal and legal, prior to 1816 see Legassick, "Griqua," chs. I to VI; Legassick, "Northern Frontier," 364–90; and Peter Kallaway, "Danster and the Xhosa of the Gariep: Towards a Political Economy of the Cape Frontier 1790—1820," in *African Studies* 41 (1982): 143–60.

36. Stockenstrom to Bird, Graaff Reinet, 24 April 1817, Cape Archives Depot (CAD), 1/GR 16/6/669. See also Kenneth Wyndham Smith, *From Frontier to Midlands. A History of the Graaff-Reinet District, 1786–1910* (Grahamstown: Institute of Social and Economic Research, Rhodes University, 1976), 42.

37. "Somerset Proclamation of November 27, 1818," in *Proclamations, Advertisements, and other Official Notices, published by The Government of the Cape of Good Hope, from the 10th January, 1806 to the 2nd May, 1825* (Cape of Good Hope: at the Government Press, 1827), 431–2. See also Bird to Baird, Colonial Office, 4 December 1818, CAD, 1/GR 8/7/149; Somerset to Bathurst, Cape Town, 28 December 1818, Public Record Office, London (PRO), C. O. 48/37/19; and Stockenstrom to Anderson, Graaff Reinet, 2 February, 1819, CAD, 1/GR 16/8/1126.

38. Bird to Baird, Colonial Office, 4 December 1818, CAD, 1/GR 8/7/149.

39. Stockenstrom to Bird, Graaff Reinet, 24 April 1817, CAD, 1/GR 16/6/669.

40. Ibid.

41. Two examples of these hawkers are Jacobus Theron and Fredrick Preller. See the memorial of Jacobus Theron, CAD, C. O. 3917/115 and 1/GR 11/6; and the memorial of Fredrick Preller, CAD, C. O. 3907/103. For a discussion of these hawkers see Neumark, *Economic Influences*, 145–51. One example of a license to trade at the Kookfontein fair is that of 22 July 1819 for Johannes Gerhardus Brummer in CAD, 1/GR 14/127.

42. Bird to Baird, Colonial Office, 4 December 1818, CAD, 1/GR 8/7/149.

43. Ibid.

44. Stockenstrom to Anderson, Graaff Reinet, 2 February 1819, CAD, 1/GR 16/8/1126. "Briqua" is the name given to the Sotho-Tswana by the Khoikhoi. See C. C. Saunders, "Early Knowledge of the Sotho: Seventeenth and Eighteenth Century Accounts of the Tswana," *Quarterly Bulletin of the South African Library* 20 (March 1966): 60–70.

45. Anderson to Stockenstrom, Griqua Town, 24 March 1819, enclosed in Stockenstrom to Bird, Graaff Reinet, 19 July 1819, CAD, C. O. 2618/62.

46. Anderson to Stockenstrom, Griqua Town, 12 April 1819, enclosed in Stockenstrom to Bird, Graaff Reinet, 19 July 1819, CAD, C. O. 2618/62.

47. *Cape Town Gazette and African Advertiser*, 26 June 1819. Baird appears to have first learned of the date for the fair from this announcement. See Baird to Stockenstrom, Beaufort, 13 July 1819, CAD, 1/BFW 11/1/272.

48. See *Cape Town Gazette and African Advertiser*, 11 September 1819.

49. Baird to Stockenstrom, Beaufort, 13 July, 1819, CAD, 1/BFW 11/1/272. George Thompson estimated that by 1823 the Griqua had obtained about 500 muskets through trade with the Boers. See George Thompson, *Travels and Adventures in Southern Africa*, ed., Vernon S. Forbes, Van Riebeeck Society (VRS), vol. 48 (Cape Town: VRS, 1967): 77.

50. Stockenstrom to Baird, Graaff Reinet, 16 July 1819, CAD, 1/BFW 9/29.

51. Ibid. Stockenstrom informed Baird that "Johs. Brummer one of the Merchants will deliver to you a Set of Scales and weights to be used at the fair." For a discussion of Brummer's application to trade at the fair see Baird to Meintjes, Beaufort, 30 July 1819, CAD, 1/BFW 11/1/289, and Brummer's permit to trade, Graaff Reinet, 22 July 1819, CAD, 1/GR 14/127.

52. Stockenstrom to Anderson, Graaff Reinet, 19 July 1819, enclosed in Stockenstrom to Bird, Graaff Reinet, 19 July 1819, CAD, C. O. 2618/62. See also Stockenstrom's letter to the Kookfontein missionary Erasmus Smit, Graaff Reinet, 19 July 1819, enclosed in Stockenstrom to Bird, Graaff Reinet, 19 July 1819, CAD, C. O. 2618/62.

53. Anderson to Baird, Griqua Town, 15 July, 1819, CAD, 1/BFW 9/57. Three days before Anderson informed the LMS in London that "the Government have requested me to supply passes to those who will be admitted to Cross," but made no mention of his intended trading. See Anderson to Burder, Orange River, 12 July, 1819, SOAS, CWM. Incoming letters, Box 8, Folder 1, Jacket C.

54. Fairs were never held on Sunday at any of the sites. Campbell quotes Baird as telling him that at this first fair the Griqua "kept regular meetings for worship, morning and evening, and some of them gave addresses from the Scriptures." He does not say whether the colonial traders followed the Griqua's example. John Campbell, *Travels in South Africa, Undertaken at the Request of the London Missionary Society; Being a Narrative of a Second Journey in the Interior of that Country*, (hereafter cited as *Second Journey*), 2 vols. (London: 1822; reprint ed., 2 vols. in 1, New York: Johnson Reprint Corporation, 1967), 1, 20–1.

55. Baird to Bird, Beaufort, 19 August 1819, CAD, 1/BFW 11/1/304. This dependency, or client, relationship is discussed in Legassick, "Griqua," chs. 4 and 5. When asked about the "Bushmen" attending the Beaufort fairs, Moffat testified that "some came as followers with the Griquas, but none for the purpose of transacting any business themselves." See "Evidence of Mr. Moffat, a Missionary, resident with the Bitchuana tribes at Latakoo," given before the Commissioners of Enquiry, 20 April 1834, *Imperial Blue Book*, no. 50 of 1835, 126.

56. Baird to Bird, Beaufort, 19 August 1819, CAD, 1/BFW 11/1/304.

57. Baird to Bird, Beaufort, 19 August 1819, CAD, 1/BFW 11/1/304. See also Baird to Stockenstrom, Beaufort, 19 August 1819, CAD, 1/BFW 11/1/305. Legassick describes the two fairs of 1819 and 1820 in more negative terms then did Baird, and attaches little significance to their existence. See Legassick, "Griqua," 238–40.

58. Stockenstrom to Bird, Graaff Reinet, 25 February 1820, CAD, 1/GR 16/9/1360.

59. Ibid. See also the advertisement for the sale of these plots of land in the *Cape Town Gazette and African Advertiser*, 25 March 1820.

60. *Cape Town Gazette and African Advertiser*, 18 March 1820.

61. Stockenstrom to Bird, Beaufort, 4 May 1820, CAD, C. O. 2625/36. This Tswana chief, Chaka, should not be confused with the famous Zulu leader of the same name. See Legassick, "Griqua," 267. Campbell reported meeting Chaka and Maklanaka on their way to this fair in March 1820. They carried "skins, assagais, knives, shields, &c to exchange for beads at the fair." Campbell, *Second Journey*, 1: 59–60.

62. Stockenstrom to Bird, Beaufort, 4 May 1820, CAD, C. O. 2625/36.

63. Ibid.

64. Philip to Burder, Cape Town, 29 July 1820, SOAS, CWM, Incoming letters, Box 8, Folder 2, Jacket B.

65. "Evidence of Mr. Moffat, a Missionary, resident with the Bitchuana tribes at Latakoo," before the Commissioners of Enquiry, 20 April 1824, *Imperial Blue Book*, no. 50 of 1835, p. 128.

66. Moffat to Burder, Griqua Town, 1820, SOAS, CWM, Incoming letters, Box 8, Folder 2, Jacket E.

67. R. Hamilton, Burder Place, near Lattakoo, entry for 22 June, 1820, Kuruman, Journal for January 7—December 29, 1820, SOAS, CWM, Journals, Box 3, Folder 75, South Africa 1821.

68. Helm to John Philip, Griqua Town, 21 June 1821, SOAS, CWM, Incoming letters, Box 8, Folder 3, Jacket B.H.

69. Helm to John Philip, Griqua Town, 2 September 1822, SOAS, CWM, Incoming letters. Box 8, Folder 5, Jacket B.

70. Melvill to Bird, Griqua Town, 27 June 1822, CAD, C. O. 164/32. Melvill was the government surveyor on the northern frontier from 1815 to 1822 when he took the post of government representative in Griqua Town. He worked for the government until about 1841 when he resigned to become a LMS missionary.

71. Moffat to Burder, Griqua Town, 1820, SOAS, CWM, Incoming letters, Box 8, Folder 2, Jacket E. See also "Evidence of Mr. Moffat, a Missionary, resident with the Bitchuana tribes at Latakoo," before the Commissioners of Enquiry, 20 April 1824, *Imperial Blue Book*, no. 50 of 1835, 128 and Melvill to Bird, Griqua Town, 27 June 1822, CAD, C. O. 164/32.

72. Philip to Burder, Cape Town, 29 July 1820, SOAS, CWM, Incoming letters, Box 8, Folder 2, Jacket B.

73. SOAS, CWM, Incoming letters, Box 8, Folder 3, Jacket A, Graaff Reinet, 6 April 1821, enclosed letter with one of Lattakoo, 10 February 1821, Hamilton to Stockenstrom who passed the letter on to A. Faure who added this comment in the letter to Philip.

74. Helm to Stockenstrom, Griqua Town, 8 November 1820, CAD, 1/GR 10/2/50.

75. Melvill to Burder, Griqua Town, 19 May 1824, SOAS, CWM, Incoming letters, Box 9, Folder 2, Jacket B.

76. Stockenstrom to Bird, Graaff Reinet, 8 February 1821, CAD, C. O. 2633/16.

77. Ellis to Stockenstrom, Colonial Office, 21 February 1821, CAD, 1/BFW 9/30.
78. Stockenstrom to Bird, Graaff Reinet, 1 March 1821, CAD, 1/GR 16/10/1693. See also Stockenstrom to Baird, Graaff Reinet, 1 March 1821, CAD, 1/GR 16/10/1694.
79. Helm to Stockenstrom, Griqua Town, 2 April 1821, CAD, 1/GR 10/2/67. See also Melvill to Baird, Beaufort, 6 May 1822, CAD, 1/BFW 9/27.
80. Kay to George Marsden, entry for 5 April 1821, Griqua Town, 30 miles north of the Great or Orange River, letter of 8 May, 1821, SOAS, MMS, Correspondence, Box 299 A. 1, Folder 4, 21, Number 13.
81. Helm to Bird, Griqua Town, 29 April 1822, CAD, 1/BFW 9/27. See also Melvill to Bird, Brak River, 27 May 1822, CAD, BFW 9/27.
82. Melvill to Bird, Griqua Town, 27 June 1822, CAD, C. O. 164/32. Melvill enclosed a list of suitable trade articles that included fabrics, carpenter and blacksmith tools, beads, and ironware such as pots, picks, and spades.
83. Ibid.
84. Melvill to Baird, Griqua Town, 18 February 1823, CAD, 1/BFW 9/27.
85. Ibid. No information about Oliver was uncovered.
86. Wyndham Smith argues that white farmers in the Graaff Reinet district cooperated with the government and only traded with Africans possessing passes, or at the fairs, while those in the Nieuweveld area of the Tulbagh district, said that oxen were the "'best passes'" the Africans could have. See Wyndham Smith, *From Frontier to Midlands*, 42. See also Stockenstrom to Bird, Graaff Reinet, 17 March 1818, CAD, 1/WOC 12/65 and Denissen to Stockenstrom, Fiscal's Office, Cape Town, 11 September 1818, CAD, 1/GR 9/11.
87. H. Helm—C. Sass, Griqua Town. Extracts of Journal of Helm and Sass. Entry for 11 May 1824, SOAS, CWM, Journals, Box 4, Folder 84, South Africa, March 14-July 31 1824. A more complete account of particular peoples and events during this period is found in Legassick, "Griqua," chs. 6, 7, and 10.
88. For a thorough description and accurate analysis of the politics of northern and northwestern frontier zones during this period, see Legassick, "Griqua," chs. 6 and 7. See also Ross, *Adam Kok's Griquas*, 15–21; and Melvill to Plasket, Cape Town, 17 December 1824, SOAS, CWM, Incoming letters, Box 9, Folder 2, Jacket E.
89. Stockenstrom to Brink, Graaff Reinet, 22 October 1824, CAD, 1/GR 16/13/3432.
90. Melvill to Plasket, Cape Town, 17 December 1824, SOAS, CWM, Incoming letters, Box 9, Folder 2, Jacket E. See also Marais, *Cape Coloured People*, 39.
91. Melvill to Plasket, Cape Town, 17 December 1824, SOAS, CWM, Incoming letters, Box 9, Folder 2, Jacket E; Legassick, "Griqua," 305.
92. Legassick, "Griqua," 310–11, 314–15; Stockenstrom to Brink, Graaff Reinet, 22 October 1824, CAD, 1/GR 16/13/3431.
93. Legassick, "Griqua," 312–14.

94. Melvill to Plasket, Cape Town, 17 December 1824, SOAS, CWM, Incoming letters, Box 9, Folder 2, Jacket E. See also Melvill to Burder, Griqua Town, 17 October 1825, SOAS, CWM, Incoming letters, Box 9, Folder 4, Jacket A.

95. Stockenstrom to Brink, Graaff Reinet, 22 October 1824, CAD, 1/GR 16/13/3431.

96. Proclamation of 27 January 1825, in *Proclamations, Advertisements, and other Official Notices*, 690–91. See also Stockenstrom to Plasket, Graaff Reinet, 13 January 1825, with enclosed regulations drawn up by the government for trade between the Griqua and the colony, CAD, C. O. 2667/8.

97. Stockenstrom to Plasket, Graaff Reinet, 13 January 1825, with enclosed regulations drawn up by the government for trade between the Griqua and the colony, CAD, C. O. 2667/8.

98. Brink to Stockenstrom, Colonial Office, 28 January 1825, CAD, 1/GR 8/15/730. It appears that Goeyman did continue to permit hawkers to traffic with the Bergenaars, at least until April 1825. See Stockenstrom to Melvill, Graaff Reinet, CAD, 1/GR 16/15/3732. J. Goeyman was a Khoi missionary assistant and his mission was to the San, but the Bergenaars had settled about the station. See Melvill to Plasket, Griqua Town, 5 September 1825, CAD, C. O. 232/242 1/2 (that is, 242 and one half).

99. Stockenstrom to Plasket, Graaff Reinet, 1 June 1825, CAD, 1/GR 16/15/3801.

100. Ibid.

101. Plasket to Stockenstrom, Colonial Office, 23 June 1825, CAD, 1/GR 8/15/781.

102. Melvill to Plasket, Griqua Town, 23 May 1825, CAD, C. O. 231/114; and Melvill to Plasket, Griqua Town, 5 September 1825, CAD, C. O. 232/242½.

103. Melvill to Burder, Griqua Town, 17 October 1825, SOAS, CWM, Incoming letters, Box 9, Folder 4, Jacket A.

104. Ibid. See also Melvill to Plasket, Griqua Town, 23 May 1825, CAD, C. O. 231/114; and Melvill to Plasket, Griqua Town, 5 September 1825, CAD, C. O. 232/242½.

105. For a more complete description of this meeting, its significance and the consequences for political hegemony on the northern frontier see Legassick, "Griqua," 318–25. John Centlivres Chase touched on many of the problems surrounding this northern border trade in the last two of a series of articles he wrote in 1825 under the penname of "Evitas." See "Evitas," "Notice on the Nature, Extent, and Promise of the Trading Intercourse with the Transgariapine Nations, and present state of some of the Tribes on the Northern Frontier of the Cape Colony," in *South African Commercial Advertiser*, 16 November and 23 November 1825.

NOTES TO CHAPTER TWO

1. K. O. Dike, *Trade and Politics in the Niger Delta 1830–1885* (Oxford: Clarendon Press 1956) 47–64; A. J. H. Latham, *Old Calabar 1600–1891* (Oxford: Clarendon Press 1973), 55–90.

2. W. E. Wariboko, "New Calabar and the Forces of Change ca 1850–1945" (Unpublished Ph.D Thesis, University of Birmingham, 1991), 73.

3. J. C. Anene, *Southern Nigeria in Transition 1885–1906* (Cambridge: Cambridge University Press 1966), 336.

4. W. I. Ofonagoro, *Trade and Imperialism in Southern Nigeria, 1881–1929* (New York: Nok, 1979).

5. W. E. Wariboko, *Planting Church-Culture at New Calabar: Some neglected aspects of missionary enterprise in the Eastern Niger Delta 1865–1918* (Bethesda: International Scholars Publications 1998), 1.

6. A. E. Afigbo, "Christian Missions and Secular Authorities in South-eastern Nigeria from Colonial Times" in *The History of Christianity in West Africa* (London: Longman 1980), 187.

7. D. M. Schreuder, "The Cultural Factor in Victorian Imperialism" *Journal of Imperial and Commonwealth History* 4, no. 3 (May 1976): 283–317.

8. J. N. Cheetham, "Nigeria—the future of the Country" *Southport Visitor* 28 May, 1914.

9. Cheetham, "Nigeria," 28 May, 1914.

10. Cheetham, "Nigeria," 28 May, 1914.

11. CA3/04/429 D.C. Crowther, "Reporting on a visit to New Calabar," 22 January 1874.

12. D. Fraser, *The Future of Africa* (1911; reprint Westport: Negro University Press 1970), 96.

13. FO 84/1882 Harry Johnston, "Memorandum on the British Protectorate of the Oil Rivers with suggestions as to its future government," 20 July 1888.

14. J. N. Cheetham, "Southern Nigeria–Missionaries and the Denationalization of the Negro," *Southport Visitor,* 23 March 1912.

15. C. W. Mills, *The Racial Contract* (Ithaca: Cornell University Press 1991), 21.

16. P. Gilroy, *Against Race: Imagining Political Culture beyond the Colour Line* (Cambridge: Cambridge University Press 2000); K. A. Appiah, "Race, Culture, and Identity: Misunderstood Connections" in K. A. Appiah and A. Gutman (eds.), *Colour Consciousness: The Political Morality of Race* (Princeton: Princeton University Press 1996); C. W. Mills, *Blackness Visible: Essays on Philosophy and Race* (London: Cornell University Press), 1998.

17. G3A3/1890/140 S. A. Crowther, "Difficulties on the way of Missionary work on the West Coast of Africa," August 1890.

18. Mills, *The Racial Contract* 128–9.

19. R. M. Nettleford, *Mirror Mirror: Identity, Race and Protest in Jamaica* (Kingston: LMH Publishing Limited 1998), xxxiv.

20. CA3/04/554 S.A. Crowther to Sir W.N.N. Hewitt 7 August 1879.

21. G3A3/1888/75 S.A. Crowther to Rev. R. Lang 31 January 1888.

22. Wariboko, "New Calabar and the Forces of Change," 267.

23. G3A3/1890/67 S. A. Crowther, 22 May 1890.

24. G3A3/1893/97 Bishop Hill to Rev. F. Baylis, November, 1893.

25. J. F. A. Ajayi, *Christian Missions in Nigeria 1841–1891: The Making of a New Elite* (London: Longman 1965), 58.

26. CA3/04/460 D. Crowther, "Letter to the Directors of the British and African Steamship Navigation Company, asking their help towards the Mission, by allowing freight free in their steamer of any box sent by the 'Missionary Leaves Association'" 28 March 1874.
27. CA3/04/748 S. A. Crowther, April 1865.
28. H. Johnston, "A Report on the British Protectorate of the Oil Rivers," 1 December, 1888.
29. G3A3/1881/38 "Rev. Walter E. Carew's letter showing the influence of heathen priests and priestesses on the King and Chiefs of New Calabar," 7 June1881.
30. G3A3/1884/139 S. A. Crowther to Rev. Lang, 6 August, 1884. (There is a hand-written copy of the "Treaty of Protection" bearing the class mark just cited).
31. G3A3/1884/139 Rev. W. E. Carew to Rev. Lang, 2 August, 1884.
32. CA3/013/20 "Conference of West African Protestant Missionaries held at Gabon" February to March, 1875.
33. CA3/04/541 Thomas Johnson to S. A. Crowther, 15, June 1876 (King Ockiya's letter to Crowther is enclosed in Johnson's letter).
34. CA3/04/544 S. A. Crowther to Hutchinson, 26 June 1876.
35. CA3/04/554 S. A. Crowther to Sir W. N. N. Hewitt (Commodore Royal Navy), "A Brief statement of advantages accruing to Protestant Christian Missions through the benign operations, and moral influence of British Government on the West Coast of Africa," 9 August, 1879.
36. CA3/04/554 S. A. Crowther to Sir W. N. N. Hewitt (Commodore Royal Navy), 9 August, 1879.
37. A. Toynbee, *Change and Habit: The Challenge of our Time* (Oxford: One World 1992), 191.
38. G3A3/1891/203 "The Oil Rivers Commissionship," *Times* 30 May 1891.
39. T. N. Tamuno, *The Evolution of the Nigerian State: the Southern phase, 1898–1914* (London: Longman 1972), 51.
40. Ofonagorc, *Trade and Imperialism*, 161.
41. S. J. S. Cookey, *King Jaja of the Niger Delta: His Life and Times, 1821–1891* (New York: Nok 1974), 106–61.
42. Tamuno, *The Evolution of the Nigerian State*, 23.
43. Wariboko, "New Calabar and the Forces of Change," 271–80.
44. G3A3/1894/49 MacDonald to Secretary, CMS, 10 May, 1894.
45. J. B. Webster, *The African Churches among the Yoruba 1882–1922* (Oxford: Clarendon Press 1964), 26.
46. Wariboko, *Planting Church-Culture at New Calabar*, 135.
47. G3A3/1905/168 Bishop Johnson, "*Journal Report*," December July 1905.
48. Afigbo, "Christian Missions and Secular Authorities," 193.
49. J. P. Kirby. "Cultural Change and Religious Conversion in West Africa" in D. T. Blakely, E. A. W. Beek, D. L. Thomson (eds.), *Religions in Africa* (London: Heinemann, 1994), 61.
50. Degdist 3/1/3 A.F.F.P. Newns, "Reorganization Report on the Kalabari Clan," May 1947.
51. G3A3/1904/54 D.C. Crowther to F. Baylis, 5 October 1905.

52. G3A3/1903/121 Thos Alvarez to Rev. F. Baylis, 10 December, 1903.
53. G3A3/1903/96 "Niger Mission Executive Committee Minutes" September, 1903.
54. *Jamaica Diocesan Magazine* VI, No. 6 [January 1932].
55. J. N. Cheetham, "In a West African Assize Court," *Southport Visitor,* 4 May 1913.
56. C. G. Baeta, "Introductory Review," in *Christianity in Tropical Africa* ed. C. G. Baeta (Oxford: Oxford University Press 1968), 12.
57. P. Bryan, *The Jamaican People 1880–1920* (London: MacMillan 1991), 252.
58. J. N. Cheetham, "Southern Nigeria–The Future of the Country," *Southport Visitor,* 5 April, 1908.
59. L. E. P. Erith, "The Pongas Mission," *The Jamaican Diocesan Magazine* Vol. VII, No.8 (March 1933).
60. W. E. Wariboko, "Why there is no West Indian Church among the Susus in West Africa today: A critique of the Pongas Mission and its Portrayal of Blackness, 1855–1935 (Unpublished conference paper, 2006). See revised version in this volume.
61. O. U. Kalu, "Christianity and Colonial Society," in O. U. Kalu (ed.), *The History of Christianity in West Africa* (London: Longman 1980), 182.

NOTES TO CHAPTER THREE

1. This research was made possible with funds from the University of Louisville's Dean's Incentive Fund, History Department's Dale Fund, and Pan African Studies Faculty research fund. I owe immense gratitude to Lee Keeling and Andrea Lauago who worked on several archival materials crucial for this paper.
2. Included among these dominant sources are Apolo Kagwa's *Ekitabo kye mpisa za Baganda* [*The Customs of Baganda in the Luganda Language*] (Kampala: Uganda Printing and Publishing Co., Ltd., 1918); and *Ekitabo kya Basekabaka be Buganda, na be Bunyoro, na be Koki, na be Toro, na be Nkole* [*History of the Kings of Buganda, Bunyoro, Koki, Toro and Ankole in the Luganda Language*] (London: Sheldon Press, 1927; reprint Kampala: Bookshop *ne* East Africa Publishing House, 1971), 129. Other important sources are found in forms of autobiographies and biographies—most of them unpublished. For a brilliant review of these memoirs, see John A. Rowe, "Myth, Memoir, and Moral Admonition: Luganda Historical Writing 1893–1969," *Uganda Journal* 33 (1969): 17–40; and also Rowe, "Eyewitness Accounts of Buganda History: The Memoirs of Ham Mukasa and His Generation," *Ethnohistory* 36, no. 1 (Winter 1989): 61–9.
3. For instance, see Roland Oliver, *The Missionary Factor in East Africa* (London and New York: Longman 1952), which represents one of the pioneer examples followed by many others after.
4. J. P. Thoonen, *Black Martyrs* (London: Sheed and Ward, 1942); J. F. Faupel, *African Holocaust* (London: Geoffrey Chapman, 1962); and Jean Brierly and Thomas Spear, "Mutesa, the Missionaries, and Christian Conversion

in Buganda," *International Journal of African Historical Studies* 21 no. 4 (1988): 601–18

5. Tarsis B. Kabwegere, "The Dynamics of Colonial Violence: The Inductive System in Uganda," *Journal of Peace Research* 9, no. 4 (1972): 303–14.

6. Michael Twaddle, "The Emergence of Politico-Religious Groupings in Late Nineteenth century Buganda," *Journal of African History* 29, no. 1 (1988): 81.

7. J. D. Y. Peel, "Conversion and Tradition in Two African Societies: Ijebu and Buganda," *Past and Present* 77 (1977), 108–41. For studies on despotism, status culture and social mobility, see Lloyd A. Fallers, "Despotism, Status Culture and Social Mobility in an African Kingdom," *Comparative Studies in Society and History* 2, no. 1 (Oct. 1959): 11–32; and Michael Twaddle, "Ganda Receptivity to Change," *Journal of African History* 25, no. 2 (1974): 303–15. The overflowing literature on martyrdom includes a more nuanced account by John A. Rowe, "The Purge of Christians at the Mwanga's Court: A Reassessment of this Episode in Buganda's History," *Journal of African History* 5, no. 1 (1964): 55–71.

8. See for instance Holger Bernt Hansen's "Church and State in Early Colonial Uganda," *African Affairs* 85, no. 338 (Jan. 1986), 55–74. Hansen's paper emerged as a response to Richard Gray's "Christianity and Religious Change in Africa," 77, no. 306 (Jan. 1978): 89–100.

9. Kagwa, *Basekabaka*, 45.

10. See Mbonu Ojike, *I Have Two Countries* (New York: The John Day Company, 1947), 208; B. A. Ojike, *Social and Political History of Nigeria for Schools and Colleges* (Aba, Nigeria: International Press, 1961), 30.

11. Mbonu Ojike, "Week-end Catechism," *West African Pilot*, 5 June 1948, 2.

12. Robert Pickering Ashe, *Chronicles of Uganda* (London: Hodder and Stoughton, 1894), 55.

13. Peel, "Conversion and Tradition," 117.

14. See Om Ham Mukasa, "Ebija ku Mulembe gwa Kabaka Mutesa [Some Notes on the Reign of Mutesa]" *Uganda Journal* 2, no. 1–4 (1934/35): 70. For an impressive explanation on this, see Benjamin C. Ray, *Myth, Ritual, and Kingship in Buganda* (New York and Oxford: Oxford University Press, 1991), 206.

15. M. S. M. Kiwanuka, *A History of Buganda: From the Founding of the Kingdom to 1900* (New York: Africana, 1972), 125, 189.

16. Donald Anthony Low, *Buganda in Modern History* (Berkeley: University of California Press, 1971), 18. For more on this assertion, see also D. A. Low, *Religion and Society in Buganda, 1875–1900* (Kampala: East African Institute of Social Research, 1957). Low maintains that the king's only serious rivals were the priests.

17. H. P. Gale, "Mutesa I—Was He a God?" *Uganda Journal* 20, no. 1 (1956): 79

18. M. S. M. Kiwanuka, *A History of Buganda: From the Founding of the Kingdom to 1900* (New York: Africana, 1972), 101.

19. Steve Feierman, *The Shambaa Kingdom: A History* (Madison: University of Wisconsin Press, 1974). A few other prominent studies include Randall

M. Packard, *Chiefship and Cosmology: An Historical Study of Political Competition* (Bloomington: Indiana University Press, 1981); George B. Ayitteh, *Indigenous African Institutions* (New York: Transnational Publishers, 1991).

20. Michael G. Kenny, "Mutesa's Crime: Hubris and the Control of African Kings," *Comparative Studies in Society and History* 30, no. 4 (Oct. 1988): 595–612.

21. For an up-to-date analysis on this, see William Idowu, "Law, Morality and African Cultural Heritage: The Jurisprudential Significance of the Ogboni Institution," *Nordic Journal of African Studies* 14, no. 2 (2005), 175–92. See also Robin Law, *Oyo Empire, c. 1600–1836: a West African Imperialism in the Era of Atlantic Slave Trade* (Oxford: Clarendon Press, 1977); Robert Sidney Smith, *Kingdoms of the Yoruba* (Madison, Wisconsin: University of Wisconsin Press, 1988), 65–82; and David D. Laitin, *Hegemony and Culture: Politics and Religious Change among the Yoruba* (Chicago: University of Chicago Press, 1986).

22. See Packard, *Chiefship and Cosmology*, 4–6, 84. Packard asserts that "African kinships have shown that kings were frequently defined by members of society as ritual mediators between society and the forces of nature . . . they were closely associated with well-being of the land and society" (6).

23. Reverend John Roscoe, *The Baganda* (London: Macmillan, 1911), 229; Wrigley, "Christian Revolution," 39. See also John Allen Rowe, "Revolution in Buganda 1856–1900" (PhD Thesis, The University of Wisconsin, 1966), 2–3.

24. Ashe, *Chronicles*, 67.

25. Gale, "Mutesa I," 72–3.

26. Twaddle, "Mutesa's Crime," 601.

27. Mackay, *Mackay of Uganda*, 148.

28. Kagwa, *Basekabaka*, 129.

29. Gale, "Mutesa I," 81.

30. Ashe, *Chronicles*, 65.

31. Gale, "Mutesa I," 82.

32. Henry M. Stanley, *Through the Dark Continent* (New York: Harper and Brothers, 1878), 206.

33. Dorothy Stanley, *The Autobiography of Sir Henry Morton Stanley edited by his wife Dorothy Stanley* (Boston and New York: Houghton Mifflin Company, 1909), 312.

34. Julien P. Gorju, *Entre le Victoria, l'Albert, et l'Edourd* [*Between Victoria, Albert and Edward*] (Rennes : Oberthur, 1920), 261–2. See also Gale, "Mutesa I," 77.

35. Brierley and Spear, "Mutesa," 613. See also A. M. Lugira, "Redemption in Ganda Traditional Belief," *Uganda Journal* 32, no. 2 (1968): 201; Thoonen, *Black Martyrs*, 57; Wrigley, "Christian Revolution," 38

36. Karugire, *History of Uganda*, 69.

37. For a detailed read on this, see John Kelly Thornton, *The Kongolese Saint Anthony: Dona Beatrice Kimpa Vita and the Antonian Movement*

1684–1706 (Cambridge: Cambridge University Press, 1998), esp. 33–51; 114–157; and also Thornton, "The Development of an African Catholic Church n the Kingdom of Kongo, 1491–1750," *Journal of African History 25*, no. 2 (1984): 147–67.

38. Samwiri Rubaraza Karugire, *A Political History of Uganda* (Nairobi and London: Heinemann, 1980), 62.

39. These sources include that by Rev. Thoonen, *Black Martyrs*, 131; CMS Archives London, Wilson Journals dated 9 May 1878.

40. See CMS Archives G3A5/03: Mackay Journals dated 17 November 1878 and 28 December 1878.

41. See for instance Michael G. Kenny, "The Stranger from the Lake: A Theme in the History of the Lake Victoria Shorelands," *Azania* 17 (1982): 1–26; C. C. Wrigley, "Kirmera," *Uganda Journal* 23, no. 1 (1959): 38–43.

42. Kenny, "Mutesa's Crime," 602.

43. Mackay, *Mackay of Uganda*, 148.

44. See Alexina Harrison Mackay, *The Story of Mackay of Uganda, Pioneer Missionary* (London: Hodder and Stoughton, 1911), 168, 246. The first edition of this work appeared under the title: *The Story of the life of Mackay of Uganda by his Sister* (Chicago: Student Missionary Campaign Library, 1898). See also Kenny, "Mutesa's Crime," 595–612. See also Robert P. Ashe, *Two Kings of Buganda* (London: Sampson Low, 1890), 75–7.

45. See Kenny, "Mutesa's Crimes," 598, footnotes.

46. Mackay, *Mackay of Uganda*, 164–5

47. See Roscoe, *Baganda*, 298; Kenny, "Mutesa's Crimes," 604; Mackay, *Mackay of Uganda*, 119, 161; Ashe, *Two Kings*, 75–77; Brierley and Spear, "Mutesa " 606.

48. Mackay, *Mackay of Uganda*, 197; and Thoonen, *Black Martyrs*, 66.

49. Actually, the passage of Mutesa signified a period of time old customs were breaking down. According to Ashe, *Kabaka* Mutesa I was the first Buganda king to be buried in grave and with a coffin. See Ashe, *Chronicles*, 66.

50. For an interesting account on one of these emergent elite who survived persecution at the palace and later became a regional leader in Uganda, see for instance Michael Twaddle, "The Nine Lives of Kakungulu," *History in Africa* 12 (1985): 325–33; and Twaddle, "Politico-Religious Groupings," 81–92.

51. Brierley and Spear, "Mutesa," 616.

52. For a detailed and graphic account of the death of Hannington, see H. B. Thomas, "The Last Days of Bishop Hannington," *Uganda Journal* 8–9, nos. 1–2 (1940–1942): 19–27; and Ashe, *Chronicles*, 73.

53. CMS Archives G3A5/03: Mackay to Stock, dated 26 June 1886. See also J. F. Faupel, *African Holocaust* (London: Geoffrey Chapman, 1962), 157; and Rowe, "Purge," 56.

54. Rowe, "Purge," 57. For an account on the murder of the Protestant Bishop, see CMS Archives G3/A5/03. Mackay to Lang, dated 10 December 1885; and also *The Church Missionary Intelligencer*, June 1886.

55. Max Gluckman, *Order and Rebellion in Tribal Africa: Collected Essays with an Anthropological Introduction* (New York: Free Press of Glencoe,

1963), 110–36; Edward Evan Evans-Pritchard, *Essays in Social Anthropology and other Essays* (New York: Free Press of Glencoe, 1962). For an interesting analysis on these concepts along with Ugandan experience with Christianity, see Kenny, "Mutesa's Crime," 596.

56. Wrigley, "Christian Revolution," 42–3.

57. Ronald Kassimir, "Complex Martyrs: Catholic Church Formation and Political Differentiation in Uganda," *African Affairs* 90, no. 360 (July 1991): 358.

58. Holger Bernt Hansen, "Church and State in Early Colonial Uganda," *African Affairs* 85, no. 338 (Jan. 1985): 56.

59. This assertion is clearly buttressed with the testimonies reserved at CMS Archives London G3A7/0: Minutes of Conference of Missionaries held between 28–30, 1899, no. 99, it was argued that it was in the interest of the missions that the position of the *Bakungu* chiefs should be firmly established in the Agreement of 1900. See also PRO, FO 2/591: Archdeacon R. H. Walker's report on mission education in Uganda, encl. in Commissioner Saddler to Marquess of Landsowne dated 2 July 1902.

60. Michael Twaddle, "The Muslim Revolution in Buganda," *African Affairs* 71, no. 282 (1972): 54–72.

61. C. C. Wrigley, "The Christian Revolution in Buganda," *Comparative Studies in Society and History* 2 (1959): 33–48; Twaddle, "Muslim Revolution," 54–55.

62. See Twaddle, "Muslim Revolution," 61, 66.

63. E. A. Ayandele, "James Africanus Beale Horton, 1835–1883: Prophet of Modernization in West Africa," *African Historical Studies* 4, no. 3 (1971): 691–6. This article was a review on Horton's *West African Countries and Peoples*, with an introduction by George Shepperson (1868; reprint Chicago: Aldine Publishers Company, 1969). Ayandele claimed that the educated elite "had more in common with the white in Europe and America, than with the multimillion unlettered Africans in the vast interior of the continent." See also Pieter Boele van Hensbroek, *Political Discourse in African Thought 1860 to the Present* (Westport, CT: Praeger Publishers, 1999), 38.

64. In April 1920, the Pope established the decree authorizing beatification of the so-called Uganda martyrs. See Thoonen, *Black Martyrs*, esp. 285.

65. Twaddle, "Muslim Revolution," 55.

66. Rowe, "Purge," 57–8.

67. Ashe, *Two Kings*, 225.

68. Ashe, *Chronicles*, 80

69. Kagwa, *Basekabaka*, 21.

70. Abbe A. Nicq, *Vie du Reverend Pere Simeon Lourdel* [*Life of Reverend Father Simeon Lourdel*] (Alger: Maison-Carree, 1932), 337; Thoonen, *Black Martyrs*, 179

71. Among the plentiful literature on Lugard's East African campaign, the best account remains that by Margery Perham, *Lugard: The Years of Adventure* 1858–1898 (London: Collins, 1956).

72. See for instance PRO FO 5433; 5867: Confidential Prints, 1890–1892; and Bodleian Library Oxford MSS. Brit. Emp. S. 30–99: Papers of Frederick Deatry Lugard, Baron Lugard of Abinger: 1871–1969.

73. Writing in his book, Lugard explains that he had to work with Mwanga because treaty without him would have been "mere filibustering." See Frederick D. Lugard, *The Rise of Our East African Empire* (London: Blackwood, 1893), 21.

74. For details on Chwa's coming of throne, Mwanga's exile and death, and the death in 1940, see F. Lukkyn Williams, "The Kabaka of Buganda," *Uganda Journal* 7, no. 4 (April 1940): 176–87.

75. See Margaret Perham, *The Diaries of Lord Lugard* (London: Faber and Faber, 1960), 11, 29, entry for 19 Dec. 1890; and Lugard, *Our East African Empire*, 11, 24.

76. For details, see PRO FO 2/297: Uganda. Sir H. Johnston East. Dispatches, 1–65 Vol. I, dated Jan-March 21, 1900.

77. See Michael Twaddle, "The Bakungu Chiefs of Buganda under British Colonial Rule, 1900–1930," *Journal of African History* 10, no. 2 (1969): 310; PRO FO 93/4/6: Agreement. Kabaka, Chiefs and Peoples of Uganda dated March 10, 1900.

78. Wrigley, "Christian Revolution," 45. For a short biography, see Georgina Anne Gollock, *Sons of Africa* (New York: Friendship Press, 1928).

79. Hansen, "Church and State," 57.

80. For the CMS demand for these special privileges, see Lugard Papers, Oxford the correspondence between the Catholic Bishop Hirth and Lugard dated Dec. 1890. See also CMS Archives, G3A7L1: Minutes of the Uganda Mission's Finance Committee, dated 25 and 27 Jan. 1894; and Minute Book of the Eastern Equatorial African Diocese.

81. See for instance PRO, G3A7/01: Minutes of Conference of Missionaries, dated 28–30 June 1899, no. 99; Archdeacon Walker's report on educational work, encl. in Commissioner Saddler to Marquess of Landsowne dated 2 July 1902.

82. Steinhart, *Collaboration*, 261.

83. Steinhart, *Collaboration*, 262. See for instance F. Barth, "Segmentary Opposition and the Theory of Games," *Journal of the Royal Anthropological Institute* 89 (1959): 5–21.

84. Steinhart, *Collaboration*, 263.

85. See Twaddle, "Bakungu Chiefs," 312–13

86. Twaddle, "Bakungu Chiefs," 313.

87. See Wrigley, "Christian Revolution," 33.

88. See for instance Mahmood Mamdani, *Citizens and Subjects: Contemporary Africa and the Legacy of Late Colonialism* (Princeton, N.J.: Princeton University Press, 1996).

89. See F. B. Welbourn, "Missionary Stimulus and African Responses," in Victor Turner (ed.), *Colonialism in Africa, 1870–1960* (Cambridge: Cambridge University Press, 1971), 319. A similar view is shared by Twaddle, "Muslim Revolution." 70.

90. Brierley and Spear, "Mutesa," 617–8.

91. David Apter, *The Political Kingdom of Uganda* (Princeton, N.J.: Princeton University Press, 1967).

NOTES TO CHAPTER FOUR

1. Research for this essay was made possible by a Fulbright IIE full grant award for dissertation research in the Democratic Republic of Congo, a

Department of Anthropology Dissertation research grant, Rackham Discretionary funds, and the Center for AfroAmerican and African Studies African Initiatives Award, used for research in Brussels.

2. Susan Reed, "The Politics and Poetics of Dance," *Annual Review of Anthropology* (1998): 506.

3. The BaKongo are the ethnic group one finds throughout the Lower Congo, who speak varying dialects of the same language, KiKongo. BisiKongo is another, more popular term that Kongo people use to describe themselves. In keeping with the terminology of the colonial period, BaKongo will be used throughout the essay. The term "Kongo" describes the cultural area of this group, which was the basis of the Kongo Kingdom, and covers parts of present day Congo-Brazzaville, Congo-Kinshasa, and Angola.

4. Ngunza is a word in KiKongo that means messenger of a chief, a protector of the clan, a clairvoyant, a prophet-healer. This term was applied by Kongo people to Kimbangu and other prophets that arose in Lower Congo. In Manianga, the term used more often is ntumwa. See Kimpianga Mahaniah, *La Maladie et la Guérison en milieu Kongo* (Kinshasa: Centre de Vulgarisation Agricole, 1982): 90–93.

5. Selection from author's ethnographic fieldnotes, 2005.

6. For more detailed information about this historical period, see John K. Thornton, "The Development of an African Catholic Church in the Kingdom of Kongo, 1491–1750," *Journal of African History* 25, no. 2 (1984): 147–67.

7. In 1865 the area of Lower Congo was transferred from the Capuchin missionaries of the seventeenth century to the Fathers of the Holy Spirit, French Catholic missionaries based in Gabon. They established posts at Landana, Boma, and Banana, but were told to leave when the area came under Leopold II's control. In 1878 Protestant missionaries of the L. I. M. (Livingstone Inland Mission) established a station at Mpalabala, near the coast. They continued to establish stations along the caravan route between Matadi and Stanley Pool. In 1881, the B. M. S. (Baptist Missionary Society of England) founded a post at San Salvador (the former capital of the Kongo Kingdom), and then Ndandanga. In the same year the first Swedish missionary of the S. M. F. (Svenska Missions Förbundet) arrived. In 1884, after encountering financial difficulties, the L. I. M. divided its stations between the A. B. F. M. S. (American Baptist Foreign Missionary Society) and the S. M. F. The first Belgian Catholic missions were established in 1888 by the Scheutists, followed by Peres of Gand (1891), Sisters of the Gand Charity (1892), Jesuits (1893), Sisters of Notre Dame of Namur and the Trappistes (1894), Priests of the Sacred Heart (1897), and the Redemptorists (1899). See Francois Bontinck, "Le Conditionnement Historique de l'Implantation de l'église Catholique au Congo," *Revue de Clerge Africain*, Tome XXIV, 2 (March 1969): 139; Kimpianga Mahaniah, *L'Impact du Christianisme au Manianga* (Kinshasa, DRC: Editions Centre de Vulgarisation Agricole, 1988), 7–20; Hugo Gotink, *Mangembo 1921–1942: Un Regard sur l'Evangelisation Catholique dans le Territoire de Luozi* (Kinshasa, DRC: Editions Centre de Vulgarisation Agricole, 1995), 7–14; Ngemba Ntime

Kavenadiambuko, *La Methode d'evangelisation des Redemptoristes Belges au Bas-Congo (1899–1919)* (Rome: Editrice Pontificia Universita Gregoriana, 1999), 33.

8. Marvin Markowitz, *Cross and Sword: The Political Role of Christian Missions in the Belgian Congo, 1908–1960* (Stanford, California: Hoover Institution Press, 1973), 7.

9. Ruth Slade Reardon, "Catholics and Protestants in the Congo," in C. G. Baeta (ed.), *Christianity in Tropical Africa* (London: Oxford University Press, 1968), 86–7. The British form of spelling has been changed to the American form in this and following quotations.

10. Markowitz, *Cross and Sword*, 17–18.

11. John Hope Franklin, *George Washington Williams: A Biography* (Chicago: University of Chicago Press, 1985), 264–79.

12. David Lagergren, *Mission and State in the Congo: A Study of the Relations between Protestant Missions and the Congo Independent State Authorities with special reference to the Equator District, 1885–1903* (Uppsala, Sweden: Almqvist & Wiksells, 1970), 147.

13. Kimpianga Mahaniah, "The Background of Prophetic Movements in the Belgian Congo: A Study of the Congolese Reaction to the Policies and Methods of Belgian Colonization and to the Evangelization of the Lower Congo by Catholic and Protestant Missionaries, from 1877 to 1921" (Ph. D diss., Temple University, 1975), 285.

14. Mahaniah, "Background," 185.

15. Mahaniah, "Background," 185–90. See also Sigbert Axelson, *Culture Confrontation in the Lower Congo: From the Old Congo Kingdom to the Congo Independent State with special reference to the Swedish Missionaries in the 1880's and 1890's* (Sweden: Gummessons, 1970), 256; Wyatt MacGaffey, "Ethnography and the Closing of the frontier in Lower Congo, 1885–1921," *Africa: Journal of the International African Institute* 56, no. 3 (1986): 266.

16. Mahaniah, "Background," 187.

17. Mahaniah, "Background," 189, and MacGaffey, "Ethnography," 271.

18. MacGaffey, "Ethnography," 271.

19. Mahaniah, "Black Americans in the Lower Congo," 411.

20. Marcus Garvey was a highly influential yet controversial Jamaican nationalist leader who created a back to Africa movement and advocated Black pride and African independence during the early twentieth century. The influence of Garveyist ideas on the Kimbanguist movement has been explored by several authors, and although interesting, is not the topic of this paper. For information on this subject, see Mahaniah, 1993; M. W. Kodi, "The 1921 Pan-African Congress at Brussels: A Background to Belgian Pressures," in Joseph Harris (ed.), *Global Dimensions of the African Diaspora* (Washington, D.C: Howard University Press, 1993), 263–88; Wyatt MacGaffey, "Kongo and the King of the Americans," *Journal of Modern African Studies* 6, no. 2 (1968): 171–81; and Efraim Andersson, *Messianic Popular Movements in the Lower Congo* (Uppsala, Sweden: Almqvist & Wiksells Boktryckeri AB, 1958), 250–7.

21. Mahaniah, "Black Americans in the Lower Congo," 412. See also Marie-Louise Martin, *Kimbangu: An African Prophet and his Church* (Great Britain: Basil Blackwell, 1975), 45. .

22. Martin, *Kimbangu*, 46; Ministère des Affaires Étrangères, Archives Africaines [hereafter AA], portefeuille Affaires Indigenes & Main d'Oeuvre [hereafter AIMO] 1630/9184, II. Q.3.a.1. 1. Dossier: Documentation Generale sur le Kibanguisme. Document 84b. Histoire de l'apparition du prophete Simon Kimbangu, found among the native population, anonymous.

23. AA portefeuille AIMO 1634/9191B, II.Q.3.c. 12. Dossier: Incidents en Territoire des Cataracts Sud (Thysville); unnumbered document; Rapport d'enquête Administrative sur les faits et incidents de Kamba (chefferie de Zundu); Thysville, 17 May 1921; to the district superintendent of Bas-Congo, Boma from the territorial administrator Morel, page 1. All French passages have been translated by the author, who alone claims responsibility for any significant errors.

24. AA portefeuille AIMO 1634/9191B, II.Q.3.c. 12. Dossier: Incidents en Territoire des Cataracts Sud (Thysville); unnumbered document, page 2.

25. Andersson, *Messianic Popular Movements*, 58.

26. AA portefeuille AIMO1630/9183, II-Q-3-a-2. 4. Dossier: Enquete du Parquet et Rapport du Substitut Cornet. Document 1 (no. 139/966D), page 6.

27. AA portefeuille AIMO 1634/9191B, II.Q.3.c. 12. Dossier: Incidents en Territoire des Cataractes Sud (Thysville) ; Unnumbered Document. Rapport sur mon voyage d'enquête vers Yanga du 13 au 16 juin 1921. Luozi, 17 June 1921. Letter to the district superintendent in Boma from L. Cariaux, the territorial administrator, page 5.

28. Andersson, *Messianic Popular Movements*, 58.

29. Andersson, *Messaianic Popular Movements*, 58. .

30. AA portefeuille AIMO 1630/9183, II-Q-3-a-2. 4. Enquete du Parquet et Rapport du Substitut Cornet. Document 1 (no. 4744). Boma, 12 July 1921. Objet: incidents dans les cataracts, pages 1–2. unsigned.

31. Susan Asch, *L'eglise du prophète Simon Kimbangu : de ses origines à son rôle actuel au Zaïre, 1921–1981* (Paris : Editions Karthala, 1983), 112; 140; Martin, *Kimbangu*, 132.

32. AA portefeuille 1630/9183, II.Q.3.a.2. 1. Dossier: Kibangu Simon. Document 33; Leopoldville, 14 October 1921; Letter to General Governer from Vice-Governor General; Subject: Kimbangu Movement, page 2; Jules Chomé, *La Passion de Simon Kimbangu* (Brussels: Les amis de la Présence Africaine, 1959), 27; Asch, *L'eglise du prophète Simon Kimbangu*, 23.

33. AA portefeuille AIMO 1634/9191B, unnumbered document, 2–4.

34. Martin, *Kimbangu*, 51.

35. Martin, *Kimbangu*, 51.

36. Andersson, *Messianic Popular Movements*, 58. Banganga is a KiKongo term used to describe priest and healers of Kongo traditional religion.

37. Mahaniah, "Background," 249.

38. AA portefeuille AIMO 1630/9184, II. Q.3.a.1. 1. Dossier: Documentation Generale sur le Kibanguisme. Document 84a. Leopoldville, 22 September

1921. Letter to the Vice Governor General from L. Morel, Territorial Administrator, Page 6.

39. AA portefeuille AIMO 1630/9183, II.Q.3.a.2. 8. Dossier: Articles des journaux. Document 64 (No. 3863) Leopoldville, 14 (July or August) 1921. Objet: Mouvement Kimbangu. Included in a letter from Dupuis, assistant district commissioner, to the governor general.

40. Chomé, *La Passion de Simon Kimbangu*, 22–4.

41. AA portefeuille AIMO 1630/9184, Document 84A, page 6.

42. Martin, *Kimbangu*, 58.

43. AA portefeuille AIMO 1634/9191B, II.Q.3.c. 12. Dossier: Incidents en Territoire des Cataracts Sud (Thysville). Documents # 17 and unnumbered following; Thysville, 2 July 1921. Letter from Guasco to Geerts, Ingenieur Director. and 5 July 1921, Letter from Geerts to the governor-general of Boma.

44. AA portefeuille AIMO 1634/9191B, II.Q.3.c. 12. Dossier: Incidents en Territoire des Cataracts Sud (Thysville). Unnumbered document. Kamba, 20 June 1921. Decision. L. Morel, Territorial Administrator.

45. Chomé, *La Passion de Simon Kimbangu*, 63.

46. Chomé, *La Passion de Simon Kimbangu*, 33.

47. AA, portefeuille 1630/9183, II.Q.3.a.2. 1. Dossier Kibangu Simon; Unnumbered document; Jugement. Conseil de guerre de Thysville, 3 Octobre 1921, pronounced by Judge De Rossi, page 2.

48. AA portefeuille 1630/9183, II.Q.3.a.2. 7. Dossier Attitude des Missionaires Etrangers; Document 24. 5 October 1921, Letter to governor general.

49. AA portefeuille 1630/9183, II.Q.3.a.2. 1. Dossier Kibangu Simon ; Document 32; Affaire Kimbangu; 12 October 1921. Letter to Governor General in Boma from the substitute public prosecutor, V. van den Broeck.

50. AA, portefeuille 1630/9183, II.Q.3.a.2. 1. Dossier Kibangu Simon; Document 42; by Albert, King of the Belgians, Article 1, Bruxelles, 15 November 1921.

51. Martin, *Kimbangu*, 67.

52. AA portefeuille 1630/9193, II.Q.3.a.2. 5. Dossier Relations avec le R.P. Dufonteny.

53. AA portefeuille 1630/9183, Dossier Enquete et Rapport Procureur du Roi, Voisin; Unnumbered Document; 6 February 1925, Kibangisme, Mesures a prendre pour enrayer le mouvement; Letter to the District Commisioner from the Governor, F.Olsen, Province du Congo-Kasai, page 2.

54. Martin, *Kimbangu*, 81.

55. Manianga territory is known today as Luozi territory.

56. National Archives, Kinshasa, DRC. AIMO. *Territoire de Manianga. Rapport Annuel, 1944.*

57. AIMO. *Territoire de Mayumbe. Rapport Annuel, 1947.*

58. AIMO. *Territoire de Manianga. Rapport Annuel, 1947.*

59. AIMO. *Territory of Luozi. Rapport Annuel, 1950.*

60. Martin, *Kimbangu*, 69.

61. AIMO. *Territoire de Luozi. Rapport Annuel, 1955.*

62. AIMO. *Territoire de Luozi. Rapport Annuel, 1957.*

63. AA portefeuille AIMO 1634/9191B, II.Q.3.c. 12. Dossier: Incidents en Territoire des Cataracts Sud (Thysville); unnumbered document; District du Bas-Congo: Decision. Thysville, le 8 aout 1921, Dupuis, assistant district superintendant.

64. This is a pseudonym. All of the names of interviewees are pseudonyms, unless otherwise noted.

65. *Kilombo* in KiKongo means a large group of people that are so numerous that they cannot be counted. In the context of the Protestant church, and other churches as well, the name is most commonly used for a choir, often large, that incorporates traditional musical instruments.

66. Tata Mukiese was born in 1934. Interview conducted by author. January 30, 2006, Luozi, Democratic Republic of Congo.

67. AIMO. *Territoire de Luozi. Rapport Annuel, 1956.*

68. Territory of Luozi, Annual Report 1957.

69. This male type of dress is called *mbokula* in kikongo.

70. Author's Ethnographic Fieldnotes, 2005.

71. Congo Belge, Gouvernement Local, *Recueil Mensuel des ordonnances, circulaires, instructions et ordres de service.* 6me annee, No. 10. Octobre 1913.

72. Congo Belge, Gouvernement Local, *Recueil Bi-Mensuel des ordonnances, circulaires, instructions et ordres de service.* 5me annee, No. 1. 15 Janvier 1912. Circulaire #14.

73. Recueil Mensuel, October 1913, circular #139.

74. Congo Belge, Gouvernement Local, *Recueil Mensuel des ordonnances, circulaires, instructions et ordres de service.* 8me annee, No. 1, Janvier 1915. Circulaire #2.

75. Axelson, *Culture Confrontation*, 285.

76. Mahaniah, "Background," 162–3.

77. Axelson, *Culture Confrontation*, 288.

78. *Au Pays de Palmiers: Récits du Congo écrits par des moniteurs indigènes* (1928), (Stockholm: Èditions Svenska Missionskyrkan, 2003), 59.

79. Ibid., 92.

80. These passages written by these instructors could have been influenced by the fact that the readership was a Swedish audience, rather than a Kongo one. However, I have also encountered other Kongo Protestants in the present who viewed dancing as inappropriate for members of the church.

81. Interview with Tata Esaie, September 29, 2005, Luozi, DRC; Interview with Tata Mbuta, September 29, 2005, Luozi, DRC; Interview with Tata Yangalala, October 30, 2005, Luozi, DRC.

82. Interview with Mama Londa, September 20, 2005, Luozi. DRC.

83. This is his real name, which I have been given permission to use.

84. Interview with Ne Nkamu Luyindula, September 20, 2005, Luozi, DRC.

85. Interview with Tata Malanda, October 28, 2005, Luozi, DRC.

86. J. Van Wing, "Les Danses Bakongo," *Congo: Revue générale de la Colonie Belge, Tome II*, 2 (July 1937): 121.

87. Ibid., 127–8.
88. See Richard F. Burton, *Two Trips to Gorilla Land and the Cataracts of the Congo. Volume II* (London: S. Low, and Searle, 1876); and Joachim John Monteiro, *Angola and the River Congo* (Volume II) (London: MacMillan and Co, 1875), 136–138.
89. Phyllis Martin, *Leisure and Society in Colonial Brazzaville* (Cambridge: Cambridge University Press, 1995), 131.
90. Wing, "Les Danses Bakongo," 128.
91. Wing, "Les Danses Bakongo, " 129.
92. Wing, "Les Danses Bakongo, " 129.
93. Wing, "Les Danses Bakongo, " 130.
94. Wing, "Les Danses Bakongo, " 131.
95. P. DeCapmaker, "Danses des BaKongo" in *La Mission et les Joies Populaires: Compte Rendu de la XVIe Semaine de Missiologie de Louvain*,(Brussels, Belgium: L'edition Universelles, S. A., 1938), 40.
96. DeCapmaker, "Danses des BaKongo,"41–4.
97. DeCapmaker, "Danses des BaKongo," 58.
98. DeCapmaker, "Danses des BaKongo," 61.
99. Father Hugo Gotink, in discussion with the author, Mbanza-Ngungu, March 11–12, 2006. This material is apparently what Decapmaker used for his own presentation at the seminar. Gotink shared with me his copies of the two dossiers on Congo dance deposited at the Archives of the Redemptorist Fathers in Rome.
100. Jean Cuvelier, "Les Missions Catholiques en face des danses des Bakongo," *Africanae Fraternae Ephemerides Romanae* 17 (June 1939): 155.
101. Cuvelier, "Les Missions Catholiques,"170.
102. Michaël Kratz, *La Mission des Rédemptoristes Belges au Bas-Congo: La Période des semailles (1899–1920)* (Brussels: Académie Royale des Sciences d'Outre-Mer, 1970), 351.
103. Tata Tuzolana, Interview by author, Ndundu Kivwila and Hippolyte Ngimbi, July 22, 2005, Mayidi, Bas-Congo, Democratic Republic of Congo. The Kongo priest in question apparently changed his mind about these issues, as he later became one of the first people to reintroduce traditional instruments into the Catholic church. Father Masamba, Interview by author and Alain Nkisi, June 3, 2005, Kinshasa, DRC.
104. Tata Mbumba, in discussion with the author, July 21, 2005, Mayidi, Bas-Congo, DRC.
105. AA portefeuille 1630/9184, II. Q.3.a.1. 1. Dossier: Documentation Generale sur le Kibanguisme. Document B. Gungu, 13 January 1924. Objet: Mouvement Kibangiste. Letter to the governor from Noirot.
106. Gotink, Hugo, *Mangembo 1921–1942: Un Regard sur l'Evangelisation Catholique dans le Territoire de Luozi*, (Kinshasa, DRC: Editions Centre de Vulgarisation Agricole, 1995), 156.
107. AIMO 1878/9981. Conference de Administrateurs Territoriaux du Bas-Congo, compte-rendu de la conference.

108. Gotink, Hugo, *Mangembo 1921–1942: Un Regard sur l'Evangelisation Catholique dans le Territoire de Luozi*, (Kinshasa, DRC: Editions Centre de Vulgarisation Agricole, 1995), 157.

109. Wing, "Les Danses Bakongo," 130.

NOTES TO CHAPTER FIVE

1. *World Missionary Conference, 1910, Report of Commission III: Education in Relation to the Christianization of National Life* (Edinburgh and London: Oliphant, Anderson and Ferrier, 1910), 213.

2. *World Missionary*, 248.

3. *World Missionary*, 250.

4. John R. Mott, *The Decisive Hour of Christian Missions* (New York: Student Volunteer Movement For Foreign Missions,1912),120.

5. *World Missionary*, 254.

6. *World Missionary*, 253.

7. *World Missionary*, 259.

8. *World Missionary*, 259.

9. *World Missionary*, 257.

10. Mott, *The Decisive Hour*, 25.

11. Gordon M. Haliburton, *The Prophet Harris* (London: Oxford University Press, 1973).

12. *World Missionary*, vii-xx.

13. *World Missionary*, 3.

14. *World Missionary*, 4.

15. *World Missionary*, 6.

16. Mott, *The Decisive Hour*, 114

17. *World Missionary*, 240.

18. *World Missionary* , 244.

19. *World Missionary*, 245, 257.

20. *World Missionary*, 245, 257.

21. Paulo Freire, *Pedagogy of the Oppressed* (New York: Continuum,1970), 58–60

22. *World Missionary* , 258.

23. Freire, *Pedagogy of the Oppressed*,181.

24. Freire, *Pedagogy of the Oppressed*, 182–3.

25. *World Missionary* , 247; see, Roswith Gerloff (ed.), *Mission Is Crossing Frontiers: essays in honour of Bongani Mazibuko* (Pietermaritzburgh: Cluster Publications,2003), 14.

26. *World Missionary*, 252.

27. *World Missionary*, 261.

28. R. Suntharalingam, *Politics and Nationalist Awakening in South India, 1852–1910* (Jaipur-New Delhi, 1980).

29. Cited in Klaus Korschorke (ed). *Transcontinental Links In the History of Non-Western Christianity* (Weisbaden: Harrasowitz Verlag, 2002), 205.

30. E. A. Ayandele, *The Missionary Impact on Modern Nigeria, 1842–1914* (London: Longmans, 1966).

31. Mott, *The Decisive Hour*,109–110

32. Mott, *The Decisive Hour*, 114.

33. J. Ade Ajayi, *Christian Missions in Nigeria; The Making of an Elite* (London: Longmans, 1965). See also John P. Ragsdale, *Protestant Mission Education in Zambia, 1880–1954* (Toronto: Associated University Press, 1986).

34. *World Missionary*, 8.

35. See a discussion in Efiong S. Utuk, *From New York to Ibadan: The Impact of African Questions on the Making of Ecumenical Mission Mandates* (New York: Peter Lang, 1991).

36. *World Missionary*, 208–211.

37. *World Missionary*, 233-ff.

38. See, Brian Stanley's article on "Church, State and Hierarchy of Civilization" and Andrew C. Ross, "Christian Missions and the Mid-Nineteenth Century Change in Attitude to Race" in Andrew Porter, ed., *The Imperial Horizons of British Protestant Missions, 1880–1914* (Grand Rapids: Eerdmans, 2003), 58–105.

39. Ross, "Christian Missions," 166.

40. Ross, "Christian Missions," 168.

41. Mott, *Decisive Hour*, 22.

42. *World Missionary*, 175.

43. *World Missionary*,180.

44. *World Missionary*, 183.

45. *World Missionary*, 187.

46. *World Missionary*, 197.

47. *World Missionary*, 197–198.

48. *World Missionary*, 203.

49. *World Missionary*, 203; see, Stormont, cited in *World Missionary*, 204.

50. W. H. Mobley, *The Ghanaians' Image of the Missionary* (Leiden: E. J. Brill, 1970); J. S. Mbiti, *Theology and Bible in Africa* (Nairobi: Oxford University Press, 1987); Lamin Sanneh, *Translating the Message* (Maryknoll, NY: Orbis, 1989); John Peel, *Religious Encounter and the Making of the Yoruba* (Bloomington, IN: Indiana University Press, 2002); P. E. H. Hair, *The Early Study of Nigerian Languages* (Cambridge: Cambridge University Press, 1967). See the chapter on translation work in N. Omenka, *Schools as Means of Evangelization* (Leiden: E. J. Brill, 1991).

51. *World Missionary*, 207.

52. *World Missionary*, 206.

53. *World Missionary*, 207.

54. *World Missionary*, 166.

55. O. U. Kalu, *Divided People of God: Church Union Movement in Nigeria, 1875–1966* (New York: NOK Publishers, 1978). Deeply impressed by the Edinburgh Conference, Wilkie of the UFC initiated the regular meetings between the CMS, Qua Iboe Mission, and the CSM in Eastern Nigeria from 1911. These inspired the church union movement.

56. William H. Taylor, *Mission to Educate* (Leiden: E J. Brill, 1996), 11.
57. Michael Foucault, *Discipline and Punishment* (Paris: Gallimand,1979), 136; V.Y. Mudimbe, *Tales of Faith: Religion as Political Performance in Central Africa* (London: The Athlone Press,1997), 50–1
58. *Record, 1911:16,* cited in Foucault, *Discipline,* 125.

NOTES TO CHAPTER SIX

1. Jurgen Osterhammel, *Colonialism: A Theoretical Overview* (Princeton: Markus Wiener Publishers, 1997), 16.
   Giuliana Lund, "Healing the Nation" Medicolonial Discourse and the State of Emergency from Apartheid to Truth and Reconciliation," *Cultural Critique* 54 (2003): 88–119.
3. W. Buhlmann, *The Coming of the of the Third Church* (New York: Orbis Books, 1978), 150–51.
4. Emmanuel Ifemegbunam Ifesieh, "Prayer in Igbo Traditional Religion: Some Traditional Models (A Case Study)" in Elochukwu E. Uzukwu (ed.), *Religion and African Culture* (Enugu: Spiritan Publications, 1988), 73-ff.
5. Leonard A. Ugbor, *Prayer in Igbo Traditional Religion: Its Meaning and Message for the Church in Igboland Today* (Rome: Pontifical University Gregoriana, 1985), 56.
6. D. Zahan, *The Religion, Spirituality and Thoughts of Traditional Africa* (Chicago: University of Chicago Press, 1979), 50.
7. M. A. Onwuejeogwu, "The Igbo Culture Area," in F. C. Okafor and E. N. Emenanjo (eds.), *Igbo Language and Culture* (Ibadan: Oxford University Press, 1975), 2–8. According to this author, "*alusi* [spirits/spiritual forces] . . . always intrudes into the lives of the members of the lineage, but the extent of their success depends on the pleasure of the dead members . . ."
8. Ogbu U. Kalu, "The Gods in Retreat: Models for Interpreting Religious Change in Africa" in Emefie Ikenga Metuh (ed), *The Gods in Retreat: Continuity and Change in African Religions,* (Enugu: Fourth Dimension Publishers, 1986), 3.
9. B. Malinowski, *The Dynamics of Culture Change: An Inquiry into Race Relations in Africa* (London: Geoffrey Cumberledge, 1945), 16.
10. Okot p'Bitek, *African Religions in Western Scholarship* (Kampala: East African Literature Bureau, 1970), 44.
11. Awolalu and Dopamu, *West African Traditional Religion* (Ibadan: Onobanjo Press & Books Industries, 1979), 11–12.
12. J. D. Y. Peel, *Religious Encounter and the Making of the Yoruba* (Bloomington: Indiana University Press, 2000), 88.
13. Jon Kirby, "Cultural Change and Religious Conversion in West Africa," in T. D. Blakely (ed.), *Religion in Africa: Experience and Expression* (London: James Currey, 1994), 60–1.
14. Kevin Shillington, *History of Africa* (New York: St Martin's Press, 1995), 291.

15. Adrian Hastings, *Church and Mission in Colonial Africa* (London: Burns and Oates, 1967), 119.
16. See for example, Ekechi, Felix K. *Missionary Enterprise and Rivalry in Igboland, 1857–1914* (London: Frank Cass, 1972); Kalu, Ogbu U. "Missionaries, Colonial Government and Secret Societies in South-eastern Igboland, 1920–1950," *Journal of the Historical Society of Nigeria* 9, no. 1 (Dec. 1977): 75–90; Kevin Shillington, *History of Africa* (New York: St Martin's Press: 1995), 292.
17. Shillington, *History of Africa*, 293.
18. E. A. Ayandele "Traditional Rulers and Missionaries in Pre-colonial West Africa," *Tarikh 9: Christianity in Modern Africa, Vol. 3* (London: Longman, 1969), 33.
19. Ayandele, "Traditional Rulers," 33.
20. Benedict XV, Maximum Illud, Apostolic Letter of Nov. 1919. AAS XI (1919): 447. (English trans. Dominican Publications).
21. Adrian Hastings, *Church and Mission in Modern Africa*, 119.
22. L. Senghor, "Negritude and Africa Socialism," in M. Minogue and J. Molloy (eds.), *African Aims and Attitudes* (London: Cambridge University Press, 1974), 231.
23. Isichei, *A History of the Igbo people*, 47.
24. R. Rweyemamu, "The Christian Mission in Africa before and after the Berlin Conference (1884–1885)" Euntes *Docete* 38 (1985): 61–3.
25. T. Fowell Buxton, *The African Slave Trade and Its Remedy* (London: Dawson of Pall Mall, 1968, First edition, 1839), 511.
26. Robert W. July, *A History of the African People*, 158.
27. Peel, *Religious Encounter*, 155–6.
28. Peel, *Religious Encounter*, 124.
29. Jehu J. Hanciles, "Bishop Crowther and Archdeacon Crowther: Inter-Generational Challenge and Opportunity in Africa Christian Encounter," in Chima J. Korieh and G. Ugo Nwokeji (eds.), *Religion, History, and Politics in Nigeria* (New York: University Press of America, 2005), 58.
30. J. P. Jordan, *Bishop Shanahan of Southern Nigeria (Dublin:* Reynolds: 1918), 33–4.
31. Jordan, *Bishop Shanahan*, 33–4.
32. Jordan, *Bishop Shanahan*, 34.
33. National Archives of Nigeria, Calabar (hereafter NAC), "Outbreak of Religious Mania in Enyong and Ikot-Ekpene Divisions" Memorandum, No 0.733/1927.
34. NAC, File No 0733/1927.
35. NAC, File No. 0733/1927.
36. NAC, File No. 63/1925.
37. J. Mullan, *The Catholic Church in Modern Africa* (London: Godfrey Chapman, 1955), 24.
38. Mullan, *Catholic Church*, 24.
39. Bishops of Onitsha Ecclesiastical Province, "Put out into Deep Water." A Pastoral Letter on the first Centenary Celebration of the Advent of the Catholic Church in Eastern Nigeria (Onitsha, 1980), 11- 12.

40. Robert Voeks, "African Medicine and Magic in the Americas," *Geographical Review* 83, no. 1 (Jan., 1993): 66 (66–78).

Moses Ochonu, "Native Habits are Difficult to Change": British Medics and the Dilemmas of Biomedical Discourses and Practice in Early Colonial Northern Nigeria," Journal of Colonialism and Colonial History 5, no.1 (2004): 17. On the extensive literature on colonial medicine, see for example, David Arnold (ed.), Imperial Medicine and Indigenous Societies (Manchester: Manchester University Press, 1988); Sheldon Watts, Epidemics and History: Disease, Power and Imperialism (New Haven: Yale University Press, 1998); Gerald W. Hartwig and David K. Patterson, eds., Disease in African History: An Introductory Survey and Case Studies (Durham: Duke University Press, 1978); D. Bagster Wilson, "Malaria in British Somaliland," The East African Medical Journal 26, no.10 (1949); K. David Patterson and Gerald F. Pyle, "The Diffusion of Influenza in Sub-Saharan Africa During the 1918–1919 Pandemic," Social Science and Medicine, 17, no.17 (1983): 1299–1307; K. David Patterson, "The Influenza Pandemic 1918–1919 in the Gold Coast," Journal of African History 24 (1983): 485–502; K. David Patterson, "Health in Urban Ghana: The Case of Accra, 1900–1940," Social Science and Medicine 13B (1979): 251–68; Marc H. Dawson, "Smallpox in Kenya, 1880–1920," Social Science and Medicine 13B (1979): 245–50; Randall M. Packard, "Maize, Cattle and Mosquitoes: The Political Economy of Malaria Epidemics in Colonial Swaziland," Journal of African History 125 (1984): 180–212; Daniel R. Headrick, The Tools of Empire: Technology and European Imperialism in the Nineteenth Century (New York: Oxford University Press, 1981); Daniel R. Headrick, ed., Colonialism, Health and Illness in French Equatorial Africa, 1885–1935 (Atlanta: African Studies Association Press, 1994); Megan Vaughan, Curing Their Ills: Colonial Power and African Illness (Stanford: Stanford University Press, 1991); Terence Ranger, "Plagues of Beasts and Men: Responses to Epidemic in Eastern and Southern Africa," in Terence Ranger and Paul Slack (eds.), Epidemics and Ideas (Cambridge: Cambridge University Press, 1992); Mariynez Lyons, The Colonial Disease: A Social History of Sleeping Sickness in Northern Zaire, 1900–1940 (Cambridge: Cambridge University Press, 1992); J. M. Janzen and Steve Feierman, "The Social History of Disease and Medicine in Africa," Social Science and Medicine 13b (1979); Roy Macleod and Milton Lewis, eds., Disease, Medicine, and Empire (London: Routledge, 1988); Alfred Crosby, Ecological Imperialism (Cambridge: Cambridge University Press, 1983). Jama Mohamed, "Epidemics and Public Health in Late Colonial Somaliland" Northeast African Studies 6 no.1–2 (1999): 45–81.

42. Ochonu, "Native Habits," 17.

43. Jonathan Sadowsky, "Psychiatry and Colonial Ideology in Nigeria," *Bulletin of the History of Medicine* 71, no.1 (1997): 94–111.

44. Sadowsky, "Psychiatry and Colonial Ideology," 98.

45. Charles M. Good, *Ethnomedical Systems in Africa: Patterns of Traditional Medicine in Rural and Urban Kenya* (New York: The Guilford Press, 1987), 38.

46. Cf. Good, *Ethnomedical*, 37.
47. Lund, "Healing the Nation," 91.
48. Cited in Lund, "Healing the Nation," 91.
49. Cited in Lund, "Healing the Nation," 90.
50. Cited in Lund, "Healing the Nation," 90.
51. Jean Comaroff, "The Diseased Heart of Africa: Medicine, Colonialism, and the Black Body," in Shirley Lindenbaum and Margaret Lock (eds.), *Knowledge, Power, and Practice* (Berkeley: University of California Press, 1993. Cited in Lund, "Healing the Nation," 90.
52. *New York Times,* "The African and Buiti," January 16, 1921, xx5.
53. *New York Times,* "Prosperity Comes to Medicine Man," May 18, 1958, 19.
54. *New York Times,* "Science, Psychiatry—or Witchery," 17.
55. Cf. Ngugi Wa Thiong'O, *Decolonizing the Mind* (London: Currey Press, 1986); Laurenti Magesa, *African Religion: The Moral Tradition of Abundant Life* (Maryknoll: Orbis Books, 1997).
56. *New York Times,* "Prosperity Comes to Medicine Man," May 18, 1958, 19.
57. Victor Turner, *The Drums of Affliction: A study of Religious Possession Among the Ndembu of Zambia* (Oxford: Clarendon Press, 1969), J. M. Janzen "Drums of Affliction: Real Phenomenon or Scholarly Chimera?" in Thomas D. Blakely, Walter E. A. van Beek, Dennis I. Thomson (eds.), *Religion in Africa*, (Portsmouth: Heinemann, 1994).
58. Relevant works include: J. O. Kokwora. *Medical Plants in East Africa* (Nairobi: East African Literature Bureau, 1976); I. U. W. Osisiogu, "Some Notes on Africa's Drug Plant Heritage," *Ikenga* 1, no. 2 (July 1972); B. Oliver, *Medicinal Plants in Nigeria* (Ibadan: The Nigerian College of Arts, Science & Technology, 1960); A. Sofowora, *Medicinal Plants and Traditional Medicine in Africa* (Ibadan: Onibonoje Press, 1979), 240.
59. Examples of African medicinal plants are cited in the following works: S. C. Chhabra, R. L. Mahunnah, and E. N. Mshiu, "Plants used in Traditional Medicine in Eastern Tanzania," *Journal of Ethnopharmacol* 39 no 2 (June 1993): 83–103. This work has fifty three angiosperm species used in many parts of East Africa. See also B. Desta, "Ethiopian Traditional Herbal Drugs: Part 11: Antimicrobial Activity of 63 Medicinal Plants," *Journal of Ethnopharmacol* 39 no. 2 (1993): 129–39, A. Sofowora, "Research on Medicinal Plants and Traditional Medicine in Africa," *Journal of Alternative Complementary Medicine* 2, no. 3 (Fall, 1961): 365–72.
60. S. N. Bye and M. F. Dutton, "The Inappropriate use of Traditional Medicines in South Africa," *Journal of Ethnopharmacol* 34 nos. 2–3 (Sept 1991): 253—9.
61. Stephen Hunt, "Doing the Stuff": The Vineyard Connection," in Stephen Hunt, H. Malcolm and Tony Walter (eds.), *Charismatic Christianity: Sociological Perspectives* (London: Macmillan Press Ltd, 1997), 85.
62. Hunt, "Doing the Stuff," 85.

63. J. E. Kunnie, "Black Churches in the United States and South Africa: Similarities and Differences," in G. C. Oosthuizen, M. C. Kitshoff, and S. W. D. Dube (eds.), *Afro-Christianity at the Grassroots: Its Dynamic and Strategies* (Leiden: E. J. Brill, 1994), 91.

64. R. H. Friesen. "Origins of the Spiritual Healing Church in Botswana," in G. C. Oosthuizen, M.C. Kitshoff and S. W. D. Dube (eds.), Afro-*Christianity at the Grassroots: Its Dynamics and Strategies* (Leiden: E. J. Brill, 1994), 42- 4.

65. S. I. Maboea, "Causes for the Proliferation of the African Independent Churches," in G. C. Oosthuizen, M.C. Kitshoff and S. W. D. Dube (eds.), Afro-*Christianity at the Grassroots: Its Dynamics and Strategies* (Leiden: E. J. Brill, 1994), 123.

NOTES TO CHAPTER SEVEN

1. NAC Calprof 5/15/145 "Christian Pagan Conflicts law 1925 Donald Kingdom to Chief Secretary Lagos" 25 February 1925.

2. See David B. Barrett, "AD2000: 350 million Christians in Africa," *International Review of Mission* 59 (1970), 39–54. For the most recent survey of African Christianity, see Ogbu U. Kalu (ed.), *African Christianity: An African Story* (Pretoria: University of Pretoria press, 2005), specially, chapter two.

3. A classic account would be Joseph Conrad, *Heart of Darkness*, originally published in 1902. For an unabridged version see the Dover Trift edition (New York: Dover Publications, 1990).

4. For the origin and persistence of such negative images of Africa, see for example, Curtis Keim, *Mistaking Africa: Curiosities and Inventions of the American Mind* (Boulder, CO.: Westview, 1999).

5. V.Y. Mudimbe, *The Idea of Africa* (Bloomington: Indiana University Press, 1994), xv.

6. *New York Tines*, "The Possible Future of Africa," 10 August, 1879, 6.

7. Richard Gray, "Christianity, Colonialism, and Communication in Sub-Saharan Africa," *Journal of Black Studies* 13, no. 1 (1982): 59.

8. John Du Plessis, *The Evangelization of Pagan Africa* (Cape Town, 1929), Preface.

9. Kenneth O. Dike, *Trade and Politics in the Niger Delta, 1830–1885* (Oxford, Publisher, 1956), 14.

10. F. K. Ekechi, *Missionary Enterprise and Rivalry in Igboland, 1857–1914* (London: Frank Cass, 1972), 1.

11. Ekechi, *Missionary*, 2.

12. Patrick Mbajekwe, "The Ambivalent Triumvirates on the Niger: European Traders, Christian Evangelism and British Imperial Politics in Southern Nigeria, 1850–1899." Abstract of paper presented at the 48th Annual Meeting of the African Studies Association, Washington DC, 17–20 November 2005.

13. Ogbu U. Kalu, "African Christianity: An Overview," in Kalu, (ed.), *African Chrsitianity*, 32.
14. Kalu, "African Christianity," 32.
15. Paul H. Gundani,"Iberians and African Clergy in Southern Africa" in Kalu (ed.), African Christianity, 176.
16. Kalu, "*African Christianity*," 35.
17. On the Berlin Conference, see for example, G. N. Uzoigwe, "Spheres of Influence and the Doctrine of the hinterland in the Partition of Africa," *Journal of African Studies* 3, no 2 (1976): 183–203; Thomas Pakenham, *The Scramble for Africa* (London, Harper Perennial, 1991).
18. Chukwudi A. Njoku, "The Missionary Factor in African Christianity, 1884–1914," in Kalu, (ed.), *African Christianity*, 243.
19. Kalu, *African Christianity*, 36.
20. V.Y. Mudimbe, *Between Tides*. trans. by Stephen Becker (New York: Simon & Schuster, 1991) [Originally *Entre les Eaux*, 1973], 82–3.
21. Michael Echeruo, "The Education of Lagosians," *West Africa Review* 3, no. 1 (2001): 1.
22. Echeruo, "The Education of Lagosians," 2.
23. Meredith Mckittrick, *To Dwell Secure: Generation, Christianity, and Colonialism in Ovamboland* (Oxford: James Currey; Portsmouth NH: Heinemann; Cape Town: David Philip, 2002).
24. Echeruo, "The Education of Lagosians," 5.
25. Echeruo, "The Education of Lagosians," 5.
26. Echeruo, "The Education of Lagosians," 7.
27. Cited in Echeruo, "The Education of Lagosians." 7.
28. NAC Calprof 5/15/145, 'Christian Pagan Conflicts law 1925 Donald Kingdom to Chief Secretary Lagos," 25 February 1925.
29. NAC Calprof 5/15/145, 'Christian Pagan Conflicts law 1925 Donald Kingdom to Chief Secretary Lagos," 25 February 1925.
30. NAC Calprof 5/15/145, 'Christian Pagan Conflicts law 1925 Donald Kingdom to Chief Secretary Lagos" 25 February 1925.
31. NAC Calprof 5/15/145, 'Christian Pagan Conflicts' DO Awgu to Resident Onitsha Province, 4 April 1925.
32. NAC Calprof 5/15/145, 'Christian Pagan Conflicts law 1925 Donald Kingdom to Chief Secretary Lagos," 25 February 1925.
33. NAC Calprof 5/15/145, 'Christian Pagan Conflicts law 1925, Resident, Calabar Province to Secretary Southern Provinces," 11 April 1925.
34. NAC Calprof 5/15/145 'Christian Pagan Conflicts law 1925 Donald Kingdom to Bishop of Lagos" 25 May 1925.
35. G. Parrinder, *Religion in Africa* (Middlesex, Penguin Books), 1969.
36. B. Jules-Russette, *New Religions in Africa* (New Jersey, Ablex Publishing Corporation, 1979).
37. Godfrey Ngumi, "The African Initiated Churches: Affirming the Identity, Challenging the Power," http://www.hs.unp.ac.za/theology/bct/aics.htm 25 June 2005.

38. Mudimbe, *Between Tides*, 108.
39. Mudimbe, *Between Tides*, 108.
40. Ralph Dumain, *Between Tides*, *AAH Examiner*-review [Newsletter of African Americans for Humanism], vol. 1, no. 4 (winter 1992): 5–6.
41. Ngumi, "The African Initiated."
42. Ngumi, "The African Initiated."
43. NAC RIVPROF 8/9/531, Christ Army Mission Stations.
44. NAC RIVPROF 8/9/531, Christ Army Mission Stations, U. U. Usen to Senior District Officer, Opobo, 27 June 1947.
45. NAC RIVPROF 8/9/531, Christ Army Mission Stations, U. U. Usen to Senior District Officer, Opobo, 27 June 1947.
46. *New York Times*, Sept. 5 1960, 31.
47. *New York Times*, Sept 5 1960, 31.
48. *New York Times*, Sept. 5 1960, 31.
49. *New York Times*, Sept. 5 1960, 31.
50. *New York Times*, Sept. 5 1960, 31.
51. National Archive, Enugu: Long Juju of Arochukwu and Okonko Society, 1920, Abadist 13/4/54. Cited in Eli Bentor, "Spatial Continuities: Masks and Cultural Interactions between the Delta and Southeastern Nigeria," *African Arts* (spring, 2002).
52. Bentor, "Spatial Continuities:"
53. Bentor, "Spatial Continuities:"
54. NAE UMPROF 5/1/138, "Okonko Society and Faith Tabernacle Disturbances," Eastern Regional Public Relations Office, Enugu, Press Release No. 3, 3/1/51.
55. NAE UMPROF 5/1/138, "Okonko Society and Faith Tabernacle Disturbances," Resident Owerri to Secretary, Eastern Province, 10 January 1951.
56. NAE RIVPROF 8/9/531, Meeting with Okonko members, 6 January 1951.

NOTES TO CHAPTER EIGHT

1. H. O. Russell, *The Missionary Outreach of the West Indian Church: Jamaica Baptist Missions to West Africa in the Nineteenth Century* (New York: Peter Lang 2000); N. Smith, *The Presbyterian Church of Ghana 1835–1960* (Accra: Ghana Univ. Press 1966); D. Jenkins, *Black Zion: Africa imagined and real, as seen by Today's Blacks* (New York: Harcourt Brace Jovanovich, 1975).
2. W. E. Wariboko, *Ruined by Race: Afro-Caribbean Missionaries and the Evangelization of Southern Nigeria, 1895–1925* (New Jersey: Africa World Press, 2006); also see W. E. Wariboko, "'I Really Cannot Make Africa My home': West Indian Missionaries as 'Outsiders' in the Church Missionary Society civilizing Mission to Southern Nigeria, 1898–1925," *Journal of Africa History* 45 (2004): 221–36.

3. P. E. Skinner, "The Dialectic between Diasporas and Homelands" in J. J. Harris (ed.), *Global Dimensions of the African Diaspora* (Washington: Howard University Press 1993), 22.

4. L. E. P. Erith, "The Pongas Mission," *The Jamaica Diocesan Magazine* 7, no. 8 (March, 1933).

5. J. B. Ellis, *The Diocese of Jamaica: A Short Account of its History, Growth and Organization* (London: SPCK 1913), 81–96; also see A.C. Dayfoot, *The Shaping of the West Indian Church 1492–1962* (Jamaica: The Press, Univ. of the West Indies, 1999), 182–3.

6. Missionary Bishop John Daley, "A Letter from the Bishop of Gambia and the Rio Pongas to the Church in the West Indies," *Jamaica Diocesan Magazine* (December, 1949).

7. W. R. Shenk, *Henry Venn- Missionary Statesman* (New York: Orbis Books, 1983).

8. S. M. Jacobs, "The Historical Role of Afro-Americans in American Missionary Efforts in Africa," in S. M. Jacobs (eds.), *Black Americans and the Missionary Movement in Africa* (Westport-Connecticut: Greenwood Press 1982), 5–29.

9. Reverend W. T. Mumford, "A Special Appeal to the Women and Girls of Jamaica," *Jamaica Diocesan Magazine* 7, no. 1 (August 1932).

10. J. A. Langley, *Pan-Africanism and Nationalism in West Africa, 1900–1945* (Oxford: Oxford Univ. Press 1978), 20.

11. Canon R. O. C. King, "Thoughts on the visit of the Bishop of Gambia," *Jamaica Diocesan Magazine* 21, no. 11 (November 1954).

12. N. Titus, "Missionaries under Pressure: The Experiences of Reverend John Duport in West Africa," *Caribbean Group for Social and Religious Studies* (CGSRS) No. 4, 1983.

13. J. B. Ellis, *The Diocese of Jamaica: A short account of its history, growth and organization* (London: SPCK, 1913), 148.

14. P. Bryan, *The Jamaica People1880–1920* (London: Macmillan, 1991), 33.

15. Reverend M. H. Waddell, *Twenty-Nine Years in the West Indies and Central Africa: A Review of Missionary Work and Adventure 1829–1858* (London: Frank Cass, 1970), 663.

16. Titus, "Missionaries under Pressure," 17.

17. L. Evans, *The 150th Anniversary of the Diocese of Jamaica, 1824–1974* (Kingston: Litho Press United, 1974), 22.

18. Evans, *The 150th Anniversary*, 25.

19. Canon Dean S. McEwen, "The Pongas Mission," *Jamaica Diocesan Magazine* 4, no. 4 (Nov. 1929).

20. Ellis, *The Diocese of Jamaica*, 148.

21. Ellis, *The Diocese of Jamaica*, 147–8.

22. Dayfoot, *The Shaping of the West Indian Church*, 183–2.

23. Titus, "Missionaries Under Pressure," 3.

24. A. Hodge, "The Training of Missionaries for Africa: the Church Missionary Society's Training College at Islington, 1900–1915," *Journal of Religion in Africa* 4, no. 2 (1971): 81–96.

25. Reverend Waddell, *Twenty-Nine Years in the West Indies and Central Africa*, 301–2.
26. Reverend Waddell, *Twenty-Nine Years in the West Indies and Central Africa*, 672.
27. J. P. Kirby, "Cultural Change and Religious Conversion in West Africa," in D. T. Blakely, D. T. Beek and E.A.W. Thomson (eds.), *Religion in Africa* (London: Heinemann 1994), 61.
28. FO84/1882 Harry Johnston, "A Report on the British Protectorate of the Oil Rivers," 1 December 1888.
29. CA3/04/554 S. A. Crowther to Sir W.N.N. Hewitt [Commodore Royal Navy], "A brief statement of advantages accruing to Protestant Christian Missions through the benign operations, and moral influence of British Government on the West Coast of Africa," 7 August 1879.
30. C. Wondji, "The States and Cultures of the Upper Guinean Coast," in *Africa from the sixteenth to the eighteenth century* ed. B.A. Ogot. California: Heinemann 1992, 368–97. (UNESCO General History of Africa Vol. V. Unabridged edition).
31. Titus, "Missionaries under Pressure," 9.
32. King, "Thoughts on the visit of the Bishop of Gambia."
33. Titus, "Missionaries under Pressure," 9
34. Titus, "Missionaries under Pressure," 17.
35. Wariboko, *Ruined by Race*, 105–11.
36. McEwen, "The Pongas Mission."
37. McEwen, "The Pongas Mission."
38. Titus, "Missionaries under Pressure," 23.
39. Erith, "The Rio Pongo Mission."
40. P. Bryan, *The Jamaican People 1880–1920* (London: Macmillan, 1991), 50.
41. Wariboko, "'I Really Cannot Make Africa My Home.'"
42. Evans, *The 150th Anniversary*, 37–46.
43. *Gleaner,* 5 November 1909.
44. *Jamaica Times,* 30 April 1910.
45. Erith, "The Rio Pongas Mission."
46. W. E. Wariboko, *Planting Church-Culture at New Calabar: Some Neglected Aspects of Christian Missionary Enterprise in the Eastern Niger Delta, 1865–1918* (Bethesda: San Francisco, 1998).
47. McEwen, "The Pongas Mission."
48. W. A. Burris, "*Jamaica Times,* 30 April 1910.
49. *Jamaica Churchman* Vol. V. No.1 (March, 1908).
50. "Making Africa New: Missionaries dethrone Nyamba," *Jamaica Times* 20 Aug., 1910.
51. "Jamaica Missionaries: The Rev and Mrs. W.A. Burris," *Jamaica Times* 10 Sept., 1910.
52. *Jamaica Diocesan Magazine* Vol. VIII, No. 2 (September 1932).
53. McEwen, "The Pongas Mission."
54. "The Pongas Mission: A Mission from Africa's Sons to Africa," *Jamaica Diocesan Magazine* 7, no. 8 (March, 1933).

55. King, "Thoughts on the visit of the Bishop of Gambia"
56. Titus, "Missionaries under Pressure," 27.
57. L. Sanneh, "The CMS and the African transformation: Samuel Ajayi Crowther and the Opening of Nigeria" in K. Ward and B. Stanley (eds.), *Church Mission Society and World Christianity* (Cambridge: William B. Eerdmans Publishing Company), 2000, 85.
58. "The Pongas Mission: A Mission from Africa's Sons to Africa"
59. Daley, "A Letter from the Bishop of Gambia and the Rio Ponga."
60. P. D. Curtin, *The Image of Africa: British Ideas and Action, 1780–1850* (Madison: The University of Wisconsin Press, 1964), 324.
61. W. D. Jordon, *The White Man's Burden* (Oxford: Oxford University Press, 1974), 6.
62. C. W. Mills, *The Racial Contract* (Ithaca: Cornell University Press, 1997), 119.
63. R. M. Nettleford, *Caribbean Cultural Identity: The Case of Jamaica* (Princeton: Markus Wiener Publishers, 2003), 159.
64. R. M. Nettleford, *Mirror Mirror: Identity, Race and Protest in Jamaica* (Kingston: LMH Publishing Limited, 1998), 36.

NOTES TO CHAPTER NINE

1. These European groups largely superseded the less powerful local imperialisms of the Kilindi clan rulers of the Shambaa kingdom, the Omani rulers of Zanzibar and Pangani Town, and various Big Men who had grown in power during the mid-century slave trade.
2. In particular, the long-serving Archdeacon of the diocese, J. P. Farler, was most vehemently vocal about the disasters German occupation brought. Farler was among those who popularized the idea in the English press that the treaties that formed the basis for German claims in the region were bogus. J. P. Farler to W. H. Penny, Letter November 8, 1885, Rhodes House, UMCA Box A1-VI-A.
3. J. P. Farler, "Misdoings of the Germans," [n.d.~1889] Rhodes House, UMCA Box A1-V-A.
4. Archdeacon Farler's letter to the *Times*, June 1887, Rhodes House, UMCA Box A1-VI-B.
5. Bateman-Jones to W. H. Penney, letter of January 13, 1889, Rhodes House, UMCA Box A1-VI-B.
6. Bishop Hine to Secretary Travers, letter of October 5, 1905, Rhodes House, UMCA Box A1-XIII.
7. J. P. Farler to W. H. Penney, letter of September 28, 1885, Rhodes House, UMCA Box A1-VI-A.
8. Reverend J. Griffen to C. A., letter of August 24, 1894, Rhodes House, UMCA Box A1-VI-B.
9. Reverend Chambers to Secretary Travers, letter of Easter 1896, Rhodes House, UMCA Box E1.

10. Karl Juhlke, *Colonial Correspondence* 18, 1886. Juhlke included sarcastic asides like: "Owing to its being mixed up in the Slave Trade question, which breaks out now and then, England was in a position to wait for a suitable moment, when it suited her to annex." Discussed by Robert Cust in letter of June 1, 1887, Rhodes House, UMCA Box C1.

11. Bishop Hine to Pastor Johansen, letter of August 18, 1903, Rhodes House, UMCA Box A1-XIII and H. W. Woodward to Secretary Travers, letter of September 4, 1903, Rhodes House, UMCA Box TC F6.

12. C. M. Yonge, "Preface," in A. E. M. Anderson-Morshead, *History of the Universities' Mission to Central Africa (1859–1909),* (London: 1909), xxi.

13. Archdeacon Farler's letter to the *Times,* June 1887, Rhodes House, UMCA Box A1-VI-B.

14. Jonathon Glassman, *Feast and Riot* (Portsmouth: 1995); Edward Steere, *Central African Mission: Its Present State and Prospects,* UMCA Pamphlet (London: 1873), 8.

15. J. P. Farler, "The Work of Christ in Central Africa: A letter to the Reverend H. P. Liddon," (London: Rivington's, 1878), 17.

16. J. P. Farler, "The Work of Christ . . . ," 20.

17. William Lowndes to Ted Lowndes, December 9, 1881, Rhodes House, UMCA Box A1-IV-A; Bishop Smythies, January 7, 1885, "Journey from Zanzibar to Magila . . . with Mr Geldart . . . description of country round Mkuzi," Rhodes House, UMCA Box A1-V-B.

18. Karl Juhlke, *Colonial Correspondence* 18, 1886.

19. On the basis of no evidence whatsoever, European geographers described the African interior as being overrun with swamps.

20. H. Meyer, *Across East African Glaciers,* 330. Meyer chastised Carl Peters' commentary, 'for extent and fertility [German East Africa] will stand comparison with any tropical colony in the world.' "I am sorry to say I cannot endorse Dr. Peters' opinion."

21. "Usambara- und Küsten-Gebiet in den Bezirken Tanga, Pangani und Wilhelmstal, 1910," *Tanzania National Archives.*

22. Archdeacon Farler's letter to the *Times,* June 1887, Rhodes House, UMCA Box A1-VI-B.

23. Charles Smith, "Exploration in Zanzibar Dominions," *Royal Geographical Society Supplementary Papers* 2 (1889), 121.

24. Farler, "The Usambara Country," 91–92.

25. H. Meyer, *Across East African Glaciers,* x.

26. *Kolonial-Politische Korrespondenz* 1 (May 1885), Berlin, 16.

27. Herman von Wissman, "Nachrichten aus den deutschen Schutzgebieten: Deutsch-Ostafrika," *Deutsches Kolonialblatt* 6.19 (1895), 479.

28. Russell Berman, *Enlightenment or Empire: Colonial Discourse in German Culture* (Lincoln: University of Nebraska Press, 1998), 2–8.

29. Berman, *Enlightenment or Empire,* 2.

30. Berman, *Enlightenment or Empire,* 1; 90–91.

31. Mary Louise Pratt, *Imperial Eyes* (New York: Routledge, 1992), 49–65.

32. Farler, "The Usambara Country," 82.

33. Farler, "The Usambara Country," 84.

34. F. R. Hodgson, "A Journey from Zanzibar to Magila," May 1877, Rhodes House, UMCA box A1-IV-A; Bishop Smythies, letter of July 9, 1884, UMCA box A1-V-B; J. P. Richardson, letter of February 27, 1896, UMCA box A1-VII.

35. Baumann, *Usambara und Seine Nachbargebiete*, 7–8.

36. J. P. Farler wrote his accounts specifically to draw in more missionaries; his own reign as Archdeacon over the mission station at Magila was fraught with problems of retention. A number of his subordinates (not to mention superiors) died during his tenure, and his style of managing the station made a number of his underlings anxious to leave. William Lowndes to Ted Lowndes, letter of June 3 1881, Rhodes House, UMCA archives, Box A1-IV-A. The squabbles between Farler and his juniors led one of them to even eat Farler's pet pigeons while he was away!

37. Alfred Bellville. "Journey to the Universities' Mission Station of Magila, on the Borders of the Usambara Country" *Proceedings of the Royal Geographical Society* 20 (1876): 74–78. Bellville traveled alongside J. P. Farler.

38. Baumann, *Usambara und Seine Nachbargebiete*, 5.

39. Herman von Wissman, "Nachrichten aus den deutschen Schutzgebieten: Deutsch-Ostafrika," *Deutsches Kolonialblatt* 6.19 (1895), 479. ("Report from the German Protectorate.")

40. Christopher Conte, *Highland Sanctuary, Environmental History in Tanzania's Usambara Mountains* (Athens: Ohio University Press, 2004), 45.

41. C. Smith, "Exploration in Zanzibar Dominions," 121.

42. H. Meyer, *Across East African Glaciers*, 16.

43. *TNA*, G8/850.

44. Hans Schabel, "Tanganyika Forestry Under German Colonial Administration, 1891–1919," *Forestry & Conservation History* (July 1990), 132.

45. Johan Ludwig Krapf, *Travels*, XLV.

46. Edward Steere, *Central African Mission: Its Present State and Prospects*, UMCA Pamphlet (London: U.M.C.A., 1873), 13–14.

47. Richard Grove, *Ecology, Climate and Empire: colonialism and global environmental history, 1400–1940* (Cambridge: White Horse, 1997), 7.

48. H. W. Woodward, letter of July 15, 1901, Rhodes -House, UMCA Box A1-VIII.

49. Richard Grove, *Green Imperialism: Colonial Expansion, Tropical Island Edens and the Origins of Environmentalism 1600–1860* (Cambridge: Cambridge University Press, 1995), 483.

50. James Scott, *Seeing Like A State*, 19. Henry Lowood, "The Calculating Forester: Quantification, Cameral Science, and the Emergence of Scientific Forestry Management in Germany," in T. Frängsmyr, J. L. Heilbron, and R. E. Rider(eds.), *The Quantifying Spirit in the 18th Century* (Berkeley: University of California Press, 1990), 319–42.

51. Letter 9 Janurary, 1905, *TNA* G8/599, *Forstwirtschaft Bezirk Pangani* [Forest Economy Pangani District] *Bd 1*, 1898–1912

52. Eduard Deininger, 22 December, 1911, *TNA* G8/804, *Waldreservate Bezirk Tanga "Mlemmabach"*[Forest Reserve "Mlemmabach" in the Tanga District].

53. D. O. Sperling, Letter 27 May, 1903, *TNA G8/801, Waldreservate Bezirk Tanga "Bassiwald" 1903–15.*

54. Lieutenant von Bieberstein, Letter on the Administration of Land Commissions in Wilhelmstal District, 11 December, 1911, *TNA G8/838, Waldreservate Bezirk Wilhelmstal "Pangani-Fluss" bei Buiko, 1912.*

55. Dr. Stier, 15 September, 1911, *TNA G8/804 Waldreservate Bezirk Tanga "Mlemmabach"* [Forest Reserve "Mlemmabach" in the Tanga District]; Also, District Officer Sperling, Letter 27 May 1903, *TNA G8/801 Waldreservate Bezirk Tanga "Bassiwald"* [Forest Reserve "Bassiwald" in the Tanga District], 1903–1915.

56. Bishop Smythies, *Proceedings: Methods of Missionary Work*, Rhodes House, UMCA Box A1-V-A, 2.

57. Bishop Smythies "Proceedings: Methods of Missionary Work," Rhodes House, UMCA Box, A1-V-A, 3.

58. Anonymous, Introduction to "Missionary Pastoral Letter" (1870) from Bishop Tozer, Rhodes House, UMCA Box A1 (I) A, 3.

59. William Lowndes to Ted, letter of January 31, 1881, Rhodes House, UMCA Box A1-IV-A; Farler to Dear Professor, letter of May 30, 1880, Rhodes House, UMCA Box A1-VI-A.

60. "An account of the sending of S. Steere and party to the Mainland (1872)," Rhodes House, UMCA Box TC E27.

61. Farler to Penney, letter of October 4, 1881, Rhodes House, UMCA Box A1-VI-A.

62. Farler to W. H. Penney, letter of December 1, 1886, Rhodes House, UMCA Box A1-VI-A.

63. Yorke to Farler, letter of the Feast of Saint Matthew, 1878, Rhodes House, UMCA Box A1-IV-A.

64. Wilson to Penney, letter of November 1, 1881, Rhodes House, UMCA Box A1-IV-A.

65. Farler to Wilson, letter of November 12, 1881; Farler to Bishop Steere, letter of November 19, 1881; Rhodes House, UMCA Box A1-VI-A.

66. J. P. Farler to H.A.B. Wilson, letter of November 19, 1881, Rhodes House, UMCA Box A1-VI-A. J. P. Farler to Bishop Steere, letter of November 23, 1881, Rhodes House, UMCA Box A1-VI-A.

67. Theodor Siebenlist, *Forstwirtschaft in Deustch Ost-Afrika* (Berlin: 1914), 39.

68. James Scott, *Seeing Like a State*, 2.

69. *TNA G 8/599, Forstwirtschaft Bezirk Pangani* [Agriculture in the Pangani District] *Bd 1, 1898–1912.*

70. A. C. Hamilton and I. V. Mwasha, "History of Resource Utilization and Management Under German Rule," in eds., A. C. Hamilton and R. Bensted-Smith, *Forest Conservation in the East Usambara Mountains Tanzania* (IUCN: 1989), 39.

71. Schabel, "Tanganyika Forestry," 131.

72. Conte "Nature Reorganized: Ecological History in the Plateau Forests of the West Usambara Mountains 1850–1935," in *Custodians of the Land,* 108.

73. Siebenlist, *Forstwirtschaft,* 55.

74. Schabel, "Tanganyika Forestry," 138.

75. *TNA,* G8/526, *Forstwirtschaft, Hauptnutzung* (Forest Economy, Principal Uses).

76. J. S. Groome, "History of the Forest Department," 3. Rhodes House Library, Mss Afr.S.1389.

77. Christopher Conte, *Highland Sanctuary.*

78. John Iliffe, *A Modern History of Tanganyika* (Cambridge: Cambridge University Press,1979), 126–27; 152.

79. Bezirkamtmann Speith, Pangani 10 February, 1909, *TNA]* G 8/599 (*Forstwirtschaft Bezirk Pangani Bd 1, 1898–1912*).

80. Thaddeus Sunseri, *Vilimani: Labor Migration and Rural Change in Early Colonial Tanzania* (Portsmouth: Heinemann, 2002), 53–67.

81. Roderick Neumann, "Ways of Seeing Africa: Colonial Recasting of African Society and Landscape in Serengeti National Park," *Ecumene* 2, no. 2 (1995): 153.

NOTES TO CHAPTER TEN

1. Ali Mazrui, "Churches and Multinationals in the Spread of Modern Education: A Third World Perspective," *Third World Quarterly* 1, no. 1 (Jan. 1979): 30-49.

2. David J. Bosch, *Believing in the Future: Toward a Missiology of Western Culture* (Valley Forge, PA.: Trinity Press International, 1995), 18.

3. See William Olsen Lowrey, "Passing the Peace, People to People: Religion and Indigenous Roles in Nuer, Sudan" (Ph.D. diss., The Union Institute, 1996).

4. See Richard L. Hill, "Government and Christian Missions in the Anglo-Egyptian Sudan, 1899-1914," *Middle Eastern Studies* 1, no. 2 (1965): 13-21.

5. Robert O. Collins, "The Establishment of Christian Missions and Their Rivalry in the Southern Sudan," *Tarikh* 3 (Jan.-March 1969): 96, 39.

6. Robert O. Collins, *Land Beyond the Rivers: The Southern Sudan, 1898-1918,* (New Haven, and London: Yale University Press, 1971), 284, 286.

7. Collins, *Land Beyond,* 1971, 287.

8. Mohamed Omer Beshir, *Southern Sudan: Background to Conflict* (London: C. Hurst & Co, 1968), 32-5; Lilian Sanderson Passmore, and Neville Sanderson, *Education, Religion, and Politics in Southern Sudan, 1899-1964,* (London: Ithaca Press, 1981), 36, 60.

9. Kenneth Henderson, *Sudan Republic,* (London: Ernest Benn, 1965), 161.

10. Cited in Abdek Rahim, "The Development of British Policy in the Southern Sudan, 1899-1947," Department of Political Science, University of Khartoum [conference paper], 1965, 6-7, quoting Khartoum, March 14, 1920. Milner Papers.

11. Rahim, "British Policy," 6-7.

12. Rahim, "British Policy," 198-9.

13. Sanderson and Sanderson, *Education, Religion and Politics,* 33.

14. Collins, *Land Beyond*, 283.
15. Oliver Albino, *The Sudan: A Southern Viewpoint* (London: Institute of Race Relations and Oxford University Press, 1970), 16-19; Sanderson and Sanderson, *Education, Religion and Politics,* 78-103.
16. Hill, "Government and Christian Missions," 119, citing Wingate to Gwynne, May 17 1911, SGA, Khartoum and Durham.
17. Abdel Rahim, "The Development of British Policy in the Southern Sudan, 1899-1947," *Middle Eastern Journal* (April 1966): 238.
18. Annual Report of 1926, Sudan No. 2 (1027) Cmd. 2991, 8.
19. Giffen, "Evangelistic Report," 83-97. Ministry of Education, "Education Report," Khartoum. SGA & SGAD, 1915, 23-7.
20. See Heather Sharkey, "Christians among Muslims: The Church Missionary Society in the Northern Sudan," *The Journal of African History* 43, no.11 (2002): 51-75; See also John Mathews, *"Memorandum of Educational Policy in the Nuba Pagan Area"* (Khartoum, 1930), cited in Lilian Sanderson, "Educational development and administrative control in the Nuba Mountains region of the Sudan," *Journal of African History* 4 (1963): 233.
21. Sharkey, "Christians among Muslims."
22. Toniolo, "The First Centenary of the Roman Catholic Mission to Central Africa, 1846-1946," *SNR* 27 (1946): 102 [99-I26].
23. Lilian Sanderson, "Education in the Southern Sudan: The Impact of Government-Missionary-Southern Sudanese Relationships upon the Development of Education during the Condominium Period, 1898-1956," *African Affairs* 79, no. 315 (April 1980): 157-70, 160. See also Charles R Watson, *The Sorrow and Hope of the Egyptian Sudan: A Survey of Missionary Conditions and Methods of Work in the Egyptian Sudan,* (Philadelphia: United Presbyterian Church of North America 1913), 134.
24. See the lengthy correspondences of "Wingate to Gwynne,"17th May, 1911, *Wingate Papers*, School of Oriental Studies, Sudan Correspondence, 300/5.
25. Edward Evans-Pritchard, *Nuer Religion* (Oxford: Clarendon Press, 1956), vii.
26. John Burton, "Christians, Colonists, and Conversion: A View from Nilotic Sudan," *The Journal of Modern African Studies* 23 no. 2 (1985): 367; See also, Francis Mading Deng, *Dinka Cosmology,* (London: Ithaca Press, 1980).
27. John Burton, "Sacrifice: A Polythetic Class of Atuot Religious Thought," *Journal of Religion in Africa* 11 (1980): 94.
28. Deng, *Dinka Cosmology,* 50-67.
29. Carson, "Evangelistic Report," 20.
30. Mohamed Beshir, *Educational Development in the Sudan, 1898-1956* (Oxford: Clarendon Press, 1969): 75.
31. Beshir, *Educational Development,* 75.
32. Beshir, *Educational Development,* 75.

33. Cited in Dunstan M. Wai (ed.), *The Southern Sudan: The Problem of National Integration* (London: Frank Cass, 1973), 175.
34. Beshir, *Educational Development*, 74.
35. Beshir, *Educational Development*, 74.
36. Sanderson and Sanderson, *Education, Religion and Politics*, 200.
37. See Vincent Battle, "The American Mission and Educational Development in the Southern Sudan, 1900-1929'" in Battle and Lyon (eds.), *Essays in the History of African Education*, (New York: Teachers College Press, Columbia University, 1970).
38. Robert O. Collins, *Shadows in the Grass: Britain in the Southern Sudan, 1918-1956* (New York: Yale University Press, 1983), 86.
39. Mohamed Beshir, *The Southern Sudan, Background to Conflict* (New York: Frederick A. Praeger, 1968), 22-7.
40. Martin Daly, "Islam, Secularism, and Ethnic Identity in the Sudan," in Gustavo Benavides and Martin Daly (eds.), *Religion and Political Power* (New York: State University of New York Press, 1989), 84-5.
41. Harold MacMichael, *The Sudan* (London: F. A. Praeger, 1955), 91-118; 137-40; Sanderson, *Education, Religion and Politics*, 111-37.
42. Sanderson, *Education, Religion and Politics*, 51-71; 147-63.
43. Oliver Albino, *The Sudan: A Southern Viewpoint*, 11-14.
44. Heather Sharkey, "Christians among Muslims," 57-8.
45. Sharkey, "Christians among Muslims," 63-4,
46. Wal Duany, "Neither Palaces nor Prisons: The Constitution of Order among the Nuer." (Ph.D. dissertation, Indiana University, 1992), 298.
47. Hill, "Government and Christian Missions," 123-4.
48. Collins, *Land Beyond*, 292.
49. Burton, "Christians, Colonists, and Conversion," 349-69.
50. "Wingate to Gwynne 17th May, 1911," *Wingate Papers*, School of Oriental Studies, Sudan Correspondence, 300/5.
51. Collins, *Land Beyond*, 291.
52. Collins, *Land Beyond*, 293.
53. The Roman Catholic missionaries therefore had to move into Southern Sudan at Lul, on the banks of the Nile. The area made the RC missionaries suffer from frequent bouts of malaria; See Arnaldo Violine, "The History of Our Mission, Lul," *The Messenger* (Feb/ March 1937), 13.
54. For a discussion of these various missionary spheres, and their relation to colonial policy, see Philip Legge Pitya, "A History of Western Christian Evangelism in Sudan, 1898-1964," (Ph.D. diss. Boston University Graduate School, 1996).
55. Roman Catholic missionaries faced the same situation at Wau, where they could not settle because British officials did not want to offend local Muslim sensibilities; See Antonio Vignato, "The History of Our Missions," *The Messenger*, May 1934, 31.
56. Sanderson and Sanderson, *Education, Religion and Politics*, 211-49.
57. Collins, *Land Beyond the Rivers*, 113-21.

58. See Arnaldo Violini, "The History of Our Missions," (Jan/Feb. 1937): March, 13, April, 23, May, 31.

59. Oliver Allison, *Pilgrim Church's Progress*, (Church of Sudan, Highway Press, 1966), 38-45, 77-85.

60. See Giovanni Vantini, *Christianity in the Sudan*, (Bologna: EMI Publishers, 1981), 253.

61. See Rev. William Carey, "Annual Report for 1939, Juba," (London, Church Missionary Society, 1939), 22-5.

62. Lamin Sanneh, *Encountering the West: Christianity and the Global Cultural Process: The African Dimension* (London: Harper Collins Publishers; Maryknoll, New York: Orbis Books, 1993), 19.

63. G. Whitehead, "Social Changes among the Bari," *SNR 5*, no. 1 (1929): 91-7; Anderson, *South Sudan*, 26-9; Angela Arpo, "History of Our Missions," (Sept. 1934): 11; Arnaldo Violini, "History of Our Missions," (Nov. 1937), 70.

64. Sanderson, "Education in the Southern Sudan,"166.

65. C. S. Equatoria, Educational Conference, Juba, 1, 2, and 4 April, 1933. See also, Sanderson, "Education in the Southern Sudan," 166.

66. Sanderson, "Education in the Southern Sudan," 166.

67. CMS G3/E/O? 1925, "Notes on Government Medical and Educational Development in the Sudan, received 11 July 1925." Cited in Sharkey, "Christians among Muslims," 68.

68. See, Albino, *The Sudan: A Southern Viewpoint*, 23-4; Abel Alier, "The Southern Sudan Question," in Dunstan M. Wai (ed.), *The Southern Sudan: The Problem of National Integration* (London: Frank Cass, 1973), 15-18.

69. Verona Fathers Mission, "The Black Book of the Sudan on the Expulsion of the Christian Missionaries from Southern Sudan: An Answer," (Milano: Istituto Artigianelli, September 1964), 75.

70. Bong, "Christian Missionaries in the South," 1.

71. *The Black Book of the Sudan*, 75.

72. *The Black Book of the Sudan*, 16-17.

73. "Relations between the Government and the Missionary Organisations during the Era of Foreign rule," in *Memorandum on Reasons that led to the Expulsion of Foreign Missionaries and Priests from the Southern Provinces of the Sudan* (Khartoum, 1964), 3-4.

74. "A Strictly Confidential Letter from Ali Baldo, Governor of Equatoria to Bishop Sisto Mazzoldi, Vicar Apostolic of Bahr el Gebel, Juba, 11 th March 1957," SP/ SCR/ 46. A.2, cited in Scopas Sekwat Poggo, "War and Conflict in the Southern Sudan, 1955-1972" (Ph.D. dissertation, University of California, Santa Barbara, 1999).

75. Bishop Mazzoldi sought to reassure Ali Baldo about the specifically religious nature of the institution, in his reply: 'I intend to assure you of opening the Mission Station as a purely religious institution for the spiritual needs of our Christians and adherents' in Nyangiya or Lotelepei.

"Letter from Bishop Sisto Mazzoldi, Vicar Apostolic, Juba, to District Commissioner, Eastern District, Kapoeta," 13th March 1957, ED/SCR/46 A 1/1, cited in Poggo, "War and Conflict."

76. Poggo, "War and Conflict."
77. "A Strictly Confidential Letter from Governor Ali Baldo, Governor, Equatoria, Juba, to District Commissioner, Eastern District, Kapoeta,' 4th Jan. 1958," EP/SCR/ 46.C.6.4, XR/ SCR/ 46.C. 6.5, cited in Scopas Poggo, "War and Conflict."
78. "Editorial Comment," *Voice of Southern Sudan* 1, no. 2 (Sudan African National Union, 1963), 9.
79. "Editorial Comment," *Voice of Southern Sudan* 1, no. 2, 9.
80. Sharkey, "Christians among Muslims," 72.
81. "The Memorandum Presented by the Sudan African National Union to the Commission of the Organization of African Unity for Refugees" (Kampala, Uganda, November 1964): 57.
82. See, for example, Gerard Prunier, *Darfur: The Ambiguous Genocide* (Ithaca, New York: Cornell University Press, 2005).
83. Oliver Albino, *The Sudan: A Southern Viewpoint*, 6. Citing "Parliamentary Proceedings: Second sitting of the first session of parliament," 1958, 3. It is important to note that Ali el Mirghani was the patron of the P. D. P. and religious leader of the Khatmiya sect, and Sadiq el Mahdi was the leader of the Ansar sect, and also, headed the Umma Party.
84. See "Relations between the Government and the Missionary Organisations during the Era of Foreign rule," in *Memorandum on Reasons that led to the Expulsion of Foreign Missionaries and Priests from the Southern Provinces of the Sudan*, 3.
85. Dr. Kamal Baghir, *Rai El Amm*, 30.9.59.
86. Veroni Fathers, *The Black Book of the Sudan*, 98-9.
87. "Editorial Comment," *Voice of Southern Sudan* 1, no. 2 (1963): 12.
88. "Editorial Comment," *Voice of Southern Sudan* 1, no. 2 (1963): 2.
89. "A Petition by East African Students in the United Kingdom and Ireland to President Ibrahim Abboud of the Republic of the Sudan During His State Visit to the United Kingdom," London, 21 May 1964, 57.
90. Bong, "Christian Missionaries in the South, How and Why Religion has Become a Problem in the South," 1.
91. Bong, "Christian Missionaries in the South," 1.
92. Victor Ramadan, "Uses of Education," *The Messenger*, Wau (Sept. 1948): 63; Joseph H. Oduho, "Senior Education," *The Messenger*, Wau (Sept. 1948), 63; William G. Gbendi and Tarcizio Ahmed, "School Fees," *The Messenger*, Wau (Sept. 1948), 63.
93. "Editorial Comment," *Voice of Southern Sudan* 1, no. 2 (Sudan African National Union, Negritude and Progress, 1963), 10.
94. "Editorial Comment," *Voice of Southern Sudan*, 10.
95. Anderson, "Minutes of the Annual Meeting of the Association, AM" (Feb. 21-28, 1958), 4-15.

96. "Editorial Comment," *Voice of Southern Sudan* 1, no. 4 (1964), 16.
97. "Letter to The Times," London, March 13, 1964, cited in *Voice of Southern Sudan* 2, no. 1 (April 1964), 7-8.
98. Veroni Fathers, *The Black Book of the Sudan,* 112.
99. For this notion, see for example, Marc Nikkel, "Dinka Christianity: The Origins and Development of Christianity among the Dinka of Sudan, with Special Reference to the Songs of Dinka Christians" (Ph.D diss., University of Edinburgh, 1993).
100. See Philip Pitya, "Christian Evangelism," 650-5.
101. Douglass Johnson, *Nuer Prophets: A History of Prophesy from the Upper Nile in the Nineteenth and Twentieth Centuries,* (Oxford: Clarendon Press, 1994), 315, 216
102. Wal Duany, *Neither Palaces,* 219.
103. Wal Duany, *Neither Palaces,* 299.
104. "Sudan Expels Missionaries," *Christian Century,* Jan. 2, 1963, 19.
105. William Olsen Lowrey, "Passing the Peace, people to people," 130.
106. Johnson, *Nuer Prophets,* 315.
107. Johnson, *Nuer Prophets,* 315, 216.
108. Pitya, "Christian Evangelism," 555.
109. Pitya, "Christian Evangelism," 586.
110. Pitya, "Christian Evangelism," 586.
111. Studies suggest that Christianity entered Nubia as early as 37 A. D, thanks to Nubian converts. Some argue that Christianity was established in Nubia in the third century A. D. by Egyptian fleeing Roman persecution. Vantini, Christianity in the Sudan, 21-5; 35-6; F. F. Gadallah, "Egyptian Contribution to Nubian Christianity," *SNR,* 40, 38.
112. For a recent discussion of a new breed of evangelical NGOs concerned with Sudan, and their supporters in Washington, see Allen Hertzke, *Freeing God's Children: The Unlikely Alliance for Global Human Rights,* (Oxford: Rowma and Littlefield, 2004), 237-300.
113. For a preliminary methodology, at least, see Katharina Hofer, "The Role of Evangelical NGOs in International Development. A Comparative Case study of Kenya and Uganda," *Afrika Spectrum* 38, no. 3 (2001): 375-98.

Selected Bibliography

Ajayi, J. Ade. *Christian Missions in Nigeria: The Making of a New Elite*. London: Longmans, 1965.

Anderson-Morshead, A. E. M. *History of the Universities' Mission to Central Africa, 1859–1909*. London: Office of the Universities' Mission to Central Africa, 1909.

Andersson, Efraim. *Messianic Popular Movements in the Lower Congo*. Uppsala, Sweden: Almqvist & Wiksells Boktryckeri AB, 1958.

Anene, J. C. *Southern Nigeria in Transition 1885–1906*. Cambridge: Cambridge University Press 1966.

Appiah, K. A. and A. Gutman, eds. *Colour Consciousness: The Political Morality of Race*. Princeton: Princeton University Press. 1996.

Apter, David. *The Political Kingdom of Uganda*. Princeton: Princeton University Press, 1967.

Asch, Susan. *L'eglise du prophète Simon Kimbangu: de ses origines à son rôle actuel au Zaïre, 1921–1981*. Paris: Editions Karthala, 1983.

Ashe, Robert Pickering. *Chronicles of Uganda*. London: Hodder and Stoughton, 1894.

———. *Two Kings of Buganda*. London: Sampson Low, 1890.

Au Pays de Palmiers: Récits du Congo écrits par des moniteurs indigènes (1928). Stockholm: Èditions Svenska Missionskyrkan, 2003.

Axelson, Sigbert. *Culture Confrontation in the Lower Congo: From the Old Congo Kingdom to the Congo Independent State with special reference to the Swedish Missionaries in the 1880's and 1890's*. Sweden: Gummessons, 1970.

Ayandele, E. A. "James Africanus Beale Horton, 1835–1883: Prophet of Modernization in West Africa." *African Historical Studies* 4, no. 3 (1971): 691–6.

———. *The Missionary Impact on Modern Nigeria, 1842–1914*. London: Longmans, 1966.

Ayitteh, George B. *Indigenous African Institutions*. New York: Transnational Publishers, 1991.

Barth, F. "Segmentary Opposition and the Theory of Games." *Journal of the Royal Anthropological Institute* 89 (1959): 5–21.

Beidelman, T. O. "The Anthropology of Colonialism: Culture, History and the Emergence of Western Governmentality." *Annual Review of Anthropology* 26 (1997): 163–183.

———. *Colonial Evangelism*. Bloomington: Indiana Univ. Press, (1981).

Bontinck, Francois. "Le Conditionnement Historique de l'Implantation de l'église Catholique au Congo." *Revue de Clerge Africain*, Tome XXIV, 2 (March 1969): 132–145.

Bowie, F., Kirkwood, D., and S. Ardener (eds.) *Women and Missions: Past and Present, Anthropological and Historical Perceptions*. Oxford: Berg, 1993.

Brierly, Jean and Thomas Spear. "Mutesa, the Missionaries, and Christian Conversion in Buganda." *International Journal of African Historical Studies* 21 no. 4 (1988): 601–18.

Burton, Richard F. *Two Trips to Gorilla Land and the Cataracts of the Congo. Volume II*. London: S. Low, and Searle, 1876.

Cheetham, J. N. "In a West African Assize Court," *Southport Visitor,* 4 May 1913.

———. "Southern Nigeria: The Future of the Country." *Southport Visitor,* 5 April, 1908.

Chomé, Jules. *La Passion de Simon Kimbangu*. Les Amis de la Présence Africaine: Brussels, 1959.

Comaroff, Jean and John Comaroff, "The Colonization of Consciousness in South Africa," *Economy and Society* 18, no. 3 (August 1989), 267–96

———. Of Revelation and Revolution Vol. II: The Dialectics of Modernity on a South African Frontier. Chicago: University of Chicago Press,

———. *Of Revelation and Revolution: Christianity, Colonialism, and Consciousness in South Africa*, vol. 1. Chicago: University of Chicago Press, 1991.

Conte, Christopher. *Highland Sanctuary, Environmental History in Tanzania's Usambara Mountains*. Athens, OH: Ohio University Press, 2004.

Cuvelier, Jean. "Les Missions Catholiques en face des danses des Bakongo." *Africanae Fraternae Ephemerides Romanae*, 17 (June 1939): 143–170.

Desta, B. "Ethiopian Traditional Herbal Drugs: Part 11: Antimicrobial Activity of 63 Medicinal Plants." *Journal of Ethnopharmacol* 39 (2) (1993): 129–39.

Dike, K. O. *Trade and Politics in the Niger Delta 1830–1885*. Oxford: Clarendon Press 1956.

Donald Anthony Low, *Buganda in Modern History*. Berkeley: University of California Press, 1971.

Ekechi, Felix K. *Missionary Enterprise and Rivalry in Igboland, 1857–1914*. London: Frank Cass, 1972.

———. "Colonialism and Christianity in West Africa: The Igbo Case," *Journal of African History* 21, no. 1 (1971): 103–15

Ellis, J. B. *The Diocese of Jamaica: A Short Account of its History, Growth and Organization*. London: SPCK 1913.

Evans-Pritchard, Edward Evan. *Essays in Social Anthropology and other Essays*. New York: Free Press of Glencoe, 1962.

Fallers, Lloyd A. "Despotism, Status Culture and Social Mobility in an African Kingdom." *Comparative Studies in Society and History* 2, no. 1 (Oct. 1959): 11–32.

Falola, Toyin. *Violence in Nigeria: The Crisis of Religious Politics and Secular Ideologies*. Rochester, NY: University of Rochester Press, 2001.

Faupel, J. F. *African Holocaust*. London: Geoffrey Chapman, 1962.

Feierman, Steve. *The Shambaa Kingdom: A History*. Madison: University of Wisconsin Press, 1974.

Foucault, Michael. *Discipline and Punish*. Paris: Gallimand, 1979.

Franklin, John Hope. *George Washington Williams: A Biography*. Chicago: University of Chicago Press, 1985.

Fraser, D. *The Future of Africa*. Westport: Negro University Press 1970.

Freire, Paulo. *Pedagogy of the Oppressed*. New York: Continuum, 1970.

Gale, H. P. "Mutesa I—Was He a God?" *Uganda Journal* 20, 1 (1956): 72–87.

Georgina Anne Gollock. *Sons of Africa*. New York: Friendship Press, 1928.

Gerloff, Roswith, ed. *Mission is Crossing Frontiers: Essays in Honour of Bongani Mazibuko*. Petermaritzburgh: Cluster Publications, 2003.

Gilroy, P. *Against Race: Imagining Political Culture Beyond the Colour Line*. Cambridge: Cambridge University Press, 2000.

Gluckman, Max. *Order and Rebellion in Tribal Africa: Collected Essays with an Anthropological Introduction*. New York: Free Press of Glencoe, 1963.

Good, Charles M. Ethnomedical Systems in Africa: Patterns of Traditional Medicine in Rural and Urban Kenya. New York: The Guilford Press, 1987.

Gotink, Hugo. *Mangembo 1921–1942: Un Regard sur l'Evangelisation Catholique dans le Territoire de Luozi*. Kinshasa, DRC: Editions Centre de Vulgarisation Agricole, 1995.

Grove, Richard *Ecology, Climate and Empire: Colonialism and Global Environmental History, 1400–1940*. Cambridge: White Horse Press, 1997.

———. *Green Imperialism: Colonial Expansion, Tropical Island Edens, and the Origins of Environmentalism 1600–1860*. Cambridge: Cambridge University Press, 1995.

Hair, P.E.H. *The Early Study of Nigerian Languages*. Cambridge: Cambridge University Press, 1967.

Haliburton, Gordon M. *The Prophet Harris*. London: Oxford University Press, 1973.

Hansen, Holger Bernt. "Church and State in Early Colonial Uganda." *African Affairs* 85, no. 338 (Jan. 1986): 55–74.

Hastings, Adrian *Church and Mission in Modern Africa*. London: Burns and Oates, 1967.

Hensbroek, Pieter Boele van. *Political Discourse in African Thought 1860 to the Present*. Westport, CT: Praeger Publishers, 1999.

Hodge, A. "The Training of Missionaries for Africa: The Church Missionary Society's Training College at Islington, 1900–1915." *Journal of Religion in Africa* IV, 2 (1971): 81–96.

Horton, Africanus Baele. *West African Countries and Peoples*, with an introduction by George Shepperson. 1868; reprint Chicago: Aldine Publishers Company, 1969.

Idowu, William. "Law, Morality and African Cultural Heritage: The Jurispruden-
    tial Significance of the Ogboni Institution." *Nordic Journal of African Studies*
    14 no. 2 (2005): 175–92.
Jacobs, S. M. "The Historical Role of Afro-Americans in American Mission-
    ary Efforts in Africa." In *Black Americans and the Missionary Movement
    in Africa,* ed. S. M. Jacobs. Westport-Connecticut: Greenwood Press, 1982,
    5–29.
Janzen, J. M. "Drums of Affliction: Real Phenomenon or Scholarly Chimera?" in
    Religion in Africa, ed. Thomas D. Blakely, Walter E. A. van Beek, Dennis I.
    Thomson. Portsmouth: Heinemann, 1994.
———. "Pluralistic Legitimization of Therapy Systems in Contemporary Zaire."
    Rural African, 26 (1974): 105–122.
Jehu J. Hanciles, "Bishop Crowther and Archdeacon Crowther: Inter-Generational
    Challenge and Opportunity in Africa Christian Encounter." In *Religion, His-
    tory, and Politics in Nigeria,* ed. Chima J. Korieh and G. Ugo Nwokeji. New
    York: University Press of America, 2005, 52–74.
Jenkins, D. *Black Zion: Africa imagined and real, as seen by Today's Blacks.* New
    York: Harcourt Brace Jovanovich, 1975.
Jordon, W. D. *The White Man's Burden.* Oxford: Oxford University Press, 1974.
Kabwegere, Tarsis B. "The Dynamics of Colonial Violence: The Inductive System in
    Uganda." *Journal of Peace Research* 9, no. 4 (1972): 303–14.
Kagwa, Apolo. *Ekitabo kye mpisa za Baganda* [*The Customs of Baganda in the
    Luganda Language*]. Kampala: Uganda Printing and Publishing Co., Ltd.,
    1918.
Kalu, Ogbu U. "Missionaries, Colonial Government and Secret Societies in South-
    eastern Igboland, 1920–1950." *Journal of the Historical Society of Nigeria* 9,
    no. 1 (Dec. 1977): 75–90.
———. "The Gods in Retreat: Models for Interpreting Religious Change in Africa."
    In *The Gods in Retreat: Continuity and Change in African Religions,* ed.
    Emefie Ikenga Metuh. Enugu: Fourth Dimension Publishers, 1986.
———. *Divided People of God: Church Union Movement in Nigeria, 1875–1966.*
    New York: NOK Publishers, 1978.
———. ed. *African Christianity: An African Story.* Pretoria: University of Pretoria
    press, 2005.
Karugire, Samwiri Rubaraza. *A Political History of Uganda.* Nairobi and London:
    Heinemann, 1980.
Kassimir, Ronald. "Complex Martyrs: Catholic Church Formation and Political
    Differentiation in Uganda." *African Affairs* 90, no. 360 (July 1991): 357–82.
Kavenadiambuko Ngemba Ntime. *La Methode d'evangelisation des Redemptor-
    istes Belges au Bas-Congo (1899–1919).* Rome: Editrice Pontificia Universita
    Gregoriana, 1999.
Kenneth Mills and Anthony Grafton, eds. *Conversion: Old Worlds and New. Stud-
    ies in Comparative History Series.* Rochester: University of Rochester Press,
    2003.
Kenny, Michael G. "Mutesa's Crime: Hubris and the Control of African Kings."
    Comparative Studies in Society and History 30, no. 4 (Oct. 1988): 595–612.

Kenny, Michael G. "The Stranger from the Lake: A Theme in the History of the Lake Victoria Shorelands." *Azania* 17 (1982): 1–26.

Kirby, Jon. "Cultural Change and Religious Conversion in West Africa," in *Religion in Africa. Experience and Expression*, eds. T. D. Blakely et al. London: James Currey, 1994.

Kiwanuka, M. S. M. *A History of Buganda: From the Founding of the Kingdom to 1900* New York: Africana, 1972.

Kodi, M.W. "The 1921 Pan-African Congress at Brussels: A Background to Belgian Pressures," In *Global Dimensions of the African Diaspora, Second Edition*, ed. Joseph Harris. Washington, D.C: Howard University Press, 1993.

Kratz, Michaël. *La Mission des Rédemptoristes Belges au Bas-Congo: La Période des semailles (1899–1920)*. Brussels: Académie Royale des Sciences d'Outre-Mer, 1970.

Lagergren, David. *Mission and State in the Congo: A Study of the Relations between Protestant Missions and the Congo Independent State Authorities with special reference to the Equator District, 1885–1903*. Uppsala, Sweden: Almqvist & Wiksells, 1970.

Laitin, David D. *Hegemony and Culture: Politics and Religious Change among the Yoruba*. Chicago: University of Chicago Press, 1986.

Langley, J. A. *Pan-Africanism and Nationalism in West Africa, 1900–1945*. Oxford: Oxford Univ. Press 1978.

Latham, A.J.H. *Old Calabar, 1600–1891*. Oxford: Clarendon Press 1973.

Law, Robin. *Oyo Empire, c. 1600–1836: A West African Imperialism in the Era of Atlantic Slave Trade*. Oxford: Clarendon Press, 1977.

Low, D. A. *Religion and Society in Buganda, 1875–1900*: Kampala: East African Institute of Social Research, 1957.

Lowood, Henry "The Calculating Forester: Quantification, Cameral Science, and the Emergence of Scientific Forestry Management in Germany." In *The Quantifying Spirit in the 18th Century*, ed. T. Frängsmyr, J. L. Heilbron, and R. E. Rider. Berkeley: University of California Press, 1990, 319–42.

Lugard, Frederick D. *The Rise of Our East African Empire*. London: Blackwood, 1893.

Lugira, A. M. "Redemption in Ganda Traditional Belief." *Uganda Journal* 32, no. 2 (1968): 199–203.

MacGaffey, Wyatt. "Ethnography and the Closing of the frontier in Lower Congo, 1885–1921." *Africa: Journal of the International African Institute* 56, no. 3 (1986): 263–79.

———. 1968. "Kongo and the King of the Americans." *Journal of Modern African Studies* 6, no. 2 (1968):171–81.

Mackay, Alexina Harrison. *The Story of Mackay of Uganda, Pioneer Missionary.* London: Hodder and Stoughton, 1911.

Mahaniah, Kimpianga. "The Presence of Black Americans in the Lower Congo from 1878 to 1921." In *Global Dimensions of the African Diaspora, Second edition*, ed. Joseph Harris. Washington, D.C: Howard University Press, 1993.

———. *L'Impact du Christianisme au Manianga*. Kinshasa, DRC: Editions Centre de Vulgarisation Agricole, 1988.

———. *La Maladie et la Guérison en milieu Kongo*. Kinshasa: Centre de Vulgarisation Agricole, 1982.

———. "The Background of Prophetic Movements in the Belgian Congo: A Study of the Congolese Reaction to the Policies and Methods of Belgian Colonization and to the Evangelization of the Lower Congo by Catholic and Protestant Missionaries, from 1877 to 1921." Ph.D. diss., Temple University, 1975.

Mamdani, Mahmood. *Citizens and Subjects: Contemporary Africa and the Legacy of Late Colonialism*. Princeton, NJ: Princeton University Press, 1996.

Markowitz, Marvin. *Cross and Sword: The Political Role of Christian Missions in the Belgian Congo, 1908–1960*. Stanford, California: Hoover Institution Press, 1973.

Martin, Marie-Louise. *Kimbangu: An African Prophet and his Church*. Great Britain: Basil Blackwell, 1975.

Martin, Phyllis. *Leisure and Society in Colonial Brazzaville*. Cambridge: Cambridge University Press, 1995.

Mbiti, J. S. *Theology and Bible in Africa*. Nairobi: Oxford University Press, 1987.

Mills, C. W. *Blackness Visible: Essays on Philosophy and Race*. London: Cornell University Press, 1998.

———. *The Racial Contract*. Ithaca: Cornell University Press 1991.

Mobley, W. H. *The Ghanaians' Image of the Missionary*. Leiden: E. J. Brill, 1970.

Monteiro, Joachim John. *Angola and the River Congo* (Volume II). London: MacMillan and Co, 1875.

Mott, John R. *The Decisive Hour of Christian Missions*. New York: Student Volunteer Movement for Foreign Missions, 1912

Mudimbe, V. Y. *Tales of Faith: Religion as Political Performance in Central Africa*. London: The Athlone Press, 1997.

Mukasa, Om Ham. "Ebija ku Mulembe gwa Kabaka Mutesa [Some Notes on the Reign of Mutesa]." *Uganda Journal* 2, no. 1–4 (1934/35): 60–70.

Mullan, J. *The Catholic Church in Modern Africa*. London: Godfrey Chapman, 1965.

Nettleford, R. M. *Caribbean Cultural Identity: The Case of Jamaica*. Princeton: Markus Wiener Publishers, 2003.

———. *Mirror: Identity, Race and Protest in Jamaica*. Kingston: LMH Publishing Limited 1998.

Neumann, Roderick "Ways of Seeing Africa: Colonial Recasting of African Society and Landscape in Serengeti National Park," *Ecumene* 2, no. 2 (1995): 153–67.

Nicq, Abbe A. *Vie du Reverend Pere Simeon Lourdel* [*Life of Reverend Father Simeon Lourdel*]. Alger: Maison-Carree, 1932.

Ofonagoro, W. I. *Trade and Imperialism in Southern Nigeria, 1881–1929*. New York: Nok, 1979.

Ojike, B. A. *Social and Political History of Nigeria for Schools and Colleges*. Aba, Nigeria: International Press, 1961.

Ojike, Mbonu. "Week-end Catechism." *West African Pilot*, 5 June 1948.

———. *I Have Two* Countries. New York: The John Day Company, 1947.

Oliver, Roland. *The Missionary Factor in East Africa*. London and New York: Longman 1952.

Omenka, N. *Schools as Means of Evangelization.* Leiden: E. J. Brill, 1991.

Ozigbo, Ikenga R. A. "An Evaluation of Christian Pioneering Techniques with particular reference to Nigeria," *Nigerian Journal of Theology* 8, no. 1 (1994): 43–62.

p'Bitek, Okot *African Religions in Western Scholarship.* Kampala: East African Literature Bureau, 1970.

Packard, Randall M. *Chiefship and Cosmology: An Historical Study of Political Competition.* Bloomington: Indiana University Press, 1981.

Peel, J. D. Y. "Conversion and Tradition in Two African Societies: Ijebu and Buganda." *Past and Present* 77, (1977): 108–41.

———. *Religious Encounter and the Making of the Yoruba.* Bloomington: Indiana University Press, 2000.

Perham, Margaret. *The Diaries of Lord Lugard.* London: Faber and Faber, 1960.

———. *Lugard: The Years of Adventure 1858–1898.* London: Collins, 1956.

Porter, Andrew ed., *The Imperial Horizons of British Protestant Missions, 1880–1914.* Grand Rapids: Eerdmans, 2003.

Ragsdale, John P. *Protestant Mission Education in Zambia, 1880–1954.* Toronto: Associated University Press, 1986.

Ray, Benjamin C. *Myth, Ritual, and Kingship in Buganda.* New York and Oxford: Oxford University Press, 1991.

Reed, Susan. "The Politics and Poetics of Dance." *Annual Review of Anthropology* 27 (1998): 503–32.

Roscoe, John (Rev.). *The Baganda.* London: Macmillan, 1911.

Rowe, John Allen. "Eyewitness Accounts of Buganda History: The Memoirs of Ham Mukasa and His Generation." *Ethnohistory* 36, no. 1 (Winter 1989): 61–9.

———. "Myth, Memoir, and Moral Admonition: Luganda Historical Writing 1893–1969." *Uganda Journal* 33 (1969): 17–40.

———. "Revolution in Buganda 1856–1900." (PhD Thesis, The University of Wisconsin, 1966.

———. "The Purge of Christians at the Mwanga's Court: A Reassessment of this Episode in Buganda's History." *Journal of African History* 5, no. 1 (1964): 55–71.

Russell, H. O. *The Missionary Outreach of the West Indian Church: Jamaica Baptist Missions to West Africa in the Nineteenth Century.* New York: Peter Lang 2000.

Sanneh, Lamin. *Translating the Message.* Maryknoll, NY: Orbis, 1989.

Schreuder, D. M. "The Cultural Factor in Victorian Imperialism." *Journal of Imperial and Commonwealth History* 4, no. 3 (May 1976): 283–317.

Shenk, W. R. *Henry Venn- Missionary Statesman.* New York: Orbis Books, 1983.

Slade Reardon, Ruth. "Catholics and Protestants in the Congo." In *Christianity in Tropical Africa*, ed. C.G. Baeta. London: Oxford University Press, 1968.

Smith, N. *The Presbyterian Church of Ghana 1835–1960.* Accra: Ghana Univ. Press 1966.

Smith, Robert Sidney. *Kingdoms of the Yoruba.* Madison: University of Wisconsin Press, 1988.

Sofowora, A. "Research on Medicinal Plants and Traditional Medicine in Africa," *Journal of Alternative Complementary Medicine* 2, no. 3 (Fall, 1961): 365–72.

———. *Medicinal Plants and Traditional Medicine in Africa.* Ibadan: Onibonoje Press, 1979.

Stanley, Dorothy. *The Autobiography of Sir Henry Morton Stanley edited by his wife Dorothy Stanley.* Boston and New York: Houghton Mifflin Company, 1909.

Stanley, Henry M. *Through the Dark Continent.* New York: Harper and Brothers, 1878.

Steere, Edward *Central African Mission: Its Present State and Prospects.* London: UMCA Pamphlet, 1873.

Summers, Carol "Tickets, Concerts, and School Fees: Money and New Christian Communities in Colonial Zimbabwe, 1900–1940." In *Conversion: Old Worlds and New. Studies in Comparative History Series,* ed. Kenneth Mills and Anthony Grafton. Rochester: University of Rochester Press, (2003),

Sundkler Bengt and Christopher Steed, *A History of the Church in Africa.* Cambridge: Cambridge University Press, 2000.

Suntharalingam, R. *Politics and Nationalist Awakening in South India, 1852–1910.* Jaipur-New Dehli, 1980.

Tamuno, T. N. *The Evolution of the Nigerian State: The Southern Phase, 1898–1914.* London: Longman 1972.

Taylor, William H. *Mission to Educate.* Leiden: E J. Brill, 1996.

Thomas, H. B. "The Last Days of Bishop Hannington." *Uganda Journal* 8–9, nos. 1–2 (1940–1942): 19–27.

Thoonen, J. P. *Black Martyrs.* London: Sheed and Ward, 1942.

Thornton, John Kelly. "The Development of an African Catholic Church in the Kingdom of Kongo, 1491–1750." *Journal of African History* 25, no. 2 (1984): 147–67.

———. *The Kongolese Saint Anthony: Dona Beatrice Kimpa Vita and the Antonian Movement 1684–1706.* Cambridge: Cambridge University Press, 1998.

Toynbee, A. *Change and Habit: The Challenge of our Time.* Oxford: One World, 1992.

Turner, Victor. *The Drums of Affliction: A Study of Religious Possession among the Ndembu of Zambia.* Oxford: Clarendon Press, 1969.

Twaddle, Michael. "The Nine Lives of Kakungulu." *History in Africa* 12 (1985): 325–33.

———. "Ganda Receptivity to Change." *Journal of African History* 25, no. 2 (1974): 303–15.

———. "The *Bakungu* Chiefs of Buganda under British Colonial Rule, 1900–1930." *Journal of African History* 10, no. 2 (1969): 309–22.

———. "The Emergence of Politico-Religious Groupings in Late Nineteenth-Century Buganda." *Journal of African History* 29, no. 1 (1988): 82–92.

———. "The Muslim Revolution in Buganda." *African Affairs* 71, no. 282 (1972): 54–72.

Ugbor, Leonard A. *Prayer in Igbo Traditional Religion: Its Meaning and Message for the Church in Igboland Today.* Rome: Pontifical University Gregoriana, 1985.

Utuk, Efiong S. *From New York to Ibadan: The Impact of African Questions on the Making of Ecumenical Mission Mandates.* New York: Peter Lang, 1991.

Waddell, M. H. *Twenty-Nine Years in the West Indies and Central Africa: A Review of Missionary Work and Adventure 1829–1858.* London: Frank Cass, 1970.

Wariboko, W. E. "'I Really Cannot Make Africa My Home': West Indian Missionaries as 'Outsiders' in the Church Missionary Society civilizing Mission to Southern Nigeria, 1898–1925." *Journal of Africa History* 45 (2004): 221–36.

———. *Planting Church-Culture at New Calabar: Some Neglected Aspects of Missionary Enterprise in the Eastern Niger Delta 1865–1918.* Bethesda: International Scholars Publications 1998.

———. *Ruined by Race: Afro-Caribbean Missionaries and the Evangelization of Southern Nigeria, 1895–1925.* New Jersey: Africa World Press, 2006.

Welbourn, F. B. "Missionary Stimulus and African Responses," in Victor Turner (ed). *Colonialism in Africa, 1870–1960.* Cambridge: Cambridge University Press, 1971.

Williams, Lukkyn. "The Kabaka of Buganda." *Uganda Journal* 7, no. 4 (April 1940), 176–87.

World Missionary Conference, 1910, Report of Commission III: Education in Relation to the Christianization of National Life. Edinburgh and London: Oliphant, Anderson and Ferrier, 1910.

Wrigley, C. C. "Kirmera." *Uganda Journal* 23, no. 1 (1959): 38–43.

———. "The Christian Revolution in Buganda." *Comparative Studies in Society and History* 2 (1959): 33–48.

Zahan, D. *The Religion, Spirituality and Thoughts of Traditional Africa.* Chicago: University of Chicago Press, 1979.

Contributors

Jude Aguwa is associate professor of Religion at Mercy College, Dobbs Ferry, New York. A graduate of Urban University Rome, he received his Ph.D. in Theological Anthropology from Pontifical College, Teresianum, Rome. He was a Senior Research fellow at the Center for Igbo Studies, Abia State University, Nigeria, and a Senior Lecturer of Religion in the University's College of Education. Since 1997, Aguwa has taught at Mercy College. Most of Aguwa's scholarship concerns African culture and religion, Christianity, Islam and politics in Nigeria. Among his books are *The Anthropological Challenges of Christianity in the Changing African Culture* (1987); *The Agwu Deity of Igbo Religion* (1995); and *Religious Dichotomy in Nigerian Politics (1993)*. He co-edited: *The Igbo and the Tradition of Politics* (1993); and *Agriculture and Modernity in Nigeria* (1998). He has contributed several book chapters including "Christianity and Nigerian Indigenous Culture" in the volume, *Religion, History, and Politics in Nigeria* (2005). He has also written several articles published in such renowned journals as, the *Anthropos*, *Dialectical Anthropology*, *PAIDEUMA*, *Bigard Theological Studies*, and *Aquinas Journal*. Aguwa's current research interests focus on African religion and medicine, and the historical impact of Western culture and science on African indigenous institutions.

Roger B. Beck received his B.A. from the University of Evansville (1969), and M.A. (1979), and Ph.D. in African History (1987) from Indiana University. He is professor of African History and World History at Eastern Illinois University. His publications include *The History of South Africa* (2000); a translation of P. J. van der Merwe's *The Migrant Farmer in the History of the Cape Colony 1657–1842* (1995); "Bibles and Beads: Missionaries as Traders in Southern Africa in the Early Nineteenth Century," *Journal of African History* (1989); "Cape Officials and Christian Missionaries in the Early Nineteenth Century," in *Christian Missionaries and the State in the Third World* (eds. Twaddle and Hansen, 2001); "Monarchs and Missionaries among the Tswana and Sotho," in *Christianity in the History of South Africa* (eds. Elphick and Davenport, 1997); and more than ninety other articles, book chapters, and reviews. He is a senior consultant for McDougal Littell's *World History. Patterns of Interaction.* (3rd ed.), and co-author of McKay, Hill, Buckler, Ebrey, Beck, *A History of World Societies* (Houghton/Mifflin, 7th ed.).

Yolanda Covington-Ward is a Ph.D. candidate in the Department of Anthropology at the University of Michigan, Ann Arbor. As an undergraduate she majored in Africana studies at Brown University. She has published a book review in *African Studies Quarterly* 7(4), 2004, an article entitled "South Bronx Performances: The Reciprocal Relationship between Hip-Hop and Black Girls' Play" in *Women and Performance: A Journal of Feminist Theory* (forthcoming 2006), and is also the author of supplemental texts for *Anthropology: The Exploration of Human Diversity* (11th edition). A recipient of numerous fellowships, including the Fulbright IIE Fellowship and Andrew W. Mellon Fellowship for Humanistic Studies, she is currently conducting ethnographic research for a year on BaKongo performance practices as embodied history in the Democratic Republic of Congo.

Ogbu U. Kalu studied at the University of Toronto, University of London, and Princeton Theological Seminary. He earned B.A. Hons, M.A., Ph.D. in History, Master of Divinity, and was awarded a Doctor of Divinity by Presbyterian College, Montreal. For over two decades he taught at the University of Nigeria, Nsukka; most of those years as a Professor of Church History. Currently, he is the Henry Winters Luce Professor of World Christianity at McCormick Theological Seminary, Chicago, and the Director of Chicago Center for Global Ministries, Catholic Theological Union, Chicago. He has published over 150 articles and edited seven books, including *The History of Christianity in West Africa* (1980), *African Church Historiography* (1988), *A Global Faith: Evangelicalism and Globalization* (1997), and *African Christianity: An African Story* (2005). He has also published a number of books including, *Divided People of God: Church Union Movement in Nigeria, 1876–1966* (1978), *Embattled Gods: Christianization of Igboland, 1841–1991* (1996), *Power, Poverty and Prayer: The Challenges of Poverty and Pluralism in African Christianity* (2000).

Chima J. Korieh holds a BA (First Class) degree in History from the University of Nigeria. He also holds masters degrees from the University of

Helsinki, Finland and the University of Bergen, Norway. He received a PhD in History from the University of Toronto, Canada in 2003. He had earlier on taught at Central Michigan University, Rowan University, and was a visiting research scholar at Imo State University, Owerri, Nigeria in 1999. He is the recipient of many academic awards and distinctions, including the Rockefeller African Internship Award and the West African Research Association Post-doctoral Fellowship. He has authored many articles and essays in journals, books, and encyclopedia. His publications include: Religion, History and Politics in Nigeria. Lanham, MD: University Press of America, 2005 co-edited with G. Ugo Nwokeji; and Aftermath of Slavery: Transitions and Transformation in Southeastern Nigeria, Trenton, NJ: African World Press, 2007), co-edited with Femi Kolapo. He is also an associate editor of Encyclopedia of Western Imperialism and Colonialism since 1450. New York: Macmillan Reference USA, 2006).

Gideon Mailer is Henry Pelling Benefactors' Scholar in History at St. John's College, University of Cambridge, United Kingdom. He is also a supervisor in American and Atlantic history with the faculty of history in Cambridge. He has written on the history, religion, and politics of Sudan, and Anglo-American involvement in the region, in several journals, including *The RUSI Journal, The Liberal, The Cambridge Review of International Affairs*, and *Diplo: A Journal of International Affairs*. He has authored chapters in upcoming books on the primacy of foreign policy in British history, the influence of covenanting religion in Anglo-American political structures, and on the structures and contours of our historical understanding of the "Atlantic world." He has authored several published book chapters, including "Britain and Africa" in John Bew, Gabriel Glickman, (eds.), *The British Moment: The Case for Democratic Geopolitics*, (Social Affairs Unit Publishers: June 2006), "The Terrorist Threat to America's Public Spaces and Individual Civil Liberties," in James Forest (ed.) *Homeland Security: Protecting America's Targets* (Westport, CT: Praeger Publishers, July 2006), "Syllogism and the Declaration of Independence," Geoff Golsen (ed.), *July 4 1776: One Day in History* (HarperCollins and Smithsonian Books, November 2006).

Michael McInneshin graduated from Duke University in 1993 with a B.A. in history and received an M.A. in history from North Carolina State University in 1998. He presently teaches history and geography at Columbia College, Missouri while completing his history Ph.D. at the University of Minnesota.

Raphael Chijioke Njoku, a first class honors graduate of University of Nigeria Nsukka, received two Ph.D.s in: (1) African History from Dalhousie University, Canada, 2003, and (2) African Politics from Free University Brussels, 2001. Before he joined the University of Louisville faculty in 2003, Njoku had taught briefly at the Department of History, Alvan Ikoku College of Education, Owerri, Nigeria. His research specialty is African history and African politics. He is the author of *Culture and Customs of Morocco* (Greenwood, 2005), and *African Cultural Values: Igbo Political Leadership in Colonial Nigeria 1900–1966* (Routledge, 2006). Njoku has also published 20 articles in scholarly journals, edited volumes, and encyclopedias. With a fellowship from the New York based Schomburg Center for Research in Black Studies, Njoku is beginning a new book project on *African Masks and Masquerades and Carnival of the Diaspora.*

Waibinte Wariboko is senior lecturer in African History at the University of the West Indies in Mona, Jamaica. He is the author of numerous book chapters and journal articles on the missionary enterprise in Southern Nigeria. He is also the author of *Planting Church-Culture at New Calabar: Some Neglected Aspects of Missionary Enterprise in the Eastern Niger Delta, 1865–1918*; and *Ruined by Race: Afro-Caribbean Missionaries and the Evangelization of Southern Nigeria, 1895–1925*(Trenton, NJ: Africa World Press, 2006).

Index

Printed in the USA/Agawam, MA
December 16, 2014

603261.005